THE MEDIEVAL MARCH (

This book examines the making of the March of Wales and the crucial role its lords played in the politics of medieval Britain between the Norman conquest of England of 1066 and the English conquest of Wales in 1283. Max Lieberman argues that the Welsh borders of Shropshire, which were first, from *c.* 1165, referred to as *Marchia Wallie,* provide a paradigm for the creation of the March. He reassesses the role of William the Conqueror's tenurial settlement in the making of the March and sheds new light on the ways in which seigneurial administrations worked in a cross-cultural context. Finally, he explains why, from *c.* 1300, the March of Wales included the conquest territories in south Wales as well as the highly autonomous border lordships. This book makes a significant and original contribution to frontier studies, investigating both the creation and the changing perception of a medieval borderland.

MAX LIEBERMAN is a post-doctoral researcher at the Historical Seminar of the University of Zurich.

Cambridge Studies in Medieval Life and Thought
Fourth Series

The series Cambridge Studies in Medieval Life and Thought was inaugurated by G. G. Coulton in 1921; Professor Rosamond McKitterick now acts as General Editor of the Fourth Series, with Professor Christine Carpenter and Dr Jonathan Shepard as Advisory Editors. The series brings together outstanding work by medieval scholars over a wide range of human endeavour extending from political economy to the history of ideas.

A list of titles in the series can be found at:
www.cambridge.org/medievallifeandthought

THE MEDIEVAL MARCH OF WALES

The Creation and Perception of a Frontier, 1066–1283

MAX LIEBERMAN

CAMBRIDGE
UNIVERSITY PRESS

The Edinburgh Building, Cambridge CB2 8RU, UK

Published in the United States of America by Cambridge University Press, New York

Cambridge University Press is part of the University of Cambridge.

It furthers the University's mission by disseminating knowledge in the pursuit of education, learning and research at the highest international levels of excellence.

www.cambridge.org
Information on this title: www.cambridge.org/9781107650046

First published 2010
First paperback edition 2013

A catalogue record for this publication is available from the British Library

Library of Congress Cataloguing in Publication data
Lieberman, Max, 1974–
The medieval March of Wales : the creation and perception of a frontier, 1066-1283 / Max Lieberman.
p. cm. – (Cambridge studies in medieval life and thought, 4th ser. ; 78)
Includes bibliographical references and index.
ISBN 978-0-521-76978-5 (hardback)
1. Welsh Borders (England and Wales)–History–To 1500. 2. March of Wales–History. 3. Border security–England–History–To 1500. 4. Welsh Borders (England and Wales)–Politics and government. I. Title. II. Series.
DA740.B7L543 2010
942.9′902–dc22
2009044691

ISBN 978-0-521-76978-5 Hardback
ISBN 978-1-107-65004-6 Paperback

In memory of Rees Davies

CONTENTS

MAPS

Some of the titles in the list above are abbreviated. Contour lines are 100 metres, 200 metres and 300 metres. If only one is shown, it is 300 metres.

The course of Offa's Dyke is indicated by a line of small triangles.

TABLES AND ILLUSTRATION

TABLES

Some of the titles in the list above are abbreviated.

ILLUSTRATION

PREFACE

This book sets out to solve a puzzle. It focuses on the period between the beginning of the Norman conquest of England (1066) and the English conquest of Wales (1283). This was when Norman and English knights and barons, having established themselves in England, encroached upon Welsh territory. It was also when the phrase 'the March of Wales' (*Marchia Wallie*) came to be widely used. However, that phrase appears not, at first, to have referred to the territories conquered in Wales (the territories known as the 'Marcher lordships' to modern-day historians of medieval Britain). Rather, the first 'March of Wales' seems to have been the Welsh border of the English county of Shropshire. It was only after a century and a half, from *c.* 1300, that all 'Marcher lordships', even those in south Wales, were normally included within the medieval March of Wales, the region known to contemporaries as *Marchia Wallie*.

This puzzle, along with some of the many others posed by the medieval March of Wales, has intrigued me for a number of years now. During that time I have benefited enormously from the help of others. I am very pleased to have the opportunity to record my thanks to them. This book is based on my Oxford DPhil. thesis, which was examined by Professor Thomas Charles-Edwards and Professor Huw Pryce. I am grateful to both for making my viva such a constructive occasion. Moreover, I found their corrections, comments and suggestions very helpful as I applied myself to revising my thesis for publication. Dr David Stephenson also read and commented on my thesis. Further, I thank Professor Christine Carpenter and Professor Rosamond McKitterick for their comments on my manuscript. Dr David Stephenson, Dr John Reuben Davies and Mr John Davies kindly sent me drafts and offprints of their articles. I am grateful to Mr M. D. Watson of the Shropshire County Council Archaeology Service, Mr C. J. Spurgeon and Mr J. R. Kenyon for their advice on castle-studies.

Collins Maps & Atlases kindly gave permission to publish the maps, which I prepared using Bartholomew mapping data.

I was able to complete this book thanks to the financial support I have received from the Swiss National Science Foundation.

I am very grateful to have been able to work on this book in Oxford and in Cambridge. For providing environments greatly conducive to study, I thank the Warden and Scholars of Merton College, Oxford, and the President and Fellows of Wolfson College, Cambridge.

Finally, I would like to record my gratitude to the late Professor Sir Rees Davies, who supervised my D.Phil. thesis. The debt I owe to his work will be evident from the pages that follow. I also owe a great debt to his teaching and guidance.

ABBREVIATIONS

Abbreviatio Placitorum	*Placitorum in Domo Capitulari Westmonasteriensi Asservatorum Abbreviatio: Temporibus Regum Ric. I., Johann., Henr. III., Edw. I., Edw. II.* (London, 1811).
AWR	*The Acts of Welsh Rulers, 1120–1283*, ed. H. Pryce, with the assistance of C. Insley (Cardiff, 2005).
Annales Cambriae	*Annales Cambriae*, ed. J. Williams ab Ithel (RS, 1860).
Arch. Camb.	*Archaeologia Cambrensis.*
BBCS	*Bulletin of the Board of Celtic Studies.*
Brenhinedd y Saesson	*Brenhinedd y Saesson: or, The Kings of the Saxons*, ed. T. Jones (Cardiff, 1971).
Brut	*Brut y Tywysogyon, or the Chronicle of the Princes. Red Book of Hergest Version*, ed. T. Jones (Cardiff, 1955).
Brut, Peniarth 20	*Brut y Tywysogyon, or the Chronicle of the Princes, Peniarth MS. 20 Version*, ed. T. Jones (Cardiff, 1952). (All references to the Red Book of Hergest version have been checked against *Peniarth 20*, and any significant divergences are noted.)
Cal. Anc. Corr. Wales	*Calendar of Ancient Correspondence Concerning Wales*, ed. J. G. Edwards (Cardiff, 1935).
Cal. Chanc. R. Var.	*Calendar of Various Chancery Rolls: Supplementary Close Rolls, Welsh Rolls, Scutage Rolls. A.D. 1277–1326* (London, 1912).
Cal. Chart. R.	*Calendar of Charter Rolls.*
Cal. Close R.	*Calendar of Close Rolls.*
Cal. Pat. R.	*Calendar of Patent Rolls.*

Cartae	*Cartae et Alia Munimenta Quae ad Dominium de Glamorgancia Pertinent*, ed. G. T. Clark, 6 vols. (Cardiff, 1910)
Matthew Paris, *Chron. Maj.*	*Matthaei Parisiensis, Monachi Sancti Albani Chronica Majora*, ed. H. R. Luard, 7 vols. RS, 1872–83).
CIPM	*Calendar of Inquisitions Post Mortem.*
Comp. Peerage	*The Complete Peerage of England, Scotland, Ireland, Great Britain, and the United Kingdom, Extant, Extinct, or Dormant*, ed. G. E. Cokayne, rev. edn (13 vols. in 14, London, 1910–59).
DB	*Domesday Book* (Phillimore edn).
DNB	*Dictionary of National Biography on CD-ROM* (Oxford, 1995).
EHD	*English Historical Documents.*
EHR	*The English Historical Review.*
Eyton	R. W. Eyton, *Antiquities of Shropshire*, 12 vols. (London, 1854–60).
Giraldus	*Giraldi Cambrensis Opera*, eds. J. S. Brewer, J. F. Dimock and G. F. Warner, 8 vols. (RS, 1861–91).
Haughmond Cart.	*The Cartulary of Haughmond Abbey*, ed. U. Rees (Cardiff, 1985).
John of Worcester	*The Chronicle of John of Worcester*, vol iii. *The Annals from 1067 to 1140 with the Gloucester Interpolations and the Continuation to 1141*, ed. and transl. P. McGurk (Oxford, 1998).
Lilleshall Cart.	*The Cartulary of Lilleshall Abbey*, ed. U. Rees (Shrewsbury, 1997).
Littere Wallie	*Littere Wallie*, ed. J. G. Edwards (Cardiff, 1940).
Mon. Angl.	*Monasticon Anglicanum; a History of the Abbies and Other Monasteries, Hospitals, Friaries, and Cathedral and Collegiate Churches, with their Dependencies, in England and Wales,* ed. W. Dugdale, new edn by J. Caley, H. Ellis and B. Bandinel, 6 vols. in 8 (London, 1817–30; repr. Farnborough, 1970).
Mont. Coll.	*Montgomeryshire Collections.*
Orderic	*The Ecclesiastical History of Orderic Vitalis*, ed. and transl. M. Chibnall, 6 vols. (Oxford, 1969–80).
ODNB (2004)	*Oxford Dictionary of National Biography* (Oxford, 2004).
Parl. Writs.	*Parliamentary Writs and Writs of Military Summons*, ed. F. Palgrave, 2 vols. in 4 (London, 1827–34).

Rot. Claus.	*Rotuli Litterarum Clausarum*, ed. T. D. Hardy, 2 vols. (London, 1833–44).
Rot. Oblat.	*Rotuli de Oblatis et Finibus, Tempore Regis Johannis*, ed. T. D. Hardy (London, 1835).
Rot. Parl.	*Rotuli Parliamentorum*, ed. J. Strachey, 6 vols. (London, 1767–77)
Rot. Pat.	*Rotuli Litterarum Patentium*, ed. T. D. Hardy (London, 1835).
RRAN, ed. Bates	*Regesta Regum Anglo-Normannorum. The Acta of William I (1066–1087)*, ed. D. Bates (Oxford, 1998).
RRAN, ii	*Regesta Regum Anglo-Normannorum, 1066–1154*, vol. ii: *Regesta Henrici Primi, 1100–1135*, eds. C. Johnson and H. A. Cronne (Oxford, 1956).
RS	Rolls Series.
Rymer	*Foedera, Conventiones, Litterae*, ed. T. Rymer, 3rd edn, 10 vols. (1745, repr. Farnborough, 1967.)
Salop. Cart.	*The Cartulary of Shrewsbury Abbey*, ed. U. Rees, 2 vols. (Aberystwyth, 1975).
Saxon Chronicles	*Two of the Saxon Chronicles Parallel*, eds. J. Earle and C. Plummer, 2 vols. (Oxford, 1892, repr. 2000).
SA	Shropshire Archives, Shrewsbury.
TNA	The National Archives (formerly the Public Record Office), Kew.
TRHS	*Transactions of the Royal Historical Society.*
TSAS	*Transactions of the Shropshire Archaeological and Historical Society.*
VCH, i	W. Page, (ed.), *The Victoria History of Shropshire*, vol. i (London, 1908).
VCH, ii	A. T. Gaydon, (ed.), *The Victoria History of the Counties of England. A History of Shropshire*, vol. ii (Oxford, 1973).
VCH, iii	G. C. Baugh, (ed.), *The Victoria History of the Counties of England. A History of Shropshire*, vol. iii (Oxford, 1979).
VCH, iv	C. R. Elrington, (ed.), *The Victoria History of the Counties of England. A History of Shropshire*, vol. iv (Oxford, 1989).
VCH, viii	A. T. Gaydon, (ed.), *A History of Shropshire. The Victoria History of the Counties of England*, vol. viii (Oxford, 1968).
WHR	*Welsh History Review.*

INTRODUCTION

More than two centuries elapsed between the Norman conquest of England and the English conquest of Wales. One year after their victory at Hastings in 1066, William the Conqueror's knights and barons had launched their first raids across the Welsh border. Yet Wales was not brought under the direct control of the kings of England until 1282–3, when Edward I fought his second Welsh war, Llywelyn ap Gruffudd, the last native prince of Wales, was killed, and Llywelyn's brother Dafydd was executed. In achieving dominion over Wales by military force, Edward I outdid his own campaigns of 1276–7 as well as all those of his Norman and Plantagenet predecessors. After William the Conqueror himself went on an expedition to St David's in 1081, Wales was attacked by William II in 1095 and 1097 and by Henry I in 1114 and 1121. Stephen was prevented by civil war from campaigning in Wales, but Henry II led armies there in 1157, 1158, 1163 and 1165. Richard I preferred the Holy Land and France as arenas for military exploits, but Wales was invaded by John in 1211 and 1212, and repeatedly, between the 1220s and the 1260s, by Henry III or his deputies. Yet none of these campaigns led to a Norman or English 'conquest' of Wales, even though some may well have aimed at doing so, notably the one which failed in 1165 and the one which was abandoned in 1212.

Nevertheless, the two centuries after 1066 were an age of dramatic change in the political geography of Wales and the borders. In that time, roughly half of Wales was conquered, albeit haltingly and in a piecemeal fashion, by Norman and English military adventurers. Many of the knights and barons who swept into Wales after 1066, especially those who built their castles along the northern and western coasts, soon saw their ambitions thwarted in the face of native opposition. But many others succeeded in securing footholds and lands for themselves and their descendants, often in places where Welsh resistance was temporarily weakened by the loss of a ruler or by rivalries between native dynasties.

A good example is the Welsh kingdom of Morgannwg in south-eastern Wales. Norman raids began there under the leadership of Robert fitz Hamo, the lord of Creully in Normandy, probably after the killing in 1093 of Rhys ap Tewdwr, the king of south Wales. By means of the conquests Robert and his successors made in Morgannwg, they gradually established the lordship of Glamorgan. However, their position remained precarious throughout the twelfth and thirteenth centuries. Until the late 1260s, they failed to dislodge the Welsh rulers in the uplands to the north. Moreover, the Welsh threat to their acquisitions periodically grew acute, for instance when military leadership was provided by the rulers of Gwynedd, Llywelyn ap Iorwerth (d. 1240) or his grandson, Llywelyn ap Gruffudd (d. 1282). Despite this, the lordship of Glamorgan survived until 1282–3, its lowlands by then bristling with castles and settled extensively by English immigrants. Meanwhile, in the borderlands adjoining Herefordshire, families like the Mortimers and the Braoses fought for generations to gain control of the Welsh principalities of Maelienydd, Elfael, Builth and Brecon. The Clares occupied Ceredigion early during the reign of Henry I, only to lose it to the Welsh in 1136–8. But lowland Glamorgan, the Gower peninsula, Pembroke Castle and parts of south-western Wales remained in foreign hands from the late eleventh century onwards.

In the 1270s and 1280s, Edward I added liberally to these conquest lordships, rewarding the captains of his Welsh campaigns with Ceri, Cedewain, Chirk, Bromfield and Yale, Dyffryn Clwyd, Denbigh, Cantref Bychan and Iscennen. The former Welsh kingdom of Powys descended hereditarily to a scion of the Welsh dynasty of southern Powys who sided with Edward I in the war against Llywelyn ap Gruffudd; it thereby became a Welsh barony held of the English king.[1] By 1284, when Edward I established his Principality of Wales in what had been the previously unoccupied northern and western part of the country, the remainder of Wales had been parcelled out into around forty castle-centred lordships varying widely in size and age. The conquest lordships created in Wales between the late eleventh and the late thirteenth centuries constitute the area known to modern-day historians as the March of Wales. After 1283, they formed an extensive patchwork of territories that separated England from Wales and also extended along the southern Welsh coast from Glamorgan to Pembroke.[2]

[1] R. R. Davies, *Lordship and Society in the March of Wales, 1282–1400* (Oxford, 1978), pp. 26–31.

[2] For a recent introduction to the medieval March of Wales, see M. Lieberman, *The March of Wales, 1067–1300: A Borderland of Medieval Britain* (Cardiff, 2008). The most recent detailed analysis of a section of the March (that adjoining Herefordshire) is B. W. Holden, *Lords of the Central*

Map 1. The Marcher lordships and the Principality of Wales in the fourteenth century

Wales was to stay divided until the end of the Middle Ages. While the Principality of Wales remained part of the private estates of the English crown, the Marcher lordships descended as hereditary domains of such families as Clare, Mortimer, Braose and Bohun, later also of Lancaster and

Marches: English Aristocracy and Frontier Society, 1087–1265 (Oxford, 2008). On Glamorgan, see J. B. Smith, 'The Kingdom of Morgannwg and the Norman Conquest of Glamorgan', T. B. Pugh (ed.), *Glamorgan County History*, vol. iii (Cardiff, 1971), pp. 1–43.

Despenser. These families claimed quasi-regal jurisdiction within their Marcher lordships, as their predecessors had begun to do by the end of the twelfth century.[3] The administrative and jurisdictional fragmentation of Wales and the March persisted throughout the fourteenth and fifteenth centuries, despite the fact that it entailed serious inconveniences and risks for the English royal government. This became glaringly obvious when it hampered the military response to the revolt of Owain Glyn Dŵr between 1400 and 1415.[4] Nevertheless, it was only in the reign of Henry VIII that the English crown set about integrating the March into the administrative and governmental system of England. The two parliamentary acts of 1536 and 1542 created a single dominion of England and Wales. They also abolished the Marcher lordships, either subsuming them within one of seven new shires or incorporating them into an existing English shire.[5]

The Marcher lordships were all compact, by contrast with the estates of baronial landholders in England, many of which were scattered over several counties. The same compactness was characteristic of a number of castle-centred lordships which directly adjoined or even overlapped with Welsh territory: the Mortimer castlery of Wigmore, for instance, or the lordships of Oswestry, Caus, Montgomery and Clun on the Welsh frontier of Shropshire, the largest inland county of England. These lordships are sometimes considered to be part of the March of Wales, even though they originated as tenurial blocks established mostly or entirely on English territory, rather than as conquests in Wales. For one thing, they are coeval with the very first Norman conquests in Wales. They are already recorded in Domesday Book, the great record of landholding in England in 1086. However, their appurtenance to the English shires became ever more debatable during the twelfth and thirteenth centuries, and during the later Middle Ages they escaped the reach of the administrative, fiscal and judicial institutions of the English kingdom, albeit to varying degrees. Henry VIII's parliamentary acts of 1536 and 1542 treated many of them in the same way as the Marcher lordships established in Wales, providing for their integration into the new Welsh shires or the English border counties.

The March of Wales can therefore be fairly precisely characterized for the purposes of the political and administrative history of England and Wales during the Middle Ages. The March consisted of the foreign-held lordships in Wales and the compact honors directly adjoining Welsh

[3] R. R. Davies, 'Kings, Lords and Liberties in the March of Wales, 1066–1272', *TRHS*, 5th ser., **29** (1979), pp. 41–61.
[4] R. R. Davies, *The Revolt of Owain Glyn Dŵr* (Oxford, 1995), pp. 256–7.
[5] W. Rees, *The Act of Union of England and Wales* (Cardiff, 1948).

territory. It therefore expanded and contracted significantly as conquests in Wales were made and lost, especially before 1167, when Ireland became a new destination for knights in search of lands to conquer. The extent of the March was also determined by the degree to which the frontier honors were withdrawn from the reach of the English state.[6] After 1283, the March became more fixed in extent than ever before. During the fourteenth and fifteenth centuries, it drove a wedge between the Principality and the English counties, while also extending across southern Wales; but in 1536–42 it was erased from the map of the political geography of the British Isles.[7]

Thus, modern-day historians of the medieval period mean by the term 'March of Wales' the congeries of lordships carved out in Wales between 1067 and 1283; and they sometimes include the compact frontier lordships within this 'March' as well. This historiographical terminology is based on a medieval precedent: the phrase *Marchia Wallie*. An early version of that phrase is found in the folios of Domesday Book. The expression becomes more common in the second half of the twelfth century. Then, in 1215, the authors of Magna Carta juxtaposed a 'March' to England on the one hand and Wales on the other. Writers in England and the March referred to the borders of Wales by other Latin terms as well.[8] But it does seem that in the voluminous records kept by the chancery and exchequer of the English crown the phrase *Marchia Wallie* acquired something of an official status. In view of this, and given that the modern historical category of the March of Wales refers to a relatively well-defined phenomenon, it might be expected that there was a contemporary concept of the March which corresponded to ours. However, the usage of the phrase *Marchia Wallie* between the late eleventh and the early fourteenth centuries suggests that the medieval concept of the Welsh March was a malleable one.

★ ★ ★

It is possible to locate Domesday Book's 'March' with some precision. The survey is arranged by counties, and the folios for Herefordshire state that both Osbern fitz Richard and Ralph de Mortimer held vills lying 'in the March of Wales'.[9] As Map 2 shows, the vills which were said to lie in

6 I will refer to the medieval English kingdom as a state, without using inverted commas. For a stimulating recent discussion of the concept and its uses for medieval historians cf. R. R. Davies, 'The Medieval State: The Tyranny of a Concept?', *Journal of Historical Sociology*, **16** (2003), pp. 280–99.

7 Davies, *Lordship and Society*, p. 16.

8 K. Mann, 'The March of Wales: A Question of Terminology', *WHR*, **18** (1996), pp. 1–13.

9 DB 183d ('in marcha de Wales'), 186d ('in Marcha de Walis').

this March were all located on the westernmost borders of Herefordshire, and formed a continuous territory through which ran Offa's Dyke. It seems natural, therefore, to wonder whether Domesday's 'Marcha' could be considered the precursor of the later March of Wales. However, unlike the later March, that of 1086 was not coterminous with lordships, or honors. Only part of the estates held respectively by Osbern fitz Richard and Ralph de Mortimer in 1086 were considered to lie in this March; their honors were not coextensive with the Domesday March, but overlapped with it. Ralph de Mortimer's main concentration of lands lay in the Teme valley, around his castle at Wigmore (he also held a number of estates north of the Teme, in Shropshire, outside the area shown on the map). Osbern's 'Marcher' estates formed a fairly compact group, but they were intermingled with Mortimer's – in this respect, the tenurial pattern in Domesday's March was similar to that generally found in the counties of England. Moreover, the focus of Osbern's honor probably lay further east, at Richard's Castle. Domesday's 'March' was really a geographical description referring to the valleys of the river Lugg and of the Hindwell Brook.

We can be confident that the phrase *Marchia Wallie* first became more common during the 1160s. This certainty is due primarily to the near-complete survival of the Pipe Rolls, the annual accounts of the royal exchequer of England, from the second year of Henry II's reign onwards. Since the Pipe Rolls record the accounts rendered annually by individual sheriffs, they reveal with some precision where the first twelfth-century March of Wales was thought to be located, which territories were subsequently included within the March, and when. The first 'March' of the Pipe Rolls was the Welsh border of Shropshire. In 1166, Geoffrey de Vere, the sheriff of Shropshire, accounted for £62 16d for 'the 100 serjeants of the castle of Shrawardine and of the March'.[10] In 1168, Geoffrey de Vere received £100 'to guard the March of Wales'.[11] The following year, he accounted for the £29 4s he had spent on sustaining 'serjeants of the March'.[12] The sheriffs of Shropshire accounted for payments for the same purpose in 1171, 1172 and 1174.[13] The Pipe Rolls show that the 'March'

[10] *Pipe Roll 12 Henry II, 1165–6* (P. R. S., 9), p. 59: 'in liberatione .c. Seruientium de Shrawurdin'. Et de Marcha a festo Sancti Michaele usque ad uigiliam Pasce .lxii. libri. et .xvi. denarii'. The one Pipe Roll to survive from before Henry II's reign dates to 1129–30. It makes no mention of a 'March' even though it does contain accounts for the border county of Gloucestershire as well as for Carmarthen and Pembroke in south Wales: *Pipe Roll 31 Henry I*, ed. J. Hunter (1833, repr. in facs. London, 1929), pp. 76–80, 89–90, 136–7.

[11] *Pipe Roll 14 Henry II, 1167–8* (P. R. S., 12), p. 199: 'ad custodiendam March' Walie'.

[12] *Pipe Roll 16 Henry II, 1169–70* (P. R. S., 15), p. 154.

[13] *Pipe Roll 17 Henry II, 1170–71* (P. R. S., 16), pp. 32, 53, 96; *Pipe Roll 18 Henry II, 1171–2* (P. R. S., 18), p. 111; *Pipe Roll 20 Henry II, 1173–4* (P. R. S., 21), p. 108.

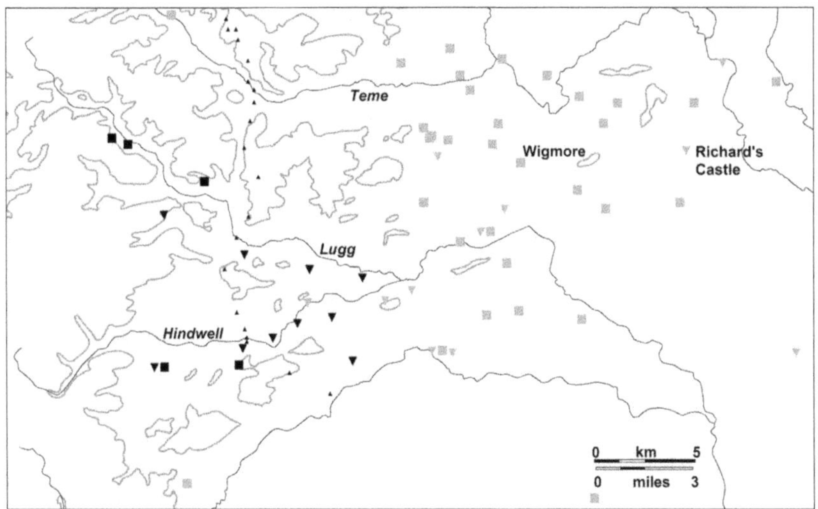

Map 2. Domesday Book's March of Wales

was clearly soon thought to encompass the southern Welsh borders as well. In 1167, the reference to 'the king's castles in the March' occurs in the Pipe Roll for Worcestershire, in 1173, 'serjeants of the March of Wales' are mentioned in Herefordshire, and in 1184, the Gloucestershire Roll shows Hywel, the lord of Caerleon, was remunerated 'for maintaining himself in the king's service in the marches of Wales'.[14] However, the close link between the 'March' and the Shropshire–Powys borders is strikingly corroborated by a contemporary royal charter. It was before 1175, and probably after 1173, that Henry II confirmed Owain Fychan, a son of the king of Powys, Madog ap Maredudd (d. 1160), in the possession of Mechain and 'five vills of the March'. Four of these vills certainly

[14] *Pipe Roll 13 Henry II, 1166–7* (P. R. S., 11), p. 64; *Pipe Roll 19 Henry II, 1172–3* (P. R. S., 19), p. 38; *Pipe Roll 30 Henry II, 1183–4* (P. R. S., 33), p. 59. The first references explicitly distinguishing between Wales and the March of Wales date to 1196: *Chancellor's Roll 8 Richard I, 1196* (P. R. S., NS 7, London, 1930), pp. 17, 19, 20; cf. Mann, 'Terminology', p. 6; Holden, *Lords*, pp. 43–5.

lay in Oswestry lordship in north-western Shropshire; the fifth may have been Sycharth, just across Offa's Dyke from the others.[15]

In view of the geographical proximity of Domesday's 'March' to Shropshire, one wonders whether a regional tradition preserved the usage of the term. The shift from *marcha* to *marchia* may have been due to the fact that the former was derived from Old English *mearc/merc*, while the latter was a Latinization of Old French *marche*.[16] Given the spread of the French language in England between the eleventh and the twelfth centuries, this may plausibly explain why it was *Marchia Wallie* that became the dominant form, and remained so in the thirteenth and fourteenth centuries. If *marcha* and *marchia* were indeed derived from different languages, this raises the question of how far the two Latin terms might have had different meanings. Both Old English *mearc* and Old French *marche* could mean 'boundary'; but the meaning of 'border district' is documented for *marche* alone.[17] The evidence of Offa's Dyke suggests that, in the eighth century, the Anglo-Saxons thought of their border with the Welsh as a line; so does the fact that, according to William of Malmesbury, Æthelstan, king of England, fixed the Wye as the boundary between the Welsh and the English.[18] Yet perhaps it would be wise not to draw too strict a distinction between *mearc*, *marche* and their Latin derivatives. After all, it seems clear from Domesday Book's usage that *marcha* could also mean a border district.[19]

Possibly, a particular regional meaning of the term *Marchia* is suggested by the ecclesiastical re-organization of north-east Wales and the adjacent borders in the mid-twelfth century. In 1291, the diocese of

15 *The Welsh Assize Roll 1277–84*, ed. J. C. Davies (Cardiff, 1940), p. 237: 'Mechen cum pertinenciis et quinque villas de Marchia'. The four 'vills of the March' of this document which are certainly identifiable are Llynclys, Llanyblodwel, Bryn and Trefonnen (see Map 3). Cf. R. Morgan, 'The Barony of Powys, 1275–1360', *WHR*, **10** (1980), p. 38, n. 2; D. Stephenson, 'The Supremacy in (Southern) Powys of Owain Fychan ap Madog: A Reconsideration', *Cambrian Medieval Celtic Studies*, **49** (2005), pp. 48–9 and n. 15. I must thank Dr Stephenson for kindly sending me an offprint of this article.

16 As is suggested by D. R. Howlett (ed.), *Dictionary of Medieval Latin from British Sources: Fascicule vi (M)* (Oxford, 2001), pp. 1717–18.

17 T. Northcote Toller (ed.), *An Anglo-Saxon Dictionary, Based on the Manuscript Collections of the Late Joseph Bosworth*, parts 1–4. A-Y (Oxford, 1898), pp. 673–4; T. Northcote Toller, *An Anglo-Saxon Dictionary: Supplement, with rev. and enlarged Addenda by A. Campbell* (Oxford, 1921), p. 633; W. Rothwell, L. W. Stone and T. B. W. Reid (eds.), *Anglo-Norman Dictionary* (London, 1992), p. 406.

18 William of Malmesbury, *Gesta regum*, ed. and transl. R. A. B. Mynors, compl. R. M. Thomson and M. Winterbottom (Oxford, 1998), i, 216 (§134.6); cf. C. P. Lewis, 'English and Norman Government and Lordship in the Welsh Borders, 1039–1087' (University of Oxford DPhil thesis, 1985), pp. 348–9.

19 Above, pp. 5–6 and Map 2.

St Asaph, alone among the four Welsh bishoprics, included a deanery of 'Marchia'.[20] The earliest evidence which establishes the boundaries of the diocese, the fiscal assessment of Welsh and English church lands known as the Norwich Valuation, dates to 1254.[21] By then, the deanery of 'Marchia' encompassed Oswestry and Whittington lordships as well as territories to the west of Offa's Dyke, to wit, the Tanat valley and surrounding uplands. The latter district clearly related to the Welsh commote of Mochnant and indeed by 1291 a new, eponymous deanery had been created for it. A new deanery of Cynllaith was also established between 1254 and 1291. As a result, at the end of the thirteenth century, the deanery of 'Marchia' comprised just the lordships of Oswestry and Whittington. The best explanation for the inclusion of these lordships within a Welsh diocese is the political situation of the 1140s and 1150s. The diocese of St Asaph was established, or perhaps re-established, in north-east Wales in 1141.[22] Oswestry Castle may have been in Welsh hands soon afterwards, and certainly was by 1149, or 1151 at the latest.[23] It is possible that the deanery of 'Marchia' was first created shortly after 1150,[24] and that it was already so named at the time.[25]

It is also, of course, conceivable that the term *Marchia* did not have any local or regional meaning, or that the usage of the English royal chancery and exchequer developed independently of such a tradition. The timing of the phrase's first occurrence in the Pipe Rolls certainly points to a specific set of historical circumstances. Henry II led an unsuccessful campaign into Wales, by way of Oswestry, in 1165.[26] And it was in the same year that Geoffrey de Vere was installed as sheriff of Shropshire and

[20] D. R. Thomas, *The History of the Diocese of St Asaph*, 3 vols. (Oswestry, 1908), i, 41; *Taxatio Ecclesiastica Angliae et Walliae Auctoritate P. Nicholai IV. circa A. D. 1291*, ed. T. Astle, S. Ayscough, and J. Caley (London, 1802), pp. 272–94, esp. pp. 285–6. For the deanery of 'Marchia' in 1535 see *Valor Ecclesiasticus*, ed. J. Caley and J. Hunter, 6 vols. (London, 1810–34), iv, 344 and map; also the map in *VCH*, ii, 24; and W. Rees, *An Historical Atlas of Wales: From Early to Modern Times*, 3rd edn (London, 1967), Plate 33.

[21] C. N. L. Brooke, *The Church and the Welsh Border in the Central Middle Ages*, ed. D. N. Dumville and C. N. L. Brooke (Woodbridge, 1986), p. 12, n. 40; cf. *The Valuation of Norwich*, ed. W. E. Lunt (Oxford, 1926), pp. 467–73, esp. pp. 471–2.

[22] M. J. Pearson, 'The Creation and Development of the St Asaph Cathedral Chapter, 1141–1293', *Cambrian Medieval Celtic Studies*, **40** (2000), pp. 35–56.

[23] *Brut*, p. 129; *Annales Cambriae*, p. 44. Below, pp. 45, 76–7, 119, 211.

[24] For this possible dating, see D. Stephenson, 'Madog ap Maredudd, *Rex Powissensium*', *WHR*, **24** (2008), pp. 14–15. Pearson, 'Creation and Development of St Asaph', pp. 47–8, suggests the period 1149–55 for the shaping of the deanery of 'Marchia'. See also J. R. Davies, 'Aspects of Church Reform in Wales, *c.* 1093–c. 1223', in *Anglo-Norman Studies*, **30** (2008), pp. 85–99. I should like to thank Dr Stephenson and Dr Davies for kindly sending me drafts of their articles.

[25] The deanery of 'Marchia' does not, however, appear to be mentioned in any of the edited twelfth-century Welsh or English episcopal acts or in any of the edited Welsh monastic charters.

[26] See index under Henry II (1165 campaign).

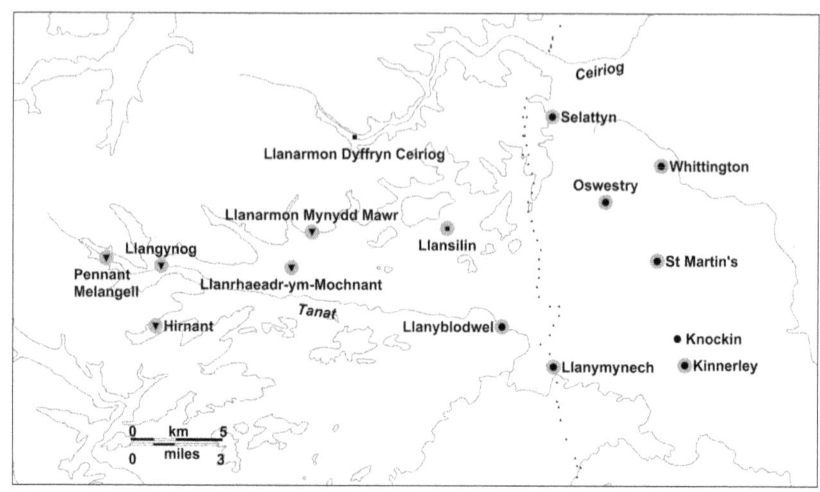

Deanery of 'Marchia' in 1254, possibly from *c.* 1150
Deanery of 'Marchia' in 1291
Deanery of Mochnant in 1291
Deanery of Cynllaith in 1291
Offa's Dyke

Map 3. The deanery of 'Marchia'

appears to have been placed in charge of a standing army of 'serjeants of the March'. As has been mentioned, after the debacle of 1165, no English king led a campaign into Wales for almost fifty years. It seems indeed as if the concept of a Welsh 'March' gained currency precisely at a time when it became more widely accepted that a military stalemate existed on the Anglo-Welsh border.[27]

Given this timing, it may be that the twelfth-century *Marchia Wallie* came to be thought of as a military buffer zone, initially on the Shropshire borders, later all along the Anglo-Welsh frontier. The connotation of a disputed border territory was widespread at the time. None other than Gerald of Wales (*c.* 1146–1223), the author of invaluable ethnographic works on Wales and Ireland, described the frontierlands between English and Irish in Ireland as 'those lands that were furthest inland and closest to the enemy, the so-called marches, which in truth could well take the name

[27] See R. R. Davies, *The Age of Conquest. Wales 1063–1415* (Oxford, 2000; first published under this title Oxford, 1991; first published as *Conquest, Coexistence and Change: Wales 1063–1415*, Oxford, 1987), p. 272.

of "the lands of Mars" from the god of war.'[28] This connotation, although based on an erroneous etymology, may also have inspired Domesday Book's earlier use of 'Marcha de Walis'. Osbern fitz Richard was the son of Richard fitz Scrob, who had been granted land in Herefordshire by Edward the Confessor, king of England, during the 1050s.[29] Richard is thought to have built the first motte in the British Isles, not far from the vills said in 1086 to lie 'in Marcha de Walis'; he may have been among the Normans who were routed by the Welsh armies of Gruffudd ap Llywelyn in 1052.[30] It is entirely possible that the Norman pioneers in Herefordshire were the first to see the Anglo-Welsh borders as a *marche*.

The idea of a militarized buffer zone is certainly consistent with the way in which *march(i)a* was used in other parts of Latin Europe at different periods. It was given the Latin gloss 'regni extremitates'; it can be traced back as far as the sixth century, at which time it referred to the uncultivated land between two properties.[31] The crucial shift in meaning occurred in the late eighth century, when the term began to be used in a new way, particularly in Charlemagne's capitularies. It was then that it came to denote a border zone of the Carolingian empire for which particular legal and military arrangements had been made in order to provide for standing armies charged with the defence of the realm. The first such marches to appear in the sources are the 'marka Tolosana' and the 'marca Hispaniae'. The local officers placed in charge of these were originally referred to as *comites*, *confinii comites* or *limitis custodes*; in the ninth century, the new-fangled term *marchio* appears.[32]

It was in this sense, then, that the term first came to be applied to different regions of medieval Europe. As a result, it played various roles in the histories of the European countries. In the case of Denmark, the term is of obvious importance on a national level. In Austria, the *marchae* are thought to have been, originally, the wooded districts contrasting with the *terrae*.[33] Thus, the *Mark* was synonymous with the *Wald*, the forest.

[28] Translation from Gerald of Wales, *Expugnatio Hibernica*, ed. A. B. Scott and F. X. Martin (Royal Irish Academy, 1978), pp. 240–1: 'terris penitimis hostique propinquioribus, que marchie dicuntur, seu potius a Marte marcie dici possent'. Cf. *Giraldus*, v, 391 (*Expugnatio Hibernica*, ii, 36), which has the reading 'a Marte martie'.

[29] Lewis, 'English and Norman Government', p. 276.

[30] Below, p. 106.

[31] K. Brunner, 'Die fränkischen Fürstentitel im neunten und zehnten Jahrhundert', in H. Wolfram (ed.), *Intitulatio II: Lateinische Herrscher- und Fürstentitel im 9. und 10. Jahrhundert (Mitteilungen des Instituts für Österreichische Geschichtsforschung, Ergänzungsband 24*, 1973), pp. 208–9.

[32] J. Dhondt, 'Le Titre du marquis à l'époque carolingienne', *Archivum Latinitatis Medii Aevi (Bulletin Du Cange)*, **19** (1948), pp. 416–17.

[33] O. Brunner, *Land und Herrschaft: Grundfragen der territorialen Verfassungsgeschiche Österreichs im Mittelalter*, 5th edn (Vienna, 1965, repr. Darmstadt, 1990), pp. 185–6.

As such, it designated a territory which had only recently been settled and brought under cultivation, and which still might develop into a fully fledged *Land*, or territory defined by its legal community of settlers. In this context, therefore, *marcha* complements the single most controversial key term in Austrian constitutional history. In high medieval northern France, one characteristic of *marchae* was their role as diplomatic arenas. The 'march' of Normandy was symbolized by the Gisors elm in the Epte valley, where parleys between the dukes of Normandy and the kings of France traditionally took place.[34] It is possible that there was a direct link between a Continental usage and the growth in fashion of the term in Britain from the 1160s. The 'march' of Normandy was of course closely familiar to the twelfth-century kings of England and their entourages, and perhaps they considered it to parallel the 'march' of Wales.[35] Moreover, it is worth noting that in 1165, Matilda, Henry II's eldest daughter, was betrothed to Henry the Lion, whose duchy of Saxony was at the time being hedged about by new *Marken*, such as the *Mark* of Brandenburg. Henry the Lion was married to Matilda in 1168, and in exile in England from 1182 to 1185 and in 1189. He failed to become margrave of Austria, but he was active in the German settlement of Slavic territory in Mecklenburg, to the north of Brandenburg.[36] Conceivably, perceived parallels to the German–Slavic frontier further encouraged the use of *marchia* in the context of the Welsh borders in the later twelfth century. In any case, whether or not Continental usages of the term can help us understand why it appears in a medieval British context, they do illustrate that it carried certain fundamental connotations which could adapt to local circumstances.

There is certainly some overlap between the originally Carolingian meaning of the term – that of a border region under the command of a deputy – and the modern historiographical concept of the March of Wales as a collection of lordships. Moreover, as early as 1168, the English exchequer, in keeping with its use of *Marchia* for the region, referred to lords of the Anglo-Welsh frontier as *marchisi*.[37] The phrase *barones Marchie*,

[34] J. F. Lemarignier, *Recherches sur l'hommage en marche et les frontières féodales* (Lille, 1945); D. Power, *The Norman Frontier in the Twelfth and Early Thirteenth Centuries* (Cambridge, 2004), pp. 16–17.

[35] See index under Normandy. In a forthcoming article in the *English Historical Review*, I shall deal more fully with the links and parallels between the 'marches' of Normandy and Wales.

[36] For the date of the betrothal see J. Ehlers, *Heinrich der Löwe: Eine Biographie* (Munich, 2008), p. 466; for a charter of Henry the Lion referring to the judicial assembly of Mecklenburg as a 'marcthinc', see *Urkunden und erzählende Quellen zur deutschen Ostsiedlung im Mittelalter*, ed. R. Buchner (Freiherr vom Stein-Gedächtnisausgabe, Band xxvi a-b), 2 vols. (Darmstadt, 1968–70), i, no. 61 (dated to 1169).

[37] *Pipe Roll 14 Henry II, 1167–8* (P. R. S., 12), p. 199; *marchiones* with reference to the lords of the Welsh borders became widespread in John's reign: cf. Holden, *Lords*, p. 229.

which begins to occur at the beginning of the thirteenth century,[38] suggests that the *Marchia* was indeed perceived as a region including, perhaps even coterminous with, the lands of an identifiable group of lords. In this respect, there is reason to believe that *Marchia Wallie* conveyed a similar meaning to both contemporaries and modern-day historians.

On the other hand, it seems clear that on one crucial point contemporary usage differed, initially, from that of the modern literature. As has been seen, the evidence suggests that the medieval 'March of Wales' was, at first, the Welsh border of Shropshire; it then came to be applied to the Anglo-Welsh frontier more generally. Moreover, the border lordships in westernmost Shropshire continued to be considered 'Marcher'. Thus, the castles of Oswestry and Clun were explicitly referred to as lying in the March in 1272; in 1306, the sheriff of Shropshire was dispatched to 'the liberty of Oswestry in the March of Wales outside the county'.[39] However, for some considerable time the medieval concept of the March does not seem to have included the conquest lordships in south Wales. Gerald of Wales, who was a clerk at the royal court from 1184 to about 1196, would have been familiar with the geographical terminology used by the chancery and exchequer, if indeed he did not play a role in shaping it. To him, south Wales, where he was born and spent his childhood, was apparently not, or at least not unequivocally, part of the March of Wales. Pembroke, he wrote, sometime between 1208 and 1216, lay in Wales; and so did Glamorgan (the diocese of Llandaf).[40] Monmouth, on the other hand, according to a text he penned in the late 1190s, was situated in the March of Wales.[41]

In fact, the case is not always so clear-cut. In Gerald's writings, as elsewhere, it is sometimes impossible to be certain whether or not references to *Marchia* in a Welsh context referred to the entire March of Wales as understood by modern-day historians. In 1194, in a well-known passage on the military prowess of his kinsmen from south Wales, Gerald referred to those kinsmen as 'gens in Kambriae marchia nutrita'.[42] A famous example may serve to illustrate further the difficulties of determining the extent of the medieval March of Wales. In Magna Carta, in 1215, King John proclaimed:

If we have disseised or deprived Welshmen of lands, liberties or other things without lawful judgment of their peers, in England or in Wales, they are to be

[38] *Rot. Claus.*, i, 12a (1204); below, esp. pp. 79–84.

[39] *Cal. Pat. R., Henry III, 1266–72*, p. 671; *The Parliament Rolls of Medieval England, 1275–1504*, gen. ed. C. Given-Wilson, 16 vols. (London, 2005), vol. ii: *Edward I (1294–1307)*, ed. P. Brand (London, 2005), p. 506; *Rot. Parl.*, i, 206.

[40] *Giraldus*, i, 21, 58–9, 61, 87 (*De rebus a se gestis*, i, 1; ii, 9, 10, 24). For the dating of Gerald's works, cf. R. Bartlett, *Gerald of Wales (1146–1223)* (Oxford, 1982), pp. 213–21 (appendix I).

[41] *Giraldus*, ii, 148 (*Gemma ecclesiastica*, ii, 51): 'in marchia Walliae apud Munemutam'.

[42] *Giraldus*, vi, 220 (*Descriptio Kambrie*, ii, 8).

returned to them at once; and if a dispute arises over this it shall be settled in the March by judgement of their peers; for tenements in England according to the law of England, for tenements in Wales according to the law of Wales, for tenements in the March according to the law of the March. The Welsh are to do the same to us and to ours.[43]

By identifying the 'March' as an area with its own law, this clause effectively places that region on a par with England and Wales. On the other hand, the first instance of *Marchia* in the clause may not refer to a region at all, but to a border. The phrase 'in Anglia vel in Wallia' also suggests that the 'March' was not quite equivalent to these other two geographical entities. However, 'in Anglia vel in Wallia' only appears as an addition at the foot of one of the four surviving originals of Magna Carta (Ci).[44] It seems that in 1215 there was still some uncertainty about the status of 'Marchia' relative to 'Anglia' and 'Wallia'. Moreover, it is impossible to tell from Magna Carta alone exactly how far Wales, England and the March were thought to extend.

Throughout the thirteenth century, royal clerks continued to be somewhat ambiguous about whether or not the conquest lordships in south Wales were part of the March. In 1216, William the Marshal, the earl of Pembroke, was referred to as one of the 'barons of the March';[45] but this does not prove conclusively that Pembroke was considered to be a Marcher lordship, since the Marshal was also lord of Chepstow on the Anglo-Welsh border. Ten years later, on 10 July 1226, Henry III wrote to the Marshal's son, also William, requesting him to deliver up the castles of Carmarthen and Cardigan, since the king proposed 'to stray into the March of Wales'. This may be read as a possible indication that those castles, though in south Wales, were considered to be Marcher.[46] It should be noted that in the following month Henry headed not to south Wales, but, once again, to Shrewsbury and Oswestry, there to negotiate with Llywelyn ap Iorwerth and other Welsh rulers.[47] On the other hand, the rebellion of Richard Marshal, which was largely restricted to the south

[43] J. C. Holt, *Magna Carta*, 2nd edn (Cambridge, 1992), App. 6, esp. pp. 466–9 (clause 56 of the 1215 text): 'Si nos disseisivimus vel elongavimus Walenses de terris vel libertatibus vel rebus aliis, sine legali judicio parium suorum (in Anglia vel in Wallia), eis statim reddantur; et si contencio super hoc orta fuerit, tunc inde fiat in Marchia per judicium parium suorum de tenementis Anglie secundum legem Anglie; de tenementis Wallie secundum legem Wallie; de tenementis Marchie secundum legem Marchie. Idem facient Walenses nobis et nostris.'

[44] *ibid.*, p. 466, n. 4. [45] *Rot. Claus.*, 270a.

[46] *Cal. Pat. R., Henry III, 1225–32*, pp. 80–1.

[47] J. E. Lloyd, *A History of Wales from the Earliest Times to the Edwardian Conquest*, 3rd edn (London, 1939; repr. in 2 vols. 1948), pp. 665–6; *Rot. Claus.*, ii, 206; T. Craib and others, *Itinerary of Henry III, 1215–1272* (Public Record Office, 1923), pp. 62–3.

of Wales, was in 1233 referred to as having taken place in the March.[48] One clear instance dates to 1268: in that year Henry III granted Payn de Chaworth two weekly markets 'at Cydweli in the March of Wales'.[49] There is no reason to believe that English royal officials were always entirely confident about the location of places in Wales and the borders. However, they probably knew where Cydweli was, given its proximity to the English kings' stronghold at Carmarthen. It may well be that by the 1260s, a century after Henry II's expedition to Wales, the idea that south Wales was part of *Marchia Wallie* was gaining ground.

On the other hand, at around this time, in *c.* 1250 × 1259, Matthew Paris marked a 'Marchia' in red ink on the most detailed of his four maps of Britain,[50] locating it just to the north of the Severn. South Wales is also marked in red, with a gloss that seems to be inspired by the writings of Gerald of Wales.[51] Given that Roman cartographical concepts and techniques were unknown in medieval Europe, Matthew's maps are astoundingly accurate in their proportions.[52] That is not to say that he did not err in filling in the topographical details: for instance, the river to the north of the 'Marchia' should of course be the Dee, but to judge from the position of Carlisle and the Roman walls, Matthew took it for the Eden.[53] Also, the erasion and re-marking of 'Cludesdale' would suggest that he was unsure about the difference between the rivers Clwyd and Clyde. He correctly identified the Severn, however, and perhaps his placing of the 'Marchia' of Wales may be explained by the usage of the phrase *Marchia Wallie* which was current in England at the time he drew his maps.

48 *Excerpta e Rotulis Finium, 1216–1272*, ed. C. Roberts, 2 vols. (London, 1835–6), i, 251–2.

49 *Cal. Chart. R.*, ii, 113; TNA C 53/57, m. 1: 'Keddewelly in March' Wall".

50 See this book's cover for a detail showing 'Wallia' and its 'Marchia'. The map is from BL Cotton Claudius D VI, f. 12v, the beginning of Matthew's *Abbreviatio Chronicorum*. Matthew's are the earliest extant detailed maps of Britain.

51 'Regio palustris montuosa nemorosa invia pastoribus accomoda. Incolas habet agiles incultos et bellicosos' ('a marshy, mountainous, woody and pathless region suitable for shepherds. It has agile, uncultivated and warlike inhabitants.')

52 P. D. A. Harvey, 'Matthew Paris's Maps of Britain', in P. R. Coss and S. D. Lloyd (eds.), *Thirteenth-Century England*, 4 (Woodbridge, 1992), p. 113; see also R. Vaughan, *Matthew Paris* (Cambridge, 1958), pp. 241–2; *Four Maps of Great Britain Designed by Matthew Paris about A. D. 1250. Reproduced from Three Manuscripts in the British Museum and one at Corpus Christi College, Cambridge*, ed. J. P. Gilson (London, 1928), Map A; S. Lewis, *The Art of Matthew Paris in the* Chronica Majora (Berkeley and Aldershot, 1987), pp. 364–72, esp. fig. 221, p. 370.

53 Matthew may have confused these two rivers owing to their similar courses: J. B. Mitchell, 'Early Maps of Great Britain', *Geographical Journal*, **81** (1933), p. 30; cf. Harvey, 'Maps', p. 117. The names Matthew gave this river remain mysterious ('Tunce' on the map discussed above, 'Gance' on his map of Britain in Corpus Christi College, Cambridge, MS 16 f. v, verso). The Dee appears in neither of the indices to the Rolls Series editions of Matthew Paris's works. See also *Four Maps*, ed. Gilson (London, 1928), Map A, pp. 7 and 11, n. 4.

We begin to gain a clearer picture from the 1230s onwards. It was then that the royal chancery started producing inquisitions *post mortem*, which conveniently group the estates of deceased magnates under geographical headings. Since they also contain escheats of Welsh territories, they are a particularly useful class of document for determining the perceived extent of the March. The inquisitions *post mortem* suggest that a distinction continued to be drawn between the lordships in the March and those in south Wales until as late as the fourteenth century. Between 1284 and 1307, places identified by escheators as lying in the March of Wales included the Vale of Montalt on the Cheshire borders, Magor (west of Caldicot on the southern coast of Gwent) and Mathern, which lies just to the east of Magor and where there was a Welsh knight's fee held of the lordship of Chepstow.[54] In the same period, the following were identified as lying in Wales: Bronllys and Glasbury in the lordship of Brecon; Radnor, and Bleddfa just to its north; the commotes of Gwrtheyrnion and Maelienydd; in south-east Wales, Merthyr Mawr, a Glamorgan knight's fee just to the north of Ogmore; and, in south-west Wales, the commotes of Iscennen and of Ystrad Tywi, as well as those of Perfedd and of Hyrfryn, where stood the castle of Llandovery.[55]

However, at the beginning of the reign of Edward II, there was some uncertainty about the situation of Pembroke. The headings 'Marchia' and 'Marchia Wallie' were added as an afterthought to the inquisitions made in 1307 into the lands of Joan de Valence, countess of Pembroke.[56] Thereafter, it became more normal to consider the lordships in south Wales as Marcher: in 1317, the inquisition *post mortem* of Nicholas d'Audley was entitled 'Llandovery in the March of Wales', even though in 1299 that castle had been considered to lie in Wales.[57] The inclusion within the March of lordships in south Wales was to prove enduring: in 1375, Glamorgan and the county of Pembroke were understood to be 'in the March of Wales adjacent to Gloucestershire'.[58] In *post mortem* inquisitions, this method of identifying sections of the March by the county on which they abutted

[54] Vale of Montalt: *CIPM*, ii, 161 (no. 284, Roger de Montalt; TNA C 133/20 (14), mm. 1–2); Magor: *CIPM*, iii, 276 (no. 415, William de Mohun; TNA C 133/79 (14), m. 5); Mathern: *CIPM*, iv, 336 (no. 446, Bogo de Knovill; TNA C 133/131/11, m. 3).

[55] Merthyr Mawr: *CIPM*, iii, 250 (no. 371, Gilbert de Clare; TNA C 133/77 (3), m. 20v); Bronllys, Glasbury, Perfedd, Hyrfryn, Llandovery: *CIPM*, iii, 419–21 (no. 544, John Giffard of Brimpsfield; TNA C 133/91 (2), mm. 6, 7, 13–15); Radnor: *CIPM*, iv, 19 (no. 41, Maud de Mortimer; TNA C 133/101 (6), m. 1); Bleddfa: *CIPM*, iv, 143 (no. 221, Hugh Mortimer of Richard's Castle; TNA C 133/113 (2), m. 5); Gwrtheyrnion and Maelienydd: *CIPM*, iv, 161–2 (no. 235, Edmund Mortimer; TNA C 133/114 (8), mm. 14–15); Ystrad Tywi: *CIPM*, iv, 233 (no. 352, John Pichard; TNA C 133/121 (12), m. 3).

[56] TNA C 134/4 (1), mm. 2 ('Marchia'), 3 ('Marchia Wallie'), 4 ('Marchia Wallie'); cf. *CIPM*, v, no. 56. The additions were made in a fourteenth-century hand.

[57] *CIPM*, vi, 42 (no. 56); cf. TNA C 134/56 (3), m. 7.

[58] *CIPM*, xiv, 220, 223–4 (no. 209, Edward le Despenser, d. 1375; TNA C 135/253 (1), mm. 3–4, 59, 61).

remained standard for the rest of the medieval period.[59] Indeed, the last *post mortem* inquisition to refer to the March of Wales was ordered and held in 1538–9, that is, *after* the first of the Acts of Union which identified and then abolished all the Marcher lordships, including those in south Wales.[60] It should be noted, however, that the old geographical nomenclature did not disappear overnight.[61] The inquisition *post mortem*, compiled in 1324, of Aymer de Valence, eleventh earl of Pembroke, son of the aforementioned Joan, records that he held no lands in north Wales, but then lists under the heading of south Wales his lordships of Upper Gwent, Pembroke, Haverfordwest and Oysterlow (Ystlwyf).[62] Abergavenny and Painscastle were deemed to lie in the March in 1313 and 1315 respectively, but Abergavenny was placed in Wales in 1325.[63] In the first years of Edward III's reign, Pembroke county, as well as commotes in Ceredigion and in the lordship of St Clare, were found to lie in Wales, and so, more surprisingly, were Ewyas Lacy, and Talgarth in the lordship of Brecon.[64]

As we have seen, phrases like *Marchia Wallie* appear in two of the key documents of English medieval history, Domesday Book and Magna Carta. Just like *Wallia* itself,[65] *Marchia Wallie* acquired considerable importance in high medieval political and legal discourse. It is a testament to that importance that the Welsh, too, began to refer to part of their country as the 'March'. The expression appears to have been communicated to the Welsh rulers early in the thirteenth century, through diplomatic channels as it were. The March is not mentioned in King John's treaty

59 See, for example, TNA C 141/2 (20) (Martin Ferrers, inquisition held in 1484); TNA C 141/6 (20) (Roger Barewe, 1485).

60 TNA C 142/59 (78) (William Edmunds: writ and inquisition refer to 'the March of Wales adjacent to Gloucestershire', inquisition finds the fees of Usk and of Caerleon to lie in the March of Wales).

61 For instance, see *Vita Edwardi Secundi*, ed. and trans. N. Denholm-Young (London, 1957), p. 119, *sub anno* 1322: '[Edward II] Rex igitur, relicta Salopia, in Marchiam transiuit, et quia nemo restitit omnia castella faciliter occupauit. Veniensque apud Herfordiam episcopum loci acriter increpauit ...' ('The king, therefore, leaving Shrewsbury, crossed to the March and as no one opposed him he easily took all the castles. Coming to Hereford, he upbraided the bishop of the place ...').

62 *CIPM*, vi, 323–4 (no. 518; TNA C 134/84, mm. 58, 60).

63 *CIPM*, v, 401 (no. 615, Guy de Beauchamp, earl of Warwick; TNA C 134/50, m. 38); *CIPM*, v, 232 (no. 412, John de Hastings the elder; TNA C 134/31 (1), m. 15r); *CIPM*, vi, 387, 390 (no. 612, John de Hastings the younger; TNA C 134/91 (1), m. 21; TNA C 134/92 (1), m. 36). John was also found to hold Cilgerran castle in Pembroke county 'as a free baron in Wales': *CIPM*, vi, 387–8; TNA C 134/91 (1), m. 22.

64 Pembroke county: *CIPM*, vii, 292 (no. 391, Aymer de Valence, 1331; TNA C 135/30 (1), m. 19); Ceredigion, commotes of Mabwynion, Perfedd and Creuddyn: *CIPM*, vii, 305 (no. 418, Goronwy ap Tudur, inquisition held in 1332; TNA C 135/31 (16)); St Clare's lordship, commotes of Amgoed and Peuliniog: *CIPM*, vii, 247 (no. 329, Morgan ap Maredudd, 1333; TNA C 135/26 (11), mm. 3–4); Ewyas Lacy: *CIPM*, vii, 71 (no. 83, Theobald de Verdon, 1327; TNA C 135/7 (1), m. 10); Talgarth: *CIPM*, vii, 143 (no. 177, Rhys ap Howel, 1328; TNA C 135/14 (3), m. 6).

65 See, for example, R. R. Davies, 'The Identity of "Wales" in the Thirteenth Century', in R. R. Davies and G. H. Jenkins (eds.), *From Medieval to Modern Wales: Historical Essays in Honour of Kenneth O. Morgan and Ralph A. Griffiths* (Cardiff, 2004), pp. 45–63.

of 1201 with Llywelyn ap Iorwerth, nor in the three agreements reached three years after Magna Carta between Llywelyn and Henry III's minority government. This is perhaps surprising, given that on both occasions the application of English and Welsh law was discussed.[66] But, by around 1230, at the very latest, the 'Marches' were part of normal discourse in cross-border communications.[67] In 1233, Llywelyn ap Iorwerth himself mentioned Henry III's 'bailiffs of the March', the earliest reference to the March to occur in the surviving Welsh acts.[68] Thereafter, the dominant concept of the March, from a Welsh point of view, would appear to have been that of Magna Carta: the March as a region with its own law, like England and Wales. It is in that legal context that 'Marchia' is contrasted to 'pura Wallia' in the letter addressed to Archbishop Pecham in October 1282, in which Llywelyn ap Gruffudd aired his grievances against Edward I and his men.[69]

In geographical terms, the usage of *Marchia* by the Welsh rulers and their scribes broadly parallels that found in English documents. In 1218, Llywelyn ap Iorwerth seems to have had no doubt that Cardigan and Carmarthen lay in south Wales.[70] Well after the initial Welsh acceptance of the term *Marchia*, Llywelyn ap Gruffudd, writing to Henry III, explicitly distinguished 'barones de Marchia' from 'ballivi vestri et barones de Sudwallia'.[71] There is no instance in the documents which have come down to us of a Welsh ruler identifying a part of south Wales as lying in the March. If Welsh usage conformed to that of twelfth- and thirteenth-century English scribes in that respect, it did not become as standardized. Llywelyn ap Gruffudd frequently referred to 'Marches' in the plural.[72] It is apparently consistent with this that there is also one striking document in his name which twice refers to the 'Shropshire March'.[73] This linguistic coinage is not paralleled in the surviving Welsh acts for any of the other border counties. It may suggest that the Powys–Shropshire borders, for Llywelyn ap Gruffudd, were just one of several 'Marches'. On the other hand, it possibly shows that the borders of Shropshire, the area around the ford of Rhyd Chwima over the Severn, had a quintessentially 'Marcher' character from the Welsh point of view as well.[74] Moreover, it indicates that in Welsh usage the imported concept of the 'March' was adapted and refined, very possibly as a result of a familiarity with local

66 *AWR*, nos. 240–2. 67 *Ibid.*, nos. 264–5.

68 *Ibid.*, no. 268. 69 *Ibid.*, no. 429.

70 *Ibid.*, no. 241. 71 *Ibid.*, no. 351 (probably 1262).

72 e.g. *ibid.*, no. 393 (1275–6).

73 *Ibid.*, no. 385 (1275–7).

74 There are numerous other instances in the Welsh acts of 'Marchia' occurring in a Powys–Shropshire context. Probably in 1262, Llywelyn ap Gruffudd included John Fitzalan II (d. 1267), lord of

and regional circumstances which was greater than that of the English chancery and exchequer scribes.

* * *

It would appear, then, that the medieval concept of the March did approximate to the modern historical category – but only belatedly, and somewhat inconsistently. Indeed, the first twelfth-century 'March of Wales' was a part of the Welsh borders where there were no conquest lordships at all. The frontier lordships on the borders of Shropshire, as has been seen, covered mostly territory that was uncontestably shire-ground in the eleventh century. Thus, the history of the medieval concept of the March of Wales presents a puzzle. That concept originally referred to a section of the borders where hardly any Welsh territory was conquered after 1066. But over the years it came to embrace both the frontier honors and the English-held lordships in Wales.

This seems particularly strange since it involved the conceptual merging of two distinct kinds of marches. The march of the Carolingian type, with defensive border commands situated on the 'hither' side of the frontier, corresponds to the compact blocks of mainly English territory found in westernmost Shropshire. On the other hand, the conquest territories in Wales parallel the Roman *limes*, which commonly consisted of a network of client territories situated on the far side of the border line.[75] It might be argued that since these two concepts are incompatible, the medieval concept of the March of Wales must have come to refer to a 'no-man's land' lying between the respective boundaries of England and of Wales. This latter concept could conceivably have gained ground after 1284, once the tripartite structure of Principality, March and English counties had become established. In any case, the history of the March

Oswestry and of Clun, among a group of *barones de Marchia* whom he contrasted with 'barones de Cateric', Staffordscir' et Sallopp'' ('barons of ?Cheshire, Staffordshire and Shropshire'): cf. *ibid.*, nos. 351–2. Cf. also *ibid.*, no. 355 (Llywelyn ap Gruffudd, probably 1262), which refers to Roger Mortimer II (d. 1282), lord of Wigmore, and Humphrey de Bohun V 'the Younger' (d. 1265), son of the earl of Hereford and lord of Brecon, as 'barons of the March'; no. 384 (Llywelyn ap Gruffudd, probably 1275–6) for the phrase 'iuxta Monte(m) Gom(er)i in Marchia'; nos. 393–4 (Llywelyn ap Gruffudd's letters to Robert, archbishop of Canterbury, on trespasses of 'Marchers', including Mortimer and Gruffudd ap Gwenwynwyn, contrasted to 'the king's barons and bailiffs of South Wales', 1275–6) and no. 605 (Gruffudd ap Gwenwynwyn, probably 1277–8), for a reference to *Marchia Wallie* on the Shropshire borders. For a recent assessment of the long-term significance of the Severn ford (Rhyd Chwima, the 'rushing ford') to 'Anglo-Welsh relations' see J. Davies, 'Rhyd Chwima – The Ford at Montgomery – Aque Vadum de Mungumeri', *Mont. Coll.*, **94** (2006), pp. 23–36.

[75] D. C. Braund, *Rome and the Friendly King: The Character of Client Kingship* (London, 1984), esp. pp. 91–103; B. Isaac, *The Limits of Empire*, rev. edn (Oxford, 1992).

indicates that a specific medieval frontier might be conceptualized and demarcated in quite different ways at different times. This provides a complementary perspective on other historical frontiers, particularly on the other political boundaries of medieval Europe.[76]

It is safest to start with the simple fact that the phrase *Marchia Wallie* was coined at all – and contrasted with *pura Wallia*. At the most basic level, this suggests that a region was understood to exist which was separate both from Wales proper and from England. The question that needs to be asked, then, is how far the creation of the Welsh March was perceived as the making of a region. The task of understanding the medieval concept of the March of Wales clearly involves investigating what characteristics were considered to be typically 'Marcher' at different times. Nothing illustrates that task better than the issue of 'Marcher' liberties. The Marcher lords' claim to quasi-regal immunity has been inextricably linked to the concept of the March of Wales at least since the sixteenth century. The link is evident, for instance, in the writings of George Owen of Henllys, an Elizabethan lawyer and antiquary who acquired the lordship of Cemais in northern Pembrokeshire and whose interest in the origins of his lordship went hand in hand with his concern to establish his own claim to Marcher immunity.[77] Marcher liberties did tie together the lordships of south Wales and those which were withdrawn from the English border counties. However, if it is accepted that Marcher liberties only became an issue in the thirteenth century,[78] it follows that they cannot have been among the distinctive characteristics of the March at the time the phrase *Marchia Wallie* was coined. The challenge, then, is to identify other features which might have set the March apart from Wales on the one hand and from England on the other.

The early history of the phrase *Marchia Wallie* reveals a unique opportunity for identifying such 'Marcher' characteristics. The borders between Shropshire and Wales, and those borders alone, were identified

[76] Frontiers, of states and of societies, have intrigued historians for well over a century. See the remarks in L. Febvre, *La Terre et l'évolution humaine* (Paris, 1922), esp. pp. 357–83. For an influential late nineteenth- and early twentieth-century view of the American 'Frontier', see F. J. Turner, *The Frontier in American History* (New York, 1921). Recent studies of frontiers include R. Bartlett and A. MacKay (eds.), *Medieval Frontier Societies* (Oxford, 1989); D. Power and N. Standen (eds.), *Frontiers in Question: Eurasian Borderlands, 700–1700* (London, 1999); W. Pohl, I. Wood and H. Reimitz (eds.), *The Transformation of Frontiers from Late Antiquity to the Carolingians* (Leiden, 2001); D. Abulafia and N. Berend (eds.), *Medieval Frontiers: Concepts and Practices* (Aldershot, 2002); P. Bauduin, *La Première Normandie (Xe–XIe siècles). Sur les frontières de la haute Normandie: identité et construction d'une principauté* (Caen, 2004); Power, *Norman Frontier*; F. Curta (ed.), *Borders, Barriers and Ethnogenesis: Frontiers in Late Antiquity and the Middle Ages* (Turnhout, 2005); see also E. O'Byrne and J. Ní Ghradaigh (eds.), *The March in the Medieval West, 1000–1400* (forthcoming).

[77] George Owen of Henllys, *The Description of Pembrokeshire*, ed. D. Miles (Llandysul, 1994), esp. ch. 3.

[78] Davies, 'Kings, Lords and Liberties', esp. p. 59.

by contemporaries as the 'March of Wales', from the time when that expression gained currency, and may indeed have been newly coined, to the time when it included foreign-held lordships in south Wales. Studying the Welsh borders of Shropshire, therefore, is the single most promising way of tracing how the medieval concept of the March originated and developed. As far as that concept is concerned, there is a good chance that what was true of the Shropshire borders was true of all the area identified as 'Marcher'. If the lordships on the Welsh borders of Shropshire displayed common features which distinguished them from the county on the one hand and Wales on the other, those features may well reveal the meaning, or meanings, of the phrase *Marchia Wallie*.

It is true that allowance needs to be made for the possibility that the concept of the March changed and the Shropshire borders simply continued to be included out of habit. In such a case, the characteristics of the Shropshire frontier would cease to reflect reliably the medieval concept of the March. Moreover, given the great political fragmentation and geographical diversity of the Welsh borders, let alone Wales, it is far from evident that *Marchia Wallie* was always a name for a region displaying certain uniform and distinctive characteristics. It cannot be assumed from the outset that there were such characteristics at all; or, to put it differently, that the March was ever perceived to exist as a region with its own identity, in the sense that it was thought to display its own, typical features. The only way not to prejudge that issue is to leave open the possibility that *Marchia Wallie* referred to a district believed to exist in a negative sense only, one that could be assigned neither to Wales nor to England: a region whose only distinctive and typical characteristic was its great diversity and fragmentation.

Thus, even if the Shropshire borders formed a region in themselves, it is conceivable that they were included in the later *Marchia* because they were not thought to belong to either England or Wales, rather than because of more positive similarities to other parts of the March. However, caveats notwithstanding, a study of the Shropshire borders holds out great promise. It is abundantly clear that those borders are of central interest to the history of the Marcher concept. But, what is more, the Shropshire borders offer an especially effective way of addressing one of the chief challenges in writing the history of the March of Wales. That challenge consists in the dilemma that studies of individual lordships, or even groups of lordships, risk not revealing what was common to the March as a whole, while studies of the whole March that are to remain manageable can consider less local and regional variation.[79]

[79] See Rees Davies's preface to his *Lordship and Society*, pp. v–vi; Lieberman, *March of Wales*, pp. 9–10.

Since the Shropshire borders were apparently taken to be the original *Marchia Wallie* and also continued to be included within that category, the ways in which they changed between 1066 and 1283 may mirror the development of the wider March of Wales during that period more faithfully than any other section of that March. Certainly, concentrating on the lordships of westernmost Shropshire will reveal the differences as well as the similarities between them. This book, then, will focus on the part of the Welsh borders that seems first to have been, and always to have belonged to, the *medieval* March of Wales. In doing so, it will discuss how far the history of the Welsh frontier of Shropshire between the late eleventh and the early fourteenth centuries provides a paradigm both for the coining of the phrase *Marchia Wallie* and for the making of the wider March of Wales. Indeed, this book aims to contribute to frontier studies more generally, by shedding light both on how a specific medieval frontier was created and on how it was perceived by successive generations.

Chapter 1

A BORDER REGION?

It may well be that the phrase *Marchia Wallie* was initially coined as a result of day-to-day political events, in the aftermath of Henry II's failed campaign of 1165.[1] But more permanent characteristics of the Welsh borders must be considered as well: the lie of the land, say, or the patterns of communications and of human settlement. The relationship between pre-modern political frontiers and the obstacles provided by terrain was far from deterministic. Boundaries of medieval European polities were generally zonal or fragmented rather than linear, and could cut across rivers, forests or mountain ranges. They were commonly overlaid and blurred by the tenurial interests and family connections of local aristocracies. Moreover, of course, they tended to shift over time, often considerably.[2] Nevertheless, it stands to reason that terrain may have played a role in demarcating the perceived and actual extent of *Marchia Wallie*. It may well be, for instance, that observers from central England would have been struck, in encountering the Welsh borders, by the transition from lower to higher land. It certainly seems possible that geographical features helped create the perception that the Welsh borders formed a distinctive region in themselves. It is therefore worth investigating how far this might have been true in the case of the original *Marchia Wallie*, to wit, the Powys–Shropshire borderlands.

TERRAIN AND COMMUNICATIONS

The Welsh borders of Shropshire were demarcated by the upland–lowland transition, but only to a certain extent. In the eleventh century, the western boundary of Shropshire quite closely followed the course of

[1] Above, pp. 9–10.

[2] P. Peyvel, 'Structures féodales et frontière médiévale: l'exemple de la zone de contact entre Forez et Bourbonnais aux XIIIe et XIVe siècles', *Moyen Âge*, **93** (1987), pp. 51–83; cf. Power, *Norman Frontier*,

Offa's Dyke. After all, the Dyke had been built in the eighth century to demarcate the western limits of the old kingdom of Mercia, and Shropshire was among the westernmost of the shires into which Mercia had been divided in the tenth century. However, it appears doubtful whether the upland–lowland divide alone determined the position of Offa's Dyke on the east–west axis. The Dyke clearly aimed at drawing a borderline running straight from north to south, and it therefore followed some boundaries of physical geography while boldly cutting across others. Thus, the river Severn runs roughly from south to north for about eight kilometres west of the Breidden range, and here it links two separate sections of Offa's Dyke, effectively replacing it as the boundary line. To the north of this stretch of the Severn, the Dyke runs along a clear highland–lowland divide. For here, the plain which extends across both Cheshire and the northern half of Shropshire abuts against part of the Welsh massif, the Berwyn mountains, which rise abruptly to over 400 metres. Yet, even here, Offa's Dyke does not follow the upland–lowland divide entirely faithfully, for it traverses the valleys of the rivers Efyrnwy (English spelling Vyrnwy), Ceiriog and Dee. Such inconsistency is even more pronounced to the south of the Breidden range, where the upper Severn valley, a broad swathe of lowland, lies to the west of the Dyke, and to its east rises what is, in terms of relief, a continuation of the Welsh upland plateau jutting out across southern Shropshire: the Stiperstones, the Long Mynd and Wenlock Edge.

There was, then, only a limited geographical logic to the course of the frontier between Shropshire and Powys in the eleventh century. This is perhaps not very surprising. After all, the shape of the shires into which Mercia was divided was dictated mainly by administrative and strategic considerations. The frontiers of Shropshire provide strong evidence that the principle which guided the partition of Mercia was to create territories with defensible sites at their centres. The boundaries between Shropshire and its adjacent counties, Cheshire, Staffordshire, Worcestershire and Herefordshire, are not marked by clear geographical features. Shropshire's original borders were probably the result of an early tenth-century emergency measure against the threat of Viking attacks.[3] They disregarded the frontiers of the Mercian sub-kingdoms such as those of the Wreoconsæte and the Magonsæte;[4] it was only to

pp. 7–8 on Normandy's lack of 'natural frontiers' apart from the English Channel; for a critical discussion of the reality of 'natural frontiers' in a later period, see P. Sahlins, 'Natural Frontiers Revisited: France's Boundaries since the Seventeenth Century', *American Historical Review*, **95** (1990), pp. 1423–51.

[3] M. Gelling, *The West Midlands in the Early Middle Ages* (Leicester, 1992), pp. 141–2.

[4] F. M. Stenton, *Anglo-Saxon England*, 3rd edn (Oxford, 1971), p. 337.

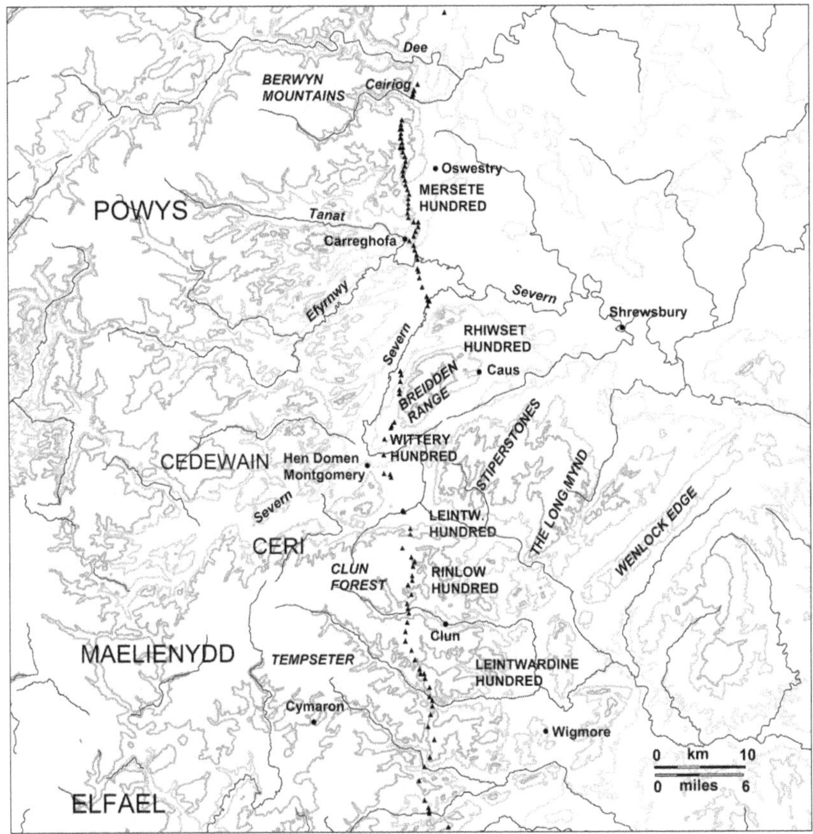

Map 4. Principalities and hundreds on the Shropshire–Powys borders

be expected that they would disregard some, at least, of the boundaries imposed by physical geography.

Similarly, the lie of the land was only one of the factors shaping communications in the Welsh border counties. The site of Shrewsbury, within a loop of the river Severn, was clearly chosen for its incomparable value as a defensible position. However, it also soon came to lie at a crossroads which was of crucial importance to the borderlands. Roman roads had converged upon Viroconium, modern-day Wroxeter, about six miles downstream.[5] But these were diverted to the new site, probably in the tenth century (Shrewsbury is first mentioned in 901).[6] Four roads which

[5] Gelling, *West Midlands*, p. 18; W. Davies, *Wales in the Early Middle Ages* (London, 1982), p. 17.

[6] P. H. Sawyer, *Anglo-Saxon Charters: An Annotated List and Bibliography* (Royal Historical Society, 1968), no. 221; *The Early Charters of the West Midlands*, ed. H. P. R. Finberg, 2nd edn (Leicester, 1972),

were of importance during the medieval period met at the new town. One ran to Shrewsbury from Chester, by way of either Ellesmere or Whitchurch; another from Bristol through Gloucester, Tewkesbury, Worcester and Bridgnorth; a third from the Wye valley and Hereford, passing Leominster, Ludlow and the Church Stretton valley; and a fourth led to the main entry-point into Wales: the gap formed in the Welsh mountains by the Severn valley.[7] This last road, like the others, was partly of Roman origin, although during the Middle Ages the preferred route lay along the edge of the alluvial plain of the Rea–Camlad vale, rather than over the Long Mountain.[8]

These four roads, together with the fact that the river Severn was navigable as far as Shrewsbury, helped ensure that town's prosperity. In 1086, Shrewsbury already had 252 burgesses, and probably over a thousand inhabitants in total, which placed it among the middle-ranking boroughs of England, with such places as Chester and Cambridge.[9] But the roads which met at Shrewsbury were of significance at a regional level, because they provided the main arteries of communication, and helped determine the direction towards which the population was oriented. To a considerable extent, Shropshire faced east and south. The importance of waterways in the medieval period meant that river drainage systems contributed towards providing communications within, and thereby unifying, regions.[10] The Severn, which drains much of Shropshire, certainly acted to encourage that county's ties with the West Midlands. This tie, moreover, was further strengthened by the road which ran to Bristol, along the Severn, by way of Bridgnorth and Worcester. This is one of the best-documented land-routes of medieval England. Its stations were detailed in William of Worcester's fifteenth-century compendium; and it is one of the roads shown on the unique map of Britain, datable to about 1360, known as the Gough map.[11] The paths to Wales, on the other hand,

no. 430; 'Anglo-Saxon Charters Relating to Shropshire', eds. W. H. Stevenson and W. H. Duignan, *TSAS*, 4th ser., **1** (1911), pp. 4–6; M. Gelling, *The Place-Names of Shropshire, Part 4: Shrewsbury Town and Suburbs and the Liberties of Shrewsbury* (Nottingham, 2004), pp. xiii–xviii.

7 F. M. Stenton, 'The Road System of Medieval England', *EHR*, **7** (1936–7), p. 5.

8 T. C. Cantrill, 'Geology', in *VCH*, i, Map facing p. 1.

9 The river Severn: R. H. Hilton, *A Medieval Society: The West Midlands at the End of the Thirteenth Century* (London, 1966), pp. 9, 254; J. F. Edwards and B. P. Hindle, 'The Transportation System of Medieval England and Wales', *Journal of Historical Geography*, **17** (1991), pp. 129–30; for the suggestion that the Severn was navigable as far as Welshpool: E. T. Jones, 'River Navigation in Medieval England', *Journal of Historical Geography*, **26** (2000), p. 63; the burgesses: DB 252a; ranking of boroughs: H. C. Darby, *Domesday England* (Cambridge, 1977), p. 307.

10 Hilton, *A Medieval Society*, pp. 10–13.

11 William Worcestre, *Itineraries*, ed. J. H. Harvey (Oxford Medieval Texts, 1969), p. 331; E. J. S. Parsons, *The Map of Great Britain circa A.D. 1360 Known as the Gough Map: An Introduction to the Facsimile*,

were fraught with difficulty. In 1165, as has been seen, Henry II tried to lead an army across the Berwyn mountains, but it was harried by Welsh archers taking cover in the woods of the Ceiriog valley and, though it reached the mountain ridge, it was forced to retreat after being caught in stormy weather.[12] In 1283, Edward I ordered the captains of his invading army to cut down the trees on either side of mountain passes around Montgomery and in northern Shropshire and to ensure that the breaches were a bowshot in breadth.[13] The Welsh continued to make use of the ancient ridgeways leading east across Offa's Dyke;[14] but, for the English, entering Wales remained a daunting prospect throughout the twelfth and thirteenth centuries.

Yet the importance to Shropshire of its westwards communications, particularly during the twelfth and thirteenth centuries, should not be underestimated. The road west, as will be seen, retained a crucial strategic importance throughout that period, while also proving indispensable to much of Anglo-Welsh diplomacy. That Shrewsbury, from very early on, looked to Wales as well as to England is perhaps shown by the fact that its Welsh name, 'Amwythig', the fortified place, seems to be a Welsh rendition of the *-bury* part of its English name; from at least the early fourteenth century on, the bridges over the Severn leading into Shrewsbury from the west and east were known as the Welsh and English bridges respectively.[15] Furthermore, apart from the Severn route, Shropshire was relatively cut off from central England. And that route could itself be effectively defended against attack from the east. In 1102, King Henry I, having moved an army along it to quell the rebellion of the earl of Shrewsbury, had first to overcome the garrison at the new castle at Bridgnorth and then chose to approach Shrewsbury by cutting a swathe through the woods on Wenlock Edge.[16]

This conveys a preliminary idea of Shropshire's contacts with Wales. But the twelfth and thirteenth centuries were also a period during which Shropshire's lifeline with the southern Welsh borderlands, the Shrewsbury–Ludlow–Hereford connection, gained importance because of the strategic challenge posed by the Welsh.[17] Indeed, that road, from

2nd edn (Oxford, 1996); B. P. Hindle, 'The Towns and Roads of the Gough Map' (1979, offprint from *The Manchester Geographer*, 1, 1980), pp. 38–9 (fig. 2, Road S3b).

12 *Brut*, pp. 144–7; above, p. 9.

13 *Cal. Chanc. R. Var.*, pp. 253, 274.

14 See below, p. 168.

15 R. Morgan, *Welsh Place-Names in Shropshire* (Cardiff, 1997), p. 49; Gelling, *Place-Names. Part 4*, pp. 9–10; 22.

16 *Orderic*, vi, 28–31; *VCH*, viii, 86 identifies Henry I's road with the route from Wenlock to Harley to Cressage.

17 Stenton, 'Road-System', p. 5.

one contemporary point of view at least, provided the main connection between Chester and Bristol. The Anglo-Norman romance known as the legend of *Fouke le Fitz Waryn*, a prose tale thought to be based on a verse romance of the late thirteenth century, is a tribute to the family of Fitzwarin, the lords of Alberbury and Whittington; its author displays a sound knowledge of local geography, particularly of the Ludlow region; it is a text that has often been said to capture the 'Marcher ethos'.[18] According to this legend, a bridge built 'of stone and chalk' in the twelfth century across the river Teme at Ludlow linked 'the high way that leads through the march, and from Chester to Bristol'.[19] To the poet of *Fouke le Fitz Waryn*, the main road from Chester to Bristol ran not along the Severn, but straight through 'the march'. It was argued above that channels of communication acted to tie regions together during the Middle Ages;[20] one of the signs that the Welsh borders came to be better defined as a region was the growth in importance of the main road running through them.

POPULATION DENSITY AND ECONOMY, *c.* 1070–1300

According to Domesday Book, Shropshire, in the second half of the eleventh century, was one of the most sparsely populated English counties.[21] The Domesday evidence suggests, furthermore, that Shropshire's Welsh borderlands included some of the emptiest districts in all of England. Thus, in the uplands to the south-west of the county, where the lordship of Clun was to be founded, population density at the end of the eleventh century has been calculated as two inhabitants per square mile.[22] This was not unparalleled within the county, as it corresponded to the population density in the stretch of moorland in the north-east; but in the north-west, in the parish of Oswestry – where the lordship of Oswestry was to be established – Domesday Book records barely one inhabitant per square mile. The national scope of the Domesday survey makes it possible to compare these numbers directly with the rest of England – and the scarcity of population, as depicted by Domesday Book, of the districts around Clun and Oswestry is well illustrated by the fact that south of the Humber, areas of less than 2.5 inhabitants per square mile were recorded

[18] *Fouke le Fitz Waryn*, ed. E. Hathaway, P. T. Ricketts, C. A. Robson and A. D. Wilshere (Oxford, 1975), pp. ix–x.

[19] *Ibid.*, p. 4, lines 12–14: 'le haut chemyn qe va parmy la marche, e de Cestre desqe Brustut'.

[20] Above, p. 26.

[21] Darby, *Domesday England*, pp. 90–3 (Figs. 34–6).

[22] V. A. Saunders, 'Shropshire', in H. C. Darby and I. B. Terrett (eds.), *The Domesday Geography of Midland England*, 2nd edn (Cambridge, 1971), p. 131 (fig. 42).

only in such places as the Fenlands, the Weald, Exmoor, Dartmoor and parts of the Cornish peninsula.[23]

It is true that Domesday Book may lead us to underestimate the population density in the Shropshire–Powys borderlands. For instance, it does not state whether the vill of Clun had any outlying settlements (berewicks). This may suggest that Clun did not belong to the area of Shropshire where multiple estates had developed before the Norman conquest, and that, apart from those places mentioned by name in the Domesday survey, no other settlements existed in 1086. However, the omission of berewicks may simply be due to inconsistency. Indeed, it is probable that there were in 1086 unnamed satellite settlements near Clun. In the area around Clungunford, in particular, we may strongly suspect that the settlements of Shelderton, Weo and View Edge, Abcott and Rowton already existed at the time of the Domesday survey. We have no evidence of these place-names earlier than the Hundred Rolls of the thirteenth century, but it is likely that the settlements they represent are included in the hides assigned to Clungunford in Domesday Book.[24] Clungunford appears to have had eight geldable hides; Clun had fifteen.[25] This alone makes it likely that unnamed settlements existed in the upper Clun valley at the time of the Domesday survey. Eyton suggested that Acton and Down were held of the lord of Clun as members of that manor.[26] Further possible satellite settlements lay in Clun Forest.[27]

It is also important to stress that Domesday Book is a problematic source for the Welsh borders (as indeed for the other frontier of the English kingdom), because the historical spotlight it throws illuminates only the area over which the Normans exerted some measure of control in 1086. It is not necessarily true that this area was coterminous with later territorial units such as counties, parishes, hundreds and lordships. This is relevant to the calculation of population densities. It has not always been explicitly recognized that in all geographical regions along the limits of the territory conquered by the Normans by 1086, there may conceivably have existed settlements, English or Welsh, which lay beyond the reach

[23] See Darby, *Domesday England*, p. 94.

[24] *Domesday Book*, gen. ed. J. Morris, vol. XXV: *Shropshire*, ed. F. Thorn and C. Thorn, from a draft translation prepared by C. Parker (Phillimore, London and Chichester, 1986), 255a and 258b; notes 4, 3, 46 and 4, 20, 24. The editors of the Phillimore Domesday also mention possible unnamed settlements in the part of the de Sai honor lying in Leintwardine Hundred: notes 4, 20, 18–27. For Picot de Sai, the Domesday lord of Clun, below, pp. 60–9.

[25] DB 258b.

[26] Eyton, xi, 242–3. Cf. J. Tait, 'Introduction to the Shropshire Domesday', in *VCH*, i, 287.

[27] Mainstone and Reilth (including Colebatch); Bettws y Crwyn (with its townships of Cefncelynnog, 'Rugantin', and Trebrodier).

of the Domesday inquest.[28] In any case, Domesday Book is no census. It provides a record of population numbers which can be shown from internal and external evidence to be neither consistently systematized nor complete.[29] These uncertainties notwithstanding, however, it does seem plausible that, as Domesday Book suggests, the Shropshire borderlands included some of the most thinly populated areas of England. The Domesday Book entries for those areas are internally consistent: thus, the lack of population is matched by a scarcity of plough-teams,[30] and with regard to arable, too, there appears to be no great discrepancy between the number of people and the number of ploughlands recorded.[31] Domesday Book's evidence for population numbers along the Shropshire–Powys frontier thus appears fairly sound. An exceptionally low population can be safely assumed to have been a distinctive characteristic of the region around 1086.

Restraints imposed on agriculture by the terrain were clearly among the reasons for this scarcity, but the distribution of soils also played a role. That much is suggested by the ways in which the Severn valley contrasted with the north-west and south-west of the county.[32] The belt of land following the course of the Severn across the county was characterized by relatively low plains and medium loam soils. Significantly, this swathe of countryside was three times as populous as the Clun region, having six inhabitants per square mile, even without counting the burgesses of Shrewsbury and Quatford. Even close to the Welsh border, the ratio of population to area was considerably higher in the Severn valley – where the lordships of Caus and of Montgomery were later to be founded – than to the north and south. The correspondingly higher number of plough-teams again corroborates the population densities, while also reinforcing the impression that the most populous areas were those best suited to arable agriculture. There is even archaeological evidence, uncovered during the excavation of Hen Domen Montgomery Castle, of an arable field system which can be dated securely to the eleventh century.[33]

[28] Thus, the maps prepared by V. A. Saunders (see nn. 22 and 30 in this chapter) compute the averages on the basis of present-day parish boundaries, which is a necessary approximation, since the precise westwards extent of the territory under Norman control in 1086 is uncertain.

[29] Darby, *Domesday England*, pp. 57–61.

[30] Saunders, 'Shropshire', p. 129 (fig. 40).

[31] *Ibid.*, p. 135.

[32] *Ibid.*, pp. 129 (fig. 40), 131 (fig. 42), 152.

[33] P. A. Barker and J. Lawson, 'A Pre-Norman Field System at Hen Domen, Montgomery', *Medieval Archaeology*, **15**, pp. 58–72. The field system is thought to have been contained within the four demesne ploughlands recorded in DB 253c.

The distribution of population density thus served, at the end of the eleventh century, to emphasize the distinction between the borders and lower, more fertile land – but the fact that the upper Severn valley was more populous than other parts of the frontier also highlights the diversity of the borderlands. We have no way of being certain whether the correlation between lower, fertile land and relatively high population also existed west of the area covered by the Domesday survey. The fact that population density in the western Severn valley was only half of what it was further east perhaps suggests that it continued to decrease westwards, as the valley narrowed, but this is no more than a plausible guess.

There is evidence that in the Welsh borders arable agriculture was practised at higher altitudes during the Middle Ages than it is today. This was certainly the case in the uplands of northern Britain.[34] Some of the evidence for the Shropshire borders dates to a very early period: the course of Offa's Dyke as it crosses the Clun valley suggests that it ran along eighth-century arable fields.[35] Even though by 1215 the hospital at Oswestry had been granted grazing rights in the 'land of Cynynion', which lies in the hills west of Offa's Dyke,[36] it seems that cattle grazing there coexisted with at least some arable: 'Cynynion' derives from the Welsh for 'shreds, small pieces', and may indicate the presence of small arable fields among the pasture.[37] Although it is also possible that the place-name refers to patches of pasture amid waste,[38] the first reading seems more probable. By the later Middle Ages Cynynion was a hybrid settlement, for it combined common fields with dispersed habitations, instead of the more usual villages or hamlets; there was arable in two separate fields.[39] In sum, arable in the hills west of Oswestry may well date back to the thirteenth century or even earlier.

Yet there can be no doubt of the great importance to the uplands' economy of pasture, and especially of cattle-rearing. As in northern Britain, there was a predominance of 'horn over corn'.[40] The early fourteenth-century Fitzalan estate surveys preserve evidence for a demesne

[34] G. W. S. Barrow, 'Frontier and Settlement: Which Influenced Which? England and Scotland, 1100–1300', in Bartlett and MacKay (eds.), *Medieval Frontier Societies*, pp. 6–7; see also W. E. Kapelle, *The Norman Conquest of the North: The Region and its Transformation, 1000–1135* (London, 1979), pp. 213–27.

[35] C. Fox and D. W. Phillips, 'Offa's Dyke: A Field Survey (Fifth Report)', *Arch. Camb.*, **85** (1930), pp. 19–28. But cf. P. L. Everson, 'Three Case Studies of Ridge and Furrow, 1: Offa's Dyke at Dudston in Chirbury, Shropshire. A Pre-Offan Field System?', *Landscape History*, **13** (1991), pp. 53–63, which concludes that the discernible traces of ridge-and-furrow here are later than Offa's Dyke.

[36] *Haughmond Cart.*, nos. 838, 840.

[37] Morgan, *Welsh Place-Names*, p. 25.

[38] *Ibid.*, p. 25.

[39] D. Sylvester, *The Rural Landscape of the Welsh Borderland* (London, 1969), pp. 308–10.

[40] Barrow, 'Frontier and Settlement', pp. 7–8.

sheep stint of 300 heads at Bicton,[41] but since the Fitzalans were avid sheep-farmers, it would appear quite possible that they introduced the practice in Clun. It is also notable that by the fourteenth century, the earl of Arundel was breeding horses at Clun,[42] a practice which may also have been an import: Gerald of Wales, in his *Journey through Wales*, notes that Robert de Bellême (earl of Shrewsbury 1098–1102) had brought horses from Spain whose stock, by Gerald's day, had made Powys famous for its horse-breeding.[43] While it would appear that sheep and horses were later additions to the local animal husbandry, there are indications that indigenous pasture originally relied on cattle. It is probable that the tribute of two *animalia* owed at Clun manor in 1086 was a traditional render of cattle, possibly Welsh in origin.[44] At that time, the lord of Oswestry claimed a tribute of eight cows from the Welshmen of Edeirnion.[45] In 1102, the men of Powys plundered 'the flocks and herds' which the earl of Shrewsbury had pastured in their country.[46] The sources reveal that by 1302 the English lord of Clun took *trethcanteidion* (a render of no less than 100 oxen) from his Welsh tenants.[47] Like other such seigneurial dues, this is a survival of a traditional Welsh tribute,[48] and therefore provides an indication that cattle formed the mainstay of the local economy at an early period.

There are further hints that cattle-rearing was particularly common in the borderlands. In 1221, King Henry III, pursuing the host of Llywelyn ap Iorwerth from Grosmont Castle towards Montgomery, 'destroyed everything belonging to Welshmen in the way of cattle and buildings'.[49] In 1241–2, the sheriff of Shropshire accounted for £20 13s 10d for ninety-five and a half cows which were owed the lord of Oswestry as a kitchen rent.[50] By that time, or shortly afterwards, the abbey of Haughmond in central Shropshire was buying cattle at Oswestry.[51] It is tempting to

[41] W. J. Slack, *The Lordship of Oswestry: A Series of Extents and Rentals Transcribed and Edited with an Introduction, 1393–1607* (Shrewsbury, 1951), p. 59.

[42] *VCH*, iv, p. 57.

[43] Gerald of Wales, *The Journey through Wales/The Description of Wales*, transl. L. Thorpe (London, 1978), p. 201 (*Itinerarium Kambriae*, ii, 12).

[44] DB 258b. [45] DB 255a. [46] *Brut*, p. 45.

[47] *CIPM*, iv, no. 90: inquisition *post mortem* of Richard Earl of Arundel (d. 1302).

[48] On the 'tax of one hundred oxen' see Davies, *Lordship and Society*, pp. 20 (n. 19), 134, 356.

[49] Matthew Paris, *Historia Anglorum*, ed. F. Madden (RS, 1866), p. 247; Matthew Paris, *Chron. Maj.*, iii, 64 (both *sub anno* 1221); Roger of Wendover, *Chronica, sive Flores Historiarum*, ed. H. O. Coxe, 4 vols. (London, 1841–4), iv, 72 (the Latin is *pecus*).

[50] *The Great Roll of the Pipe, 26 Henry III, 1241–2*, ed. H. L. Cannon (New Haven and London, 1918), p. 8 (possibly a commuted and slightly adjusted 'tax of one hundred oxen', in which case this may be evidence for the importance of cattle at an earlier date).

[51] *Haughmond Cart.*, p. 11.

suggest that those cattle were driven eastwards from the Welsh hills, and that market towns such as Oswestry derived some of their border aspect from functioning as centres for the exchange of a typically upland commodity. Certainly, in 1274, the burgesses of Ludlow complained that the constable of Wigmore Castle had his men capture forty of their cattle 'on the king's highway, at Edgton … coming from the market at Montgomery', and drive them 'from the barony of Clun to Wigmore Castle'.[52]

We also catch glimpses of the centrality of cattle to the Powysian economy during the twelfth and thirteenth centuries. The tribute payments which Henry I demanded from the rulers of Powys in 1121 were reckoned in thousands of heads of cattle, and in 1110 he had ransomed Iorwerth ap Bleddyn, a member of the Powysian ruling family, for 'three hundred pounds of silver in whatever form he might come by them, whether in horses or in oxen or in any form he might come by them'.[53] The charters of the Cistercian abbey of Ystrad Marchell, in recording grants made to it by Welsh lords of Powys in the years after its foundation at the end of the twelfth century, make abundant references to pasture and the importance of cattle.[54] Although Cistercian houses in Wales generally exploited marginal lands,[55] and grants of upland pasture to them are therefore unsurprising, the Ystrad Marchell charters do provide further evidence that arable agriculture was not predominant in Powys.

Rather, the evidence points to a mixed economy. According to the Welsh laws, the food renders due to a Welsh king from manors in his realm included produce from arable such as loaves of bread made from wheat or groats.[56] Arable agriculture certainly was not unknown in the valleys of Powys during the Middle Ages: 124 instances of ridge-and-furrow submitted to the Sites and Monuments Records for Powys, Denbighshire, Flintshire and Wrexham have been assigned to the medieval period.[57] These cannot be dated very closely, but there is some documentary evidence for arable in Powys or adjacent parts of Wales

[52] *Rot. Hund.*, ii, 99 (the Latin is *averia*).

[53] *Brut*, p. 109 (*sub anno* 1121); p. 65 (*sub anno* 1110).

[54] e.g. *The Charters of the Abbey of Ystrad Marchell*, ed. G. C. G. Thomas (Aberystwyth, 1997), nos. 34 (1201, grants all pastures in Powysian principality of Cyfeiliog); 41 (1204/5, grants all pastures in Mochnant); no. 54 (1207, grants all pastures in Arwystli).

[55] D. H. Williams, *The Welsh Cistercians: Aspects of Their Economic History* (Pontypool, 1969), pp. 13–14; the same, *The Welsh Cistercians*, 2 vols. (Tenby, 1984), i, ch. 1; ii, *passim*.

[56] See, for instance, the section on *dawn bwyd* (food gift) and *gwestfa* (hospitality, food render) in *The Law of Hywel Dda*, ed. and transl. D. Jenkins (Llandysul, 1986), pp. 128–9. For a discussion of these food-renders, which were owed respectively by bondmen and land-holding nobles, see T. M. Charles-Edwards, *Early Irish and Welsh Kinship* (Oxford, 1993), pp. 370–95.

[57] Not including a further 191 instances tentatively assigned to the Middle Ages.

during the twelfth and thirteenth centuries. In 1109, raiders of the lands of Cadwgan ap Bleddyn, ruler in Powys and Ceredigion (d. 1111), burned 'the houses and the barns and the corn' belonging to that ruler. Around 1280, Llywelyn ap Gruffudd ap Madog, the lord of Powys Fadog, complained to Edward I that the Fitzalan lords of Oswestry and their men had 'entered the houses of Llywelyn's villeins, cut the crops and carried them away'.[58] If arable was common in Powys, the same was true of pasture in Shropshire. Haughmond Abbey, by the second half of the thirteenth century, was running several cattle-farms both within the county and in the borders.[59] In 1260, the lords of Knockin, of Whittington and of southern Powys were accused of leading a band of Welshmen to attack the manor of Ford, only eight kilometres west of Shrewsbury, of killing, wounding or taking prisoner 28 men, and of carrying off as booty a total of 260 oxen and cows, 80 sheep and 57 horses.[60] It is impossible to quantify the relative importance of arable and pasture in Powys, the borderlands and Shropshire. But the evidence suggests that, during the twelfth and thirteenth centuries, a mixed economy prevailed.

It was seen above that population and settlements were concentrated in the Severn valley at the beginning of the period under consideration. This raises the question of how far the Shropshire–Powys frontierlands might have formed a region of settlement expansion thereafter, during the twelfth and thirteenth centuries. Parallels provided by other parts of Welsh border country, such as Dyfed, suggest that the arrival of colonists from Normandy and Flanders in the early twelfth century stimulated the establishment of new settlements, which were often named after their founder.[61] The same was true of Ceredigion in the late eleventh and early twelfth centuries, where English settlers were said to have been brought in 'to fill the land, which before that was almost completely empty from a scarcity of people'.[62] On the Continent, the creation of new villages was one of the hallmark features of the eastwards movement of German settlers after around 1125.[63] A characteristic of High Medieval frontier

58 *Brut*, p. 61; *AWR*, no. 535 (dated 1277 × March 1282), cf. also no. 534; *Cal. Anc. Corr. Wales*, p. 98. Note that Dr Stephenson has recently argued that the lands raided in 1109 lay in Ceredigion, not Powys: cf. D. Stephenson, 'The "Resurgence" of Powys in the Late Eleventh and Early Twelfth Centuries', *Anglo-Norman Studies*, **30** (2008), p. 192 and n. 71. I should like to thank Dr Stephenson for kindly sending me a draft of this article.

59 *Haughmond Cart.*, p. 11. 60 *Close R., 1259–61*, pp. 180–1.

61 I. W. Rowlands, 'The Making of the March: Aspects of the Norman Settlement in Dyfed', *Anglo-Norman Studies*, **3** (1981), pp. 146–8; K. Murphy, 'Small Boroughs in South-West Wales: Their Planning, Early Development and Defences', in N. Edwards (ed.), *Landscape and Settlement in Medieval Wales* (Oxford, 1997), p. 145.

62 *Brut*, p. 93 (*sub anno* 1116).

63 R. Bartlett, *The Making of Europe: Conquest, Colonization and Cultural Change 950–1350* (London, 1993), ch. 5.

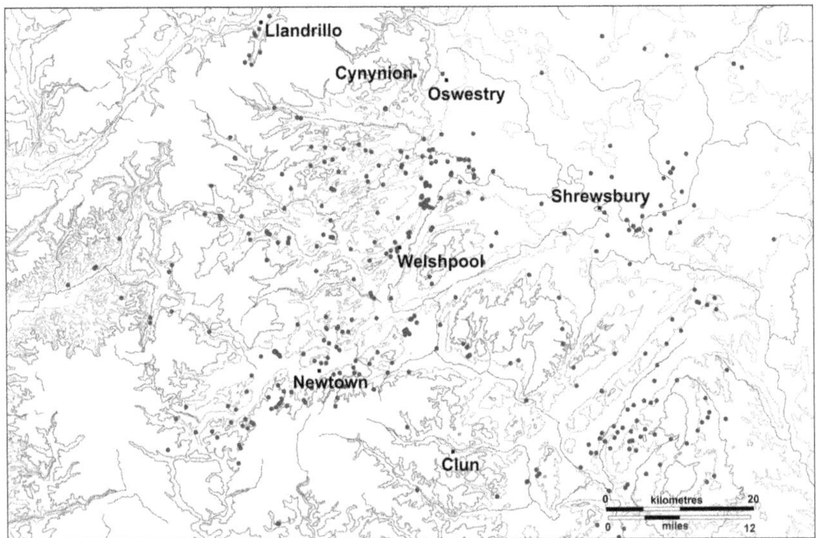

Map 5. Possible and probable instances of medieval ridge and furrow in Shropshire and Powys

regions, then, was that they tended to be areas where new settlements were founded, and it is therefore worth discussing whether the Shropshire borderlands displayed this feature as well.

The main type of evidence that can be used to assess the age of settlements is that of place-names. It is true that, where place-names cannot be corroborated with evidence from other sources, relying on their testimony carries the risk of post-dating settlements, as place-names were often not recorded until long after they began to be used. Besides, an exhaustive analysis of Shropshire and Powys place-names would be far beyond the scope of this chapter. However, since Margaret Gelling has collected and dated the spellings of all ancient Shropshire parish place-names,[64] it is possible to map at least one category of place-name appearing for the first time in our records after 1086 and before 1300.

The Shropshire parish place-names which were first recorded between 1087 and 1300 are certainly not restricted to the territory that came to be coterminous with the Marcher lordships. Rather, they are distributed to the north and south of a corridor of lower land just over ten kilometres wide that follows the course of the Severn – roughly the same belt of

[64] Gelling, *Place-Names. Part 1.* This volume also lists spellings for the place-names first mentioned in Domesday Book.

countryside in which settlements and population were concentrated in 1086.[65] It should be emphasized again that the first occurrence of these names between 1087 and 1300 need not necessarily mean that all, or even any, of the settlements were newly established during that period. However, given that there is such a clear correlation between less desirable land and more recently recorded place-names, their distribution does seem to reflect more than just the state of the surviving evidence. It is reasonable to suggest that these names were not documented until after 1086 because it was only after that date that the places to which they refer came into existence or grew in importance.

Settlement growth between 1087 and 1300 illustrates again that the border country between Shropshire and Powys was not homogeneous. The evidence of the parish place-names suggests that new settlements were quite common in the north-west. But they were almost absent from the area around Caus, and most numerous in the hilly southern half of the county, both close to the Welsh border and in the east. This is only a rough impression, and it is very possible that it will be amended as further research into lesser place-names of Shropshire and the borders is conducted. Meanwhile, however, it is possible to gain a more differentiated picture by asking whether first recordings of place-names were particularly common in the borderlands at any given time during the twelfth and thirteenth centuries.

Thus, considering the chronological layers on Map 6 does provide a further perspective on the borderlands. During the earliest period, between 1087 and 1150, the countryside closest to Wales was distinctively lacking in any newly recorded place-names. Thereafter, names are first recorded in roughly even numbers in the borderlands and the county. In the latest period, the second half of the thirteenth century, parish place-names which are first documented are disproportionately more common close to the frontier than in Shropshire proper. Any interpretations which could be advanced on the basis of this evidence concern the nature of the surviving sources as much as the actual development of settlements in Shropshire and the borderlands. Yet, as was observed above, the newly recorded parish names did show a clear correlation with the areas less favourable to settlement in 1086. It does seem, then, that place-name evidence is a rough indicator of settlement expansion, and that the Shropshire–Powys borderlands were an area unfavourable to the growth of existing settlements, or the establishment of new ones, during the late eleventh century and the first half of the twelfth. Between about 1150 and 1250, frontier settlements developed roughly on a par with those in

[65] See maps in Saunders, 'Shropshire', referred to in this chapter, nn. 22, 28 and 30.

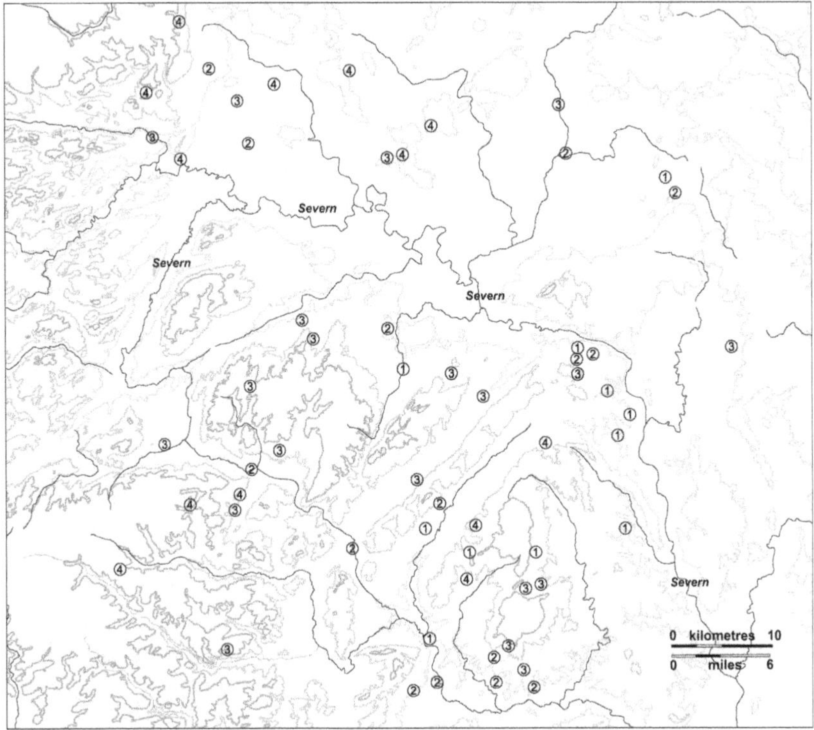

① First recorded between 1087 and 1150 ② First recorded between 1151 and 1200
③ First recorded between 1201 and 1250 ④ First recorded between 1251 and 1300

Map 6. Shropshire parish place-names first recorded between 1087 and 1300

the county proper, while during the latter half of the thirteenth century the borderlands surpassed the county as an area still offering possibilities for further settlement expansion. This would suggest that limitations on arable such as relief and soils were not the only factor slowing settlement growth to the north and south of the Severn valley between 1087 and 1300. The evidence of the Shropshire parish place-names indicates that proximity to Wales may have delayed settlement expansion by about half a century.[66]

If we turn from the evidence of the parish place-names to that of the boroughs, the borders appear more clearly as an area of settlement expansion.[67] Overwhelmingly, the boroughs on the Shropshire–Powys

[66] That would fit the evidence of the borderlands' castles. See below, Chapter 4, esp. pp. 151–72; Conclusion, p. 256.

[67] See Map 7, below, p. 40.

frontier were plantations, that is, they were established on sites previously uninhabited, or scarcely inhabited. In no case were boroughs created by bestowing burghal privileges on existing towns.[68] This was, of course, because so many of the boroughs close to Wales grew up next to castles, whose sites were frequently chosen purely for strategic reasons. Oswestry Castle, for instance, is almost certainly identical with the castle named *L'oeuvre* in Domesday Book.[69] Although it is recorded under the entry for the manor of Maesbury, its site lies some four kilometres to the north of the vill of that name. It may be that it was built on one of Maesbury's five unnamed satellite settlements. However, it is just as possible that the site was chosen purely because it offered strategic advantages,[70] such as a combination of water supply and control over communications and the surrounding countryside. At Oswestry the symbiosis between castle and new town could hardly be more evident: the first burgage plots nestled within the shelter of the castle bailey.[71] The case of Caus is exactly parallel. The choice of its site may have been influenced by the existence of a berewick, in this case belonging to the manor of Worthen. Yet it seems clear that the prime considerations were defensibility and the views of the upper Severn valley afforded by its hilltop position; the town was probably entirely enclosed by the castle's outer bailey.[72] The small borough of Bishop's Castle originated in a similar way, a settlement growing up next to the castle which the bishop of Hereford built near his manor of Lydbury. As for the borough at Clun, this was clearly associated with the castle to the north of the river, and may have been an addition to a pre-existing Anglo-Saxon settlement centred on the church to the river's south.[73] The present-day town of Montgomery was founded in 1227, its site being determined not by an existing settlement, but by the proximity of the rocky outcrop on which Henry III decided to build a castle in 1223.[74] In the case of Welshpool, or Y Trallwng, a Welsh ecclesiastical settlement may have preceded the castle, which was probably built in

[68] For the distinction, see Bartlett, *Making of Europe*, pp. 167–72; on towns in medieval Herefordshire, see Holden, *Lords*, pp. 36–7.

[69] DB 253c.

[70] This was the explanation favoured by Eyton: Eyton, x, 319–20.

[71] R. A. Griffiths (ed.), *Boroughs of Medieval Wales* (Cardiff, 1978), p. vii; Ll. B. Smith, 'Oswestry', in Griffiths (ed.), *Boroughs*, pp. 219–42. In 1272, the burgage plots at Oswestry within and without the castle bailey were distinguished in the *post mortem* inquisition of John Fitzalan III: Eyton, x, 330.

[72] M. Beresford, *New Towns of the Middle Ages*, 2nd edn (London, 1988), pp. 480–1.

[73] *Ibid.*, pp. 478–83.

[74] Matthew Paris, *Historia Anglorum*, p. 247; Matthew Paris, *Chron. Maj.*, iii, 64 (both *sub anno* 1221); Roger of Wendover, *Flores Historiarum*, iv, 72; J. K. Knight, 'Excavations at Montgomery Castle', *Arch. Camb.* **141** (1992), pp. 97–180; *Cal. Chart. R., 1226–57*, p. 10; *ibid.*, p. 101: Hubert de Burgh grants privileges to both New and Old Montgomery in 1229; cf. Eyton, xi, 134–5.

the first half of the twelfth century; but it seems clear that, if a church settlement existed, it cannot have been large.[75] Further south, on the Shropshire–Herefordshire border, two further striking examples are to be found. These were Richard's Castle, a petty borough which grew up around what is thought to be the first castle built by Normans in the British Isles, and Ludlow, often referred to as a classic Norman plantation.[76] In all these places, settlement growth was galvanized in good part by the erection of castles, often on previously empty sites or next to isolated settlements.

Urban plantation was, of course, not limited to the borderlands. The town of Bridgnorth even paralleled the border boroughs in that it was associated with a Norman castle. It was clearly a plantation, for it came to replace the Domesday borough at Quatford.[77] Wenlock, which had thirty-nine burgesses by 1247, was a monastic foundation, much like Atcham, although the latter failed, despite being situated by a bridge over the Severn.[78] Newport was a borough established during the reign of King Henry I;[79] its suggestive name does not appear in Domesday Book. Newport lay within the manor of Edgmond, which suggests that it may have paralleled Oswestry or Caus as a development of a satellite settlement. However, it was no castle-borough: its economic origins, and to some extent the grant of burghal privileges, were related to the royal fishponds nearby.[80] The castle-plantations, as opposed to the non-fortified plantations, were overwhelmingly a frontier phenomenon in Shropshire and the borderlands during the twelfth and thirteenth centuries.

The survival of towns was not guaranteed by the presence of a castle, as is shown by the evidence of Hen Domen Montgomery. By 1201, Chirbury priory held a burgage plot by Hen Domen castle, which implies that there were others there too – an Ystrad Marchell charter of the year 1215 refers to the 'uilla de Muntgumeri', which must be Hen Domen, as the new town was not founded until after 1223.[81] However,

75 R. Morgan, 'The Foundation of the Borough of Welshpool', *Mont. Coll.*, **65** (1977), pp. 7–9. First mention of Welshpool castle: *Brut*, p. 177 (*sub anno* 1196); note that *Brut, Peniarth 20*, p. 35, mentions that Madog ap Rhirid intended to build a castle at Welshpool as early as 1111.

76 Beresford, *New Towns*, pp. 637–41; 481–2; R. Shoesmith, 'Ludlow town', in R. Shoesmith and A. Johnson (eds.), *Ludlow Castle: Its History and Buildings* (Logaston Press, 2000), pp. 5–13; for Richard's Castle, see below, p. 143, n. 15.

77 Beresford, *New Towns*, pp. 479–80; for the settlement history in the area, see J. F. A. Mason, *The Borough of Bridgnorth, 1157–1957* (Bridgnorth, 1957), pp. 1–3; the same, 'The Norman Castle at Quatford', *TSAS*, **57** (1961–4), pp. 37–62.

78 Eyton, iii, 257; Atcham: *VCH*, iv, 67.

79 Eyton, ix, 129–36.

80 Beresford, *New Towns*, p. 482.

81 *Innocentii III, Romani Pontificis, Opera Omnia*, ed. J.-P. Migne, 4 vols. (*Bibliotheca Patrum Latina*, 214–18, Paris, 1855), i, col. 944; *Ystrad Marchell Charters*, ed. Thomas, no. 25.

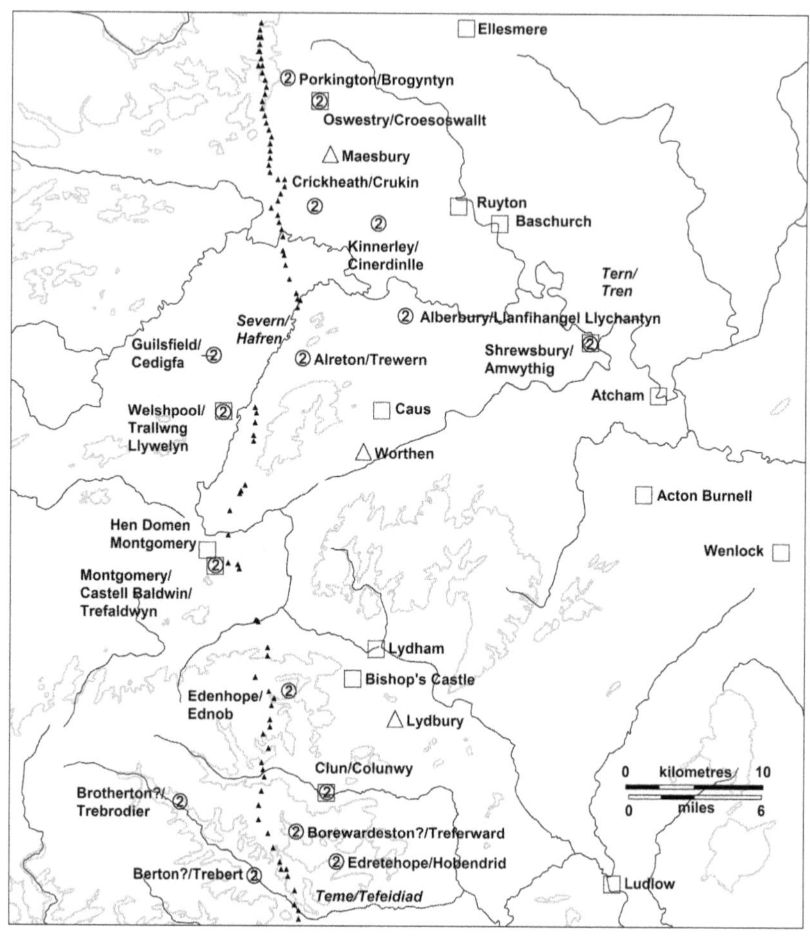

Map 7. Boroughs and dual place-names in Shropshire and the borders to *c.* 1300

the castle and nascent borough at Hen Domen were destroyed by the Welsh in around 1215; they may have been abandoned until about 1223.[82] Moreover, the twelfth-century castellan family had died out in 1207, and

[82] P. A. Barker, 'Timber Castles on the Welsh Border with Special Reference to Hen Domen, Montgomery', in *Les Mondes Normands (VIIIe–XIIe siècles)* (Caen, 1989), pp. 139, 145.

a royal borough was founded nearby, all of which conspired to doom Hen Domen, or Old Montgomery, to failure as a town.[83]

The burgeoning of petty boroughs along the Shropshire–Powys frontier was not encouraged solely by the proliferation of castles, but also, in some cases, by grants of burghal privileges. The laws of Hereford and Breteuil, which had been introduced to the border counties almost as soon as the Normans arrived there, may well have been bestowed on Clun and on Oswestry by the end of the twelfth century (having been derived from Shrewsbury). They were granted to Ellesmere early in Henry III's reign, possibly to the new town at Montgomery in 1227,[84] and certainly to Welshpool in the early 1240s.[85] The boroughs of westernmost Shropshire thereby became members of that pioneering 'family of urban law' to which belonged such colonizing ventures as the town at Rhuddlan on the northern Welsh coast and several of the English urban plantations in Ireland.[86] The growth of the border plantations, as far as we can see, was closely connected with grants of privileges. It began after the middle of the twelfth century, and gathered momentum even later, keeping pace with the delayed expansion of settlement on the borders. Around the castle at Caus, 28 burgage-tenements had been founded by 1274; that number rose to 34 in 1300, and to 58 in about 1349.[87] Clun, in 1272, was already a town of 183 burgages held by 101 burgesses, with an additional 22 burgages in assarts.[88] Although the individual boroughs were small, their cumulative effect transformed the demography of what had once been almost empty districts, while also stimulating local trade. Welshpool had no fewer than 225 burgages by 1322, which made it one of the largest towns in Wales and the borders.[89]

As for the physical layout of the boroughs, the development of towns on the border seems often to have followed a similar pattern, in that streets were arranged in a regular grid between the castle and the church. Sometimes this appears to have been the result of planning, as at New Radnor, and possibly at Ludlow.[90] Although regular street grids are, of

[83] See the decline of Caus in the fifteenth century, discussed below, p. 153.

[84] M. Bateson, 'The Laws of Breteuil, Part II: The English Evidence (Continued)', *EHR*, **15**, no. 59 (1900), pp. 522–3, 520; Eyton, x, 324–5; *Cal. Chart. R., 1226–57*, p. 10. The Fitzalan lord of Oswestry and Clun granted the laws of Breteuil to Ruyton (near Oswestry) in 1308: M. Bateson 'The Laws of Breteuil (Continued)', *EHR*, **15**, no. 58 (1900), p. 316.

[85] Morgan, 'Welshpool', pp. 7–9.

[86] Bartlett, *Making of Europe*, pp. 172–7; Rhuddlan: DB 269a; Beresford, *New Towns*, pp. 37, 551.

[87] TNA C 133/7 (8), m. 1r; C 133/94 (6), m. 2r; *VCH*, viii, 310, n. 99, citing Longleat MSS. unbound 3846.

[88] TNA C 132/42 (5), m. 6r.

[89] See Beresford, *New Towns*, pp. 255–6, for further examples and comparisons.

[90] R. Silvester, 'New Radnor: The Topography of a Medieval Planned Town in Mid-Wales', in Edwards (ed.), *Landscape and Settlement*, pp. 157–64; Beresford, *New Towns*, pp. 481–2; A. L. Poole,

course, found in many plantations in England, the specific combination of a grid with a castle and a church is so widespread in the Welsh borderlands as to be almost characteristic of that region. Some, but not all, of these characteristic elements can be discerned in the morphology of the towns on the Shropshire frontier. It has to be conceded that most, especially Oswestry, lacked a rectilinear street grid, although Clun, for example, displays a classical street grid laid out between church and castle. By far the clearest physical feature of the Shropshire border towns was, and is, the presence of a castle.

THE TRANSFORMATION OF THE ETHNIC FRONTIER

Throughout the period under consideration, the western border of Shropshire was a frontier of peoples. It therefore seems possible that one 'Marcher' characteristic was an overlap between English and Welsh settlements. At the end of the eleventh century, considerably more than sixty Welshmen were recorded as tilling the soil on a total of eighteen of the manors listed in the Domesday Book entries for Shropshire.[91] Vills wholly or partly populated by Welshmen were most common in the lowlands to the north-west, around the newly built castle at Oswestry, but Welshmen were also settled further south, at Churchstoke, Bausley, Trewern, Kempton and Clun. In most of these places, English, Welsh and indeed 'French' settlers intermingled (although no English settlers are mentioned at Churchstoke, Bausley, Maesbrook, Melverley, Aston and the unidentified 'Tibeton'). Thus, the Shropshire–Powys border does appear to have been a region of mixed settlement at this period. In this respect, it perhaps contrasted with Herefordshire, where the districts of Ewias and Archenfield, which had a strong Welsh identity in 1086, were fairly clearly separated from the English-populated part of the county.[92] Shropshire itself, in the eyes of the Domesday inquiry, was adjacent to Welsh districts, 'fines Walensium', which presumably were inhabited by Welshmen only. Such, plausibly, was the case in the 'finis terrae Walensis' which 'Tuder, a certain Welshman' was said to hold; and also in Cynllaith and Edeirnion, the two 'fines' supposedly held 'in Walis' by the Norman lord of Oswestry.[93] However, it seems clear that, between these 'fines'

Medieval England, 2 vols. (Oxford, 1958), i, 58 (fig. 20); R. Shoesmith, 'Ludlow Town', pp. 5–13, esp. p. 14.

91 DB 253b; 253c (two entries); 253d; 254d (four entries, of which 'Tibeton' has not been identified); 255a (four entries); 255c; 256b; 258a; 258b; 259b; 259c; 259d.

92 C. W. Watkin, 'Herefordshire', in Darby and Terrett (eds.), *Domesday Geography of Midland England*, pp. 75, 77; *Alecto County Edition of Domesday Book*, Map 14, 'Herefordshire and Worcestershire' (London, 1988); compare *ibid.*, Map 20, 'Shropshire' (London, 1990).

93 DB 253c; 255a.

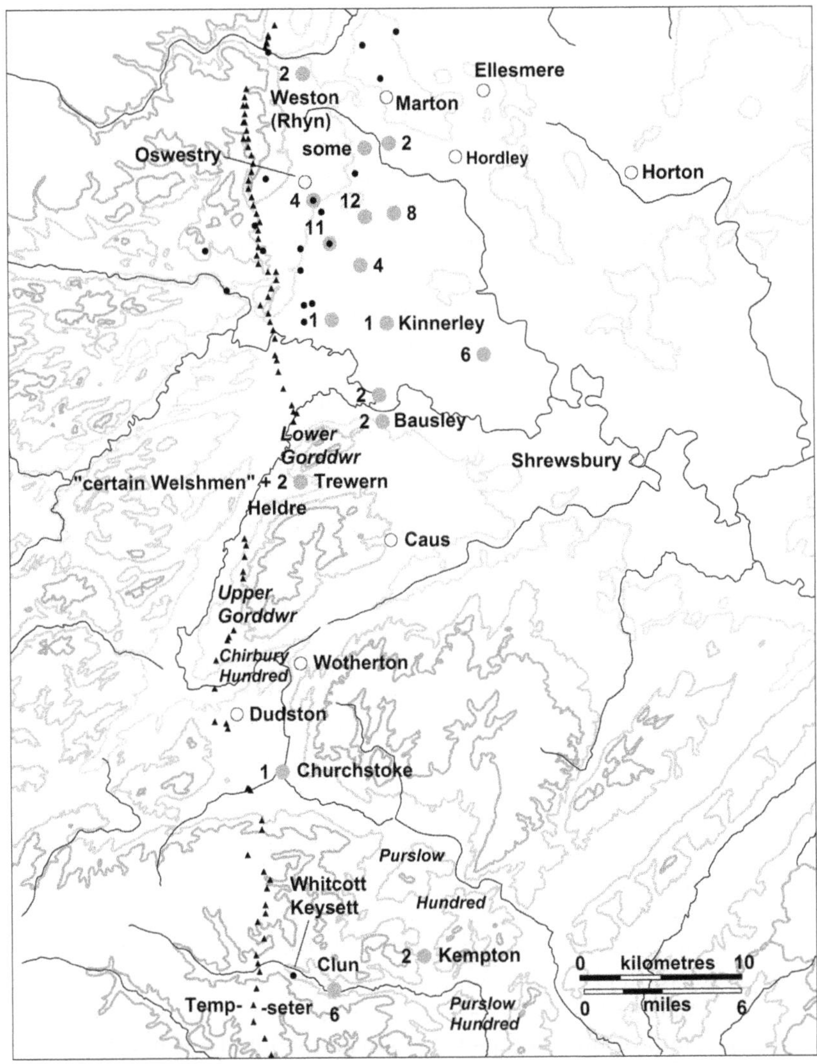

Map 8. Welsh population in the Powys–Shropshire borders, 1086–*c.* 1300

and English-inhabited Shropshire, lay a zone of mixed population. The frontier of peoples in western Shropshire was a permeable one in the late eleventh century.

Domesday Book's Shropshire Welshmen were agricultural labourers integrated within the English manorial system,[94] although it seems possible that their social and legal status was less well defined than that of their various English counterparts. How permeable was the Shropshire–Powys frontier for Welsh freemen? In 1109, Cadwgan ap Bleddyn, who had married the daughter of the first Norman lord of Clun, moved to 'a township which he had received from his wife', but he seems to have required the permission of King Henry I to do so.[95] It is possible that this was purely for political reasons, and that mixed settlement zones were still common. In the 1150s, Gilbert Foliot, the bishop of Hereford, granted to Grent son of Llywelyn the land in Linley which his uncle had held, on terms of castle-guard service.[96] But, from shortly afterwards, we have evidence for the efforts of Englishmen to prevent or reverse Welsh settlement. In the 1190s, William Fitzalan II, the lord of Oswestry and sheriff of Shropshire, proclaimed that he had granted to William Lestrange land which had been forfeited by 'Iago filius Warneri', presumably a Welshman, 'lest Welshmen occupy it as if by hereditary law.'[97] In the 1220s, Hamo of Wotherton granted to Alan of Boullers land in Dudston, near where the new castle at Montgomery was being built.[98] Hamo stated that the land had been held by 'Grifinus de Dudiston', but in bestowing it on Alan he insisted that the new tenant was free to assign land there to whomever he wished, 'except to Welshmen'. It is quite possible that such clauses became widespread, even standard, in land transactions near the Welsh border. They certainly show that Englishmen and Welshmen were perceived as rivals in staking out claims to land.

Such an outlook need not necessarily have affected the settlement pattern. But there can be no doubt that the legal clauses in the charters often masked an increasingly bitter and polarized struggle. The progress of both Welsh and English settlement was often linked to the vicissitudes of military campaigns. Just how complex the situation could be is illustrated by a case of novel disseisin brought at the Shrewsbury assizes in 1221.[99] The property in question lay at Hordley, on the boundaries between Pimhill (formerly Baschurch) hundred and the lordship of Oswestry, and the case was brought by the descendants of one 'Eynon' by his English wife against

[94] Lloyd, *History of Wales*, p. 389. [95] *Brut*, p. 63.
[96] *Haughmond Cart.*, no. 700.
[97] *Salop. Cart.*, no. 302b.
[98] *Lilleshall Cart.*, no. 139.
[99] *Rolls of the Justices in Eyre, 1221, 1222*, ed. D. M. Stenton (Selden Society 59, 1940), no. 1002.

his descendants by his Welsh wife. The Welsh heirs claimed that their English half-siblings 'never had seisin of that land save by the intrusion they made in time of war'. The jurors then determined that the English party had had seisin 'until Llywelyn came towards Shrewsbury in the war', a reference to the occupation of the county town by Llywelyn ap Iorwerth, the prince of Gwynedd, in 1215.[100] Migration in the wake of military campaigns appears to have continued unabated throughout the thirteenth century. Between 1241 and 1269, and probably between 1265 and 1269, eleven Welshmen quitclaimed land in Weston Rhyn, effectively being forced to admit that they had 'occupied it unjustly'; this occupation may have been linked to the Welsh attacks on the Shropshire borderlands led by Llywelyn ap Gruffudd, the prince of Gwynedd, in the early 1260s.[101] After Edward I's Welsh wars of 1282–3, Roger Lestrange, to whom the king had granted the manor of Ellesmere, evicted forty-one Welshmen from Marton and Horton within that manor on the grounds that, as supporters of Llywelyn ap Gruffudd, they had forfeited their land; he then granted the property to one of his English tenants.[102] It was only eight years later that sixteen of the evicted Welshmen won the right to a commission of *oyer* and *terminer* to judge whether their forfeiture had been legal.[103]

The link between politics and migration may go back to the mid-twelfth century. It has been suggested that the country around Oswestry Castle experienced extensive Welsh settlement when that fortification was temporarily occupied by Madog ap Maredudd, the lord of Powys (d. 1160), in the late 1140s and early 1150s.[104] It seems that, during this settlement, the land which came to be occupied by Welshmen was parcelled out among them and subsequently descended according to the Welsh hereditary law which applied to freely held land, with the original parcels being subdivided among male heirs. At the end of the fourteenth century, and indeed beyond, the original parcels, held by agnatic kin groups known as *gwelyau* (literally: 'beds', later 'families'), persisted as the units for seigneurial taxation and assessment of the Welsh population of Oswestry lordship.[105] Map 8 plots these fourteenth-century *gwelyau*. It will be seen that they covered a compact territory, mainly of dispersed

[100] Below, p. 127.

[101] *Salop. Cart.*, no. 368f; for Llywelyn's attacks, see below, pp. 131–2.

[102] *Cal. Chanc. R. Var.*, p. 285.

[103] *Cal. Pat. R., 1281–92*, p. 521. The case sheds interesting light on the stance of the English state towards Welshmen at the end of the thirteenth century: see below, p. 244.

[104] *Brut*, p. 129; and see below, p. 119 and n. 91 there; Ll. B. Smith, 'The Welsh Language before 1536', in G. H. Jenkins (ed.), *The Welsh Language before the Industrial Revolution* (Cardiff, 1997), pp. 18–19; Ll. B. Smith, 'The Lordships of Chirk and Oswestry, 1282–1415' (University of London PhD thesis, 1971), pp. 21–2, 263–70; below, pp. 76–7, 119, 211.

[105] Davies, *Lordship and Society*, pp. 359–62; Slack, *The Lordship of Oswestry*, pp. 153–70.

settlement, situated within the area which according to Domesday Book had been among the most sparsely populated districts of England. The *gwelyau* can be seen to be concentrated west of the region which was wholly or partly Welsh-populated in 1086.[106] On the evidence above, it seems entirely plausible that they were the result of a new migratory movement of free Welshmen eastwards into the lowlands which took place in the mid-twelfth century. It is conceivable that this substantial Welsh advance in the 1140s and 1150s provoked the efforts by the Fitzalan lord of Oswestry, who was reinstated by Henry II at Oswestry Castle in 1155, to stem the tide of Welsh immigration.[107]

Despite the complexities, it is possible to paint a general picture of how the ethnic frontier between Shropshire and Powys developed. It seems clear that, overall, districts of Welsh and English settlement became not only more populous, but better defined and more segregated, and that, as a result, the frontier of peoples became more clearly delineated. As will be argued below, the thirteenth century was a period of efforts by the lords of the border castles to organize their Welsh and English tenants into separate administrative units increasingly referred to as 'Welshries' and 'Englishries'.[108] A Welshry was attached to the lordship of Alberbury by the 1260s,[109] and to the lordship of Oswestry by 1272.[110] The lord of Clun was said in 1267 to have held 'much Welshry'; in 1292, that Welshry was first referred to as 'Tempseter'.[111] This might indicate that the district had become more firmly established by the later date. On the other hand, it may be that administrative or geographical terms like 'Tempseter' were much older than their first appearance in the documents. The district east of the Severn which was partly populated by Welshmen in 1086 and which included the manors of Trewern and of Bausley was known, by the late twelfth century, as the Gorddwr, 'the land beyond the water'.[112] It thereafter frequently changed hands between Welsh rulers and the Corbet lords of Caus;[113] in 1281 a jury found that 'Le Gordur' lay 'in the Welshry and outside the county'.[114] In 1300, the Corbet lord of Caus was found to have held both Upper and Lower Gorddwr and a minor intermediate district referred as 'Baghaltreff' (Bachelldre, modern-day Heldre).[115] By that time,

[106] See Map 8. [107] Above, p. 44.

[108] Below, pp. 189–217. [109] Eyton, vii, 83.

[110] *CIPM, Henry III*, no. 812, p. 279.

[111] TNA C 132/35 (18), m. 3r; *A Concise Account of Ancient Documents Relating to the Honor, Forest and Borough of Clun*, ed. T. Salt (Shrewsbury, 1858), p. 6: in 1292, 'Richard Earl of Arundel and Lord of Clonne' grants hunting rights 'to all our men the Welchmen of Tempsett'.

[112] J. E. Lloyd, 'Border Notes', *BBCS*, **11** (1941–4), pp. 48–51.

[113] C. J. Spurgeon, 'Gwyddgrug Castle and the Gorddwr Dispute in the Thirteenth Century', *Mont. Coll.*, **57** (1962), part ii, 125–36.

[114] *Cal. Chanc. R. Var.*, p. 204. [115] *CIPM*, iii, no. 600, TNA C 133/94 (6), m. 2r (1300).

the Gorddwr was thoroughly Welsh: in 1300, there were forty-four Welsh free tenants in Lower Gorddwr, twenty-eight in Upper Gorddwr and ten in Bachelldre. By contrast, Chirbury hundred, on which the Gorddwr bordered, was almost exclusively English in 1327, at least according to the picture conveyed by the lay subsidy roll for that year.[116] The same was true of Purslow hundred, just to the south of Chirbury, although there were some Welshmen living at Bishop's Castle, Broughton, Wentnor and Ratlinghope. Purslow hundred lay to the east of the Welsh hill-district of Tempseter that has already been mentioned. The strongly Welsh character of that region is evident from the exceptional collection of fourteenth-century court rolls from the lordship of Clun.[117] Fifty-five out of sixty-one names mentioned in the minutes of that court's session of 18 August 1337 were Welsh; in 1345, forty-eight free Welshmen were amerced for giving false testimony in the court of Tempseter.[118] In 1374, there were at least five *gwelyau* in the upper Clun valley, in Whitcott Keysett.[119] Since it was much simpler to hold courts in a single language, those courts had long acted to create separate communities of Englishmen and Welshmen. In 1200, one Ralph son of Picot was being paid by two Welshmen to be responsible for the suit of Llywelyn and 'Kenenard' to Purslow hundred court and the court of Lydbury manor.[120] Thus, the creation of Welshries and Englishries came to delineate more clearly the ethnic frontier in western Shropshire.

The overall impression, then, is that, by the late thirteenth and early fourteenth centuries, districts overwhelmingly settled by Welshmen were adjacent to regions of almost exclusively English settlement.[121] The place-name and indeed the field-name evidence for the area around Oswestry certainly corroborates the view that that borough's hinterland was thoroughly Welsh.[122] To give a striking example, the Old English place-name of Porkington acquired a Welsh phonetic rendering, 'Brogyntyn', and as such became the sobriquet of the Welsh lord of Penllyn and Edeirnion, Owain Brogyntyn, one of the sons of Madog ap Maredudd (d. 1160) of Powys.[123] Further south, the history of settlement in the Clun valley

[116] *The Shropshire Lay Subsidy Roll of 1 Edward III (1327)*, ed. W. G. D. Fletcher (Oswestry, 1907 – repr. from *TSAS*, various). Some Welsh names are recorded at the vills of Marton, Walcot, Hope, Mucklewick and Wotherton. Rhyston and Brompton were Welsh settlements.

[117] Preserved in the Shropshire Archives in Shrewsbury. See G. E. A. Raspin, 'Transcript and Descriptive List of the Medieval Court Rolls of the Marcher Lordship of Clun Deposited in the Salop Record Office by the Earl of Powis' (University of London thesis for Diploma in archive administration, August 1963).

[118] SA 552/1/7, m. 13r; 552/1/10, m. 10r. [119] SA 552/1/18, m. 2r.

[120] *Haughmond Cart.*, no. 743. [121] See Map 7.

[122] H. D. G. Foxall, *Shropshire Field-Names* (Shrewsbury, 1980), pp. 68–70.

[123] *Ystrad Marchell Charters*, ed. Thomas, no. 9 (dated to after 1183).

certainly involved moving frontiers and successive occupations, as will become clearer once the complex mix of Brythonic, later Welsh and English place-names has been disentangled by further scholarship.[124] The place-name evidence here bespeaks an English advance beyond Offa's Dyke, with a later tide of Welsh resettlement. 'Tempseter', the name of the Welshry of Clun, probably originally referred to Anglo-Saxon settlers in the hills between the Teme and Clun rivers.[125] It is also notable that several of the English place-names beyond Offa's Dyke were turned into their Welsh equivalents: 'Berton' became 'Trebert', Domesday's 'Edretehope' became 'Hobendred', and 'Treverward' seems to indicate an original 'Burwardeston'.[126] The evidence for Welsh field-names in Clun and Bettws-y-Crwyn is almost as strong as in the Oswestry area.[127] Moreover, as the case of Marton shows, vills of which we know only the English name could have been Welsh-populated in the twelfth and thirteenth centuries.[128]

In addition to the cases where Welsh names replaced earlier English forms, variants of place- or river-names in both languages could coexist. Shrewsbury and the Severn were also known as Amwythig and Hafren because of their regional importance. Smaller settlements probably had names in both English and Welsh because they were places of regular contact between the two peoples. This is very likely to have been true for the border towns. Their dual place-names fit in well with evidence suggesting that these boroughs remained English islands for some time, but later experienced Welsh immigration.[129] Gerald of Wales records that, in 1188, he was entertained at Oswestry by the lord of the castle 'in splendid fashion with English sumptuousness'.[130] However, the town at Oswestry had a mixed population by the end of the fourteenth century.[131] By the 1330s, there were Welshmen living in the borough of Clun.[132] In the case of Trallwng Llywelyn/Welshpool, where the Welsh name occurs before the English one, the place-name evidence may indicate the introduction of English burgesses into a Welsh town. The castle-boroughs of the Shropshire borders provide an interesting parallel to medieval frontier towns on the continent, like Cracow; in both cases,

[124] Sylvester, *Rural Landscape*, pp. 321, 328–32.

[125] Lloyd, 'Border Notes', pp. 53–4, derives 'Tempseter' from AS 'Temede' (Ekwall, *English River-Names* (Oxford, 1928), p. 441) and '–sete'.

[126] Lloyd, 'Border Notes', pp. 53–4.

[127] Foxall, 'Field-Names', p. 69. [128] Above, p. 45.

[129] Towns in Wales were largely English-populated before the fourteenth century: Davies, *Lordship and Society*, pp. 324–8.

[130] *Giraldus*, vi, 142 (*Itinerarium Kambrie*, ii, 12).

[131] Slack, *The Lordship of Oswestry*, pp. 143–52.

[132] SA 552/1/6, m. 2r (1335); 552/1/9, m. 6r (1340).

Table 1. *English/Welsh place-names on the Shropshire–Powys borders (cf. Map 7)*

	First documented English/Welsh name	Reference[i]	Pages
Alberbury/Llanfihangel Llychantyn	1086/1265	Morgan, *Welsh Place-Names*	15
Alreton/Trewern	1086/1311	Charles, *Non-Celtic Place-Names*	188
Berton?/Trebert	?/1284	Morgan, *Welsh Place-Names*	53
Borewardeston?/Treferward	?/1284	Morgan, *Welsh Place-Names*	54
Brotherton?/Trebrodier	?/1284	Morgan, *Welsh Place-Names*	53
Clun/Colunwy	1233/C14 (*Brut*)	Morgan, *Welsh Place-Names*	23
Crickheath/Crukin	1272/1302	Morgan, *Welsh Place-Names*	24
Edenhope/Ednob	1086/*c.* 1155–*c.* 1195	Morgan, *Welsh Place-Names*	27
Edretehope/Hobendrid	1086/1284	Morgan, *Welsh Place-Names*	32
Guilsfield/Cedigfa	1275–81/*c.* 1253	Charles, *Non-Celtic Place-Names*	189–90
Kinnerley/Cinerdinlle	1086/1307	Morgan, *Welsh Place-Names*	33
Montgomery/Castell Baldwin/Trefaldwyn	1220s?/C14/1440	Charles, *Non-Celtic Place-Names*	183–4
Oswestry/Croesoswallt	*c.* 1180/C13	Gelling, *Place-Names, Part 1* Morgan, *Welsh Place-Names*	229 43
Porkington/Brogyntyn	1161/1232–3	Morgan, *Welsh Place-Names*	18
Severn/Hafren	C12, perhaps earlier	Thomas, *Enwau Afonydd* Ekwall, *English River-Names*	115 358–9
Shrewsbury/Amwythig	910/C12	Morgan, *Welsh Place-Names*	49
Teme/Tefeidiad	*c.* 757–75/LC13	Morgan, *Welsh Place-Names*	52
Tern/Tren	*c.* 1200/C9–10	Morgan, *Welsh Place-Names*	52–3
Welshpool/Trallwng Llywelyn	1253/1108	Charles, *Non-Celtic Place-Names*	190

[i] Morgan, *Welsh Place-Names*; Gelling, *Place-Names, Part 1*; B. G. Charles, *Non-Celtic Place-Names in Wales* (London, 1938); R. J. Thomas, *Enwau Afonydd a Nentydd Cymru* (Cardiff, 1938); Ekwall, *English River-Names* (Oxford, 1928).

burghal privileges attracted burgess immigration from two peoples.[133] They are also a reminder that there were exceptions to what seems to have been the general rule: the increasingly clear separation of English and Welsh settlements.

The reasons for the segregation of Welsh and English settlements are perhaps easier to see than those for the geographical distribution of the two ethnic groups along the Shropshire–Powys frontier. Overall, there is a remarkable consistency in this respect between the eleventh century and the fourteenth. Three main observations support this view. First, areas where some Welsh population existed in 1086 very largely retained or strengthened their Welsh character. Purely in terms of the geographical distribution of peoples, the Domesday Welshmen of Trewern and of Bausley were the forerunners of the Welshmen of the Gorddwr; those of Clun paved the way for the Welshry of Tempseter. Even to the north, in the lowlands east of Oswestry, we continue to hear of Welshmen throughout the thirteenth century. Secondly, areas which were, to the best of our knowledge, almost empty in 1086 became filled in, over the following two centuries, by a significant wave of eastwards migration by Welshmen. Indeed, both in the hills around Clun and the lowlands around Oswestry, this process was probably well under way, if not completed, well before the end of the twelfth century. Moreover, it does not seem to have been reversed during the medieval period. Thirdly, there does seem to have been rivalry for land between English and Welsh landholders, but as far as we can tell, this very often took the form of quarrels between individuals over single properties. It would appear that, by the thirteenth century, the age of large-scale population movements had passed, and the frontier of peoples on the Shropshire–Powys borders had become fixed.

As will be argued below, the English kings acted to keep the lid on Anglo-Welsh hostilities on the Shropshire borders, particularly during the later twelfth and early thirteenth centuries.[134] This certainly contributed towards the stabilization of the ethnic frontier, and the lords of the border castles of Oswestry, Caus and Clun played their part too. Their response to the advance of Welsh settlement was, as has been seen, varied. On the one hand, there were attempts to curtail it; on the other hand, lordship adapted to the influx of Welshmen through the formation of Welshries (although, as will be seen, this was also due to greater administrative and judicial precision in seigneurial government).[135] Moreover, the lords of the Shropshire borders were not blind to the advantages that Welsh settlement could offer. Welsh tenure afforded lords greater control over the

[133] Bartlett, *Making of Europe*, pp. 177–82; cf. Davies, *Lordship and Society*, pp. 447–8.
[134] Below, pp. 122–6. [135] Below, pp. 201–8, 211–17.

land market, since it precluded sub-enfeoffments among tenants as well as inheritance by or transmission of land through women.[136] In 1274, the English tenants of the lordship of Caus complained that Thomas Corbet, their lord, had forced them to hold their lands 'by Welsh law' for the past thirty years, even though previously they had 'held by English law and followed the king's peace as Englishmen'.[137] Yet the evidence for the advance of Welsh settlement at Oswestry and Clun suggests that the influence of the lords, indecisive as it seems to have been, was not the main factor shaping the geographical distribution of peoples. These districts of relatively poor soils and difficult terrain, which only supported – at best – highly dispersed settlement and limited arable agriculture, simply never attracted English settlers as strongly as, say, the fields and meadows in the Vale of Glamorgan.

SETTLEMENT TYPES AND PATTERNS

Settlement features may, conceivably, have helped to lead contemporaries to consider the Shropshire–Powys frontier as a borderland. It was commonly believed during the High Middle Ages that the English and the Welsh could be distinguished partly by the nature of their habitations. Gerald of Wales wrote of the Welsh: 'They do not live together in towns, villages or castles, but inhabit the woods like hermits (*solitarii*).'[138] At the end of the thirteenth century, the Welsh, according to Archbishop Pecham, did 'not live together but far from each other', while, according to Leland, in Denbigh in the sixteenth century the people dwelled not '*vicatim*, but al *sparsim*.'[139] There is ample evidence to reveal that such absolute statements were exaggerations,[140] although in the borders, a contrast between the settlements of the Welsh and English may indeed have existed where the latter clustered together for defensive purposes.[141] Whatever the origin of the stereotypical views of Welsh habitations may have been, it does seem that they were quite widespread throughout the period under consideration and beyond. It is reasonable to suppose,

136 Conversely, on the advantages of English tenure to Welsh peasants, see Davies, *Lordship and Society*, pp. 449–55.

137 *Rot. Hund.*, ii, 96.

138 *Giraldus*, vi, 200 (*Descriptio Kambriae*, i, 17).

139 *Registrum Epistolarum Fratris Johannis Peckham, Archiepiscopi Cantuarensis*, ed. C. T. Martin (RS 1882–5), iii, 776–7; *The Itinerary of John Leland in or about the Years 1536–1539*, ed. L. T. Smith, 5 vols. (London, 1906, repr. 1964), iii, 93 (referring to Denbighshire). In 1305, the men of North Wales petitioned Edward I to allow that when the hue and cry was raised in a Welsh vill, the neighbouring four vills should not be amerced if they did not answer it, 'cum ville Walenses sint disperse': *The Record of Caernarvon*, ed. H. Ellis (1838), p. 212.

140 Davies, *Age of Conquest*, pp. 150–1.

141 Sylvester, *Rural Landscape*, pp. 192–6, 350–1, 498–9; Holden, *Lords*, p. 7.

therefore, that the distribution of villages, hamlets and isolated farmsteads would have mattered to contemporary observers, and may have helped define which parts of the landscape were considered typically Welsh, English or 'Marcher'.

A discussion of nucleation and dispersal is manageable within the remit of this chapter, since Dorothy Sylvester has charted the distribution of hamlets and nucleated villages in the Welsh borderlands. The relative distribution of nucleated villages (including small towns), hamlets and isolated, or dispersed, settlements on the Shropshire borders is shown on Map 9.[142] The classification of hamlets and villages on the map largely reflects Sylvester's use of nineteenth-century Ordance Survey maps. For England, such maps, where they have been corroborated with documentary sources, archaeological evidence and aerial photography, have repeatedly proved a reliable guide to the overall character of medieval settlement patterns.[143] The following map, therefore, conveys a rough but not entirely unreliable picture of the settlement pattern in Shropshire and Powys in the twelfth and thirteenth centuries. It should be noted, however, that, while the area roughly to the east of Offa's Dyke was encompassed by the Domesday survey and the Hundred Rolls of 1255 and 1274, very few contemporary records survive for the lands further west. Similarly, the coverage of archaeological research and place-name studies is as yet uneven for the region shown. As for the dispersed settlements, which were not individually mapped by Sylvester, these may well have been more or less numerous, and distributed differently, than Map 9 suggests. This is particularly true of Wales. By the nineteenth century, Welsh villages such as Meifod were parochial centres with outlying townships of dispersed settlement.[144] However, there can be no doubt that the settlement pattern of Wales, particularly the distribution of dispersed habitations, has changed markedly since the medieval period.[145]

The kaleidoscopic mix of villages, hamlets and farmsteads in Shropshire and Powys would no doubt have seemed confusing to Gerald of Wales and Archbishop Pecham. Dispersed settlements, it is true, predominated in such Welsh areas as the Gorddwr and the hills around Clun (the Welshry of Tempseter). Yet the same was true of much of the fertile Severn belt

[142] Sylvester, *Rural Landscape*, pp. 39–44 and ch. 9, esp. figs. 3, 20–1 and table viii. See also the map in *VCH*, viii, 4, 182 and the remarkable *Map of South Wales and the Border in the Fourteenth Century* (Ordnance Survey, 1932) by W. Rees. Map 9 is also based on archaeological data retrieved from the online versions of the Sites and Monuments Records for Powys, Denbighshire, Flintshire and Wrexham.

[143] For instance, cf. C. Lewis, P. Mitchell-Fox and C. Dyer (eds.), *Village, Hamlet and Field: Changing Medieval Settlements in Central England* (Manchester, 1997), pp. 71–2.

[144] Sylvester, *Rural Landscape*, pp. 448–9.

[145] Charles-Edwards, *Early Irish and Welsh Kinship*, pp. 433–46.

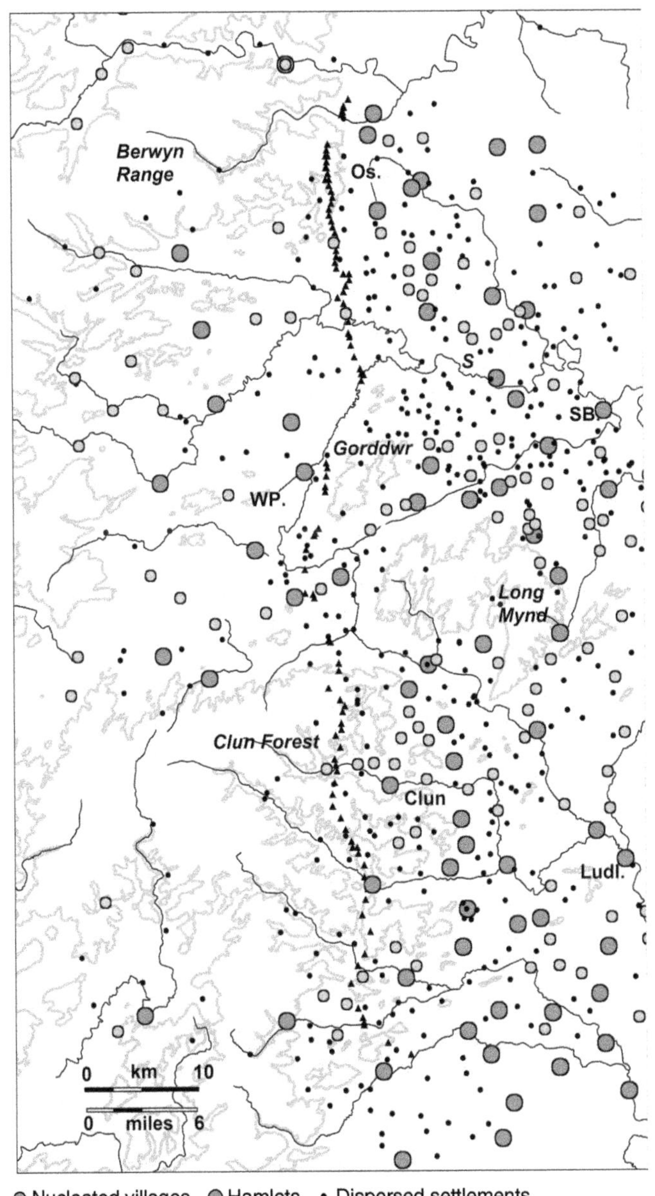

Map 9. The distribution of nucleated villages, hamlets and dispersed settlements in Shropshire (west of a line through Shrewsbury and Ludlow), *c.* 1200–1300

which traverses central Shropshire, where the countryside surrounding the town of Shrewsbury was dotted with a galaxy of isolated farmsteads. Moreover, hamlets were common in the largely Welsh districts around Oswestry and in the upper Clun valley; while Welshpool/Y Trallwng was a large nucleated settlement founded by a Welsh prince. In sum, relief, soils and altitude had a far greater impact on the settlement pattern than did the distribution of Englishmen and Welshmen. On both sides of Offa's Dyke, settlements were extremely scarce above the 300 metre contour line: the western Clun Forest, the Berwyn range and the Long Mynd appear as blank spaces on the settlement map. Much of the Shropshire–Powys borderlands would have seemed, to outsiders coming from central or south-eastern England, like a part of Wales, though one that was being colonized by Englishmen. On the other hand, Powys itself, with regard to its settlement pattern, increasingly came to look like a borderland.

A BORDER REGION?

The features considered in this chapter changed slowly, if at all. Several of them may have contributed to setting the Welsh borders of Shropshire apart from the county on the one hand and Powys on the other; but several others had the opposite effect, or tended to increase the diversity of the borderlands themselves. The Dyke dissected various landscapes. There was no neat division between Shropshire and Powys with regard to settlement patterns or agricultural systems; rather, the main contrast in these respects was between the Severn valley and the lands to its north and south, which were less favourable to arable agriculture and more sparsely populated. It would appear that, when population levels started to rise in the twelfth century, the borderlands to the north and south of the Severn gap initially lagged behind in terms of settlement expansion, although this meant that there remained proportionally more scope on the borders for the creation of new settlements and the growth of existing ones in the second half of the thirteenth century. In the case of the lowlands around Oswestry, and of the hills around Clun, settlement expansion was linked not to the advance of English colonizers, but to the infilling by Welsh immigrants of districts which were probably almost empty in 1086. The main exception to this was the petty castle-boroughs which multiplied along the Welsh border during this period, although these too only started to develop in the second half of the twelfth century. Because these boroughs were initially English-dominated, the districts around Clun and Oswestry maintained a truly frontier character in that they became areas where the geographical distribution of English and Welsh settlers overlapped. Apart from the English boroughs and their Welsh hinterlands, however, the frontier between peoples which had already existed by 1086, and remained fairly permeable at first, became more consolidated and segregated, particularly after the second half of the twelfth century. Zones of mixed settlement tended to become the exception rather than the rule on the Welsh border of Shropshire.

All in all, it does not seem clear that these elements sufficed to create a separate, 'Marcher', regional identity. Although frontiers of settlement expansion and of peoples existed during the twelfth and thirteenth centuries, in other respects there was a continuum between Powys and Shropshire. Above all, the lie of the land contributed towards erasing the differences between English- and Welsh-settled areas. Thus, the numerous important valleys leading into the Powysian hills from the eastern plains, together with the upland regions of southern Shropshire, explain the many similarities between economic practices in the Welsh kingdom and the English county; and there was no stark contrast in what were believed to be English or Welsh settlement patterns. Indeed, it seems difficult to argue that the gradually changing features discussed in this chapter made it inevitable that a 'Marcher' region should have been perceived to exist between Shropshire and Wales. The decisive factors, it would appear, have yet to be identified.

Chapter 2

THE MAKING OF A BORDER ARISTOCRACY

The medieval concept of the March of Wales is closely linked to the Norman and English aristocratic families who held land in Wales and on the border.[1] As was observed in the introduction, the March may have been perceived as a discrete territory because it was seen to coincide with the lands of a certain group of lords: those who had come, by the beginning of the thirteenth century, to be recognized as, and called, *barones Marchie*. The Welsh March was not exceptional in this respect. By 1172, the clerks of the English exchequer and chancery also referred to the frontier of Normandy as a *marcha*,[2] and that 'march', too, was densely settled by local castellan families.[3] Indeed, several familial links were forged, in the late eleventh and twelfth centuries, between the marches of Wales and of Normandy.[4] Meanwhile, on the eastern limits of the Holy Roman Empire, new *Markgrafen* (margraves) were being established in the twelfth century, for instance in the *Mark* of Brandenburg. The contacts between the Plantagenets and Henry the Lion, the duke of Saxony, have already been mentioned.[5] The idea that a 'march' was a territory under the command of a select group of border lords must have been current in twelfth- and thirteenth-century Britain. It is therefore indispensable to ask whether it could be said that the families of the Shropshire borders 'shaped the March and, were, in turn, shaped by it'.[6]

* * *

It could be argued that a frontier aristocracy existed in Shropshire even before the Normans arrived. In the eleventh century, Shropshire was a

[1] Davies, *Lordship and Society*, ch. 2.

[2] E.g. *Red Book of the Exchequer*, ed. H. Hall, 3 vols. (RS, 1896), ii, 628, 643; *Rot. Pat.*, p. 24b (1203); Power, *Norman Frontier*, pp. 13–15.

[3] Power, *Norman Frontier*, esp. chs. 5–7. [4] Above, p. 12; below, pp. 64–8.

[5] Above, p. 12. [6] Davies, *Lordship and Society*, p. 36.

part of the province of Mercia,[7] and bordered on the Welsh kingdom of Powys. Cross-border contacts between the ruling families of Mercia and Powys certainly pre-dated the Norman conquest. In 1055, Ælfgar (d. 1062), son of Leofric, the earl of Mercia (d. 1057), allied himself with Gruffudd ap Llywelyn of Gwynedd, who had ruled over Powys since 1039 at the latest.[8] After succeeding to the earldom of Mercia on the death of his father, Ælfgar gave his daughter in marriage to Gruffudd.[9] These ties between the leaders of Mercia and of Powys endured after 1066. When the sons of Ælfgar, Edwin, earl of Mercia, and Morcar, earl of Northumbria, rebelled against William I in 1068, they were supported by an army of Welshmen led by Bleddyn ap Cynfyn.[10] Bleddyn and his brother Rhiwallon were half-brothers of Gruffudd ap Llywelyn, and had become rulers of Gwynedd and Powys after Gruffudd's death in 1063.[11] Nor was this border nexus between the leading men of Powys and Shropshire restricted to the families of earls and princes. In 1067, Bleddyn and Rhiwallon raided Herefordshire in the company of the Shropshire-based English rebel known to posterity as Eadric the Wild.[12] Eadric also joined Welshmen and the men of Chester in besieging the Norman garrison at Shrewsbury, probably in 1069.[13] A Shropshire thegn who, before the Norman conquest, held around fifty manors, including several estates on the Welsh frontier,[14] Eadric has a very good claim to representing the Anglo-Saxon version of a Shropshire frontier aristocrat.

It appears quite possible that Eadric was a representative member of a group. He may, for instance, have felt a special affinity with Siward, who before 1066 held several estates in Mersete hundred, as well as a share

[7] *VCH*, iii, 5.

[8] *Saxon Chronicles*, i, 184 (Anglo-Saxon Chronicle, C version (Abingdon MS), *sub anno* 1055) and *ibid.*, i, 187 (Anglo-Saxon Chronicle, E version (Laud MS), *sub anno* 1055); Lloyd, *History of Wales*, p. 359.

[9] *The Gesta Normannorum Ducum of William of Jumièges, Orderic Vitalis, and Robert of Torigni*, ed. and transl. E. M. C. van Houts, 2 vols. (Oxford, 1992–5), ii, 162–3; *Orderic*, ii, 138, 217; cf. K. L. Maund, 'The Welsh Alliances of Earl Ælfgar of Mercia and his Family in the Mid-Eleventh Century', *Anglo-Norman Studies*, **11** (1989), 181–90, and her *Ireland, Wales, and England in the Eleventh Century* (Woodbridge, 1991), pp. 129–40.

[10] *Orderic*, ii, 217.

[11] *Saxon Chronicles*, i, 191 (Anglo-Saxon Chronicle, D version (Worcester MS), *sub anno* 1063); Lloyd, *History of Wales*, pp. 372, 374.

[12] On Eadric see S. Reynolds, 'Eadric Silvaticus and the English Resistance', *Bulletin of the Institute of Historical Research*, **54** (1981), pp. 102–5.

[13] *Orderic*, ii, 228–9.

[14] *John of Worcester*, iii, 4–5; Lewis, 'English and Norman Government', 1985), pp. 82–3, 105–6 and Maps 13 and 20. Eadric's border estates included: DB 253c (Lydham, near Bishop's Castle), probably Clun, Hopton Castle and Hopesay, Ackhill, Lingen, Hope Bendrid; Wattlesborough, Melverley, Loton, Wootton, Halston; DB 256a Middleton, later held by Robert Corbet. He also probably held seven smallish manors in Herefordshire.

in the hunting preserve on the Welsh borders around the site where the castle of Hen Domen Montgomery was founded after 1070.[15] Nor should it be assumed that this frontier aristocracy was doomed to extinction after the battle of Hastings in 1066. William the Conqueror was, initially, content to accept the submission of Earl Edwin of Mercia and, by 1069, he had appointed the abbot of Evesham, Æthelwig, to a position of judicial responsibility over all the midland counties, including Shropshire.[16] That William initially did not remove the Englishmen who had played a role in the government of Shropshire is entirely in keeping with his general preference in the early years after the battle of Hastings.[17] The ruling elite in Shropshire was fundamentally changed, both in structure and in personnel, only after William and his advisers had come to perceive this peripheral county as a military problem.

Tenurial changes provide the main evidence for this. The way in which Norman lords were established in Shropshire was determined by the needs of a military occupation force. According to the Evesham Chronicle, William the Conqueror waged a war of devastation in Shropshire, Cheshire and neighbouring counties 'in the earliest days of his reign'. Orderic tells us that William, after attacking the north of England in 1069–70, 'suppressed all risings throughout Mercia with royal power'.[18] It was in such circumstances that William abandoned his original vision of ruling England through the surviving personnel of the Old English state.[19] The way in which a new aristocracy was put in place in Shropshire is particularly indicative of this new outlook. Shropshire was annexed by the Normans in a way typical of the border counties of western England. In Shropshire, Herefordshire and Cheshire, William began by appointing one of his followers from the Continent as commander-in-chief over entire counties. William fitz Osbern, a lifelong friend of the Conqueror's, wielded comital authority over Herefordshire by 1069, possibly already by 1067.[20] The earldom of Chester was first given to a Flemish ally of the Conqueror's named Gerbod, but by 1071 he had been succeeded by Hugh, son of the *vicomte* of Avranches.[21] In Shropshire, the choice fell upon William the Conqueror's kinsman Roger II de Montgomery, who

[15] DB 255a, 254a.

[16] *Orderic*, ii, 194–5; *Chronicon Abbatiae de Evesham*, ed. W. D. Macray (RS, 1863), p. 89; *VCH*, iii, 7.

[17] C. P. Lewis, 'The Early Earls of Norman England', *Anglo-Norman Studies*, **13** (1990), pp. 216, 218–19.

[18] *Chronicon Abbatiae de Evesham*, pp. 90–1; *Orderic*, ii, 230–3 and 237.

[19] Lewis, 'Early Earls', pp. 218–19.

[20] *John of Worcester*, iii, 4–5; *Saxon Chronicles*, i, 200 (Anglo-Saxon Chronicle, D version (Worcester MS), *sub anno* 1066); *Orderic*, ii, 261; W. E. Wightman, *The Lacy Family in England and Normandy, 1066–1194* (Oxford, 1966), p. 167 and n. 1; cf. Lewis, 'Early Earls', p. 217.

[21] *Orderic*, ii, 260–1.

took his name from his family castle in Montgommery, was *vicomte* of the Hiémois and had acted as governor of Normandy during William's English campaign in 1066.[22] How far this distinctive arrangement was a planned scheme for the defence of the border counties which was put into practice at one stroke is not easy to determine with final certainty.[23] Yet it is clear that the three 'border' earls were created by William the Conqueror. No separate earldom of Shropshire appears to have existed before 1066.[24] Cheshire, too, was not a pre-Conquest earldom.[25] The earldom of Hereford had, in 1057, been merged into the earldom of Wessex held by Harold Godwineson.[26] It is possible that William the Conqueror aimed to fill the gap in this earldom left by the death of Harold when he appointed William fitz Osbern earl of Hereford in 1067.[27] However, it appears clear that the three Norman 'border' earls of the 1070s did not replace a trio of Anglo-Saxon earls. Rather, they constituted the highest level of a novel frontier aristocracy.

Moreover, the way in which Earl Roger, in turn, distributed the Shropshire estates among his own followers meant that, in effect, he created a new kind of subsidiary frontier aristocracy on the western borders of his county. Earl Roger was in a position to dispose of almost all the land in the county and nowhere, in granting land to lay followers or in making endowments to churches and monasteries, did he take much notice of the pattern of landholding of English predecessors.[28] Yet the chain of compact tenurial blocks which he established along the western borders represented the most radical changes which he made to the political landscape of Shropshire. Here, he seems to have distributed estates to three of his men more or less by assigning whole hundreds. We may identify these three original grantees by reading backwards from Domesday Book. Thus, Warin, nicknamed by Orderic 'the Bald', was clearly originally granted the lands, including Mersete hundred, which were held in 1086 by Domesday Book's 'Rainaldus *vicecomes*'.[29] Not only does Rainald

[22] J. F. A. Mason, 'Roger de Montgomery and his Sons (1067–1102)', *TRHS*, 5th ser., **13** (1963), pp. 1–28; K. Thompson, 'The Norman Aristocracy before 1066: The Example of the Montgomerys', *Historical Research*, **60** (1987), pp. 251–63.

[23] J. A. Green, *The Aristocracy of Norman England* (Cambridge, 1997), p. 69.

[24] *VCH*, iii, 5. It is possible that Shropshire was subsumed under the earldom of Hereford in the 1050s, but this arrangement, if it existed, lapsed with the death of Earl Ralph of Hereford in 1057.

[25] C. P. Lewis, 'The Formation of the Honor of Chester, 1066–1100', in A. T. Thacker (ed.), *The Earldom of Chester and its Charters: A Tribute to Geoffrey Barraclough* (Chester, 1991), p. 39.

[26] Stenton, *Anglo-Saxon England*, p. 574.

[27] Lewis, 'Early Earls', p. 217.

[28] Green, *Aristocracy*, p. 159.

[29] *Orderic*, ii, 262; for the holdings in Mersete of Rainald, Warin's successor: DB 253c, 254d–255a.

appear to have assumed the position of Earl Roger's representative in Shropshire which was originally held by Warin, he also married Warin's widow, Amieria, who was Earl Roger's niece, and in Henry I's charter to Shrewsbury Abbey (dated 1121) he was said to have succeeded to Warin's *honor*.[30] The second original Norman frontier lord was undoubtedly named Corbet. A compact group of estates in the hundreds of Rhiwset and Whittery was held in 1086 by Roger and Robert, sons of Corbet. It is possible to prove conclusively that these estates represent a single grant by Earl Roger which was subsequently divided between two of Corbet's male heirs.[31] The third Norman frontier lord, Picot, who was set up over Rinlow and Leintwardine, had probably himself first received those lands from Earl Roger.[32] There is every reason to believe that this situation developed during the 1070s. Earl Roger had been created earl of Shrewsbury by 1074.[33] By that time, his sons were already leading raids deep into Wales,[34] and it seems plausible that the occupation of Shropshire did not lag far behind. Earl Roger would not have been unusual in speedily granting land on the Welsh borders to his followers. Earl William fitz Osbern, who died in Flanders in 1071, had by that time begun distributing land in Herefordshire to the Lacy family.[35] At an early stage, then, Warin, Corbet and Picot were set apart from the other followers of Earl Roger by virtue of acquiring in each case an important, and distinctive, territorial interest on the Shropshire–Powys borders.

It is true that from this first stage of the Norman occupation of Shropshire until the forfeiture of the Montgomery-Bellême family in 1102, the men of the frontier hundreds would have shared with almost all the men receiving land in that county the sense that they were followers of Earl Roger and his sons. It does seem, though, that the frontier hundreds were bestowed on those of the Montgomery men who were both relatively substantial and very closely associated with the Montgomeries in Normandy. It is not easy to trace Warin the Bald back to Normandy,

[30] *Salop. Cart.*, p. 33: 'Rainaldus qui post mortem predicti Warini uxorem illius cum eius honore suscepit.' It is uncertain whether *honor* here refers to Warin's office, his lands, or both. Warin gave tithes from manors later held by Rainald to the abbey of St-Évroult: Eyton, vii, 203–5.

[31] Lewis, 'English and Norman Government', p. 226: the vills of Marsh and Rorrington were divided equally between the two brothers, to the point that each held half a deer-hedge in Rorrington: DB 255d, 256a. For the holdings of Roger and Robert, Corbet's sons, in Rhiwset and Wittery: DB 255c–256a. Roger also shared with his brother '20 shillings from Wales': DB 253c.

[32] For Picot's holdings in Rinlow and Leintwardine: DB 258a–b. Earl Roger kept in demesne a compact group of manors in Wittery hundred and adjoining territory in Wales. These formed the *castellaria* of Montgomery: DB 253c.

[33] *VCH*, iii, 7; Mason, 'Roger de Montgomery and his Sons', pp. 3–4.

[34] For instance, see *Annales Cambriae*, p. 26.

[35] Wightman, *Lacy Family*, pp. 117–23; contrast C. P. Lewis, 'The Norman Settlement of Herefordshire under William I', *Anglo-Norman Studies*, **7** (1984), pp. 203–5; below, pp. 67, 73.

unless he were identical with the 'Warinus curvisus' or 'Guarinus curvis' who is found witnessing two versions of a charter describing a plea between Roger de Montgomery and Bishop Robert of Sées brought before Duke William at Rouen sometime during the 1070s.[36] If Warin can indeed be so identified, this would show that he held a position of eminence among Earl Roger's men both in Normandy and in England. In England, he certainly held such a position in 1085,[37] but it does not seem possible to say with any certainty from where Warin came.[38] His successor, Rainald, on the other hand, is taken to be identical with the Rainald who held land of Earl Roger in Normandy, in Bailleul-en-Gouffern.[39] The Gouffern, to the south of Falaise, formed part of the heartland of the Montgomery possessions in Normandy.[40] In any case, it is quite clear that Warin and Rainald were the chief men of Earl Roger in Shropshire. The size of the fief which they received, apparently almost entirely from Earl Roger, is indicative of the leading position they occupied among the earl's tenants. The large tenurial complex of which Mersete hundred came to form part was by far the most extensive and valuable of those Earl Roger created in Shropshire for his followers. In 1086, the lands of Rainald *vicecomes* in Shropshire were valued at £93 annually, more than the second and third largest Shropshire fiefs together. Moreover, the total value of the lands Rainald held in Sussex, Warwickshire and Staffordshire equalled about half that of his Shropshire fiefs.[41] Among Earl Roger's tenants in England, only Robert fitz Tetbald, who appears to have been the *vicecomes* of a Sussex rape allotted to Earl Roger by William the Conqueror,[42] had a fief more valuable than that originally held by Warin.[43]

36 *RRAN*, ed. Bates, no. 29, version I: (1070 × 1079, poss. 12 iv 1071 × 1079), p. 185; *ibid.*, no. 29 version II: (same dates). There is no entry for 'curvisus' in L. Favre (ed.), *Glossarium Mediae et Infimae Latinitatis, Conditum a Carolo du Fresne, Domino du Cange*, new edn., 10 vols. (Niort, 1883–7) or in the British Academy's *Dictionary of Medieval Latin from British Sources*, various eds. (8 fascicules, London, 1975–2003). Note also the 'Guarinus de Mara' who can be seen endowing St-Martin's of Sées in 1078 × 1089: *Livre blanc de St Martin de Sées*, ff. 61r–71v, ed. K. M. Thompson, 'The Cross-Channel Estates of the Montgomery-Bellême Family, *c.* 1050–1112' (University College Cardiff M.A. thesis, 1983), p. 246.

37 V. H. Galbraith, 'An Episcopal Land-Grant of 1085', *EHR*, **44** (1929), p. 372.

38 J. F. A. Mason, 'The Officers and Clerks of the Norman Earls of Shropshire', *TSAS*, **56** (1957–60), p. 246.

39 L. C. Loyd, *The Origins of Some Anglo-Norman Families* (Harleian Soc., **103**, 1951), pp. 11–12; *VCH*, i, 296.

40 A. Vallez, 'La Construction du comté d'Alençon (1269–1380): Essai de géographie historique', in *Annales de Normandie*, **22** (1972), pp. 25–6.

41 Lewis, 'English and Norman Government', pp. 227–8.

42 Mason, 'Officers', p. 246.

43 Robert fitz Tetbald's tenurial and official position in Sussex was comparable to that of Rainald in Shropshire: Robert held lands worth over £150 in Sussex (Lewis, 'English and Norman Goverment', p. 227).

In their close association with the Montgomery family and their leading position among the earl's men, then, Warin and Rainald stood out. Much the same was true of that other frontier lord, Picot. Orderic allows us to trace Picot back to Normandy. According to Orderic, on 25 February 1083, Picot 'de Saia', and others of Earl Roger's chief followers witnessed Earl Roger's foundation of Shrewsbury Abbey.[44] It was probably during the 1080s that a Robert, nicknamed Picot, de Sai, together with his wife Adeloya, made a grant to the abbey of St Martin in Sées.[45] That this Picot actually came from Sai, a place near Argentan, on the river Orne, is probable, since the land granted to St Martin's Abbey lay in Jouvigny, near Sai. Nor can there be much doubt that he was identical with the Shropshire Picot. Sai lay in the Hiémois, the *vicomté* of Roger de Montgomery; St Martin of Sées was founded by Earl Roger, who appears as a witness to Picot's grant to that abbey.[46] It seems clear that, in the late 1080s, Picot de Sai was one of the chief men of Earl Roger, active not only in Shropshire, but also in the Hiémois. Thus, in 1089, Robert 'Picot' de Sai twice bears the title *dapifer* in charters to the abbey of St Martin.[47] Picot has been seen as a leading member of the family deriving its name from Sai. Though no traces of a castle survive in Sai today,[48] this should not be taken as conclusive proof that this family ranked lower socially than castellan families such as the Géré.[49]

Corbet, father of the Roger and Robert holding the frontier hundreds north of Picot's, also seems to have been one of Earl Roger's chief men in Normandy. He is very probably identical with the 'Corbet' who witnessed, sometime between 1079 and 1083, and possibly in the summer of 1080, an attestation of Duke William of a charter granting to the abbey of Troarn land held of the Montgomery lordship.[50] His brother, who witnesses the same charter, is called Robert, which was a particularly common name in the Corbet family. Moreover, this Troarn attestation is very probably contemporary with another of Duke William's attestations to

[44] *Orderic*, iii, 146: 'Rogerus comes [...] Guarinum uicecomitem et Picotum de Saia caeterosque proceres suos [...] conuocauit'.

[45] The editors of *Gallia Christiana* assigned this charter to 1060; however, since Picot de Sai sued in court for his right to enjoy the dower of his wife Adeloya in 1086, the St Martin charter is probably closer to the later date.

[46] J.-M. Bouvris, 'Aux premiers temps d'une grande abbaye normande au XIe siècle: les chartes de fondation de St-Martin de Sées', *Annales de Normandie*, **39** (1989), pp. 452–4.

[47] G. Louise, *La Seigneurie de Bellême, Xe–XIIe siècles: évolution des pouvoirs territoriaux et construction d'une seigneurie de frontière aux confins de la Normandie et du Maine à la charnière de l'an mil*, 2 vols. (Flers, 1990), ii, 102, citing the unpublished cartulary of St-Martin de Sées, nos. xiii and xxix.

[48] Louise, *Bellême*, ii, 108.

[49] P. Bauduin, 'Une famille châtelaine sur les confins normanno-manceaux: les Géré (Xe–XIIIe s.)', *Archéologie Médievale*, **22** (1992), pp. 309–56.

[50] *RRAN*, ed. Bates, no. 283 (p. 859).

that abbey, which confirmed a grant of land from the Beaumont lordship, and has a different group of witnesses. Since the charters are similar in format, the two different groups of witnesses probably represent the men of the Beaumont and Montgomery retinues.[51] If so, Corbet and his brother Robert can, like Warin, Picot and Rainald, be shown to have been Montgomery followers active in Normandy during the 1080s.

Nor was Corbet more distantly connected with the Montgomeries than Picot. Admittedly, the Corbets are widely believed to have come from the Pays de Caux, a part of coastal Normandy north of the Seine, and this would not associate them closely with the territorial base of the Montgomery-Bellême lordship. However, the evidence for their original connection with the Pays de Caux is confined to the name of the Corbet castle and lordship, Caus, and this has been deemed inconclusive by recent place-name studies.[52] The difficulty of locating the Corbet family in Normandy can be overcome by turning to later evidence. In May 1204, Philip Augustus, the king of France, was engaged in conquering Normandy from John, king of England.[53] At that time, he is found granting away 'all the Corbet fee such as Robert Corbet held it of Robert, the count of Alençon'.[54] On chronological grounds, it seems entirely possible to identify this Robert Corbet with the baron of Caus of that name who was dead by 1222.[55] It is even possible to say with considerable certainty that the 'feodum Corbet' was centred around the village of Crocy, near Falaise. A Robert Corbet appears as lord of 'Croceium' in 1190. This may well have been the nephew and heir of Roger Corbet of Caus, for a Roger Corbet is recorded in 1189 × 90 as having once been lord of 'Croceium'.[56] This place-name has been identified with modern-day Croisi-sur-Eure (near Évreux),[57] and an unlocated 'Croucy'.[58] However, given that Philip Augustus' 1204 grant of the 'Corbet fee' was made to the mayor of Falaise, Crocy, which lies just under ten kilometres east of that town, is the best identification of the 'Croceium' of 1189–90. This is of crucial interest in our context, of course, since Crocy lies in the Gouffern, not far from Argentan, Bailleul and Sai, which, as has been mentioned, formed the

51 *RRAN*, ed. Bates, no. 282, and p. 858.

52 M. Gelling, *The Place-Names of Shropshire, Part 2: The Hundreds of Ford and Condover* (Nottingham, 1995), pp. 56–7.

53 F. M. Powicke, *The Loss of Normandy*, 2nd edn (Manchester, 1961), pp. 260–1.

54 *Cartulaire normand de Philippe-Auguste, Louis VIII, Saint Louis et Philippe-le-Hardi*, ed. L. Delisle (Caen, 1882, repr. Geneva, 1978), no 76: 'totum feodum Corbet sicut Robertus Corbet illud de Roberto Comite de Alençon tenebat'.

55 For the date of his death see Eyton, vii, 17; *Curia Regis Rolls*, vol. x: *1221–2* (London, 1949), p. 8.

56 *Calendar of Documents Preserved in France*, ed. J. H. Round (London, 1899), nos. 604 and 601.

57 A. Le Prévost, *Dictionnaire des anciens noms de lieu du département de l'Eure* (Évreux, 1839), p. 96.

58 Delisle, *Cartulaire normand*, p. 357.

core of the Montgomery possessions in Normandy. All these places lie in the valley of the river Dives, which flows from Exmes, the chief town of Earl Roger's Hiémois *vicomté*, towards his abbey at Troarn.[59] The fact that in 1204 Robert Corbet's Norman fee could be referred to simply as the 'feodum Corbet' strongly suggests that it was an ancient patrimony, rather than a recent acquisition. Moreover, Count Robert III of Alençon (d. 1217), of whom Robert Corbet held the 'feodum Corbet' in 1204, was a direct descendant of Roger de Montgomery, earl of Shrewsbury.[60] All the evidence therefore supports the view that the Robert Corbet of the early thirteenth century had inherited his Norman fee from the Corbet who followed Earl Roger to Shropshire in the late eleventh century, and held it of the descendants of Earl Roger until he lost it in 1204. If so, Corbet, the lord of Rinlau and Wittery hundreds, was just as closely associated with the new earl of Shrewsbury as were Picot de Sai and Rainald de Bailleul. Moreover, it appears clear that they were neighbours both in Normandy and on the Shropshire borders. Thus, especially from 1085, when Rainald de Bailleul arrived, the frontier lords of Shropshire formed a tightly knit group within the Montgomery retinue, with a common lord and closely linked landed interests.

It also seems possible that Earl Roger chose to staff the Shropshire frontier with men who fulfilled a border function in Normandy. The concept of border lords may well have existed in Normandy: Orderic's usage of the term *marchio* to describe Robert de Bellême is one indication of this.[61] The Gouffern, moreover, lies across the main approach from France, by way of Argentan, towards Falaise, Caen and the Bessin; this was the road which Philip Augustus took during his invasion of Normandy in May 1204.[62] Picot appears to have owed allegiance also to the earl's eldest son, Robert, the lord of the *seigneurie* of Bellême.[63] In May 1086, Picot de Sai attended Robert's court at Bellême, suing for his wife's dower; the narrative charter recording the settlement refers to Picot as one of the 'barons' of Robert de Bellême.[64] Picot's double allegiance to both Earl Roger and the earl's eldest son illustrates the close links between the Hiémois and the lordship of Bellême at this time.

[59] The interests of the Montgomery family in the Dives valley are reflected in the location of their endowments to the abbeys Troarn and Almenêches: Thompson, 'Cross-Channel Estates', pp. 48–9.

[60] Vallez, 'La Construction', p. 45.

[61] *Orderic*, iv, 160; cf. also his description of arrangements in Normandy after Henry I's death in 1135: 'Guillelmus de Rolmara et Hugo de Bornaco aliique marchisi ad tutandos patriae fines directi sunt' (*ibid.*, vi, 450).

[62] Powicke, *Loss of Normandy*, p. 257.

[63] Robert appears to have taken control of all the lands of his mother, Mabel de Bellême, after her death in 1077: *Orderic*, iv, 132, n. 4; cf. *ibid.*, iii, 136.

[64] Loyd, *Origins of Anglo-Norman Families*, p. 96; *Cal. Docs. France*, ed. Round, no. 654.

Table 2. *Franco-Norman descendants of Earl Roger de Montgomery, the 'feodum Corbet' and 'Croceium'*

Roger de Montgomery, earl of Shrewsbury (d. 1094)
lord of Corbet (occ. 1071–1079 × 1083)
|
Robert de Bellême (d. 1114)
last Montgomery earl of Shrewsbury (forfeited 1102)
|
William, count of Alençon and Ponthieu (d. 1171)
|

John, count of Alençon (d. 1191) Robert Corbet (prob. lord of Caus, d. 1222) holds 'Croceium' of him in 1190	Gui, count of Ponthieu
| Robert, count of Alençon (d. 1217) Robert Corbet (prob. lord of Caus, d. 1222) holds 'feodum Corbet' of him in 1204	

Many of the members of Robert de Bellême's household came from the Hiémois.[65] It is of high interest that Picot was associated with the lord of that northern French frontier lordship, the *seigneurie* of Bellême.[66] It should be noted also that Picot appeared in Robert's seigneurial court at Bellême to sue 'in the sight of the forty knights or more' regarding lands that lay more than seventy kilometres distant, near Argentan. This appears to have been a snub to ducal power, for Argentan may have been garrisoned by the men of the duke of Normandy at the time.[67] Thus, it seems that Picot was associated from an early date with the independent policy pursued in Normandy by the Robert who was to rebel against Henry I

[65] Louise, *Bellême*, ii, 102.

[66] On the topographical frontier nature of the lordship of Bellême, and on the Bellême lords' multiple allegiances and aim to establish a seigneury under the direct lordship of the king of France, see Lemarignier, *Hommage en marche*, pp. 63–7; D. C. Douglas, *William the Conqueror* (London, 1964), pp. 57–8; more recently and fully: Louise, *Bellême, passim*.

[67] Robert de Bellême was to eject the duke's garrisons from Argentan in 1087, after he heard of Duke William's death: *Orderic*, iv, 112–14. On seigneurial courts in Normandy in the late eleventh century: M. Chibnall, *Anglo-Norman England, 1066–1166* (Oxford, 1986), pp. 167–8.

in 1102. Accordingly, the first Norman lord of Clun personifies the links between the Normandy–Bellême frontier in northern France and the frontier situation in western Shropshire, links which are symbolized by the castles and earthworks built under the auspices of Earl Robert both in Shropshire and in Bellême. It may be that Picot, and indeed the other Shropshire frontier lords as well, belonged to a core group within the Montgomery household which participated particularly closely with the efforts of that family to extend and entrench the frontiers of its base of influence in both France and the British Isles.

The contrast between these frontier lords and some of the other Shropshire tenants of Earl Roger was certainly heightened by their provenance from within Normandy. Roger of Courseulles came from the Calvados coast,[68] and had a very different stake in England. The lands he held of Earl Roger lay in central Shropshire and were worth only about £3 annually, as against the £163 he gained from the Somerset fief he held in chief.[69] Yet the claim to distinctiveness of the frontier lords was not based purely on their Norman provenance. Gerard of Tournai was a neighbour of Rainald de Bailleul in Normandy, but his Shropshire estates lay mostly in the centre of the county.[70] Odo of Bernières, on the other hand, came from the Calvados, but held a 'frontier' estate in Mersete hundred.[71] It would seem that Earl Roger chose his frontier lords as much for their substance and ability as their provenance. Warin, Corbet and Picot were, by a comfortable margin, the most affluent landholders in Earl Roger's Shropshire, in a separate league, in terms of wealth, from the next layer of Shropshire tenants, Robert fitz Tetbald, William Pantulf, Gerard de Tournai, Helgot, Norman the huntsman, Turold de Verley and Robert fitz Corbet, who all held lands worth between £12 and £16.[72]

It is true that the frontier lords were not identical in every respect. Warin and his successor Rainald held a clear position of leadership in Shropshire, and were also distinct from Picot and Corbet in holding lands elsewhere in England.[73] Nevertheless, despite these differences, the coherence of the Shropshire frontier lords was perhaps highlighted, at this time, by the contrasts and similarities with the Mortimer lord holding the border estates just to the south, on the Hereford–Shropshire frontier. Ralph de Mortimer did hold some land of Earl Roger, but most of his Shropshire estates, and in particular those on the borders, were held in

[68] *RRAN*, ed. Bates, no. 146 and pp. 848, 854; *VCH*, i, 298.
[69] DB 256b; Lewis, 'English and Norman Government', p. 222.
[70] DB 258d. [71] DB 257d.
[72] Lewis, 'English and Norman Government', p. 227. [73] *Ibid.*, p. 222.

chief.[74] It appears possible that he was installed on the Welsh borders by King William I even before Earl Roger was put in charge of Shropshire.[75] However, it seems clear that Wigmore Castle was added to Ralph's border estate only after 1075, when it had been forfeited by Roger, the earl of Hereford and son of William fitz Osbern.[76] In these respects, Ralph de Mortimer differed from the lords of the Shropshire border. On the other hand, the Mortimer family took its name from a Norman border castle, Mortemer-sur-Eaulne, in the *pays* of Talou, over fifty kilometres north-east of Rouen. It is true that Ralph's father had forfeited the castle in 1054,[77] but de Mortimer had in common with his neighbours to the north both a compact landed interest lying adjacent to Welsh territory and an association with the frontier of Normandy.

In keeping with this, there is some little evidence that these frontier lords may have taken their first steps towards forging a common identity. The occasion was the rebellion against William Rufus of 1088.[78] In that year, Ralph de Mortimer conspired with a very select and distinctive group of barons. One of these, just like Ralph, was named after a frontier castle of Normandy which his father had forfeited.[79] Bernard de Neufmarché had recently married the daughter of Osbern fitz Richard, the lord of Richard's Castle, and in 1088 was beginning his inroads into the Welsh principality of Brycheiniog.[80] Another rebel was Roger de Lacy, the son of the Walter who was the first lord of the Herefordshire honor of Weobley. The other party to the conspiracy is less clearly identifiable, being referred to simply as the 'men of Earl Roger of Shrewsbury'. We cannot be certain which of Earl Roger's men took part in the unsuccessful raid on Hereford. Perhaps the fact that they are not identified as separate from the other Shropshire tenants of Earl Roger may serve as a reminder that, in the eyes of contemporaries, their most obvious distinction was not that they held compact border territories, but that they were followers of Earl Roger. Moreover, their co-operation may have been partly due to the fact that they, and their lords, held lands in Normandy as well, and were therefore more likely to support Duke Robert's claim to the throne of England.[81] However, it is noticeable that they enlisted

[74] DB 256d–257a, 260b; Lewis, 'English and Norman Government', Map 34; the same, 'Norman Settlement of Herefordshire', p. 210.

[75] Green, *Aristocracy*, pp. 70–1.

[76] Lewis, 'Norman Settlement of Herefordshire', p. 210; the same, 'Ralph (I) de Mortimer (fl. *c.* 1080–1104)', in *ODNB* (2004). Note that the Mortimer family chronicle has Ralph installed in the borders after suppressing the revolt of Eadric the wild: *Mon. Angl.*, vi, p. 1, pp. 348–9.

[77] *Orderic*, iv, 86–9. [78] *John of Worcester*, iii, 52–5.

[79] *Orderic*, ii, 130. [80] Lloyd, *History of Wales*, p. 397.

[81] On the motivation of the magnates opposing William Rufus in 1088, see Green, *Aristocracy*, p. 275.

the help of Welshmen, and it does seem that their co-operation with each other is a sign that their principal interests lay on the frontier, and that this meant that their frontier neighbours came to represent the men with whom they most commonly interacted.

Nor was this the only crisis of the reign of William Rufus in which the border aristocracy of Shropshire may have acted together against the central English authority. In 1095, both Roger de Lacy and Hugh de Montgomery, the second son of Earl Roger and his successor as earl of Shrewsbury, seem to have participated in the rebellion led by Robert de Mowbray, the earl of Northumbria.[82] The evidence is indirect; Orderic tells us only that both Roger de Lacy and Hugh de Montgomery were punished by William Rufus. The rebels of 1095 were linked neither by kinship nor by geographical proximity, being concentrated near the Welsh borders and in northernmost England. Many of them had already risen against the king in 1088, but this was the only obvious connection between them.[83] It is, however, notable that during the reign of William Rufus the lords who were most inclined to rebellion were those holding land on the periphery of the English kingdom.

However, if we move on to the rebellion of 1102, there is little indication that it was a co-ordinated uprising of an aristocracy on the peripheries. Robert de Bellême, who succeeded his younger brother Hugh as earl of Shrewsbury after Hugh's death in 1098, did, apparently, make efforts to win the support of his 'neighbours'.[84] But it seems clear that he made little headway,[85] and could depend upon his brothers alone: certainly Arnulf and possibly Roger the Poitevin.[86] The fact that he was forced to rely rather too heavily on the Welsh lords of Powys over whom he claimed overlordship reinforces the impression that Robert was, in 1102, acting without the support of his neighbours on the Welsh borders. His new castle at Bridgnorth was in fact garrisoned by his Shropshire tenants, among them Roger, son of Corbet, ancestor of the lords of Caus.[87] The uprising of 1102 was strictly a Montgomery rebellion, and it was focused on Shropshire.

Nevertheless, it is perhaps not an exaggeration to say that the political geography in the British Isles was restructured in the wake of the

[82] *Orderic*, iv, 285.
[83] F. Barlow, *William Rufus* (London, 1983), p. 348.
[84] *Orderic*, vi, 21; the term used is *affines*.
[85] *Orderic*, vi, 23.
[86] *Orderic*, vi, 30–3; *John of Worcester*, iii, 100–3; *Brut*, pp. 40–7; C. W. Hollister, 'The Campaign of 1102 against Robert of Bellême', in C. Harper-Bill, C. J. Holdsworth, J. Nelson and J. Laughland (eds.), *Studies in Medieval History Presented to R. Allen Brown* (Woodbridge, 1989), pp. 193–202.
[87] *Orderic*, vi, 25.

Montgomery forfeitures of 1102.[88] In any event, Henry I's banishment of Robert de Bellême and his brothers had a dramatic, and immediate, effect on the position of the Shropshire frontier lords. The earldom of Shrewsbury was not preserved. However, it seems as if, at first, Henry I took care not to transform the Montgomery settlement in Shropshire too much. As his representative in Shropshire, he chose Richard, a former servant of the Montgomeries, who came from Beaumais, near the centre of the Montgomery estates.[89] Moreover, as far as we know, all three lords of the Shropshire frontier retained their lands. In the case of Picot de Sai, this seems certain, since his tenancies descended to his son Henry.[90] As for Roger fitz Corbet, Orderic tells us that, during Robert de Bellême's rebellion, Roger had been in charge of the garrison holding Robert's new castle at Bridgnorth against Henry I.[91] However, Roger agreed to surrender the castle when Henry I threatened him with hanging and bribed him with the promise of adding land worth £100 to his estates.[92] Whether or not this story is true – there is no sign that Roger Corbet actually received additional lands after 1102 – there is little reason to believe that it was unusual for him to be allowed to retain his estates after the forfeiture of Earl Robert. In fact, in Anglo-Norman England, subtenants were generally permitted to keep their lands even if their lord lost his.[93] It is therefore relatively safe to assume that the other Shropshire frontier lord remained in place as well. Hugh, the son of Warin the Bald, had replaced Rainald de Bailleul by 1098 and seems not to have suffered confiscation.[94] In any case, the Shropshire frontier lords now joined the growing group of *barones* who held their English lands directly of the king. The stage was now set for their border estates to establish themselves as baronies in their own right. It has been estimated that by 1166 the Shropshire baronies of Oswestry, Caus and Clun were among fifty or so baronies that had originated as subtenancies.[95]

Another way in which the fall of the Montgomeries changed the character of the Shropshire frontier aristocracy was that new families were now introduced to the region. This was largely the result of royal

[88] On the wide-ranging connections of the Montgomeries in the later eleventh century see below, pp. 108–12.

[89] *VCH*, iii, 10.

[90] *Salop. Cart.*, no. 47d.

[91] *Orderic*, vi, 25.

[92] *Orderic*, vi, 26–9.

[93] J. C. Holt, 'Politics and Property in Early Medieval England', in J. C. Holt, *Colonial England* (London, 1997), p. 138.

[94] *VCH*, iii, 10. For the subsequent fate of his lands, see below, p. 70.

[95] J. C. Holt, 'Feudal Society and the Family in Early Medieval England. I: The Revolution of 1066', in his *Colonial England*, p. 175.

patronage and part of the large-scale restructuring of the Anglo-Norman aristocracy undertaken by Henry I before 1125.[96] By far the most striking change to the make-up of the Shropshire frontier aristocracy came with Henry I's disposal of the lands of Hugh son of Warin. As has been seen, in the absence of evidence to the contrary, and given that the Corbets and other Montgomery men who had participated in the 1102 revolt were allowed to retain their lands, it is relatively safe to assume that Henry I did not seize Hugh's lands, but that at his death, apparently without issue, they escheated to the crown. Henry, however, granted them wholesale, probably by 1109, to a Breton named Alan fitz Flaald who cannot have had the slightest claim to them.[97] Alan was the younger brother of Jordan, the *dapifer* of Dol;[98] his grandfather had held the same office. Dol is near western Normandy, from where many of Henry I's new men originated.[99] Alan was not the only Breton from around Dol who was destined to be endowed with lands in England by Henry I. Orderic tells us that in 1091, when the future Henry I fortified Coutances and Avranches against his older brothers, he had Breton supporters;[100] clearly, they were Henry's associates while he was lord in the Cotentin.[101] Alan was probably for a time a member of Henry I's household, but before 1107 × 1114, he acquired a fief in Norfolk (the future honor of Mileham).[102] Nor was Alan the only newcomer to the Shropshire frontier in the early twelfth century. It seems entirely possible that the Lestranges acquired their estates around Knockin at about this time;[103] their ancestor, Rualdus Extraneus, certainly was associated with Alan fitz Flaald in Norfolk.[104]

There was also a newcomer at Hen Domen Montgomery. We may assume that Henry would have been particularly careful in deciding on whom he should bestow this key castle, whose garrison had been overcome by the Welsh as recently as 1094. Earl Roger and his sons had

96 C.W. Hollister, *Henry I* (New Haven and London, 2001), p. 346.

97 Eyton, vii, 209–11; 220; *Salop. Cart.*, pp. 258–9: 'Alanus filius fladaldi qui honorem vicecomitis Warini post filium eius suscepit.'

98 The early history of the Fitzalans is fully discussed in J. H. Round, 'The Origin of the Stewarts', in J. H. Round, *Studies in Peerage and Family History* (London, 1901), p. 129; moreover, J. H. Round and T. F. Tout published several articles on the Fitzalans in the *Dictionary of National Biography*.

99 Round, 'Origin', pp. 124–5: Henry I's 'new men' from near Dol included Richard of Reviers, the ancestor of the earls of Devon; the Hayes of Haye-du-Puits, who were to become lords of the honor of Halnaker in Sussex; and Aubigny, afterwards earls of Arundel, a fief in Norfolk. Cf. also J. Le Patourel, *The Norman Empire* (Oxford 1976), pp. 341–6.

100 *Orderic*, iv, 250–1.

101 Round, 'Origin', pp. 124–5; Henry as lord of Cotentin: *Orderic*, iv, 118–20.

102 Eyton, vii, 217–18; *The Charters of Norwich Cathedral Priory. Part 2*, ed. B. Dodwell (P. R. S., NS 46, London 1985), no. 364.

103 As is suggested by R. R. Davies, 'Henry I and Wales', in H. Mayr-Harting and R. I. Moore (eds.), *Studies in Medieval History Presented to R. H. C. Davis* (London, 1985), p. 143.

104 *Mon. Angl.*, v, 51, no. ix.

kept the *castellaria* of Montgomery in their demesne, so it must have escheated to Henry I in 1102. It is virtually certain that Henry granted it to one of his followers. That much was recorded in 1225, when the honor of Montgomery was being disputed and one of the rival claimants stated that 'Henricus senex' had granted the lands of Montgomery to one Baldwin 'de Bollers' along with the hand of Sybil of Falaise, Henry I's *neptis*.[105] There seems to be no reason to doubt this statement,[106] particularly given that a Baldwin 'de Bollers' witnessed Henry I's 1121 confirmation to Shrewsbury Abbey in the company of several Shropshire notables.[107] It is probable that Baldwin had by then already been installed at Montgomery. It has recently been suggested that Baldwin hailed from Flanders.[108] It is quite possible that he was a member, probably a younger son, of the Flemish aristocratic family based at Boelare, south-west of Aalst, near the Flemish-French border.[109] 'Bollers', the form appearing in the 1121 Shrewsbury charter, is a common spelling of the Boelare family toponymic in contemporary sources.[110] Moreover, 'Baldwin' was the ancestral first name of the comital family of Flanders, and was commonly used by the Boelare family during the twelfth century, much as 'Alan' was favoured by the family of Alan fitz Flaald because it was a hereditary first name of the counts of Brittany. First-name evidence also gives us a link to Flanders of a different sort: 'Stephen' was used both by the Bollers of Montgomery and by the Flemish family of that name, even though it was an unusual name in Flanders at the time.[111] It would not have been exceptional for Henry I to have chosen a Flemish aristocrat, possibly a younger son of the Boelare family, as hereditary castellan of Montgomery. Gerbod the Fleming, who was the first man to be put in charge of Chester by William the Conqueror, provided a precedent for the translation of a

[105] *Curia Regis Rolls*, vol. xii: *1225–6* (London, 1957), no. 761.

[106] Eyton, xi, 120–1.

[107] See *Salop. Cart.*, no. 35, for 'Balduinus de Bollers' witnessing with William Peverel, Roger and Robert fitz Corbet, Herbert fitz Helgot and Ralph of Condover.

[108] R. Higham and P. Barker, *Hen Domen, Montgomery: A Timber Castle on the English–Welsh Border – A Final Report* (Exeter, 2000), p. 143.

[109] On the Boelare family, see E. Warlop, *The Flemish Nobility*, 4 vols. (Kortrijk, 1975–6), iii, no. 28, and iv, 1249 (and entries indexed there).

[110] For an example, see P. Chaplais, *Diplomatic Documents Preserved in the Public Record Office* (London, 1964), no. 8. 'Boulers', the alternative spelling for the Boelare surname noted by Warlop, *Flemish Nobility*, iv, 1250, also appears in contemporary documents referring to the lords of Montgomery, e.g. *Pleas before the King or his Justices, 1198–1212*, vol. iii: *Rolls or Fragments of Rolls from the Years 1199, 1201, and 1203–1206*, ed. D. M. Stenton (Selden Society 83, 1967), p. 69 (1203): 'Robertus de Boulers crucesignatus obiit ante iter arreptum. Et nescitur quis habuit catalla sua.' It is true that there are numerous other spellings. However, a search of French gazetteers has produced no place-names matching any of them.

[111] Warlop, *Flemish Nobility*, i, 51, 146; iii, 689.

Flemish military leader to the Welsh borders.[112] Moreover, in 1101 and 1110, Henry I renewed a contract with the count of Flanders, which had first been concluded by William the Conqueror, and which provided for Flemish mercenaries to be dispatched to England or Normandy in case of need.[113] Finally, there is evidence that Henry I settled Flemish colonists in Dyfed as part of a deliberate policy.[114] That Baldwin de Bollers, the lord of Montgomery, came from Flanders is a distinct possibility.

If Baldwin was indeed a younger son of the Boelare family, this would have provided Henry I with a concrete incentive for choosing Montgomery as an appropriate castle to grant him. For the Boelare family, by 1100, could look back on generations of service to the counts of Flanders as frontier castellans, fulfilling a function, at least symbolically, similar to that of margraves: guarding the borders of their lord's realm. By the late twelfth century, they had been appointed hereditary constables of Flanders.[115] Thus, Baldwin de Bollers provides another reason, albeit tentative, for thinking that Henry I chose to put the western Shropshire castles in the charge of men who had a frontier family background. This would certainly parallel the policy pursued by Earl Roger, who, as has been seen, granted the western hundreds of Shropshire to those among his followers who held lands on the southern borders of his domains.[116] Henry I's choice of 'new men' in Shropshire may show that the castles of Oswestry and Montgomery were thought of as 'frontier' fortifications from the first two decades of the twelfth century onwards.

The effects of the Montgomery forfeiture, and of Henry I's introduction of new men, could be summarized by observing that the situation in Shropshire now approximated to that of Herefordshire, while losing its similarities with Cheshire. The earldom of Chester went to successive heirs of Hugh d'Avranches until it was absorbed by the crown in 1237; the barons holding land in that exceptionally independent county were to derive their identity in good measure from their position and role within the nascent 'palatinate' of Cheshire.[117] However, in Herefordshire, as in Shropshire, the Norman border earl forfeited his lands and title after an unsuccessful rebellion against the king. Here, the flash-point came less than a decade after Hastings, in 1075, when Roger de Breteuil, the

[112] *Orderic*, ii, 260–1. [113] *Diplomatic Documents*, ed. Chaplais, nos. 1 and 2.

[114] Rowlands, 'Making of the March', p. 147.

[115] Warlop, *Flemish Nobility*, i, 141–2. [116] Above, pp. 59–68.

[117] G. Ormerod, *The History of the County Palatine and City of Chester*, 3 vols. (London, 1882); B. E. Harris, 'The Earldom of Chester 1070–1301', in the same (ed.), *A History of the County of Chester*, vol. ii (Oxford, 1979), pp. 1–8; A. D. M. Phillips and C. B. Phillips (eds.), *A New Historical Atlas of Cheshire* (Chester, 2001); P. Morgan, *War and Society in Medieval Cheshire, 1277–1403* (Manchester, 1987).

son of William fitz Osbern, rose against the Conqueror.[118] Here, too, the earldom was not preserved, former subtenants became tenants-in-chief at a stroke, and the king introduced new men to the region. Thus, as has been seen, Ralph de Mortimer probably received Wigmore after 1075, although it is likely that he was dispatched to the Welsh borders earlier.[119] After 1075, moreover, Clifford Castle was bestowed on Ralph de Tosny, and Monmouth was placed in the custody of the Breton Wihenoc, the uncle of William fitz Baderon, who was in charge of the castle by 1086, and from whom the castellan family descended. Soon after 1086, Bernard de Neufmarché and William de Braose came, respectively, to Brycheiniog and Radnor.[120] Meanwhile, Walter de Lacy held on to his compact group of border estates centred on Weobley;[121] indeed, having been actively involved in suppressing the revolt of Roger de Breteuil, he was probably rewarded with further estates after 1075.[122] It has been suggested that William fitz Osbern's earldom was not revived because Walter de Lacy was considered powerful enough to fulfil the part of border guardian, but not so redoubtable as to pose a threat to the English king.[123] It may well be that Alan fitz Flaald, as successor to Hugh son of Warin, was considered to be in a comparable position in Shropshire.[124]

Essentially, then, the situation which was to prevail until the end of the thirteenth century – and indeed beyond – was created in the aftermath of the 1102 forfeiture. All the lords of the Shropshire frontier now found themselves in the position of the Mortimers to their south. As has been seen, it was not in itself very unusual that they had come to hold directly of the king.[125] By contrast with other baronies which had originated as subtenancies, however, the honors of westernmost Shropshire formed a compact group of estates immediately bordering on, indeed overlapping with, Welsh territory. There was also a fundamental change in

[118] Wightman, *Lacy Family*, pp. 123–4.

[119] Above, p. 66–7.

[120] DB 183b, 180d; Holden, *Lords*, pp. 11, 13.

[121] It should be noted that C. P. Lewis has argued that Walter de Lacy, though he had been granted some lands by William fitz Osbern, was not the man of that earl, or of his son: cf. his 'Norman Settlement of Herefordshire', pp. 203–5; the same, 'Walter de Lacy (d. 1085), magnate', in *ODNB* (2004).

[122] *John of Worcester*, iii, 24–5. Earl Roger de Breteuil is stopped at a ford of the Severn, among others, by 'Waltero de Laceio, cum copiis suis'.

[123] Wightman, *Lacy Family*, p. 166.

[124] This may have been true even though, as Lewis has observed, de Lacy's Herefordshire lands did not constitute a border block comparable to those of westernmost Shropshire: see his 'Norman Settlement of Herefordshire', p. 205. Certainly, by 1217, Ralph de Lacy's descendant, Walter II, numbered among the 'barones de Marchia': *Cal. Pat. R. 1216–25*, pp. 108–9; cf. Holden, *Lords*, *passim*, esp. pp. 8–11; below, p. 81 (n. 168).

[125] Above, p. 69.

border personnel. It is true that the lords who had participated in the 1102 rebellion kept alive the memory of the Montgomery border county well into the twelfth century: Roger Corbet, for example, may have survived until the early days of Stephen's reign.[126] On the other hand, the introduction to Shropshire of Alan fitz Flaald and a number of other newcomers profoundly changed the character of the Shropshire frontier. It was now no longer a land occupied by men tied together by the bonds of common lordship, united in the pursuit of the Montgomery cause, but simply a group of neighbouring estates. As neighbours, the frontier lords were more likely to pursue their own family concerns, and their relationship could be expected to be determined by rivalry as much as by common interest. It was argued above that the men of Earl Roger had begun co-operating with other frontier lords by 1088.[127] But it was only after the Montgomery forfeiture that they truly fitted the profile of lords of the Welsh frontier. An important part of their territorial interests lay on the borders; they were tenants-in-chief; but they had little else in common. They now truly were part of the prototypical Marcher aristocracy.

As was to remain the case for all the families on the Welsh borders, the lords of the Shropshire frontier had territorial interests in other parts of England and Normandy. Yet there are clear signs that western Shropshire was where they began to put down roots. Picot de Sai had, by 1109, given his daughter in marriage to Cadwgan ap Bleddyn, one of the Welsh lords of Powys.[128] Gerald of Wales comments that marriages with Welsh dynasties were generally contracted by the Norman colonists at this stage with a view to establishing themselves more firmly as local landlords,[129] and it seems probable that Picot was hoping for such a result. Ecclesiastical and monastic endowments provide another indication of the territorial priorities of aristocratic families at this time. William, the son of Alan fitz Flaald, was certainly taking steps towards establishing a monastic community at Haughmond in 1125 × 1136, and the work may have been begun by him, or his father, as early as 1110.[130] The Lestranges were to become equally important benefactors to Haughmond during the late twelfth and thirteenth centuries.[131] The de Bollers and Fitzwarins founded religious houses in western Shropshire, at Chirbury and Alberbury respectively, in the late twelfth and early thirteenth centuries.[132] Similarly, Ralph de

[126] *Salop. Cart.*, no. 288. [127] Above, pp. 67–8.
[128] *Brut*, pp. 62–3.
[129] *Giraldus*, vi, 91 (*Itinerarium Kambrie*, i, 12).
[130] *Haughmond Cart.*, p. 5 and no. 900; *VCH*, ii, 62–3; for a recent survey of Norman ecclesiastical foundations in Herefordshire and the adjoining conquest lordships, see Holden, *Lords*, pp. 38–41, 81–4, 113–15.
[131] *VCH*, ii, 64–5. [132] *VCH*, ii, 59–62, 47–50.

Mortimer (d. after 1104) established three prebends in the parish church of Wigmore in 1100, according to the Latin chronicle of his family.[133] Moreover, on the initiative of the steward of Ralph's son Hugh I (d. 1148 × 1150), a community of canons had come into existence at Shobdon, near Wigmore, by 1140. After moving to various different locations, this community was finally installed at Wigmore in the 1170s by Hugh II (d. after 1181).[134] Hugh II was the first of the Mortimers to be buried in the new priory, and it is a testimony to the frontier orientation of his family that his heirs continued to be buried there, without exception, throughout the twelfth and thirteenth centuries.[135]

Meanwhile, Henry I's own agents in the border counties seem to have contributed towards further reinforcing the sense that the lords of the Welsh borderlands shared a common lot. Payn fitz John and Miles of Gloucester, favourites of Henry I's who by the 1120s had acquired the shrievalties of Herefordshire, Shropshire and Gloucester, were explicitly perceived as exercising their overweening power 'from the river Severn to the sea, all along the border between England and Wales'.[136] The borderlands were increasingly coming into focus as a discrete territorial unit, in part as a result of the activities of these two men. This must have helped to shape the outlook of the Shropshire frontier lords as well. It seems that, when the Corbet castle of Caus was burned in 1134, it was in the custody of Payn fitz John, then sheriff of both Herefordshire and Shropshire.[137] There is in fact a case for seeing Payn as the new leader of the border lords. It is a fitting epitaph for him that he should have been killed, in 1137 while in pursuit of a band of Welsh raiders, probably in the area around Caus.[138]

A prototypical Marcher aristocracy may have been created on the Shropshire borders during Henry I's reign, but whether that situation would persist was another question, and an outcome which was by no means certain. During the contest for the English throne between Stephen of Blois and the Empress Mathilda, which lasted from 1138 to 1153, the composition of the Shropshire aristocracy was again radically

133 *Mon. Angl.*, vi (i), 349a.

134 'The Anglo-Norman Chronicle of Wigmore Abbey', eds. J. C. Dickinson and P. T. Ricketts, *Transactions of the Woolhope Naturalists' Field Club* 39 (1969), pp. 415–18. The striking sculpture at Shobdon Arches belongs to this period: N. Pevsner, *The Buildings of England: Herefordshire* (London, 1963), pp. 288–9.

135 *DNB*; *Comp. Peerage*.

136 *Gesta Stephani*, ed. and transl. K. R. Potter, with introduction and notes by R. H. C. Davis (Oxford, 1976), p. 24. On Payn see Lloyd, *History of Wales*, esp. p. 443 and n. 165, 477; on Miles, *ibid.*, esp. pp. 438–9, 474, 478, 495 and n. 40; Holden, *Lords*, esp. pp. 19–25.

137 *Orderic*, vi, 442–3.

138 *Orderic*, vi, 442–3; Lloyd, *History of Wales*, p. 477.

altered. Partly this was due to English politics. William Fitzalan I, having unsuccessfully attempted to hold Shrewsbury Castle against Stephen, was forced to flee, probably to the court of Earl Ranulf of Chester and certainly, later, to that of the Empress.[139] But potentially the greater threat to the border aristocracy was posed by the Welsh. During the 1140s, after Fitzalan had abandoned control of his border castle of Oswestry, it was occupied by Madog ap Maredudd of Powys. Since Madog had been persuaded by Earl Ranulf of Chester to lead a host of Welshmen against Stephen at the battle at Lincoln in 1141, it seems quite possible that an agreement had been made permanently to bestow that border castle on the Welsh lord. But there are also clear signs of cross-border hostility. In 1152, Madog's son Llywelyn killed Stephen fitz Baldwin, son and heir of the de Bollers lord of Montgomery.[140] Both the Mortimers of Wigmore and the de Sais of Clun were engaged in bitter fighting with the Welsh lords of Maelienydd and Elfael. In the latter case, the Marchers appear to have retained the upper hand. Nevertheless, at the end of Stephen's reign, it seemed far from certain that all of the Marcher families and frontier baronies on the western Shropshire border would become securely entrenched through successive inheritances.

For this reason, Henry II's treatment of the lords of the border castles at the beginning of his reign may rank in importance beside that of Henry I in the history of the establishment of a frontier aristocracy in western Shropshire. In 1155, Hugh Mortimer of Wigmore refused to surrender the royal castle at Bridgnorth when requested to do so by Henry II, and only succumbed after the young king had laid simultaneous siege to the three castles of Bridgnorth, Cleobury and Wigmore.[141] Hugh was alone among those English magnates who resisted Henry II at the beginning of his reign in submitting to actual force, rather than the mere threat of it.[142] His actions are perhaps to be explained by the support his father, Hugh the elder, had lent King Stephen.[143] It is striking, however, that in 1155 the Mortimer castles do not seem to have been razed, in contrast to those of Henry of Blois, bishop of Winchester, who

139 Eyton, vii, 234; *Gesta Stephani*, pp. 128–9 and n. 8.

140 *Brut*, p. 131.

141 *The First Four Books of the Historia Rerum Anglicarum of William of Newburgh*, in *Chronicles of the Reigns of Stephen, Henry II and Richard I*, ed. R. Howlett, 2 vols. (RS, 1884–5), i, 105; *The Historical Works of Gervase of Canterbury*, ed. W. Stubbs, 2 vols. (RS, 1879), i, 161–2; *The Chronicle of Battle Abbey*, ed. E. Searle (Oxford, 1980), pp. 158, 160.

142 Warren, *Henry II* (London, 1973), pp. 59–62.

143 The lands of Hugh Mortimer I were exempt from Stephen's grant of Herefordshire to Robert, earl of Leicester in 1140 × 1144: *Regesta Regum Anglo-Normannorum, 1066–1154*, vol. iii: *1135–54 (King Stephen, Empress Mathilda and Geoffrey and Henry, Dukes of Normandy)*, eds. H.A. Cronne and R. H. C. Davis (Oxford, 1968), no. 437.

had quietly left England to seek asylum in the abbey of Cluny. Henry II's decision to leave the Mortimer castles intact may indicate that he saw the Welsh frontier as a military challenge and leaving a local frontier lord in his castle as the best possible means of countering it. The favour Henry II bestowed on William Fitzalan I is certainly notable. William had been in Henry's entourage since at least 1153; previously he had supported the cause of the Empress stalwartly, as far as is known.[144] Nevertheless, this alone need not have guaranteed Henry II's favour. That much is perhaps demonstrated by the uncompromising attitude the young king displayed towards Earl Roger of Hereford in 1155: the earl was forced to surrender the royal castles in his charge against his will and, although he was allowed to keep his earldom, it lapsed after his death later that year. By contrast, Henry II certainly wished the reinstatement of William Fitzalan I to be a memorable occasion: William recovered all his Shropshire estates, including Oswestry Castle, in a ceremony at which his tenants did homage to him as if he had entered into his inheritance for the first time.[145] It is possible that Madog ap Maredudd's occupation of Oswestry was seen as an instance of the acquisition of land by adherents of Stephen which Henry II aimed to reverse.[146] Nevertheless, the homage ceremony seems extraordinary, given that William had already succeeded to his father's estates during the reign of Henry I. Henry II also, very probably, arranged, or assented to, the marriage between William Fitzalan II and Isabel de Sai, the heiress of Clun, and reappointed William sheriff of Shropshire. None of the frontier lords of this time ranked as high in prestige and power as the earls, but all still ruled over intact border castles and the surrounding compact districts. Henry II had recreated the judicious measure of aristocratic power on the Welsh borders which his grandfather and great-grandfather seem to have wished to establish by allowing the frontier earldoms to lapse.

When one compares the lords of the Shropshire frontier to other families ruling over lordships on the Welsh borders and in southern Wales during the second half of the twelfth century, a striking contrast emerges. The invasion of Ireland from the late 1160s onwards saw a lively participation by members of the 'Marcher' aristocratic families of southern Wales; indeed, it was spearheaded by Richard Fitzgilbert de Clare, who was earl of Pembroke and lord of Strigoil, and a band of close relatives of Gerald of Wales, a prime eyewitness and chronicler of the events. Later,

[144] Eyton, vii, 288.

[145] *Haughmond Cart.*, no. 1371. See Stenton's description of the occasion as a 'dramatic ceremony' in his *The First Century of English Feudalism, 1066–1166*, 2nd edn (Oxford, 1961), p. 163, n. 1.

[146] J. C. Holt, '1153: The Treaty of Winchester', in his *Colonial England*, pp. 271–90.

such families as the Lacies, the Marshals and the Braoses would number among the leading figures in the establishment of the thirteenth-century lordship of Ireland.[147] Ireland's becoming the favoured prospect for landed conquest for the acquisitive aristocracy of the Welsh borders was one of the most important reasons why the military pressure from England on Wales abated considerably between *c.* 1170 and 1211. It could be argued that, for a large section of the Welsh frontier aristocracy, conquest in Ireland became one of the features that gave them a common identity.

However, the lords of the Shropshire borders demonstrated a conspicuous lack of interest in following their fellow frontiersmen to Ireland. The Mortimers remained intent on adding Maelienydd to their dominions, and pursued their ambition in a succession of private military campaigns.[148] But, as far as we know, their neighbours to the north appear to have given up the project of territorial conquest in Wales and focused instead on entrenching their position as a county aristocracy. For the Fitzalans, this was already a family tradition, and it was certainly honoured by William Fitzalan II (d. *c.* 1210). We cannot tell whether he was involved in the government of Shropshire during the reign of Henry II: Gerald of Wales, who was entertained by William in Oswestry in 1188, does not mention whether his host held any royal office, merely describing him as a 'hospitable young nobleman'.[149] However, soon after Richard I succeeded to the throne, in the summer of 1189, William Fitzalan II was appointed justice in eyre for Shropshire, Herefordshire, Staffordshire and Gloucestershire.[150] Eyton believed that it was in January 1190 that William fined 60 marks to receive the shrievalty of Shropshire.[151] Possibly William bid for the shrievalty because he believed that he had a hereditary right to the office, or because he wished to establish such a right; it seems clear that he grasped the opportunity that presented itself when Richard I replaced virtually all the sheriffs in his kingdom, shortly after 16 November 1189,[152] in a move motivated by a royal wish to raise funds for the impending crusade.[153] William remained sheriff until Easter 1201,

[147] R. Frame, *The Political Development of the British Isles 1100–1400*, 2nd edn (Oxford, 1995), ch. 3.

[148] On the Mortimers in the later twelfth and thirteenth centuries see J. J. Crump, 'The Mortimer Family and the Making of the March', in M. Prestwich, R. H. Britnell, and R. Frame (eds.), *Thirteenth-Century England*, 6 (1997 for 1995), pp. 117–26.

[149] Gerald of Wales, *Journey through Wales*, transl. Thorpe, pp. 200–1. Cf. *Giraldus*, vi, 142 (*Itinerarium Kambrie*, ii, 12).

[150] *The Great Roll of the Pipe for the First Year of the Reign of King Richard I*, ed. J. Hunter (London, 1844), pp. 95, 144, 248, 168.

[151] Eyton, vii, 242: William was at King Richard's court at Westminster on 1 January 1190.

[152] W. Stubbs, *The Constitutional History of England*, 3 vols. (Oxford, 1874–1903), i, 534.

[153] On Richard's crusader fundraising see J. Gillingham, *Richard the Lionheart* (London, 1978), pp. 115–16.

when he appears to have relinquished the office by order of King John.[154] It might be argued that the Mortimers, in pursuing their military ambitions on the periphery, contrasted less with the southern Welsh families involved in conquest in Ireland than with the Fitzalans, who became increasingly assimilated to landowning society in Angevin England by being employed in the Plantagenet system of government.[155]

Nevertheless, the proximity of the Welsh frontier was to continue to shape the lives of all castellans of westernmost Shropshire. King John, who as a young man had been a frontier lord in south-east Wales, was familiar with the workings of Anglo-Welsh relations, and greatly increased the use of written instruments in their management – a development also evident from his use of documents, especially treaties, in defining relationships with Welsh princes.[156] Moreover, in 1201, King John sent Hubert de Burgh to the Welsh frontier with a retinue of 100 knights and a brief to keep the peace.[157] This may in fact have been intended to quell the rebellion of Fulk Fitzwarin, as is suggested by that family's legend.[158] On the other hand, it does seem as if, by the beginning of the thirteenth century, royal commissions were coming into more general use as a means of addressing the challenges posed by the Welsh frontier. Hubert de Burgh, admittedly, was still an outsider in the March. But it was not long before the lords of the Shropshire frontier became indispensable agents of the increasingly bureaucratized diplomacy taking place between the English kings and Welsh leaders. In 1204, William Fitzalan II was requested to provide safe-conduct to Llywelyn ap Iorwerth, apparently for negotiations conducted at the royal court prior to Llywelyn's marriage to King John's illegitimate daughter Joan. William, together with John Lestrange II, was also involved in the custody of hostages in the same year; indeed, it would appear that he was in charge of co-ordinating a group of 'barones Marchie' that had been appointed by the king personally to safeguard Llywelyn's hostages.[159]

True, these were ad hoc commissions. It seems that William was to command a ship in the fleet assembled for John's abortive campaign to Poitou in 1205; he certainly was not envisaged as holding an office which would require his permanent presence on the Welsh frontier.[160]

154 *Pipe Roll 4 John, 1202* (P. R. S., NS 15), p. 41.

155 Holt, *Magna Carta*, ch. 2.

156 Davies, *Age of Conquest*, pp. 293–4.

157 *Chronica Rogeri de Houedene*, ed. W. Stubbs (RS, 1871): 'Et rex tradidit Huberto de Burgo camerario suo centum milites, et constituit eum custodem finium Angliae et Valliae.'

158 *Fouke le Fitz Waryn*, eds. Hathaway *et al.*, p. 26, lines 16–20.

159 *Rot. Pat.*, p. 39; *Rot. Claus.*, i, 12a; for 1205 as the date of the marriage see Lloyd, *History of Wales*, p. 616.

160 *Rot. Claus.*, i, 46b.

Moreover, the impression that the lords of the Shropshire frontier became far more closely involved in a minutely organized diplomatic machine during the thirteenth century certainly owes much to the state of documentation. Yet it must have been a sign of innovation that, when William Fitzalan II was advised to deliver Welsh hostages to King John's officials in 1206, those hostages were known by name to the royal administration.[161] Because of the loss of Normandy, John's reign marked a turning point in that English kings became more focused on the British Isles than they had been since the Norman conquest. It seems highly possible that it also ushered in a period during which the crown encouraged the involvement of the Shropshire *barones Marchie* with frontier affairs to an unprecedented degree.

Certainly Robert Corbet of Caus, John Lestrange II of Knockin and William Fitzalan II of Oswestry and Clun all appear among the witnesses to the treaty concluded with Gwenwynwyn, the son of Owain Cyfeiliog, lord of Powys, in 1208.[162] No doubt they were also present at the parleys at Shrewsbury at which the terms of that treaty had been agreed. Robert Corbet wrote to King John the following year to notify him that he had received sureties from one of Gwenwynwyn's men, and that, beyond that, he was holding a hostage at Caus 'for greater security'.[163] John continued to dispatch high-ranking courtiers to the Welsh borders to guard what he referred to as 'his' March of Wales.[164] However, the lords of the Shropshire frontier acted as indispensable cogwheels in John's diplomatic machine.

That the machine already appears well oiled by John's reign suggests that acting on the king's behalf in his dealings with Welsh lords was something the Shropshire castellans had already been specializing in for some time. At a basic level, it could be said that the lords of the castles on the Powys–Shropshire frontier always had a role to play in Anglo-Welsh relations – they were bound to, given that they had some control, however it was defined at different periods, over the local military resources which shaped both the conflicts and the diplomacy between English and Welsh kings. To observe that William Fitzalan I headed a contingent of archers from the Shropshire borders in the army Henry II led to northern Wales in 1157,[165] or that Robert Corbet received a gift of 10 marks from King Richard 'to maintain himself in the king's service in the parts of Wales' in

[161] See the two instances in *Rot. Claus.*, i, 65a.

[162] *AWR*, no. 576; Rymer, I, i, 48.

[163] *Rot. Pat.*, p. 91b.

[164] *Rot. Pat.*, pp. 88a (1208): 'ad custodiendum marchiam nostram Wallie'; *ibid.*, p. 109 (1214).

[165] As is suggested by Lloyd, *History of Wales*, p. 497; cf. *The Pipe Rolls of 2, 3 & 4 Henry II*, ed. J. Hunter (1844, repr. in facs. London, 1930), p. 108.

1196,[166] is to realize that the lords of the Shropshire frontier were already acting in diverse ways as royal agents in Anglo-Welsh relations during the reigns of the first two Angevin kings of England. It is to the same period that the first mentions of royal expenditure on the garrisoning and maintenance of seigneurial border castles can be dated: Caus was garrisoned in 1165, and its refurbishment paid for by the crown in 1198; the Mortimer castles at Cymaron and Bleddfa were also garrisoned at royal expense during the 1190s.[167]

The evidence that leads us to think that from the later twelfth century the lords of the border castles were increasingly given specific tasks connected with cross-border relations correlates chronologically with the increased usage, primarily in royal sources, of terms like *Marchia Wallie* and *barones Marchie.*[168] It was argued above that these terms became more widespread after it was accepted that Wales would remain a country that was only partly conquered.[169] It is plausible that the new concept of a 'Marcher' buffer zone between England and Wales helped make the lords of the frontier appear more distinctive. The growth of the royal awareness of Wales as a military and diplomatic problem in need of a solution may well have been the basis for the conceptualization of the border lords as a group by the crown and its agents. It is true that this impression is partly due to the improved survival rate of royal documents. But the notion that there was a group of 'Marchers' can only have been strengthened by the *rapprochement* between the kings of England and native Welsh rulers after *c.* 1171. This new situation may have made it necessary for the crown to distinguish between two groups of lords playing a role in Anglo-Welsh relations: the Welsh and the 'Marchers'.

Certainly, during the reign of Henry III, we find the lords of the Shropshire frontier at the heart of Anglo-Welsh diplomacy. Hugh Mortimer and John Fitzalan I, who had taken opposing sides during the

[166] *The Chancellor's Roll for the Eigth Year of the Reign of King Richard the First. Michaelmas 1196*, ed. D. M. Stenton (P. R. S., NS 7, London, 1930), p. 42.

[167] *Pipe Roll 11 Henry II, 1165* (P. R. S., 8), p. 98; *Pipe Roll 10 Richard I, 1198* (P. R. S., NS 9), p. 108; *Pipe Roll 3&4 Richard I, 1191–2* (P. R. S., NS 2), pp. 77, 81; *Pipe Roll 7 Richard I, 1195* (P. R. S., NS 6), pp. 9, 13, 108.

[168] For an early occurrence of the term 'barones Marchie' in a Shropshire context see King John's 1204 letter to William Fitzalan II: *Rot. Claus.*, i, 12a: 'Rex etc. Willelmo filio Alani etc. Si illi qui liberaverunt nobis obsides pro Lewelino locuti fuerint cum Barones Marchie qui coram nobis nominati fuerunt ad eos custodiendum, [ita quod] velint obsides illos salvo custodire, bene placet nobis quod ipsi eis libenter [custodiend']. Et si locuti fuerint inde cum aliis nobis scire faciatis eorum nomina et nos inde operabimur per consilium nostrum. T. etc.'. 'Barones de Marchia' first appears in 1217: *Cal. Pat. R. 1216–25*, pp. 108–9. Cf. Davies, *Lordship and Society*, p. 34; Mann, 'The March: Terminology', *passim*; Holden, *Lords*, p. 8; above, pp. 56, 73; and the remarks in the introduction to this book.

[169] Above, pp. 9–10.

conflicts at the end of John's reign, were both involved in arranging for the safe conduct of Llywelyn ap Iorwerth and the princes of northern Wales to Worcester in 1218.[170] Hugh Mortimer, Henry Audley and John Lestrange II were all ordered to conduct the Welsh princes of north Wales to Worcester in the same year.[171] The wealth and complexity of issues generated by the interactions between English and Welsh created opportunities for local lords to distinguish themselves in royal service. The Audleys are one example of a family which rose from relatively obscure Staffordshire origins to occupy a surprising number of offices in Shropshire, and subsequently to intermarry with a Welsh princely family.[172] The Audleys could almost be said to have been attracted to the borders by the promise of advancement. The Lestranges had held the frontier castle of Knockin of the Fitzalans of Oswestry since the early twelfth century, but they, too, made the most of the career opportunities offered by the permanent need for competent royal agents on the Welsh borders. In 1232, John Lestrange III was appointed, together with John Fitzalan I, to oversee the terms of Henry III's truce with Llywelyn ap Iorwerth 'in the parts of Shropshire'; both lords also were given the responsibility of treating with Llywelyn's envoys in order to settle a dispute with Thomas Corbet of Caus.[173] John Lestrange III, in turn, can be found witnessing the charter recording Dafydd ap Llywelyn's homage to Henry III at Gloucester in 1240; the following year, Henry III appointed him justiciar of Chester.[174] As such, John reported to the king on the political and military situation in Shropshire and Wales, and acted as the crown's representative in treating with Dafydd ap Llywelyn of Wales in 1244–5.[175] In 1269, referring to him as John Lestrange 'senior', Henry III insisted that he attend a muster at Hereford 'pro consilio habendo'.[176] By dint of their expertise and commitment, the Lestranges came at least to equal the Fitzalans in their importance to border diplomacy during Henry III's reign.

The partnership between crown and Marcher lords in conducting cross-border affairs was not always quite voluntary. In mid-June 1233, Henry III took the precaution of obtaining hostages from John Fitzalan I,

[170] *Cal. Pat R., 1216–25*, p. 149; *AWR*, nos. 240–2; Rymer, I, i, 75; only Mortimer is known to have been present at Worcester.

[171] *Cal. Pat R., 1216–25*, p. 142.

[172] R. F. Walker, 'The Anglo-Welsh Wars, 1216–67' (University of Oxford DPhil thesis, 1954), pp. 202–3; *Cal. Chart. R., 1226–57*, p. 55; Eyton, vii, 184–92; *AWR*, nos. 515 and 516.

[173] Rymer, I, i, 110–11; *Cal. Close R., 1231–34*, p. 139.

[174] *AWR*, no. 291; Rymer, I, i, 136; *Excerpta e Rotulis Finium*, ed. Roberts, 2 vols., i, 352.

[175] *Cal. Anc. Corr. Wales*, pp. 21–2; Rymer, I, i, 150; 152.

[176] *Cal. Close R., 1261–4*, p. 275.

Thomas Corbet, Henry Audley, Ralph Mortimer, Walter Lacy and other 'barones de Marchia' 'until the kingdom be so secure that there be firm peace in the realm of England'.[177] This was probably so that they would keep the truce that was then in force with Llywelyn, rather than because they sympathized with Richard Marshal, the sixth earl of Pembroke, and his rebellious entourage.[178] In any case, after the Marshal rebellion had subsided, it was not long before the border lords were once again deemed above suspicion. Richard Marshal was killed in Ireland in April 1234; Corbet's hostage was released in June;[179] by July, Corbet, Audley, Fitzalan and other Marchers were ordered to take Grosmont, Skenfrith and White Castle into the king's hand.[180]

The fact that such tasks were delegated to them indicates that the lords of the Shropshire frontier as a group came to be seen, or to see themselves, as guardians of the English realm. The *Legend of Fulk Fitzwarin* testifies to the self-image of Marcher barons as the descendants of the men posted on the Welsh frontier by William the Conqueror.[181] Already by 1236, Ralph Mortimer II and John Fitzalan I were claiming, at the coronation of Eleanor of Provence, a right to the same ceremonial privileges as the lords of the Cinque Ports. Their claim was considered 'frivolous',[182] but it reflects both that these lords had a sense of common purpose and that they considered themselves to fulfil a role comparable to that of the guardians of the chief English harbours.

Moreover, it was a part the crown increasingly came to expect them to play. In 1260, the year in which Llywelyn ap Gruffudd recaptured Builth, Henry III placed Ralph Mortimer's son Roger in command of a very specific group of 'barones de Marchia' who had been required personally to attend to the defence of the Welsh borders.[183] Such delegations of military command were, of course, not merely determined by the fact that a given lord held estates on the borders. The relationship of individual lords to the king and personal ability mattered too. It was Roger Mortimer's loyalty to the crown that earned him a key role in the Welsh campaigns of Edward I. Moreover, the involvement of non-Marchers in Anglo-Welsh relations should not be forgotten. As has already been

[177] *Cal. Close R., 1231–4*, pp. 312–13.

[178] R. F. Walker, 'The Supporters of Richard Marshal, Earl of Pembroke, in the Rebellion of 1233–1234', *WHR*, **17** (1994–5), pp. 54–5.

[179] *Cal. Pat. R., 1232–47*, p. 56.

[180] *Cal. Close R., 1231–4*, pp. 462–3. Cf. J. Meisel, *Barons of the Welsh Frontier: The Corbet, Pantulf, and Fitz Warin Families, 1066–1272* (London, 1980), p. 16; Lloyd, *History of Wales*, p. 679 (n. 136); Holden, *Lords*, pp. 207–14.

[181] *Fouke le Fitz Waryn*, ed. Hathaway *et al.*, p. 3, lines 22–6.

[182] *Red Book of the Exchequer*, ed. H. Hall (RS, 1896), p. 756.

[183] *Cal. Close R. 1259–61*, pp. 23–4.

mentioned, in 1208, King John sent his half-brother William, earl of Salisbury, to guard what John called 'his' March of Wales.[184] John de Grey (d. 1266), the royal councillor, was appointed to military command on the Welsh borders in 1255 and in 1263.[185] It is also true that, if a military emergency coincided with a minority, the seigneurial border castles were of course garrisoned by royal troops.[186] Nevertheless, while noting the involvement of outsiders, it should be borne in mind that the state of the surviving evidence, with its emphasis on royal documents, may lead us to underestimate the contribution made by the frontier lords to military and diplomatic efforts on the borders. One indication of their importance may be the fact that there was never a permanently established office of 'warden of the March', as there was on the Scottish border in the fourteenth century. In part this was no doubt due to the fact that the Welsh military border ceased to exist before ad hoc appointments could evolve into such an office.[187] But in part, too, such an office was rendered redundant by the barons of the March, because their routine involvement in border diplomacy and warfare had become part of their recognized group identity. After all, this was a notion that endured after the conquest of Wales. Both Richard Fitzalan I and Edmund Mortimer were enjoined to reside on their estates on the Welsh borders during the revolt of Rhys ap Maredudd in 1287–8;[188] and even during the rebellion of Owain Glyn Dŵr in the early fifteenth century, it was the barons of the March who were seen as responsible for the defence of the Welsh borders.[189]

★ ★ ★

Marital alliances provide another type of evidence for discussing how far individual families, or groups of families, came to be focused on the Welsh borderlands. They are a useful guide to the range of social contacts and the geographical horizon of individual families.[190] Without allowing

[184] *Rot. Pat.*, p. 88a. See above, p. 80, n. 164.

[185] *Cal. Pat. R. 1247–58*, p. 553; *Cal. Pat. R. 1261–4*, p. 279. For details on Grey's campaigns in the latter year, see *Cal. Anc. Corr. Wales*, pp. 17–19.

[186] As happened at Oswestry during Edward I's campaign against Llywelyn ap Gruffudd in 1276–7, during the minority of Richard Fitzalan I, the future earl of Arundel: TNA E 372/121, m. 21r; *Cal. Pat. R., 1272–81*, p. 187.

[187] See F. C. Suppe, *Military Institutions on the Welsh Marches: Shropshire AD 1066–1300* (Woodbridge, 1994), ch. 4.

[188] *Parl. Writs*, i, 599; 250–5; *Cal. Chanc. R. Var.*, pp. 321–2.

[189] *The Parliament Rolls of Medieval England, 1275–1504*, gen. ed. C. Given-Wilson (16 vols., London, 2005), vol. viii: *Henry IV (1399–1413)*, ed. C. Given-Wilson (London, 2005), pp. 459–60; *Rot. Parl.*, iii, 624–5.

[190] R. Frame, 'Aristocracies and the Political Configuration of the British Isles', in R. R. Davies (ed.), *The British Isles 1100–1500: Comparisons, Contrasts and Connections* (Edinburgh, 1988), p. 148; for the marriage strategies of the Herefordshire marchers, see Holden, *Lords*, pp. 84–6, 119–24.

genealogical detail to proliferate unduly, it is possible to make a rough comparison between the Mortimers of Wigmore and the Fitzalans of Oswestry. In the case of the twelfth-century descendants of Alan fitz Flaald, we may postulate that the marriages of the leading family members reflect an orientation towards the frontier. William (d. 1160), Alan's son and heir, was first married to Christina, whom Orderic describes as the *neptis* of Robert, earl of Gloucester.[191] Christina appears not to have survived the Anarchy of Stephen's reign, and early in the reign of Henry II William contracted his second marriage, this time to Isabel de Sai, the heiress to the Shropshire frontier barony of Clun (d. *c.* 1199).[192] Their son William II (d. *c.* 1210), heir to the lordships of Clun and Oswestry, in turn married a daughter of Hugh II de Lacy (d. 1186), lord of Weobley in Herefordshire and Meath in Ireland. What we know of the twelfth-century Mortimer marriages suggests a less unambiguous frontier fixation. The wife of Hugh (d. 1148 × 1150), the son of Ralph de Mortimer, the Domesday lord of Wigmore (d. after 1104), is unfortunately unknown. Hugh's younger son and eventual heir, also named Hugh (occ. 1172), married Maud, the daughter and coheiress of William Meschin, of Skipton-in-Craven in Yorkshire.[193] As William was the earl of Chester's brother, there is a possible border connection there. Hugh Mortimer's son Roger, however, took to wife Isabel, daughter of Walkelin, lord of Ferrières-St-Hilaire and of Oakham in Rutland.[194] On the basis of what little evidence we have, it seems possible to say that the twelfth-century Mortimers, despite the location of their main territorial interests, had well-established social contacts outside the Welsh borderlands.

However, if the comparison between the Mortimers and the Fitzalans is continued into the thirteenth century, the picture is dramatically reversed. All the Mortimer marriages then betrayed a clear Marcher orientation, with highly conspicuous links to the Braose family.[195] The change in orientation appears to have been brought about by the marriage of Ralph Mortimer to Gwladus Ddu, the daughter of Llywelyn ap Iorwerth and either Joan, the natural daughter of King John, or Tangwystl, daughter of Llywarch Goch.[196] The Fitzalans also made a crucial marriage, but this, if anything, diminished the importance to them of their estates on

191 *Orderic*, vi, 520. Orderic uses *neptis* primarily in the sense of 'niece' or 'granddaughter', though also more loosely of other kinswomen (*Orderic*, vi, 520 n. 6; *ibid.*, i, 332).

192 Eyton, vii, 237, xi, 228–9, 235–6; *Lilleshall Cart.*, no. 258.

193 *Curia Regis Rolls*, vol. xviii: *1243–1245*, ed. P. Brand (London, 1999), no. 1401.

194 *Cal. Close R.*, *1251–3*, pp. 82–3.

195 See genealogical diagrams on following pages, and sources cited there.

196 *Annales Monastici*, ed. H. R. Luard, iv, 421 (Annals of Worcester, s a. 1230). On the problematic parentage of Gwladus Ddu see N. Jacobs, 'Animadversions on Bastardy in the Red Book of Hergest: *Early Welsh Gnomic Poems*, IV.6', *Cambrian Medieval Celtic Studies*, **55** (2008), p. 59 (n. 25).

the Shropshire borders. The betrothal of John Fitzalan I to Isabel, the sister of Hugh d'Aubigny, the earl of Arundel, brought the thirteenth-century Fitzalans a quarter of the d'Aubigny inheritance, including the castle of Arundel and, eventually, the title of earls.[197] It is worth noting, however, that John Fitzalan III (d. 1272) married Isabel, a daughter of Roger Mortimer II of Wigmore.[198] In sum, it seems that the Fitzalans were focused on the frontier in the twelfth century, perhaps because of their need to establish themselves among the former Montgomery men. The Mortimers, being frontier lords from the outset, sought originally to extend their web of connections, possibly with an emphasis on the north of England. Both families then made a key marriage which helped determine their priorities during the thirteenth century.

How do these patterns compare to the marital alliances of the lesser frontier families? It seems possible that the Corbets, like the Fitzalans, first restricted themselves to the Shropshire marriage market,[199] and that, once this had given them some substance, they looked further afield. Thomas Corbet's marriage to Isabel, the daughter of Reginald de Vautort, lord of Trematon, created a link to Cornwall, another instance of families with estates on the Welsh borders allying themselves with families located within the English kingdom.[200] The Fitzwarins, too, seem initially to have sought to establish themselves by marrying locally, though they did not restrict themselves to the county of Shropshire. They may also have pioneered the revival of Anglo-Welsh marriages which is a hallmark of the lesser Marcher barons of Shropshire during the thirteenth century.[201] This revival was also heralded by Baldwin de Bollers' marriage to one Gwenllian Deg in the early thirteenth century. Cross-cultural marriages certainly served to distinguish the Marcher barons of that period from both their English and their Welsh contemporaries.[202]

[197] *CIPM, Henry III*, nos. 684 and 812.

[198] *Cal. Close R., 1268–72*, pp. 505–15.

[199] Eyton suggested that the Robert Corbet who died in 1222 married Emma Pantulf: Eyton, vii, 21; ix, 167.

[200] See M. Lieberman, 'Striving for Marcher Liberties: The Corbets of Caus in the Thirteenth Century', in M. Prestwich (ed.), *Liberties and Identities in the Medieval British Isles* (Woodbridge, 2008), p. 150 (n. 51).

[201] Plans were afoot in 1215 × 1227 for a marriage between Fulk, probably the son of Fulk Fitzwarin III, to Angharad, the daughter of a Madog ap Gruffudd, who was either the lord of northern Powys or, Dr Stephenson has suggested, of Kinnerley. Cf. *Cal. Anc. Corr. Wales*, pp. 2–3; D. Stephenson, 'Welsh Lords in Shropshire: Gruffydd ap Iorwerth Goch and His Descendants in the Thirteenth Century', *TSAS*, **78** (2002), pp. 32–7. I would like to thank Dr Stephenson for kindly sending me a copy of this article.

[202] Such marriages also assimilated the English Marcher barons to such Welsh lords as Gwenwynwyn (d. *c.* 1216), son of Owain Cyfeiliog, who married a Corbet, his son Gruffudd ap Gwenwynwyn of southern Powys (d. 1286), who married a Lestrange, and Gruffudd ap Madog of northern

As the varying marriage links show, it should not be assumed prima facie that the lords of the Shropshire frontier formed a social network. Other evidence would also suggest that the social circle of these barons was by no means limited to the borders or the county. In 1207, when Fulk Fitzwarin III (d. 1258), who had rebelled against King John in 1200–3, needed pledges for the fine he owed for permission to marry Mathilda le Vavasour, the wealthy widow of Theobald Walter, he did not turn to his immediate neighbours.[203] Instead, his chief pledges were his brother William and Mathilda's father, Robert le Vavasour, who held, of the honor of Skipton (Yorkshire), manors owing the service of half a knights-fee which were mainly situated in the Wharfe valley east of Skipton.[204] All the same, among the forty-two other men who consented to act as pledges for Fulk there were several with landed interests on the Welsh borders. They included Walter II de Lacy (d. 1241), the lord of the Lacy honor of Weobley in Herefordshire, as well as the lordship of Meath in Ireland;[205] Walter II de Clifford, lord of the frontier barony of Clifford (Herefordshire); and William Braose, the lord of Brecon, and his son William. But if, as Sir James Holt has argued, the best evidence for the aristocratic networks of northern England in John's reign is the records of such financial pledges, Fulk's suggests a lack of close local associates.[206] Mortimer, Fitzalan and Corbet, whose frontier estates were nearest to Fulk's, are all conspicuous by their absence, while his other pledges included such men as Robert de Courtenay, the lord of Okehampton (Devon)[207] and Alan Basset, a close confidant of King John's.[208] There was also William Pantulf, a cousin of Hugh, the lord of the Shropshire barony of Wem, which did not adjoin Welsh territory. Perhaps too much weight should not be put on this solitary pledge list. Yet it does seem that, although Fulk was indeed a member of a network of frontier aristocrats, he looked to the borders of Herefordshire rather than of Shropshire.

Powys (d. 1269), who took an Audley to wife: Eyton, x, 274–5. In this sense, there also were Welsh Marcher lords. Note the reference in 1267 × 1276 to 'English Marchers' (*Anglici marchiani*) in *AWR*, no. 364, which might suggest that a distinction was being made between English and Welsh marcher lords.

203 *Rot. Oblat.*, pp. 405–6, 459–60; cf. also the list of pledges on *Pipe Roll 9 John, 1207* (P. R. S., NS 22), pp. 111–12.

204 On the Vavasour fee, see *Early Yorkshire Charters*, vol. vii: *Honour of Skipton*, ed. C. T. Clay, (Wakefield, 1947), pp. 166–77.

205 Walter had, at this time, forfeited his Irish lordship and been summoned from Ireland to England. See *DNB* article by C. L. Kingsford (published 1892).

206 J. C. Holt, *The Northerners. A Study in the Reign of King John* (Oxford, 1982), p. 73.

207 I. J. Sanders, *English Baronies: A Study of their Origin and Descent, 1086–1327* (Oxford, 1960), pp. 69–70.

208 *DNB* article by J. H. Round (published 1885).

Table 3. *The Fitzalans of Oswestry*

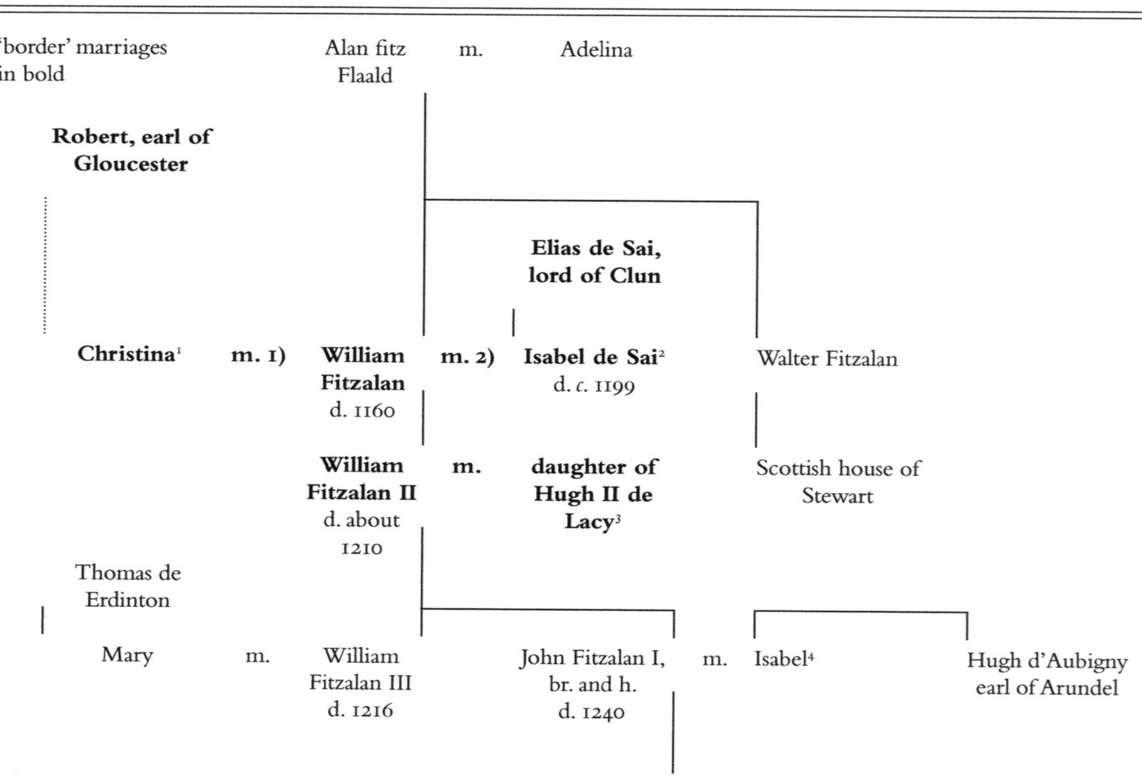

John Fitzalan II, s. and h. d. 1267	m.	Maud
		Roger Mortimer, lord of Wigmore
John Fitzalan III d. 18 March 1272	**m.**	**Isabel**[5]
Richard Fitzalan I d. 1302	m.	Alice

[1] *Orderic*, vi, 520; relation to Robert either niece or natural daughter.
[2] Eyton, vii, 237, xi, 228–9, 235–6; *Lilleshall Cart.*, no. 258.
[3] Eyton, vii, 241–2.
[4] *CIPM, Henry III*, nos. 684 and 812.
[5] *Cal. Close R., 1268–72*, pp. 505–15.

Table 4. *The Mortimers of Wigmore*

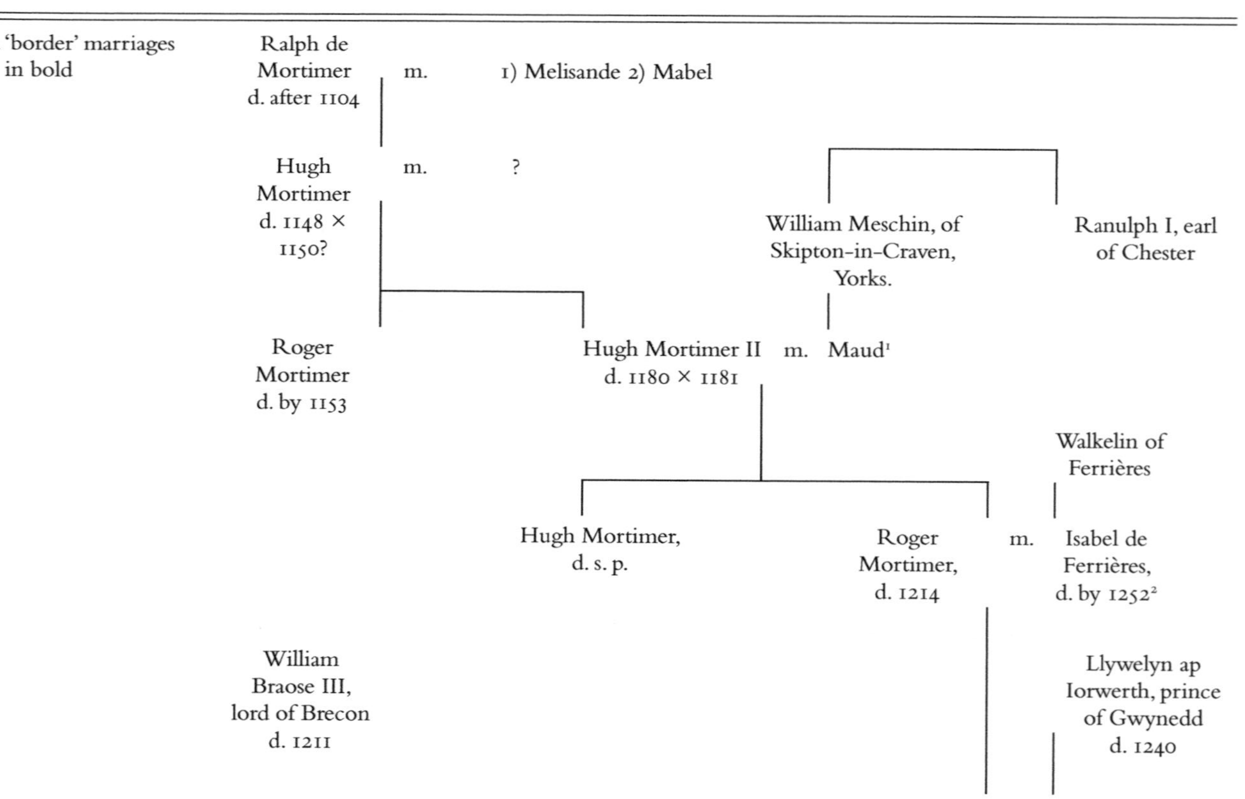

Annora[3] m. **Hugh Mortimer III**
d. 10 xi 1227

Ralph Mortimer II m. **Gwladus Ddu**[4]
d. 6 viii 1246

William Braose
V, lord of Brecon
d. 1230

Roger Mortimer II m. **Maud**[5]
d. shortly bef.
30 × 1282

1 Ralph
d. 1275

2 Edmund m. Margaret de Fiennes
d. July 1304 b. before 1286

3 Roger Mortimer, lord of Chirk m. Lucia
d. 1336

Isabella Mortimer[6] m. **John Fitzalan III**
b. 1260 d. 27 March 1271

1 *Comp. Peerage*, ix, 271, note e).
2 *Rot. Oblat.*, p. 209.
3 *Cal. Pat. R., 1225–32*, p. 501.
4 *Annales Monastici*, ed. H. R. Luard, iv, 421 (Annals of Worcester, s a. 1230).
5 *Cal. Pat. R., 1247–58,* pp. 8, 156.
6 *Cal. Close R., 1268–72*, pp. 505–15.

Table 5. *The Corbets of Caus*

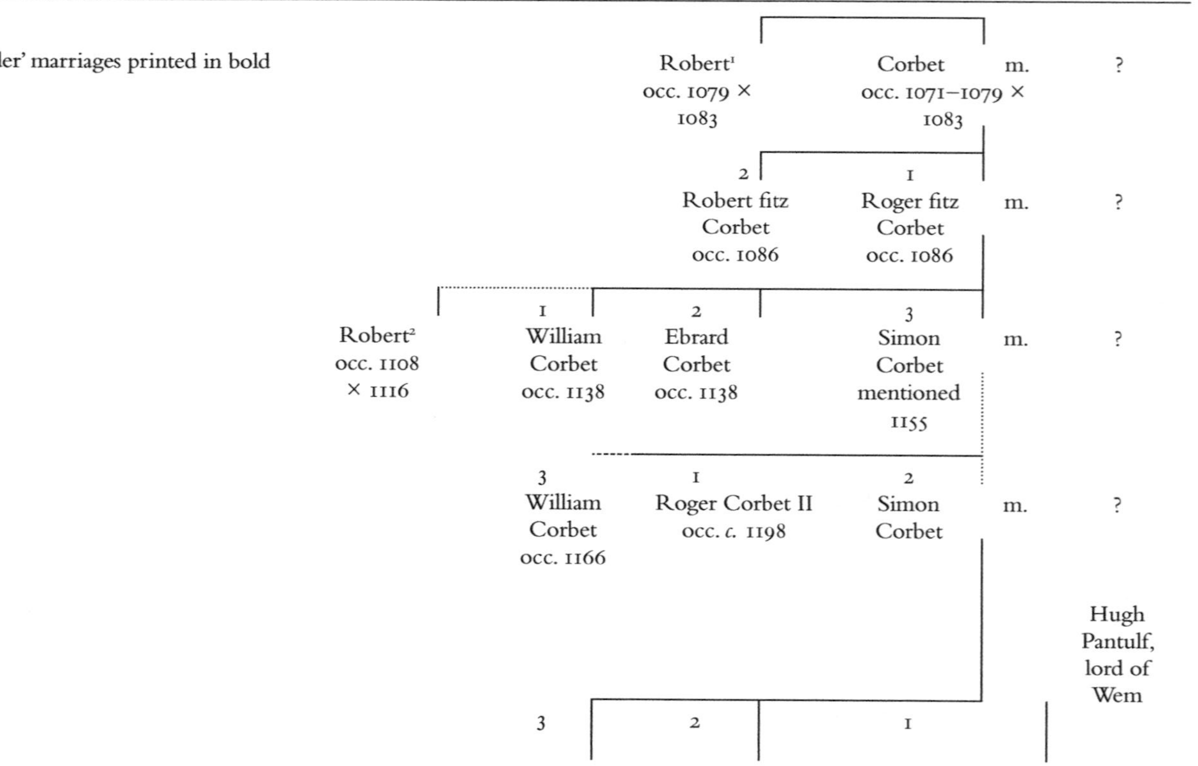

William Corbet occ. c. 1203 — Hugh Corbet occ. c. 1198 — **Robert Corbet** d. 1222 m. **Emma?**[3]

Reginald de Vautort, lord of Trematon, Cornwall.

5 William Corbet, occ. 1215–21 — **Gwenwynwyn of Powys**[4] m. 4 **Margaret** — 3 Hugh Corbet — 2 Robert Corbet — 1 Thomas Corbet, d. c. Sept. 1274 m. Isabel[5]

Brian of Brompton III d. c. 1287 m. 3 **Emma Corbet** d. 1284 — Robert Stafford d. 1282 m. 2 Alice Corbet — Joan born before 1265 m. 1) 1 Peter Corbet I d. c. July 1300 m. 2) Alice

Stafford family

Peter Corbet II d. 1322 m. Beatrice

[1] *RRAN*, ed. Bates, no. 283 (1079 × 1083).

[2] *RRAN*, ii, no. 1051 (1108 × 1116).

[3] Eyton, vii, 21; ix, 167.

[4] *Registrum Ricardi de Swinfield, Episcopi Herefordensis*, ed. Capes, p. 209.

[5] Eyton, vii, 31; *Comp. Peerage,* iii, 417.

Table 6. *The Fitzwarins of Alberbury and Whittington*

							Warin 'de Metz'[1]	m.	Melette		
Known 'border' marriages are printed in bold											
			Ralph?[2] occ. 1114		1 Roger occ. 1139 × 1146		2 Fulk Fitzwarin I d. 1170 × 1171	m.	?		3 William Fitzwarin of Burwardsley
									Joceas de Dinan		
			2 Ralph	3 Richard	4 Warin d. *c.* 1180		1 **Fulk Fitzwarin II** d. 1197	**m.**	**Hawise**[3] occ. 1198		
									Robert le Vavasour		
2 William	3 Philip	4 John / Ivo	5 Richard	6 Alan	Clarice de Auberville 1250	m. 2)	1 **Fulk Fitzwarin III** d. 1258	**m. 1)**	**Matilda**[4]	m. 1)	Theobald Walter d. 1205?

2			3	4	5	1		
Fulk Glas of Alberbury	William Pantulf baron of Wem	m.	Hawise	Joan	Eva Fitzwarin	Fulk Fitzwarin IV k. 14 May 1264 (Lewes)	m.	Constancia
Fulk Glas II								**Gruffudd ap Gwenwynwyn, lord of southern Powys**
						Fulk Fitzwarin V d. 1314	m.	**Mable**[5]

[1] *Fouke le Fitz Waryn*, ed. Hathaway *et al.*, eg. p. 8, l. 27; poss. *Cal. Pat. R., 1348–50*, p. 186.
[2] *RRAN*, ii, no. 1042.
[3] *Pipe Roll 10 Richard I, 1198* (P. R. S., NS 9), p. 72.
[4] *Rot. Claus.*, i, 92.
[5] Eyton, xi, 41; *Cal. Inq. Misc.*, i, 329.

Table 7. *The Lestranges of Knockin*

(Only main line shown, based mainly on Eyton, x, 262–3; known 'border' marriages printed in bold)

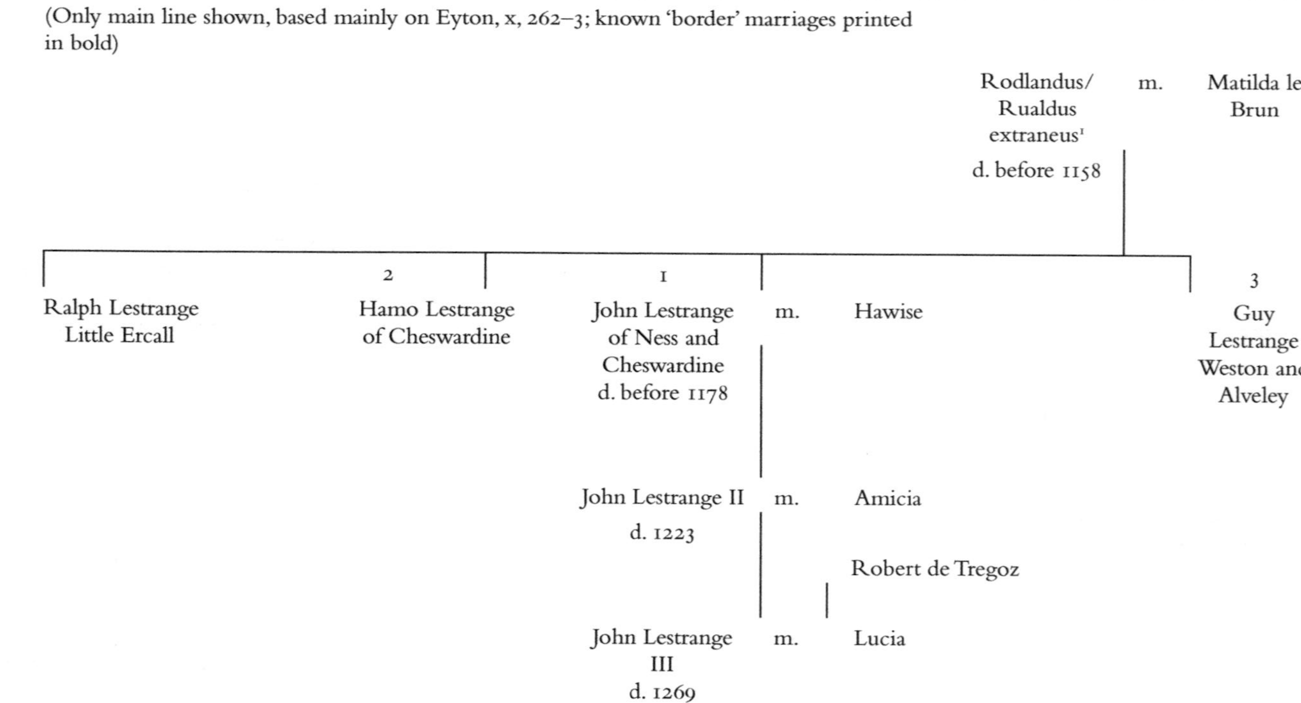

Roger de Somery

Gruffudd ap Gwenwynwyn, lord of southern Powys **m.** **Hawise**[2]

John Lestrange IV d. 1275 m Joan

Roger d'Eiville

Alienore m. 1) John Lestrange V d. 1309 m. 2) Maud

[1] *Mon. Angl.*, v, 51, no. vii; *Mon. Angl.*, v, 51, no. ix.

[2] Eyton, x, 263; 274–5.

A variety of explanations for Fulk's choice of pledges may be offered. The minimal overlap between the 1207 guarantors and the fifty-one outlaws whom John pardoned together with Fulk III in 1203 suggests that Fulk looked for pledges outside the circle of his former fellow rebels.[209] The presence of de Lacy is particularly striking. According to the Fitzwarin family legend known as *Fouke le Fitz Waryn*, a character named Fulk had grown up as a foster child of Joce de Dinan, the lord of Ludlow Castle, and joined his foster-father in fighting a character named Walter de Lacy.[210] The historical basis for these events has been situated in the 1140s, when the Joce de Dinan of history was engaged in conflict with Gilbert de Lacy; the Fulk of legend has been identified with Fulk II (d. *c.* 1197).[211] Events in Herefordshire during Stephen's reign may then explain why, over fifty years later, we find the grandson of Gilbert de Lacy acting as pledge for the son of Fulk II. It might be pointed out that the border distribution of some of Fulk's pledges merely reflected the fact that the most important local magnates were those holding frontier estates. However, the prevalence of high-ranking barons associated with Fulk III in 1207 is unusual; debtors to the crown more commonly sought their guarantors in the shire court, and often approached the sheriff or other local agents of the king.[212] Since Fulk and other 'Marcher' lords were beginning to proclaim more assiduously their independence from royal government at around this time, this may provide another part of the explanation for Fulk's choice of Marcher pledges in 1207 from among the greater lords who were not his immediate neighbours. In any case, it seems quite plausible that the very proximity of the estates of the lords of the Shropshire frontier created rivalry rather than close links. It comes as no surprise to find the Shropshire barons divided into different factions in 1215, just as the Mortimers and the Fitzalans had taken opposing sides during Stephen's reign.[213]

The families of the Shropshire frontier were unusual because of their long survival in the male line. By the mid-thirteenth century, the

[209] *Rot. Pat.*, p. 36.

[210] *Fouke le Fitz Waryn*, eds. Hathaway *et al.*, pp. 11–20.

[211] Wightman, *Lacy Family*, pp. 181 and 187; B. Coplestone-Crow, 'From Foundation to Anarchy', in R. Shoesmith and A. Johnson (eds.), *Ludlow Castle. Its History and Buildings* (Logaston Press, 2000), pp. 31–4.

[212] J. C. Holt, 'Feudal Society and the Family in Early Medieval England, III: Patronage and Politics', in his *Colonial England*, pp. 232–3.

[213] Above, pp. 75–7; Eyton x, 326–7 (letter from the sheriff of Shropshire to King John detailing the king's supporters – Hugh Mortimer, Walter Lacy, Walter Clifford and John Lestrange – and his opponents – John Fitzalan I, Fulk Fitzwarin, Bartholomaeus Turet, Baldwin de Hodnet, Vivian de Roshale, Thomas de Constantine and Radulfus de Sanfort). See K. Mann, 'A Microcosm of Civil War – The Border Shires', *TSAS*, **73** (1998), pp. 8–12.

Corbets of Caus and the Mortimers of Wigmore had held on to their border estates for about 180 years; the Fitzalans of Oswestry, and quite possibly also the Lestranges of Knockin and the Fitzwarins of Alberbury and Whittington, descended from ancestors who had arrived only a generation later than the Corbets and Mortimers. For Marcher families, this kind of familial longevity was certainly exceptional. In other parts of the Welsh borderlands, many colonial aristocratic families died out in the male line during Henry II's reign in the 1170s and 1180s. Another such wave of male mortality swept through the Marcher families during the middle decades of the thirteenth century.[214] Indeed, a very high turnover of male family heads was characteristic of the entire Norman aristocracy of England.[215] The Shropshire frontier lineages stood out, in this respect, among all the baronial families owing allegiance to the English king.

This did not pass unnoticed. The thirteenth-century family chronicles of the Mortimers and the Fitzwarins are structured along the unbroken succession of male ancestors. The link with the past is evoked in these accounts by the way the ancestral first names – Fulk, Hugh, Roger or Ralph – echo down the generations. In a society obsessed with *lignages*, there can be no doubt that the families of western Shropshire derived a keen sense of distinctiveness, as well as pride, from their exceptionally long list of ancestors. In 1250–1, Thomas Corbet demonstrated as much when he proclaimed that he refused to pay relief for his lands 'because none of his five predecessors had ever paid it'.[216] Twenty-five years later, the limit of legal memory was to be set at 1189.[217] To consider that is to appreciate the weight that Thomas' claim must already have carried in the middle of the thirteenth century. The long ancestries of the Shropshire frontier families did not only confer title to land; it helped them think of themselves as families of a distinctive kind.

* * *

The lords of the honors in westernmost Shropshire may not have been conquerors of Welsh lands, but they were certainly lords of the frontier. Their position did indeed have roots that went back to the days of William the Conqueror, as was so proudly asserted by the legend of Fulk

214 Davies, *Age of Conquest*, pp. 271, 280.
215 Holt, 'Feudal Society and the Family, I', in his *Colonial England*, p. 174.
216 TNA E 368/24, m. 12v; cf. Eyton, vii, 24.
217 P. Brand, ' "Multis Vigiliis Excogitatam et Inventam": Henry II and the Creation of the English Common Law', in his *The Making of the Common Law* (London, 1992), p. 77.

Fitzwarin and the Mortimer chronicles. Earl Roger, in distributing lands among his followers, laid the foundations of family estates which were to demarcate central Shropshire from Powys. It would even appear that the men whom he posted on the western borders of his English county came, without exception, from the heartland of his Continental possessions, itself arguably a frontier dominion. However, the Montgomery forfeiture of 1102 was the key event in assimilating the Shropshire families to the Mortimers and to the other dynasties whose outlook was to be shaped, over the following four or five generations, by a border existence. The Corbets, de Sais, de Bollers and Fitzalans became, at a stroke, the leading families in Shropshire. But they also now numbered among a group of tenants-in-chief whose estates bordered on Wales. In effect, the lords of the Shropshire–Powys frontier came, after 1102, to share a common identity with the other barons whose descendants came to be known as the lords of the March.

This common identity was cemented over the following two centuries, both in practice and in perception. The term *barones Marchie* became more fashionable towards the end of the twelfth century, possibly because by then the kings of England had accepted that the total conquest of Wales was not to be achieved within the foreseeable future, and that the lords holding lands on the Welsh borders therefore had a special function to fulfil in Anglo-Welsh relations.[218] The role of the Fitzalans, the Mortimers and families of lesser rank as defenders of the border and frontier diplomats certainly became so firmly entrenched as to pre-empt, in Wales, the creation of a permanent office of 'warden of the March'. The marital strategies of these families, admittedly, serve in part to remind us that the Shropshire lords always had horizons that stretched beyond the borders, and the same is true of the Fitzwarin pledge list of 1207. Almost all of the Shropshire lords retained territorial interests elsewhere in England. Moreover, if the Shropshire frontier barons and the neighbouring Mortimers can, after 1102, be seen as part of a group, in the sense that they all held compact frontier honors in chief, then this was a highly fractious group which never presented a united front during political crises. It seems that this rivalry increased after the Montgomery forfeiture placed all these families on a more equal footing. On the other hand, marriage links to the Welsh set the families of the Shropshire borders apart from their peers in England, while reinforcing their similarity to such distinctive border dynasties as the Mortimers. The siting of their ancestral tombs and familial monastic

[218] Above, p. 81.

endowments shows a clear frontier orientation. The dominant families within the Shropshire aristocracy remained tied in with the wider affairs of the English kingdom throughout the twelfth and thirteenth centuries, but their idea that they formed part of a distinctive 'Marcher' group was soundly based on facts.

Chapter 3

WARFARE AND DIPLOMACY

The effects of medieval warfare on regional economies and societies could be severe. Armies preyed on the estates of their enemies partly in order to sustain themselves, partly to cut off their adversaries' supplies.[1] It is often difficult to tell how much destruction was due to ravaging (rather than, say, the weather), and for how long the effects were felt, but prolonged warfare could certainly have cumulative and long-term detrimental effects on entire districts. In northern England, the devastations of the Scottish raids conducted after 1311 were still reflected twenty years later in the reduced profitability of estates.[2] Some agriculturally productive areas of France, particularly the vineyards of the Bordelais, took decades to recover from the destruction wrought by English and French armies during the fourteenth and fifteenth centuries. Fifteenth-century Silesia was gradually abandoned by a large part of its peasant populace because of the effects of prolonged warfare compounded by bad weather.[3] During the medieval period, it was quite possible for armed conflict to have a profound and lasting impact on regions.

Moreover, there is reason to believe that militarization affected the ways in which regions were perceived. The military connotation of the term *marchia*, for instance to Gerald of Wales in an Irish context, was noted above.[4] It is true that gauging the degree to which perceptions reflected realities is no straightforward task. Gerald's view of the Irish

[1] M. Strickland, *War and Chivalry: The Conduct and Perception of War in England and Normandy, 1066–1217* (Cambridge, 1996), ch. 10.

[2] J. Scammell, 'Robert I and the North of England', *EHR*, **73** (1958), pp. 385–403.

[3] R. Boutruche, 'The Devastation of Rural Areas During the Hundred Years War and the Agricultural Recovery of France', in P. S. Lewis (ed.), *The Recovery of France in the Fifteenth Century* (New York and London, 1971), esp. pp. 45–50. R. C. Hoffman, 'Warfare, Weather and a Rural Economy: The Duchy of Wroclaw in the Mid-Fifteenth Century', *Viator*, **4** (1973), pp. 273–405.

[4] Above, pp. 10–11. For an instance of King John referring to his lands 'in the march' in Ireland see *Calendar of Documents Relating to Ireland*, ed. H. S. Sweetman *et al.*, 5 vols. (London, 1875–86), i, no. 576 (1215). For later Medieval references to and perceptions of Irish 'marches', see R. Frame, 'War

marches may not have been shared by all his contemporaries. The border regions between the English- and the Gaelic-settled parts of high and late medieval Ireland are frequently referred to in our sources as the 'lands of war', and as such were contrasted to the 'lands of peace'.[5] However, the implied perception was that of the colonial government at Dublin, and therefore is only one measure, and scarcely an unbiased one, of how war-torn the Irish marches indeed were.[6] Contemporaries probably also had conflicting views of how militarized the Welsh borders were. Thus, it seems important to investigate how far the actual and perceived impact of warfare on the Welsh borders helped to shape the concept of the March of Wales. But, any discussion of the military distinctiveness of the March of Wales needs to guard itself against presenting a one-sided picture. A historical account of the borders which restricted itself to enumerating the occasions when hostilities flared up would hardly do justice to the complexity and dynamics of what may be termed Anglo-Welsh relations. As noted, the Norman 'march' of the twelfth and early thirteenth centuries, the Epte valley, was heavily fortified and frequently disputed, but it was also a diplomatic arena.[7] When discussing how far specific military challenges set the Shropshire–Powys borders apart from the county, the periods of relative peace are just as relevant as those of relative warfare. What follows is therefore a chronological analysis of Anglo-Welsh relations on the Shropshire–Powys frontier which aims to strike an adequate balance.

* * *

As has been seen, the shire named after Shrewsbury was probably established early in the tenth century.[8] By then, the country north and south of the Severn gap had long been a borderland. The valleys leading into the Welsh hills here formed a settlement frontier in the early Middle Ages. Shropshire was to be founded on part of the land colonized by the English people of the Mercians, who may well have derived their name and identity from living on the Welsh frontier.[9] It

and Peace in the Medieval Lordship of Ireland', in J. Lydon (ed.), *The English in Medieval Ireland* (Dublin, 1984), pp. 118–41.

5 Cal. Docs. Ireland, ed. Sweetman (first mention of 'land of peace', 1248); *ibid.*, ii, no. 930 (first mention of 'land of war', 1272); see J. Lydon, 'A Land of War', in A. Cosgrove, (ed), *A New History of Ireland*, vol. ii: *Medieval Ireland 1169–1534* (Oxford, 1987), p. 240.

6 R. Frame, 'Power and Society in the Lordship of Ireland, 1272–1377', *Past & Present*, **76** (1977), p. 4.

7 Above, pp. 12, 56; below, pp. 247, 249, 259–61; Lemarignier, *Hommage en marche*; Power, *Norman Frontier*, pp. 16–17.

8 Above, pp. 24–5; D. C. Cox, 'County Government in the Early Middle Ages', in *VCH*, **3**, p. 2; Stenton, *Anglo-Saxon England*, p. 337.

9 Stenton, *Anglo-Saxon England*, p. 40. Mercia was a Latinized form of *Mierce*, itself derived from Old English *mearc*, 'boundary, march'.

does not necessarily follow that this implied the existence of a military frontier; the Mercian settlers were not permanently at war with the Welsh kingdom of Powys.[10] Indeed, Penda (d. 655), a heathen king of the Mercians, appears in the year 642 to have drawn on the support of Welsh allies when he defeated the Northumbrian king Oswald after whom Oswestry is named.[11] However, we do catch echoes of days when the Mercians were pushed back by force of arms. A stone cross which stands in the Dee valley, and after which Valle Crucis Abbey was named, was inscribed to the memory of Eliseg, a Powysian king of the mid-eighth century, who 'annexed the inheritance of Powys throughout nine (years?) from the power of the English.'[12] Quite soon afterwards, by the second half of the eighth century, the men of Powys would appear to have represented a very specific kind of strategic concern for the Mercian king. The monumental boundary earthwork whose building is attributed to Penda's successor Offa (d. 796) is today believed to have been a defensive or in any case defensible boundary, at least in part. Like Wat's Dyke, which is more difficult to date, the course of Offa's Dyke, together with its height and the ditch on its western side, suggests that it was designed as a barrier against raiders of cattle coming from the west.[13] Given the staggering effort which was considered warranted to defend against such attacks, they were very probably both persistent and damaging during the eighth century. It is important to note, in the context of the prehistory of the March of Wales, as it were, that the course of Offa's Dyke can be traced with the greatest assurance along the stretch of border country which was later to coincide with the western frontiers of southern Cheshire, Shropshire and northern

[10] T. M. Charles-Edwards, 'Wales and Mercia, 613–918', in M. P. Brown and C. A. Farr (eds.), *Mercia: An Anglo-Saxon Kingdom in Europe* (London and New York, 2001), pp. 89–105.

[11] As is suggested by H. P. R. Finberg, 'Mercians and Welsh', *Lucerna: Studies of Some Problems in the Early History of England* (London, 1964), p. 73. Cf. the following, more recent discussion: C. Stancliffe, 'Where was Oswald Killed?', in C. Stancliffe and E. Cambridge (eds.), *Oswald: Northumbrian King to European Saint* (Stamford, 1995), pp. 84–96. Cf. *Bede's Ecclesiastical History of the English People*, eds. B. Colgrave and R. A. B. Mynors (Oxford, 1969), pp. 240–2. 'Oswestry' derives from the Old English for 'Oswald's tree', probably commemorating a wooden cross dedicated to St Oswald. Maserfelth, the site of his battle with Penda, is traditionally identified with Oswestry, but has not been exactly located; see Gelling, *Place-Names. Part 1*, p. 192.

[12] D. Hill, 'Offa's Dyke: Pattern and Purpose', *Antiquaries' Journal*, **80** (2000), p. 202. The inscription is now worn away, but was recorded in 1696.

[13] P. Wormald, 'Offa's Dyke', in J. Campbell (ed.), *The Anglo-Saxons*, pbk. edn (London, 1991; originally Oxford, 1982), p. 121; M. Worthington, 'Wat's Dyke: An Archaeological and Historical Enigma', *Bulletin of the John Rylands University Library of Manchester*, **79**:3 (1997), p. 195. For the view that Wat's Dyke had not a military purpose, but was intended as a territorial boundary, see J. Cane, 'Excavations on Wat's Dyke at Pentre Wern, Shropshire in 1984/5', *TSAS*, **71** (1996), pp. 10–21; D. Hill and M. Worthington, *Offa's Dyke: History and Guide* (Stroud, 2003), pp. 108–12.

Herefordshire, while Wat's Dyke is restricted to the northern part of that boundary.[14] The geographical area which is to be considered in what follows formed part of the most distinctive strategic frontier of the British Isles in the second half of the eighth century.

The distinctiveness, in military terms, of this country is likely to have been reduced in the following centuries. The Vikings, for both the Welsh and the Mercians, became the most pressing problem during the late ninth and early tenth centuries. In 893 or 894, English and northern Welsh armies even joined forces to win a victory in a pitched battle against the Danes at Buttington, on the Severn near Welshpool.[15] The earliest recorded battle that took place in the Severn gap thus saw the English and Welsh co-operating against a common enemy. Correspondingly, it is thought to have been in defence against the Norse, not the Welsh, that Mercia was hidated and divided into shires, probably in the early tenth century, under the increasing influence of the West Saxons.[16] The *burh* of Shrewsbury was founded around this time, and the choice of its site, in a loop of the Severn river, no doubt was due to strategic considerations, as was argued above.[17] Thus, it is notable that the Welsh name for Shrewsbury, 'Amwythig', means 'defended place, fortification'.[18] The advantages of the site even warranted diverting the course of the Roman north-south road, which had previously run through Wroxeter, about ten kilometres to the south-east. In origin, therefore, the creation of Shropshire was intended to provide for the defence of Shrewsbury. To that extent, the foundation of the shire shows that the regional military focus, from the English point of view, had shifted eastwards from the Welsh frontier in the early tenth century.

As the introduction of West Saxon instruments of governance worked towards the establishment of clearer administrative boundaries, the English based in Shropshire seem to have renewed westwards expansion with added confidence. The small *burh* of Chirbury was founded in 915 on an elevated position surveying the Camlad valley, probably as part of a programme of erecting fortified settlements in Mercia which was

[14] Indeed, whether the Dyke built by Offa reached 'from sea to sea' at all, as stated by Asser, or whether it marked only the frontier of Mercia, is currently a matter of controversy. For the latter view see Hill and Worthington, *Offa's Dyke*, *passim*; for the debate see the review by I. Bapty in *Studia Celtica*, **38** (2004), pp. 201–2.

[15] *Saxon Chronicles*, i, 87 (Anglo-Saxon Chronicle, A version (Parker MS), *sub anno* 894).

[16] Cox, 'County Government', pp. 3–5; F. R. Thorn, 'Hundreds and Wapentakes', in A. Williams and R. W. H. Erskine (eds.), *The Shropshire Domesday* (Alecto County Edition of Domesday Book, 19, 1990), p. 29.

[17] Above, p. 25.

[18] B. G. Charles, 'The Welsh, their Language and Place-Names in Archenfield and Oswestry', in *Angles and Britons: O'Donnell lectures* (University of Wales Press, 1963), p. 87; above, pp. 27, 48–9.

implemented by Æthelflæd, the lady of Mercia (d. 918).[19] It was probably intended as a hundredal head; yet it may also have had a military purpose. That it was a defended settlement is suggested by the place-name element –bury, deriving from Old English *burh*. Moreover, Æthelflæd, who led a raid on Brycheiniog in 916, clearly took an aggressive stance towards the Welsh. Chirbury, lying two kilometres east of Offa's Dyke, may represent an effort at bringing frontierland back under English control. Yet Anglo-Welsh relations during the tenth century were not always confrontational. English kings such as Æthelstan (d. 939) and Edgar (d. 975) exerted a considerable degree of authority over the Welsh princes.[20] Moreover, the second half of the tenth century was the peak period of Danish raids on Wales.[21] These conditions were favourable for short-term alliances between English and Welsh, as had been the case in 893 × 894. During the first century of Shropshire's existence, it seems as if the military significance of its western border was toned down, compared to its novel importance as an administrative and political frontier.

It became very clear during the eleventh century, and especially after Gruffudd ap Llywelyn seized power in Gwynedd and Powys in 1039,[22] that the country west of Shrewsbury once again formed a military borderland. In 1039, Gruffudd's first victory over an English army was won at Rhyd-y-groes, a ford across the Severn near Welshpool.[23] Yet Shropshire appears to have escaped the worst of the attacks on English territory mounted by Gruffudd, for his most spectacular raids targeted Herefordshire.[24] The inroad of 1052 was possibly directed against the Normans who were building castles on the Herefordshire borders at the time, and that of 1055, in which the city and cathedral of Hereford was burnt, was actually undertaken by Gruffudd in coalition with Ælfgar, the earl of Mercia. Rhuddlan, where Gruffudd had set up court, and which had previously belonged to the earls of Mercia, appears to have been another focus of frontier aggression at this period, and further diverted that aggression away from Shropshire. It was on Rhuddlan, by way of

19 *Saxon Chronicles*, i, 99–100 (Anglo-Saxon Chronicle, C version (MS Tiberius B. i), *sub annis*. Also in B version); Lloyd, *History of Wales*, p. 331, n. 43 identifies 'Cyric byrig' with Chirbury, later head of the Shropshire hundred of the same name.

20 On these kings see Lloyd, *History of Wales*, pp. 336, 353; 348–9; H. R. Loyn, 'Wales and England in the Tenth Century: The Context of the Æthelstan Charters', *WHR*, **10** (1980–1), pp. 283–301.

21 *Brut*, pp. 12–19.

22 *Brut*, p. 23; Lloyd, *History of Wales*, p. 359.

23 *Brut*, p. 23; Lloyd, *History of Wales*, p. 359.

24 *The Chronicle of John of Worcester*, vol. ii: *The Annals from 450 to 1066*, eds. R. R. Darlington and P. McGurk, transl. J. Bray and P. McGurk (Oxford, 1995), pp. 566–7 (*sub anno* 1052); 576–7 (*sub anno* 1055); *Saxon Chronicles*, i, 176, 185, 187 (Anglo-Saxon Chronicle, D version (Worcester Chronicle), *sub annis*).

Chester, that Earl Tostig led a sudden raid on Gruffudd in 1063, after the death of Gruffudd's Mercian ally Ælfgar.[25] Nevertheless, the frontier status of Shropshire, poised precariously between Hereford and Rhuddlan, can hardly have been in doubt at this time. It may well have been at Westbury, a mere sixteen kilometres west of Shrewsbury, that an English border patrol was killed by Welshmen in 1053.[26] It is possible that raids by the men of Gruffudd ap Llywelyn paved the way for Welsh settlement of English-occupied land around Oswestry, just as they seem to have done in Herefordshire.[27] Certainly Domesday Book, in recording the specific duty for military service in Wales owed by the burgesses of Shrewsbury, demonstrates that the sheriff of Shropshire was not complacent about frontier security in the eleventh century.[28] On the eve of the Norman conquest, the western borders of Shropshire had already had a richly complex and chequered history as a military frontier. Perhaps more importantly for our present topic, they also presented a current concern for the authorities of the Old English state.

After Hastings, it was inroads led by Eadric, an English landed magnate in Shropshire, Earl Edwin of Mercia and their Welsh allies on Shrewsbury and Hereford which pushed the Welsh frontier up the military agenda of William of Normandy.[29] William the Conqueror's response, as has been seen, was to create a buffer zone between Wales and the English lowlands by appointing Roger de Montgomery earl of Shrewsbury and by founding two further Norman earldoms with bases at Hereford and at Chester.[30] Thus, the Norman response to the challenge posed by the Welsh frontier involved, at first, the entire territory of the border counties.

Yet it was probably not long before a narrower strip of borderland became singled out as a specific military concern by the Normans who installed themselves as the new military elite in Shropshire. The creation of the three compact tenurial blocs for Warin, Corbet and Picot suggests that the establishment of Norman military control was fraught with particular difficulty along the western borders of that county.[31] It may be that

[25] *Saxon Chronicles*, i, 191 (Anglo-Saxon Chronicle, D version (Worcester Chronicle), *sub anno* 1063); DB 269a.

[26] *Saxon Chronicles*, i, 184 (Anglo-Saxon Chronicle, C version (Abingdon Chronicle), *sub anno*).

[27] Charles, 'The Welsh, their Language and Place-Names', p. 99.

[28] DB 252a; M. R. Powicke, *Military Obligation in Medieval England: A Study in Liberty and Duty* (Oxford, 1962), p. 10 and notes 5 and 8.

[29] *Saxon Chronicles*, i, 200 (Anglo-Saxon Chronicle, D version (Worcester MS), *sub anno* 1067); *Orderic*, ii, 216, 234.

[30] Above, pp. 58–9. On the Montgomery earls of Shrewsbury, see Mason, 'Roger de Montgomery and his Sons', pp. 1–28; Thompson, 'Norman Aristocracy', pp. 251–63; Lewis, 'Early Earls', pp. 207–23.

[31] Above, pp. 59–67.

Earl Roger was here, at first, constrained to assigning estates prospectively. Quite possibly, areas such as the Clun valley, a stronghold of Eadric the Wild, or Mersete and Baschurch hundreds, where both Eadric and Edwin had estates, were the target for specific reprisals undertaken collectively or individually by Norman raiders. Whether or not this was so, Earl Roger appears to have distributed land along the western limits of his earldom by hundreds rather than as individual estates, as has been seen. Thus, Corbet was given command over the hundreds of Rhiwset and Whittery, Picot set up over Rinlow and Leintwardine, and Warin the Bald over Mersete hundred.[32] It seems probable that this happened before work began on the castle of Montgomery, whose first building stage was certainly completed by 1086, and which formed an advanced outpost in Welsh territory.

The frontier, in tenurial terms at least, thus took on a radically new shape soon after the Normans first arrived in Shropshire. However, in military terms, the occupation of the frontier hundreds only set the stage for the first Norman step beyond Shropshire into Welsh territory. Earl Roger arrived in Shropshire by 1071 at the latest and during the following two decades the frontier with Powys, insofar as it had any military relevance, looked set to be eliminated, just as borders elsewhere in the British Isles were being erased or redrawn with the creation of new power structures. The Norman conquerors led by Earl Roger of Shrewsbury maintained a formidable momentum as they crossed Offa's Dyke into Wales. As early as 1072, Roger's son Hugh led a devastating raid up the Severn valley and into Ceredigion.[33] The following year, both Ceredigion and Dyfed were targeted by Normans, most probably coming from Shropshire, and another raid into Ceredigion occurred the next year.[34] Not long afterwards, and definitely before 1081, Earl Roger's right-hand-man, Warin, joined Earl Hugh of Chester, Walter de Lacy, Robert of Rhuddlan and other Norman border adventurers in a brutal plundering campaign that ranged as far as the Llŷn peninsula on the western Welsh coast.[35]

These early raids were intended to harass the Welsh into recognizing the military superiority of the newcomers. They also provided a vent for youthful ambition. Hugh de Montgomery can hardly have been of age in the early 1070s, for his elder brother Robert was knighted at Fresnay in Normandy in 1073.[36] He and his brother Arnulf are prime representatives

[32] Above, pp. 59–61. [33] *Annales Cambriae*, p. 26.

[34] *Brut*, p. 29; Mason, 'Roger de Montgomery and his sons', p. 12.

[35] *The History of Gruffudd ap Cynan*, ed. A. Jones (Manchester, 1980), pp. 122–5; *Historia Gruffud vab Kenan*, ed. D. Simon Evans (Cardiff, 1977), pp. 12–13; *A Mediaeval Prince of Wales. The Life of Gruffudd ap Cynan*, ed. D. Simon Evans (Llanerch, 1990), p. 34; *Vita Griffini Filii Conani: The Medieval Latin Life of Gruffudd ap Cynan*, ed. P. Russell (Cardiff, 2005), pp. 66–7 (§16).

[36] *Orderic*, ii, 306 and n. 3.

of the group of *iuvenes* responsible for much of the territorial conquests originating in northern France in the High Middle Ages. They were typical of the sort of younger sons who could hope for no share of the paternal inheritance, and who therefore had to carve out territories of their own.[37] These young men eagerly competed not only for land but also to prove their worth as leaders or members of such boisterous households as that headed by Earl Hugh 'the Fat' of Chester.[38]

Earl Roger clearly intended to maintain lasting control over some, at least, of the Welsh territories over which his sons and men were roving. The Norman move into Wales was driven not only by a reckless sense of adventure, but also by an appetite for land which had no doubt been sharply whetted by the huge territorial grants being doled out by William the Conqueror. In the case of the Montgomeries, it also formed part of a highly ambitious family enterprise. One of the castles Earl Roger had built beyond Offa's Dyke by 1086 was named after Montgommery, his ancestral home in Normandy.[39] In an age where lineages often derived their names, and some of their identity, from their family castle, this was a symbolic gesture.[40] It was also a way of staking out a familial claim to Welsh territory at a time when the Normans on the Welsh borders were vying with each other for land in Wales, or at least domination over Welsh lands.[41] A chain of mottes extending up the Severn valley from Hen Domen most probably stands as testimony to Earl Roger's plan. There is no reason to doubt that the building of fortifications began almost immediately. We have good evidence that William fitz Osbern erected a string of castles from Wigmore in the north to Chepstow in the south, and he died on a campaign in Flanders in 1071.[42] Earl Roger

[37] G. Duby, 'Youth in Aristocratic Society', in his *The Chivalrous Society*, transl. C. Postan (London, 1977), pp. 112–22; R. R. Davies, *Domination and Conquest: The Experience of Ireland, Scotland and Wales 1100–1300* (Cambridge, 1990), pp. 33–4.

[38] Vividly described in *Orderic*, iii, 214–17.

[39] DB 253c, 254a.

[40] Roger had, in about 1043–8, issued a charter to Jumièges which shows him pioneering the new aristocratic fashion for family names derived from castles: 'Ego Rogerius quem dicunt de Monte Gummeri': *Recueil des actes des ducs de Normandie, 911–1066*, ed. M. Fauroux (Caen, 1961), no. 113. See J. C. Holt, 'What's in a Name? Family Nomenclature and the Norman Conquest', in his *Colonial England*, p. 188. The castle named after Montgommery is identified with Hen Domen Montgomery by Higham and Barker, *Hen Domen Montgomery. A Final Report*, p. 11. For the suggestion that Earl Roger aimed to recreate the motte he had at Montgommery in Normandy, see C. J. Spurgeon, 'The Castles of Montgomeryshire', *Mont. Coll.*, **59** (1965/6), pp. 30–1.

[41] The case that hereditary toponymic surnames came to make a claim to hereditary tenure of land in eleventh- and twelfth-century England and Normandy is made in Holt, 'What's in a Name?', esp. p. 185.

[42] D. F. Renn, 'The First Norman Castles in England (1051–1071)', *Château Gaillard*, **1** (1964), pp. 125–32, and Map 14, below, p. 146.

very probably built the particularly strong motte known as the Gro Tump, which survives around twelve kilometres beyond Montgomery in Welsh territory.[43] It is just possible that the castle which the Welsh chronicle says was built by Earl Roger at Dingeraint, on the Teifi estuary, dates from 1073.[44] Dingeraint may have been meant primarily to keep open communications and supply lines between the Montgomery conquests in south-west Wales and the base in Shropshire. It may be, however, that after 1081, when William I appears to have come to terms with Rhys ap Tewdwr, the prince of southern Wales, Earl Roger and his men were constrained to restrict their ambitions to Powys.[45] The castles in the upper Severn valley suggest that by then, at the latest, this agriculturally promising land came to be marked out for a very direct kind of territorial control and exploitation, essentially of the same nature as the Normans aimed at achieving in Shropshire.

Although it seems improbable that Earl Roger and his men were intent on extending such a level of control over all of native Wales, they seem to have been quite successful in asserting their overlordship over Powys and the minor principalities bordering on it to the east.[46] The motte at Llandinam suggests that Earl Roger did indeed have some military structures to back up his claim, made in 1086, to overlordship over Arwystli.[47] The Norman earls of Shrewsbury were working towards establishing alliances with, and ultimately hegemony over, the Welsh dynasty of Powys. Gwrgeneu ap Seisyll, a lord of Powys, led his men in the joint attack on Gruffudd ap Cynan in the late 1070s in which Warin 'of Shrewsbury', Walter de Lacy and the earl of Chester also participated.[48] By 1102, Earl

[43] Spurgeon, 'Castles of Montgomeryshire', pp. 30–1.

[44] *Brut*, p. 73, *sub anno* 1110. Cf. Mason, 'Roger de Montgomery and his Sons', p. 13, n. 2. Cf. also, however, A. H. A. Hogg and D. J. C. King, 'Early Castles in Wales and the Marches', *Arch. Camb.*, **112** (1963), p. 107, and Spurgeon, 'Mottes and Castle-Ringworks in Wales', in J. R. Kenyan and R. Avent (eds.), *Castles in Wales and the Marches: Essays in Honour of D. J. Cathcart King* (Cardiff, 1987) p. 29, which suppose the castle to date to 1093. Earl Roger's castle may have been built on the site of Cardigan Castle, or it may be the 'scarped and embanked riverside knoll' (Spurgeon) at Old Castle Farm, SN164464, a mile down the Teifi. The latter is not a typical motte or ringwork. Both sites are about 150 km from Hen Domen Montgomery.

[45] Mason, 'Roger de Montgomery and his Sons', p. 12.

[46] See, for example, the Norman claim to tribute from Cynllaith and Edeirnion in Domesday Book, where these districts or commotes are referred to as 'fines': 'Isdem Rainaldus habet in Walis duos fines, Chenlei et Derniov. De uno habet lx solidos de firma. De alio octo uaccas a Walensibus.' (DB 255a).

[47] DB, 269b. Llandinam, the site of a motte most likely attributable to Earl Roger, is said to lie in Arwystli in 1162: *Brut*, p. 143. On Llandinam motte see Spurgeon, 'Castles of Montgomeryshire', pp. 14–15; and see his 'Mottes and Castle-Ringworks', p. 28 on Llandinam and the other mottes between it and Hen Domen.

[48] *Gruffudd ap Cynan*, ed. Jones, pp. 122–5; *Historia Gruffud vab Kenan*, ed. Simon Evans, pp. 12–13; *Life of Gruffudd ap Cynan*, ed. Simon Evans, p. 34; *Vita Griffini Filii Conani*, ed. and transl. Russell, pp. 66–7 (§16). Gwrgeneu ap Seisyll was killed in the battle of Mynydd Carn in 1081: *Brut*, p. 31.

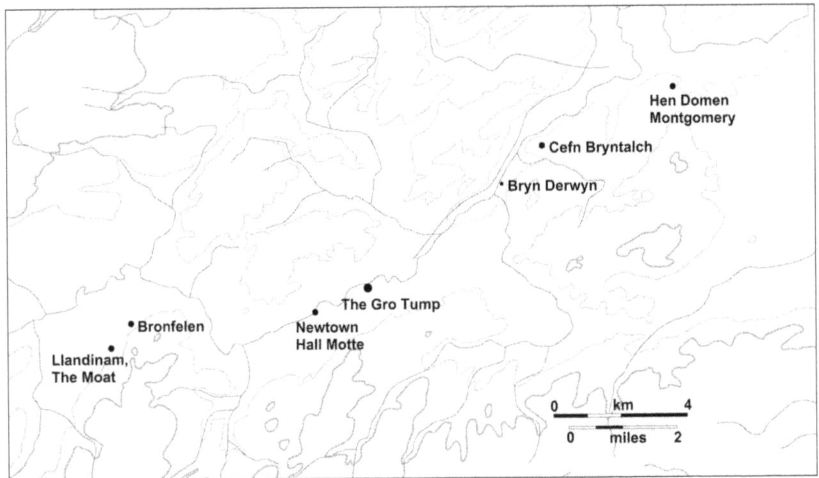

• Classified by Cathcart-King as motte type E1: 'earthworks of exceptionally fine type'
• Classified as E2: 'earthwork of average strength'
• Classified as E3: 'feeble or damaged earthworks'

Map 10. The Severn Valley west of Hen Domen, showing castles probably existing around 1086. The size of dots indicates relative strength.

Robert of Shrewsbury and his brother Arnulf, when preparing to resist the forces of Henry I of England, could call on the support of the men of Powys, or, as the Welsh chronicle puts it, 'the Britons who were subject to them and in their power, together with their chiefs, to wit, Cadwgan, Iorwerth and Maredudd, sons of Bleddyn ap Cynfyn'.[49] There is no reason to doubt that the Montgomery enterprise aimed ultimately at gaining permanent control, or at least overlordship, over Powys (perhaps paralleling Robert of Rhuddlan in Gwynedd). If the Montgomeries had succeeded in their designs, the Shropshire frontier might therefore have survived as an ethnic or administrative boundary. As a military frontier, it would have become obsolete.

It was not to be. Orderic, in his epitaph on Earl Roger, highlighted how successful the earl had been in providing inheritances for all his sons, and observed ruefully that those sons had proceeded to squander them.[50] The Montgomery enterprise may have carried the Norman earls of Shrewsbury to the furthest reaches of Wales. Yet it had its risks. In 1098,

[49] *Brut*, p. 43; above, pp. 32, 68. [50] *Orderic*, iv, 302–3.

Hugh, the second earl of Shrewsbury, was killed by Vikings while leading a ravaging campaign in Anglesey.[51] His brother Arnulf, at that time, was showing how rich the pickings could be for ambitious young Normans. He not only claimed a part of Dyfed, but was also granted Holderness in northern England when it was forfeited in 1095, and in 1102, in preparing to rebel against Henry I, he successfully obtained the support of Muirchertach, the king of Munster in Ireland, by marrying his daughter.[52] Yet, well before 1102, when he and his brother Robert suffered defeat, forfeiture and exile at the hands of Henry I, the Norman advance up the Severn valley beyond Hen Domen was repelled by the Welsh. In 1094, Earl Hugh of Shrewsbury managed to rout a Welsh attack, but the following year, Hen Domen itself was overthrown, Earl Hugh's men being killed. The successful raid on Montgomery's new castle prompted the English king himself to lead a campaign into Gwynedd.[53] But the tide of the Norman conquest of Welsh territory west of Shropshire had turned; throughout Wales, and especially in the northern and central borders, the Norman advance was grinding to a halt, or being reversed, by the late 1090s.[54] The survival of the Welsh principalities despite the fearful onslaught of the Normans meant that in effect a military frontier, however ill-defined, survived between English and Welsh lands.

At first the existence of this military frontier may not have been very clear. The fall of the Montgomery earls of Shrewsbury in 1102 removed the prime driving force behind any concerted effort at further territorial conquest in the neighbouring Welsh territories. This certainly lessened, for a time, the character of western Shropshire as a strategic border. The Normans, by 1102, had apparently already accepted the loss of their castles in the upper Severn valley, probably in 1095, when Hen Domen Montgomery was attacked. As we have seen, after 1102, Henry I decided not to appoint a successor to the earldom of Shropshire, although he did maintain the distinctive tenurial pattern on the western Shropshire frontier, since the chain of compact lordships provided a welcome source of territorial grants with which to reward his followers. The Norman impetus was thus both weakened and fragmented. Henry I's creation of a frontier aristocracy at this time was discussed above.[55] At Hen Domen Henry I installed Baldwin de Bollers. To the north, where Alan fitz Flaald soon received Oswestry, Carreghofa was to mark the limit of realistic Norman aspirations in the Tanat valley for the rest of the twelfth century.

[51] *Brut*, pp. 37–9. [52] *Brut*, pp. 43, 45.
[53] *Saxon Chronicles*, i, 230–1 (Anglo-Saxon Chronicle, E version (Laud MS), *sub annis* 1094–5).
[54] Davies, *Age of Conquest*, pp. 35–6.
[55] Above, pp. 74–5.

A strong Norman seigneurial interest which would have driven attempts at conquest up the Dee valley was lacking. To the south of the Severn, too, there was probably a lull in open hostilities. Even the Mortimers may have been slowed down, although the fact that Ralph I died after 1104 is no guarantee for this, since his heir, Hugh I (d. 1148–50) may well have succeeded to Wigmore Castle immediately.

The change in the way in which power was distributed at this time was momentous. It amounted to the creation of a new balance. The potential military reach of the locally based Anglo-Continental settlers was now reduced to a level where no military decision, not even radical military changes, could be achieved without the interference of external powers. This new military stalemate may or may not have been intended by Henry I, who engineered it by omitting to create a new earl of Shrewsbury. It certainly took a few years to materialize, and it may or may not have been immediately evident to the local lords. Yet in 1102 the road to a permanent military settlement was closed off, while the potential for further, smaller-scale military confrontation remained. The situation had, in that sense, reverted to the status that had existed before the arrival of the Montgomeries and their camp-followers. This meant that one ingredient in the creation and entrenchment, during the twelfth and thirteenth centuries, of a marcher area on the western Shropshire frontier was to be that that frontier remained, at least potentially, a military borderland.[56]

In truth, the new balance of powers quickly led the Shropshire lords to pursue non-military avenues of cross-border politics. Indeed, by 1102, the channels of inter-cultural relations which came to the fore in the early twelfth century had already begun to materialize. The Welsh chronicles, which for this period offer an unrivalled amount of information on the Powys dynasty (the descendants of Bleddyn ap Cynfyn), portray a complex world of cross-border politics.[57] As has been seen, the account of the rebellion of Robert de Bellême, earl of Shrewsbury, against Henry I in 1102 reveals that already, by then, the Norman lords of Shropshire could call on the princes of Powys for support.[58] Picot de Sai of Clun, however, seems to have pioneered the creation of cross-cultural ties. As has been seen, he created an alliance with Cadwgan ap Bleddyn, one of the leading members of the Powys dynasty, by marrying his daughter to Cadwgan.[59] This may well have been common practice among the first

[56] See the general remarks about the creation of the March of Wales as a military borderland in the early twelfth century in Davies, 'Kings, Lords and Liberties', p. 45.

[57] *Brut*, pp. 41–113 (*c. sub annis* 1100–1135).

[58] Above, pp. 32, 68, 111. [59] Above, pp. 44, 74.

Normans to claim territory in Wales and the borders. At about the same time, Gerald of Windsor, the castellan of Pembroke and grandfather of Gerald of Wales, took to wife Nest, the daughter of the prince of southern Wales, Rhys ap Tewdwr, 'with the object of giving himself and his troops a firmer foothold in the country'.[60] These marital alliances, it is true, have to be seen in perspective. Cadwgan ap Bleddyn, who married Picot's daughter, also had sons by at least four, and possibly five, daughters of Welsh chieftains, over a period of around twenty years.[61] This was a time when the descendants of Bleddyn ap Cynfyn were propelled to a dominant position among the Welsh dynasties. That position was due to the recent death of Rhys ap Tewdwr in 1093 and the continued weakness of Gwynedd, but it was also a legacy of Gruffudd ap Llywelyn.[62] In part at least, this explains why Cadwgan had sons by so many different women. During the late eleventh and early twelfth centuries, there was an abundance of Welsh dynasties seeking to establish alliances with the heirs of Bleddyn ap Cynfyn.

It is striking all the same that Picot de Sai should, by marrying his daughter to Cadwgan ap Bleddyn, have followed exactly the same tactic as various Welsh princes of his time, including Gruffudd ap Cynan of Gwynedd and Cedifor ap Gollwyn of Dyfed. It demonstrates that the position of his lands, far from pitting him irreconcilably against his Welsh neighbours, had drawn him onto the main stage of Welsh dynastic politics. The French name of one of his two grandsons, Henri, shows how quickly marital alliances fostered cultural exchange between the Welsh and the Normans. Strikingly, in 1110 Henry I accepted Henri ap Cadwgan as a hostage to guarantee that Iorwerth ap Bleddyn, Henri's uncle, would pay the 'vast sum' Henry I had demanded in return for releasing Iorwerth from prison and reinstating him as lord over a share of Powys; it is also remarkable that Henri's Welsh relations did indeed pay the sum to free him.[63] The Norman-Welsh aristocratic network in Shropshire and the borders may have been quite wide-ranging. In 1102, William Pantulf, the lord of Wem in north-eastern Shropshire, was sent by Henry I on an embassy to Iorwerth ap Bleddyn of Powys, on whose support Robert de Bellême was depending in mounting his opposition

[60] Translation from Gerald of Wales, *Wales*, ed./transl. Thorpe, p. 149 and n. 239. Cf. *Giraldus*, vi, 91 (*Itinerarium Kambrie*, i, 12).

[61] See diagram on following page, and compare that in Davies, *Age of Conquest*, p. 60. Cadwgan is first mentioned in the Welsh chronicles in 1088; he was killed 23 years later, in 1111 (*Brut*, pp. 31, 75). Some of the marital alliances he contracted may have dated to before 1088; all the sons resulting from these alliances were apparently of age in 1116, when the lands of Owain ap Cadwgan were partitioned between his half-brothers (*Brut*, pp. 99–101).

[62] Lloyd, *History of Wales*, p. 411; Stephenson, 'The "Resurgence" of Powys'.

[63] *Brut*, p. 65.

Table 8. *The sons of Cadwgan ap Bleddyn of Powys (d. 1111), their mothers and mothers' fathers*

Mother's father	Mother	Son
1. ? (not named)	? (not named)	Owain (d. 1116)
2. Gruffudd ap Cynan, prince of Gwynedd (d. 1137)	Gwenllïan[1]	Madog (last ment. 1121)
3. Dyfnwal	Sannan	Einion (d. 1124)
4. Cedifor ap Gollwyn, lord of Dyfed (d. 1091)	Ellylw	Morgan (d. 1128 on crusade)
5. Picot de Sai, lord of Clun	'the Frenchwoman'	Henri (ment. 1110 and 1116)
		Gruffudd (ment. 1116)
6. Hoeddlyw ap Cadwgan ab Elystan (Buellt?)	Euron	Maredudd (d. 1125)

[1] Gerald of Wales mentions two separate Gwenllïans, one the daughter of Madog ap Maredudd of Powys, who married Einion Clud of Elfael in 1188 (*Giraldus*, vi, 15; *Itinerarium Kambrie*, i, 1); this Gwenllïan is the other, who after Cadwgan ap Bleddyn married Gruffudd ap Rhys ap Tewdwr of Deheubarth, and was killed by Maurice de Londres in 1136 (*Giraldus*, vi, 79; *Itinerarium Kambrie*, i, 9).

against the king of England. William's success in persuading Iorwerth to renege on his allegiance to Robert de Bellême, could, we may speculate, have been due to a previous acquaintance with Iorwerth. In any case, it seems plain that in this world, the military frontiers between the Norman and the Welsh lords of Shropshire and Powys were well on their way to being overlaid, and obscured, by cross-cultural alliances.

Although the English crown had removed the earls of Shropshire, cross-border politics did not entirely devolve to the lords of the frontier hundreds. Shrewsbury became, at this time, one of the prime bases from which the English crown and its agents exercised influence in Wales. For example, Richard de Beaumais, bishop of London and Henry's representative at Shrewsbury, intervened in 1109 when Owain ap Cadwgan ap Bleddyn kidnapped Nest, the Welsh wife of the steward of Pembroke, from the castle of Cenarth Bychan. Tellingly, this intervention did not take a military form. Rather, Richard bribed Ithel and Madog, Owain's cousins, to seize or banish Owain, promising them his lands in reward.[64]

[64] *Brut*, pp. 54–9.

Richard was so well-informed about the rival camps among Welsh dynasties that he was able effectively to co-ordinate the Welsh enemies of Owain, encouraging Ithel and Madog to join forces with the rulers of Arwystli and of Meirionydd.[65] The Welsh coalition created by Richard invaded Ceredigion and soon drove Owain ap Cadwgan into a brief Irish exile.[66] Owain's father, Cadwgan, secretly escaped to Powys and negotiated with Richard de Beaumais permission to reside in a township, possibly in Shropshire, which had been the dower of Picot de Sai's daughter.[67]

This success of Richard de Beaumais' divide and rule strategy, it would appear, was to ensure that it became established practice. In 1116, Henry I succeeded in persuading Owain ap Cadwgan, the very man who had earlier been the target of a similar royal stratagem, to lead a campaign against Gruffudd, the son of Rhys ap Tewdwr, who was at the time trying to resurrect his father's rule over southern Wales.[68] Again, the English crown created a coalition of Welsh forces to pursue its interests in Wales, for Henry promised Owain the support of Llywarch ap Trahaearn of Arwystli. Owain's pursuit of Gruffudd ap Rhys led him as far as Ystrad Tywi and Carmarthen Castle, but, unlike the campaign which had been directed seven years previously against himself this one ended in disaster. Indeed, the plans of the English crown were thwarted by Gerald, the steward of Pembroke, who, in revenge for the rape of his wife in 1109, engineered the killing of Owain at the hands of the Flemings of Pembroke. (this is particularly striking because, on the Montgomery forfeiture, Pembroke had become another royal stronghold). It would also appear that the agents of the king of England sought to destabilize further the situation in Powys by releasing Welsh prisoners at strategic moments. In 1124, Ithel ap Rhirid ap Bleddyn was freed from the king's prison after the death of Einion ap Cadwgan, his cousin, possibly to fan the flames in the dispute over Einion's share of Powys. This ploy, if such it was, had only a short-term success, since Ithel was killed the following year.[69] These episodes, along with similar examples, convey the clear impression that the English crown concentrated more on fomenting violence between the members of the Powys dynasty than on renewing the push for military conquest in Wales.

The success of such methods of control ensured that they were not restricted to the Powys dynasty. The rulers of Gwynedd and of

[65] *Brut*, p. 59.

[66] *Brut*, p. 61. Owain returned later that year: *Brut*, p. 63.

[67] Ithel and Madog indeed seized Owain's lands, but 'they were not peaceful among themselves.' *Brut*, p. 63.

[68] For the following episode, see *Brut*, pp. 96–9.

[69] *Brut*, p. 109.

southern Wales during Henry I's reign were also summoned to the English king's court; inter-dynastic rivalries were provoked through English agency in all parts of Wales; and Henry I sought to demonstrate that all Welsh princes, not just those of Powys, exercised control over their territories by his consent.[70] Powys, however, bore the brunt of this intensification of the English king's overlordship, and this was where these techniques were elaborated. This impression is not entirely due to the fact that the Welsh chronicles, at this period, are the most informative for this region. It was also a matter of the geographical position of Powys, which gave it the longest frontier with England, and meant that it straddled one of the main geographical gateways into the Welsh heartland. Moreover, the Montgomery rebellion in 1102 had ensured that, when Henry I's attention was first attracted to Wales, it was with the princes of Powys that he had to deal. Henry had acquired a vast landed interest in Shropshire through the Montgomery forfeiture; as at later stages in the history of English-Welsh relations, the situation of the English king's landed interests affected where his influence was most heavily felt.[71] Iorwerth ap Bleddyn was cited before the king's council at Shrewsbury in 1103, made to answer for disputes and actions which had arisen against him and imprisoned, 'not according to law but according to power.'[72] His release in 1110 provided Henry with an opportunity to demonstrate his dominance once more by charging a huge sum in recompense.

Henry was also increasingly successful in effectively outlawing those members of the Powys dynasty who persisted in disobeying him, and in asserting his right to settle disputes between rival claimants to territory in Wales. In 1110, Iorwerth ap Bleddyn refused to receive his nephew Madog ap Rhirid in Powys because he was afraid of incurring Henry I's disapproval.[73] The following year, Madog ambushed and killed two of his own uncles, first Iorwerth and then Cadwgan ap Bleddyn. After doing Iorwerth to death, he 'lurked in the woods', having realized that he 'had committed an unlawful act against the king'; and, after killing Cadwgan, he sent messengers to Richard de Beaumais at Shrewsbury, who considered his claim and gave him control of the land, 'because he knew the ways of the people of that land, that they were all of them slaying one another'.[74] In the same year, Maredudd ap Bleddyn also sued to the king for possession of territory in Powys.[75]

[70] Davies, 'Henry I and Wales', pp. 138–41.

[71] By contrast, the crown had comparatively little demesne in Herefordshire: Holden, *Lords*, pp. 150–1.

[72] *Brut*, p. 49. [73] *Brut*, pp. 67, 73.

[74] *Brut*, p. 75. [75] *Brut*, p. 77

By 1121, Henry I's overlordship over Powys was so well established that Gruffudd ap Cynan, the lord of Gwynedd, refused a specific request of the leaders of Powys for support against the advancing English armies.[76] Throughout the 1120s, Henry and his agents helped ensure that the male members of the Powys dynasty were caught up in some of the most violent family feuding to feature in the Welsh chronicle accounts, as well as fighting with the rulers of Arwystli, as in the late 1120s.[77] Divide-and-rule stratagems continued to pay off in a variety of ways. In 1128, Maredudd ap Bleddyn seized one of his great-nephews, Llywelyn ab Owain ap Cadwgan, and handed him over to Payn fitz John, who sent him to prison in the castle of Bridgnorth.[78] The English administrators based at Shrewsbury were highly successful in ensuring the co-operation of Powysian princes, and generally managed to keep fighting restricted to one side of the Anglo-Welsh frontier.

Nevertheless, there can be no doubt that at this period, as at others, border raids may well have been more frequent than our sources reveal. The Welsh chronicles for the period after 1100 were most probably written at Llanbadarn Fawr monastery, for an audience with a close interest in the conflicts between the rival members of the Welsh ruling family of Powys.[79] Conflicts which involved the foreign newcomers rarely enter the limelight, although the frontier lords do figure in the accounts, once they became, like Picot de Sai, involved in the kin-based struggles which were of the greatest relevance to the chroniclers. The episodes involving the English king form an exception to this rule, and so it is that the Welsh chronicle does provide glimpses of the cross-border hostilities which continued after 1102. For one thing, the Powys princelings Owain ap Cadwgan and Madog ap Rhirid were, around 1110, raiding into English territory from their bases in Powys.[80] Cadwgan ap Bleddyn, the lord of parts of Powys and Ceredigion, found himself summoned permanently to Henry I's court and stripped of his lands in 1110 expressly because he had failed to keep his son's comrades from killing the English king's men in his territory.[81] It was probably due to the activities of such Powysian troublemakers that Henry I's 1114 Welsh campaign targeted Gwynedd 'and above all' Powys,[82] and that of 1121 was directed solely against Powys.[83] Henry I's campaigns do not seem to have been full-blown attempts at conquering that kingdom. He contented himself with

[76] *Brut*, p. 105. [77] *Brut*, pp. 110–13.
[78] *Brut*, p. 111.
[79] J. E. Lloyd, 'The Welsh Chronicles', *Proceedings of the British Academy*, **14** (1928–9), p. 383.
[80] *Brut*, pp. 66–7. [81] *Brut*, p. 71.
[82] *Brut*, p. 79. [83] *Brut*, p. 105.

the exaction of hostages, one-off payments in cash or kind, or a tribute of ten thousand cattle.[84] But his campaigns do suggest that the threat of Welsh raids never quite subsided on the Powys border during his reign.

Nevertheless, as elsewhere in Wales, the importance of the dominant figure of Henry I in reducing the level of conflict between English and Welsh becomes apparent retrospectively after that king's death in 1135.[85] According to one account, indeed, Caus Castle was burned by the men of Powys even shortly before Henry I's demise.[86] Certainly the Shropshire frontier was soon to become one of the areas where hostilities between the English and Welsh were most sustained and bitter. This situation was heralded in 1137, for it was probably in the country around Caus that Payn fitz John, the sheriff of Shropshire and Herefordshire, was killed, having been struck in the head by a Welsh arrow.[87] During the years when the English royal succession was being disputed between Stephen of Blois and the Empress Maud, the lords of Clun and Wigmore were caught up in murderous conflict with the rulers of Maelienydd and Elfael. Elias de Sai was involved in the killing of two sons of Madog ab Idnerth (d. 1140),[88] while Hugh Mortimer claimed further victims from that family as he fought successfully to retain his grip on Cymaron.[89] Hugh Mortimer rebuilt Cymaron Castle in 1144, which implies that it had been captured by the Welsh in the early 1140s.[90] As we have seen, by 1149 × 1151, Madog ap Maredudd (d. 1160), the ruler of Powys, held Oswestry Castle.[91] He may have achieved this through negotiation, but the killing of Stephen de Bollers by Madog's son Llywelyn in 1152 hints at conditions not dissimilar to those on the borders of Maelienydd and Elfael.[92] Moreover, twelfth-century Welsh bardic poetry dedicated to Owain Cyfeiliog vividly preserves the memory of raids led by him on Caus, the Gorddwr and the lower Camlad valley, very possibly during

[84] *Brut*, p. 109.

[85] Henry I's role in this respect is reflected by his epitaph in the Welsh chronicles: King 'Henry, the man who had tamed all the chieftains of the island of Britain through his might and power [...] the man against whom none can contend save God Himself ...' (*Brut*, p. 91).

[86] *Orderic*, vi, 442–3; Lloyd, *History of Wales*, p. 477.

[87] As is suggested by Lloyd, *History of Wales*, p. 477. Cf. *Gesta Stephani*, p. 24.

[88] *Annales Cambriae*, p. 43 (1142).

[89] *Brut*, p. 119.

[90] As is suggested by Lloyd, *History of Wales*, p. 477. Cf. *Brut*, p. 119.

[91] Above, pp. 45, 76–7; below, p. 211. In 1149, according to *Brut*, p. 129, Madog 'built' Oswestry Castle; *Annales Cambriae*, p. 44, states that he 'rebuilt' it in 1151 (C version: 'Madauc filius Maredut Croes Oswald reaedificavit'). Since there was a castle at Oswestry in 1086, it seems that the wording, if not the date, of the *Annales Cambriae* is here more reliable. In any case, it seems probable that Madog seized or received Oswestry sooner than 1149, for William Fitzalan I was in exile after 1138: *John of Worcester*, iii, 250–1 (*sub anno* 1138); *Orderic*, vi, 520.

[92] Ll. B. Smith, 'Lordships of Chirk and Oswestry', pp. 16–25, 262–9; *Brut*, p. 131.

Stephen's reign.[93] By the end of the civil war in England, the vulnerability of the Shropshire frontier may have been more evident than at any time since the arrival of the Normans.

Like Henry I, Henry II was drawn to Shropshire early in his reign on a mission to defeat a rebellious magnate. In 1102, the castles at Shrewsbury and Bridgnorth had been garrisoned in defiance of the English king by the men of Robert de Bellême; in 1155, Bridgnorth, along with the castles at Wigmore and Cleobury, were fortified against Henry II by Hugh Mortimer. Henry II's tactics, moreover, bear some resemblance to those of his predecessor. He reasserted the domination of the English crown over Shropshire by a demonstration of force, taking Mortimer's castles by siege, as has been seen.[94] However, he appears, at first, to have taken a diplomatic approach towards the rulers of Powys. William Fitzalan II was reinstated at Oswestry, but Madog ap Maredudd's retreat from that castle does not appear to have been won by force of arms. By 1156–7 Madog ap Maredudd and other chieftains of Powys were receiving payments from the English crown,[95] and Henry II's Welsh campaign of 1157 was directed against Owain, the prince of Gwynedd. Although the Welsh chronicle has Madog ap Maredudd leading a host northwards to oppose Henry II in 1157, Madog may actually not have supported Owain Gwynedd, with whom he had clashed at Coleshill in 1150.[96] It appears quite possible that Henry II, in the earliest years of his reign, successfully reduced the military threat from Powys by winning an ally in Madog ap Maredudd.

This strategy allowed Henry to concentrate his attention on Gwynedd in 1157 and on the rising power of the Lord Rhys of Deheubarth in 1158 and 1163.[97] However, the following year, he began preparations for a third Welsh campaign, and in 1165 it was at Shrewsbury that he assembled an army summoned from the whole Plantagenet empire.[98] Gerald of Wales notes the neat correspondence of Henry II's three Welsh campaigns to the three Welsh kingdoms.[99] However, as has been observed, we should

93 G. A. Williams, 'Welsh Raiding in the Twelfth-Century Shropshire/Cheshire March: The Case of Owain Cyfeiliog', *Studia Celtica*, **40** (2006), pp. 89–115, esp. pp. 104–5 and n. 121. See also D. Crouch, 'The March and the Welsh Kings', in E. King (ed.), *The Anarchy of King Stephen's Reign* (Oxford, 1994), pp. 256–89.

94 Above, pp. 76–7.

95 Lloyd, *History of Wales*, pp. 496 (and n. 45), 508; *Pipe Rolls 2, 3, 4 Henry II, 1155–8*, ed. J. Hunter (London, 1844, repr. in facs. London, 1930), pp. 89, 170 for crown payments through the sheriff of Shropshire to 'Maddoch' and others in 1156–8.

96 *Brut*, p. 129.

97 *Brut*, pp. 135, 139. For maps and discussions of Henry II's 1157 campaign, see D. J. C. King, 'Henry II and the Fight at Coleshill', *WHR*, **2** (1965), pp. 367–73; J. G. Edwards, 'Henry II and the Fight at Coleshill: Some Further Reflections', *WHR*, **3** (1966–7), pp. 251–63.

98 T. K. Keefe, 'The 1165 Levy for the Army of Wales', *Notes and Queries*, NS, **29**:3 (1982), pp. 194–6.

99 *Giraldus*, vi, 137–8 (*Itinerarium Kambrie*, ii, 10).

not assume that Powys was perceived as a threat on a par with Owain's Gwynedd and the Deheubarth of Rhys ap Gruffudd.[100] In 1165, Henry II was opposed by a Welsh army to which all three of the Welsh kingdoms contributed, and the scale of his operation indicates that he aimed at securing, at the least, the submission of all the leaders of Wales.[101] That it was the Shropshire frontier which witnessed this confrontation may indicate that Henry was responding to trouble on those borders, just as Henry I apparently did in 1114 and 1121. Soon after the death of Madog ap Maredudd in 1160, his heir, Llywelyn, had been killed, and Powys come to be divided among five coheirs.[102] Although this reduced the potential military strength that could be mustered by any one ruler of Powys, the death of a strong Powysian ruler who had been sympathetic to the crown meant that the incidence of border warfare actually increased. Carreghofa Castle, having been refurbished by the crown in 1159–62,[103] was captured in 1163 by a coalition of two of Madog's coheirs, Owain Cyfeiliog and Owain Fychan, and Maredudd ap Hywel, the lord of Edeirnion.[104] Henry II had certainly backed up his Powys diplomacy with a good measure of military clout, refurbishing and garrisoning the Shropshire border castles of Clun and Oswestry while they were in his custody during the Fitzalan minority (1160–75).[105] Thus, Shropshire may well have been singled out as the launch-pad for the best-planned of Henry II's Welsh campaigns because of the demise, in 1160, of a strong Powysian prince who had chosen a non-confrontational stance vis-à-vis the king of England. Henry's venture into Wales by way of Oswestry and the Ceiriog valley ended in disaster. After being harried by Welsh archers near Dyffryn Ceiriog and buffeted by gales and rain on the Berwyn range, he and his army were forced to retreat to the English lowlands.[106] The memory of this Welsh victory apparently won through divine intervention was treasured by men of Powys, the path followed by Henry's

[100] P. Latimer, 'Henry II's Campaign against the Welsh in 1165', *WHR*, **14**:4 (1988), p. 534.

[101] *Ibid.*, p. 537.

[102] J. B. Smith, 'Dynastic Succession in Medieval Wales', *BBCS*, **33** (1986), pp. 210–12.

[103] *Pipe Roll 5 Henry II, 1158–9* (P. R. S., 1), p. 62; *Pipe Roll 6 Henry II, 1159–60* (P. R. S., 2), p. 26; *Pipe Roll 7 Henry II, 1160–61* (P. R. S., 4), p. 38; *Pipe Roll 8 Henry II, 1161–2* (P. R. S., 5), p. 15.

[104] See the genealogical diagram in Davies, *Age of Conquest*, p. 60; *Brut*, p. 143; Lloyd, *History of Wales*, p. 509 and n. 86. For the suggestion that it was Owain Gwynedd, not Owain Cyfeiliog, who was involved in this capture of Carreghofa see Stephenson, 'Supremacy', p. 46, n. 6.

[105] *Pipe Rolls Henry II: 6*, p. 27; *7*, pp. 39–40; *8*, pp. 15–16; *9*, pp. 3–4; *10*, p. 9; *11*, pp. 90–1; *16*, p. 134; *17*, pp. 33–4; *18*, p. 112; *19*, pp. 109–10; *20*, pp. 110–11; *21*, pp. 38–9. It should be noted that the crown did not spend money on the Fitzalan castles in 1166–9, that is, during three of the four years that Geoffrey de Vere was sheriff of Shropshire (1166–70). However, this was probably not a sign of *détente*; rather, it would seem that Geoffrey had himself to pay for garrisoning and upkeep of the Fitzalan castles, for he had married Isabel of Clun, the mother of the minor William Fitzalan II.

[106] *Brut*, pp. 144–7. After moving his army to Chester, Henry II hired a fleet from Dublin and other Irish towns, but on finding it inadequate he abandoned his campaign. *Ibid.*, p. 147.

host being named 'Ffordd y Saeson', the English road.[107] The site of the last campaign to be led into Wales by an English king for over forty years became a frontier landmark.

Other concerns, such as the Becket crisis, the alarming progress made by the English invaders in Ireland and the rebellion of his sons, led Henry II to adopt a more conciliatory stance towards the rulers of Wales by the early 1170s, while asserting his mastery over the lords of the Welsh frontier.[108] In 1179, he jailed Roger Mortimer because Cadwallon ap Madog, the ruler of Maelienydd, had been killed by Roger's men.[109] Yet such drastic measures were primarily directed against the lords of the southern Welsh frontier. The Shropshire–Powys borders, at this time, became the stage for less heavy-handed royal diplomacy, much as they had been during most of the reign of Henry I. For one thing, Henry II built on the tactic of Henry I, who had installed his own men as the local landed class on the borders. Taking this strategy a step further, Henry II began to use the small lordships on the Shropshire borders as counters in the game of cross-border politics. In 1165, he resumed Whittington from Geoffrey de Vere, granting him land in Shropshire in return, and bestowed it on Roger de Powis, a descendant of the 'Tudur' who in 1086 was lord of 'a Welsh district', probably Maelor Saesneg.[110] At the council of Oxford in 1177, Ellesmere was granted from the royal demesne to Dafydd, the son of Owain Gwynedd, who in 1174 had married Henry II's half-sister Emma of Anjou.[111] Lands in Shropshire began to be granted to Welshmen on terms of serjeanty by this time at the latest. A descendant of the de Powis family received land for the serjeanty of acting as translator or interpreter in dealings with the Welsh; another for the service of leading prisoners from Powys to the court at Shrewsbury.[112] The Welsh serjeanties illustrate the emphasis placed by the crown on diplomatic efforts, and complement

[107] Lloyd, *History of Wales*, p. 517; Gerald of Wales saw Henry II's defeat as divine retribution: *Giraldus*, vi, 143–4 (*Itinerarium Kambrie*, ii, 12).

[108] As he did at the council of Gloucester in 1175: *Gesta Regis Henrici Secundi*, ed. W. Stubbs (RS, 1867), i, 92.

[109] *Brut*, p. 169; Ralph of Diss, *Opera Historica*, ed. W. Stubbs, 2 vols. (RS, 1876), i, 437; *Pipe Rolls 25 Henry II, 1178–9* (P. R. S., 28), p. 39; Holden, *Lords*, pp. 143–4.

[110] DB 253c; Eyton, xi, 30–1, with reference to 'Welsh genealogists'; F. C. Suppe, 'Who was Rhys Sais? Some Comments on Anglo-Welsh Relations before 1066', *Haskins Society Journal*, **7** (1995), fig. 16 (p. 66); F. C. Suppe, 'Roger of Powys, Henry II's Anglo-Welsh Middleman, and his Lineage', *WHR*, **21**:1 (2002), pp. 1–23.

[111] Ralph of Diss, *Opera Historica*, i, 397–8. *Brut*, p. 165, places this marriage in 1175, as does *Brut, Peniarth 20*, p. 70; *Chronica Rogeri de Houedene*, ed. Stubbs, ii, 134.

[112] *Red Book of the Exchequer*, ed. Hall, ii, 453; *Liber Feodorum. The Book of Fees Commonly Called Testa de Nevill*, 3 vols. (London, 1920–31), i, 147; Eyton, xi, 24, surmised that Henry II bestowed Kinnerley on Iorwerth Goch, brother of Madog ap Maredudd, for his services as *latimer*, or translator. Cf. Stephenson, 'Welsh Lords in Shropshire', p. 26.

the picture provided by the military serjeanties of Shropshire.[113] However, these territorial grants increasingly created rivalling claims to the border lordships. They led to the rebellion of Fulk Fitzwarin early in John's reign and were probably to blame, in part, for the border raids of Llywelyn ap Iorwerth conducted in this area in the 1220s. At first, however, they probably helped create a stalemate between the frontier lordships and the small segments into which Powys was being broken up at this period.[114]

They also bought Henry II and his sons some support from the leading men of northern Wales. Meurig, the son of Roger de Powis, can be found in 1194 receiving payments for doing the king's business in Wales.[115] Dafydd ab Owain survived as one of the rulers of Gwynedd (until 1197), but seems to have refrained from hostilities against the English for the rest of his life. After being defeated and briefly imprisoned by his nephew, Llywelyn ap Iorwerth, during the 1190s, Dafydd lived out his days in English exile, dying in 1203, quite possibly at Ellesmere.[116] The lords of Powys also came to enjoy Henry II's patronage, after about 1171, by other means than through grants of land on the Shropshire borders. Owain Cyfeiliog, the poet-prince of southern Powys, had participated in the capture of the royal castle at Carreghofa in 1167, but supported Henry II during the rebellion of 1173–4.[117] Henry II entertained him at his court at Shrewsbury, possibly in 1175 or 1176.[118] Nor were the signs of *détente* on the Shropshire frontier restricted to the policies of the English king. In 1188, Gerald of Wales accompanied Baldwin, the archbishop of Canterbury, on a recruitment mission for the Third Crusade which led him safely on a circuit around Wales and through northern Powys, before he became William Fitzalan II's guest at Oswestry.[119] Clun was held throughout Henry II's reign by William's mother, Isabel de Sai, who was married, after William Fitzalan I's death in 1160, to a succession of Shropshire magnates before her own death early in the thirteenth century. There is every reason to believe that she did little to maintain the pressure on Ceri and Maelienydd which had been exerted by her father. Finally, the rulers of Powys continued to be plagued by the old curse of family feuding. Owain Fychan, the lord of Mechain, was done to

[113] E. G. Kimball, *Serjeanty Tenure in Medieval England* (New Haven, 1936), pp. 78–9.

[114] See Map 24, below, p. 166.

[115] *Pipe Roll 7 Richard I, 1195* (P. R. S., NS 6), p. 244.

[116] *Brut*, pp. 175, 184–7.

[117] *Gesta Regis Henrici Secundi*, ed. Stubbs, i, 51, n. 4.

[118] *Giraldus*, vi, 144–5 (*Itinerarium Kambrie*, ii, 12); Henry II may have been at Shrewsbury witnessing charters to Shrewsbury and Haughmond Abbeys respectively in July 1175 and January 1176: R. W. Eyton, *Court, Household, and Itinerary of King Henry II: Instancing Also the Chief Agents and Adversaries of the King in his Government, Diplomacy, and Strategy* (London, 1878), pp. 193, 198.

[119] *Giraldus*, vi, 142 (*Itinerarium Kambrie*, ii, 12).

death in 1187 by the two sons of Owain Cyfeiliog 'through betrayal and treachery by night at Carreg Hofa'.[120] During the latter part of Henry II's reign, royal diplomacy and Welsh inter-dynastic rivalries conspired to reduce frontier hostilities at least as effectively as they had done during the reign of Henry I.

The death of Henry II in 1189 did not unleash a wave of Welsh attacks on the Shropshire borderlands, as happened in the mid-1130s. However, in south Wales, the Lord Rhys of Deheubarth, who had from the early 1170s contributed significantly to the Anglo-Welsh *détente*, launched a successful offensive against English-held castles.[121] Diplomatic efforts, at this time, were therefore also probably concentrated on southern Wales; it may well have been to the Lord Rhys that Gerald of Wales went on his embassy in 1189.[122] The truce in Powys appears to have been due primarily to the restraint of Owain Cyfeiliog for, after he retired to his newly founded abbey at Ystrad Marchell in 1195, the depredations of his son Gwenwynwyn (d. 1216) prompted a campaign under the leadership of Hubert Walter in 1196.[123] Allegiances between the Welsh and English frontier lords may also have helped to reduce the incidence of border raids in northern Herefordshire and Shropshire. In 1191, when William Longchamp, Richard I's justiciar, banished Roger Mortimer, seizing his castles at Wigmore and in Shropshire, Roger had been accused of conspiring with the Welsh against the king.[124] Given the Mortimer tradition of rebelliousness, there may have been some truth in these allegations. By 1196, however, Roger had renewed his offensive against the Welsh of Maelienydd. The castles at Knighton, Norton, Cymaron and Bleddfa, which were instrumental in Mortimer's campaigns, were garrisoned at royal expense, which marks a significant change in the royal attitude towards aristocratic conquests in Wales, no doubt brought about by the attacks which the Lord Rhys had launched on the southern borders.[125] The defeat, in 1196, of Mortimer's invasion force by a Welsh alliance under the leadership of the Lord Rhys near Radnor demonstrates that the stakes in the enterprise of Welsh territorial conquest had been raised by that prince's domination of the dynasties of Elfael, Gwrtheyrnion and

[120] *Brut*, p. 171 (here called Owain ap Madog).

[121] *Brut*, pp. 170–3. For recent discussions of the circumstances leading to Rhys' attacks see J. Gillingham, 'Henry II, Richard I and the Lord Rhys', *Peritia*, **10** (1996), pp. 225–36; Holden, *Lords*, pp. 167–8.

[122] *Giraldus*, i, 84 (*De Rebus a Se Gestis*, xxi).

[123] *Brut*, p. 177. (For 'Henry' read 'Hubert'): Lloyd, *History of Wales*, p. 583.

[124] *The Chronicle of Richard of Devizes of the time of King Richard the First*, ed. J. T. Appleby (London, 1963), pp. 30–1.

[125] *Pipe Roll 3&4 Richard I, 1191–2* (P. R. S., NS 2), pp. 77, 81; *Pipe Roll 7 Richard I, 1195* (P. R. S., NS 6), pp. 9, 13, 108.

Maelienydd.[126] Campaigns such as these made a deep impression on Roger Mortimer: in 1199, he granted lands in Gwrtheyrnion and Maelienydd to the abbey of Cwmhir for the souls of his family, his men and 'those who had died in the conquest of Maelienydd.'[127] The brief hegemony of Powys, among Welsh kingdoms, during the reign of Gwenwynwyn, along with the Mortimer offensive, may also have put the lordship of Clun into a state of heightened alarm: the castle of 'Matefelun' garrisoned in 1195 can possibly be identified with Newcastle near Clun.[128] Yet, after 1195, Gwenwynwyn sought to extend his dominion southwards, over Arwystli and Elfael, and the Shropshire borders seem to have been spared by the Powysian prince who 'sought to restore to the Welsh their [...] bounds'.[129] Indeed, in 1197, Gwenwynwyn conveyed Gruffudd, the son of the Lord Rhys, to an English prison. Since Gwenwynwyn received the border castle of Carreghofa in return, it seems very possible that he was continuing the practice of handing over Welsh prisoners to the royal gaolers at Shrewsbury.[130] Gerald of Wales was no doubt right when he noted that Gwenwynwyn was, by about 1202, well disposed towards the English because of his rivalry with Llywelyn ap Iorwerth of Gwynedd.[131] Gwenwynwyn's marriage to Margaret, the daughter of Corbet of Caus, further demonstrates that accommodation, rather than confrontation, was, in general, the watchword on the Shropshire frontier, even during the brief hegemony in Wales enjoyed by the lords of Powys around the turn of the twelfth and thirteenth centuries.[132]

John's reign witnessed, at first, a continuation of the royal diplomatic approach towards Powys. John knew Wales better than his predecessor, having succeeded to the lordship of Glamorgan in 1189.[133] It comes as no surprise to find him astutely continuing the policies which had proved effective in ensuring some influence over the Welsh leaders. The small lordships on the western Shropshire frontier continued to provide

[126] *Brut*, p. 177.

[127] See 'An Early Charter of the Abbey of Cwmhir', ed. B. G. Charles, *The Transactions of the Radnorshire Society*, 40 (1970), pp. 68–73; comments in J. B. Smith, 'The Middle March in the Thirteenth Century', *BBCS*, **24** (1970–2), pp. 80–1; and below, pp. 181, 185.

[128] *Pipe Roll 7 Richard I, 1195* (P. R. S., NS 6), p. 244: 'Matefelun' was a *domus* of William 'de Boterels', the third husband of Isabel, lady of Clun. See D. J. C. King, *Castellarium Anglicanum: An Index and Bibliography of the Castles in England, Wales and the Islands*, 2 vols. (New York, 1983), ii, 434, 563; on 'de Boterels' see Eyton, vii, 160–2; xi, 229.

[129] *Brut*, pp. 180–3.

[130] *Brut*, p. 179; *Annales Cambriae*, p. 61.

[131] *Giraldus*, iii, 226 (*De Jure et Statu Menevensis Ecclesiae*, iv).

[132] *Registrum Ricardi de Swinfield, Episcopi Herefordensis*, ed. W. W. Capes (Canterbury and York Society 6, 1909), p. 209; see R. Morgan, 'Trewern in Gorddwr: Domesday Manor and Knight's Fief, 1086–1311', *Mont. Coll.*, **64** (1976), p. 131 for the marriage of Gwenwynwyn to Margaret Corbet around 1200.

[133] I. W. Rowlands, 'King John and Wales', in S. D. Church (ed.), *King John: New Interpretations* (Woodbridge, 1999), pp. 273–87; compare Holden, *Lords*, ch. 6.

bargaining chips for that purpose. Llywelyn ap Iorwerth, with whom John had concluded a peace treaty,[134] was granted Ellesmere as the dower of his wife Joan, a natural daughter of John's.[135] By 1216, the lordship of Montgomery had been granted to Gwenwynwyn in a bid to divert his alliance from Llywelyn to the English crown.[136] The terms to which Llywelyn had to agree in 1211 show that the English king was seeking to approximate the tenurial status of portions of Powys to that of these small lordships: Llywelyn acknowledged that Edeirnion had always been held of the English king.[137]

On the occasions when John succeeded in asserting his mastery in Wales, it was, as far as Powys and Shropshire were concerned, also largely by resorting to tried and tested methods. Shrewsbury continued to fulfil its wonted function as a gaol for Welsh princes: Gwenwynwyn was held there in 1208.[138] Like his father in 1157, John succeeded in exploiting the rivalry between Powys and Gwynedd, allying himself with the lords of Powys and Cedewain when he launched his two campaigns against Llywelyn ap Iorwerth in 1211.[139] Accordingly, Oswestry, on the frontier with Powys, again provided a convenient mustering point for his second expeditionary force in 1211, while Carreghofa Castle was rebuilt in the same year, and a royal garrison placed in the castle of Tafolwern by the following one.[140] In August 1212, John was back in Shrewsbury, making preparations for an invasion of Wales on such a vast scale as to suggest that he was aiming for a permanent settlement of the Welsh problem.[141] In the end, his military operations in Wales in that year were restricted to an intervention in Powys, when he came to the rescue of Robert de Vieuxpont, who was being besieged by the coalition forces of Gwenwynwyn and Llywelyn ap Iorwerth in the castle at Mathrafal.[142] Shortly after lifting that siege, John abandoned his grand plans for dealing

[134] In 1201: edited in *Rot. Pat.*, pp. 8b–9a, and, with discussion, in I. W. Rowlands, 'The 1201 Peace between King John and Llywelyn ap Iorwerth', *Studia Celtica*, **34** (2000), pp. 149–66; cf. *Acts of Welsh Rulers*, ed. Pryce, no. 221.

[135] Eyton, x, 236; *Rotuli Chartarum*, ed. T. D. Hardy (London, 1837), p. 147.

[136] *Rot. Claus.*, i, 246b. For the charter in which Gwenwynwyn describes himself as 'lord of Montgomery' see *AWR*, no. 578.

[137] For the 1211 treaty, see J. B. Smith, 'Magna Carta and the Charters of the Welsh Princes', *EHR*, **99** (1984), pp. 355, 361.

[138] *Rymer*, I, i, 48.

[139] *Brut*, p. 191; Rowlands, 'King John and Wales', p. 286.

[140] For John's 1211 Welsh campaigns, see *Brut*, pp. 190–3; for Oswestry's role, see Roger of Wendover, *Flores Historiarum*, iii, 235; for Carreghofa and Tafolwern: ' "Cronica de Wallia" and Other Documents from Exeter Cathedral Library MS. 3514', ed. T. Jones, *BBCS*, **12** (1946), pp. 34–5.

[141] P. M. Barnes, in her introduction to *Pipe Roll 14 John, 1212* (P. R. S., NS 30, 1955), pp. xiv–xvii.

[142] *Brut*, p. 195; cf. Lloyd, *History of Wales*, p. 638.

with Wales after receiving news that a plot to assassinate him was being hatched by Eustace de Vescy and Robert fitz Walter.[143]

John's reign also witnessed the beginning of a dramatic resurrection of border raiding in Shropshire. This was a direct result of the rise to power in Wales of Llywelyn ap Iorwerth (d. 1240). From 1216 to Llywelyn's death the lords of Powys did not enter into the equation, for Gwenwynwyn, the son and heir of Owain Cyfeiliog (d. 1197), was exiled from Wales in 1216 by Llywelyn ap Iorwerth in retribution for coming to terms with John,[144] and his son Gruffudd failed to succeed to southern Powys until 1241.[145] His kinsman, Madog ap Gruffudd Maelor (d. 1236), did become lord of northern Powys in 1191, and of Maelor Saesneg in 1197,[146] but he lacked the resources to pursue a cause independent of both Llywelyn and the crown, and as a result he posed little or no threat to English territory.[147] The lesser ruling families of central Wales – those of Cedewain, Ceri, Maelienydd, Gwrtheyrnion and Elfael – accepted the sole ruler of Gwynedd as their protector as early as 1208, when the king strengthened Llywelyn's position in Wales by pardoning him for capturing the castles and lands of Gruffudd ap Gwenwynwyn; Llywelyn was able to entrench his hegemony further after King John's death in 1216.[148] While Gwenwynwyn harried Llywelyn in Powys from a base in the Corbet lands after 1208, and his son Gruffudd, together with his Corbet relatives, led attacks on Powys from England after 1228,[149] the Welsh agency disturbing the peace on the Powys borders in the first half of the thirteenth century was, overwhelmingly, Llywelyn ap Iorwerth. This role had been dramatically foreshadowed in May 1215, when Llywelyn led an army of Welshmen to Shrewsbury, occupying the town without meeting any resistance.[150] This unprecedented *coup*, the first Welsh attack on a border county town since the mid-eleventh century, must have had a significant psychological effect on the population of Shropshire. That Llywelyn's rise to power had ushered in a new era of border warfare was further demonstrated in 1234, when Llywelyn's armies, allied with those of the Marshal, again raided the country around Shrewsbury, burning part of the county town itself.[151]

[143] Barnes, introduction to *Pipe Roll 14 John*, p. xvii.

[144] *Brut*, pp. 106–9. [145] *Brut*, p. 237.

[146] *Brut*, p. 173; Lloyd, *History of Wales*, pp. 583–4; 'Valle Crucis Abbey. Its Origin and Foundation Charter', ed. M. C. Jones, *Arch. Camb.*, 3rd ser., **12** (1866), p. 414.

[147] Davies, *Age of Conquest*, pp. 235, 244.

[148] *Brut*, p. 189; *Rot. Pat.*, p. 88; *Brut*, p. 207. For a recent detailed account of the south-eastern March during the years of Henry III's minority government, see Holden, *Lords*, pp. 193–203.

[149] D. Stephenson, 'The Politics of Powys Wenwynwyn in the Thirteenth Century', *Cambridge Medieval Celtic Studies*, **7** (1984), pp. 52, 45.

[150] *Brut*, p. 203.

[151] Roger of Wendover, *Flores Historiarum*, iv, 291; Matthew Paris, *Chron. Maj.*, iii, 264. It seems clear that the lords of the Shropshire border sided with the king during the rebellion of Richard

Yet these campaigns took place in exceptional circumstances, when Llywelyn was in allegiance with Marcher lords. Thus, while Shrewsbury most definitely remained a border town during his reign, it was more often in a political than a military sense. Llywelyn was open to diplomatic negotiations, and although in 1218 it was at Worcester that he negotiated with Henry III's emissaries,[152] from 1219 to 1221 Shrewsbury provided the venue for parleys with Llywelyn. It was there that he met Pandulf, the papal legate and member of Henry III's council, in 1220.[153] The same year, Llywelyn specifically suggested Shrewsbury, rather than Worcester, for a meeting with Pandulf, the justiciar Hubert de Burgh and the archbishop of Canterbury.[154] In 1221, Llywelyn met the king and the Marcher lords at Shrewsbury to negotiate a settlement between him and Rhys Ieuanc of Deheubarth (d. 1222).[155] Shrewsbury retained its status as one of the foremost points of contact of the court of the English king with leaders from all of Wales during the minority of Henry III.

Although the county town did not escape the range of Llywelyn's military operations, there can be no doubt that it was the borders that bore the brunt of his raids. In 1223, Llywelyn led a campaign into the lowlands around Oswestry, capturing the castles of Kinnerley and Whittington.[156] His motivation for doing so is unclear,[157] but he may already have been insisting on the claim to Whittington which was asserted by his grandson, Llywelyn ap Gruffudd, in 1267.[158] In 1228, he protested against the grant of the lordship of Montgomery to Hubert de Burgh by laying siege to the newly erected stone castle there.[159] Montgomery had become a focal point for the rivalry between Llywelyn and Hubert de Burgh, who

Marshal, sixth earl of Pembroke, in 1233–4: see above, pp. 82–3; Lloyd, *History of Wales*, p. 679 (n. 136). Holden, *Lords*, pp. 207–14 analyses the impact of the Marshal rebellion on Herefordshire and the south-eastern March.

152 *AWR*, nos. 240–2. Cf. *Rymer*, I, i, 75–6.

153 *Royal and Other Letters Illustrative of the Reign of Henry III*, ed. W. W. Shirley (RS, 1862), i, 136, 142.

154 *AWR*, no. 245; *Cal. Anc. Corr. Wales*, p. 8.

155 *Brut*, p. 223.

156 *Rymer*, I, i, 89; *Cal. Pat. R., 1216–25*, p. 481; *Annales Monastici*, ed. Luard, iii, 82 (Annals of Dunstable). The attack was quite possibly launched from Montgomery; Llywelyn had been allowed to retain Montgomery, along with Ceri and Cedewain, on the terms of the 1218 Treaty of Worcester. See D. A. Carpenter, *The Minority of Henry III* (London, 1990), p. 313. Llywelyn had to surrender Montgomery to the crown in 1223: *Annales Monastici*, ed. Luard, iii, 83 (Annals of Dunstable). See also D. Stephenson, 'Llywelyn the Great, the Shropshire March and the Building of Montgomery Castle', *TSAS*, **80** (2005), pp. 52–8. I should like to thank Dr Stephenson for kindly sending me a draft of this article.

157 Lloyd, *History of Wales*, p. 661.

158 In the treaty of Montgomery: *AWR*, no. 363, p. 539; *Littere Wallie*, p. 2. Cf. D. Stephenson, '*Fouke le Fitz Waryn* and Llywelyn ap Gruffydd's Claim to Whittington', *TSAS*, **78** (2002), pp. 26–31.

159 Roger of Wendover, *Flores Historiarum*, iv, 172–4.

appears to have aimed to acquire for himself a position in south Wales to equal that of Llywelyn in the north.[160] In 1228 Hubert attempted to join Ceri commote to his lordship of Montgomery. This plan, despite being backed by the young English king in person, was foiled by Llywelyn.[161] Nor did the other Marcher lordships on the Powys–Shropshire borders escape the effects of Llywelyn's hegemony. Llywelyn became the prime obstacle to Mortimer's bid to dominate Maelienydd. By 1227 at the latest, possibly as early as 1218, Mortimer was seeking to recover the manors of Knighton and Norton in the lower Teme valley, which Llywelyn claimed to have acquired by marriage.[162] Most strikingly, the perilous position of the Shropshire border castles was demonstrated in 1231 and 1233, when Clun, Oswestry, Montgomery and possibly Bishop's Moat were destroyed in punitive raids specifically directed at the Marcher lords.[163] It was the borders of Shropshire which were revealed as particularly exposed and vulnerable in the days of Llywelyn ap Iorwerth, although all of the county may well have been, on occasion at least, in a state of alarm.

With the ascendancy of Henry III in Wales and the marches during the 1240s and the early 1250s came a considerable easing off of the threat of warfare in the borders adjoining Shropshire.[164] Petty frontier disputes, it is true, persisted. Gwenwynwyn of Powys had received the territory of Gorddwr, regarded as the Welshry of Caus lordship, from Robert Corbet II as a marriage portion, and this claim, in part, led to a state of more or less cold war between their sons, Gruffudd ap Gwenwynwyn and Thomas Corbet.[165] However, after 1237, and particularly after 1241, the extension of crown control over Cheshire had opened a new front for royal military operations against the northern Welsh, as was demonstrated by Henry III's campaign against Dafydd ap Llywelyn of Gwynedd in 1245, which was launched from Chester. Shropshire did not retreat from the main stage of Anglo-Welsh relations: during the fighting in 1245 there was also a bloody battle at Montgomery.[166] But, in general, Shropshire was less exposed during this period. In 1241, an English army, moved against

160 R. F. Walker, 'Hubert de Burgh and Wales, 1218–1232', *EHR*, **87** (1972), p. 465; see also Holden, *Lords*, pp. 203–7.

161 *Brut*, pp. 226–9.

162 *AWR*, no. 244 (dated October 1218 × November 1227); *Cal. Anc. Corr. Wales*, p. 23.

163 On 1231: Roger of Wendover, *Flores Historiarum*, iv, 220–3. Walker, 'Hubert de Burgh and Wales', p. 486, for the view that Llywelyn's raid of 1231 was a planned campaign aimed primarily against Hubert de Burgh's ambitions in Wales rather than an immediate reaction to the battle at Montgomery. See *Brut*, p. 231 for the 1233 raid.

164 For Herefordshire and the adjoining March in those decades, see Holden, *Lords*, pp. 214–18.

165 See, for example, *AWR*, no. 596 (c. 1247 × 1259), where Gruffudd complains that Thomas had hanged three of his men without judgment or cause. Cf. *Cal. Anc. Corr. Wales*, pp. 19–20.

166 *Brut*, p. 239; *Rymer*, I, i, 152; Matthew Paris, *Chron. Maj.*, iv, 423; *ibid.*, iv, 407 for the English massacre of 300 Welsh at Montgomery in 1245.

Wales by way of Shrewsbury, had secured the submissions of the minor dynasties of the central March to the king.[167] The effective measure of influence exerted over these families, however short-lived, is shown by the existence of a Welsh royal seneschal active in Elfael and Maelienydd in 1252.[168] The ruler of southern Powys, Gruffudd ap Gwenwynwyn, owed his succession to his inheritance to the English king.[169] In 1248, outstanding fines due from the chieftains of Cedewain and of Ceri for succession to their lands were recorded by the English exchequer, the royal bailiff at Montgomery being enjoined to obtain pledges.[170] Northern Powys, after the death of Madog ap Gruffudd Maelor in 1236, had been divided between Madog's four sons.[171] Both Gruffudd ap Gwenwynwyn and Gruffudd, the senior of the sons of Madog, had by now married daughters of English Marcher lords. The lord of southern Powys was married to Hawise Lestrange, the daughter of the lord of Knockin,[172] while his counterpart in northern Powys (Gruffudd, lord of Powys Fadog) had taken to wife Emma, a daughter of Henry Audley.[173] The level of control exercised by the English crown over the rulers of Powys reached a new pitch. We should however note that the channels through which that control was exercised remained largely the same, while cross-cultural ties multiplied.

It appears to have been the high-handed behaviour of the Lord Edward in the Perfeddwlad in northern Wales after he succeeded to the crown possessions in Wales in 1254 that sparked Welsh hostilities again. Though it began in the north, the Shropshire borders did not remain unaffected for long by the new outbreak of warfare. Llywelyn ap Gruffudd, the sole ruler in Gwynedd since 1255, had raided up the Severn valley and burnt Pool as early as 1257, expelling Gruffudd ap Gwenwynwyn from Wales. In 1263, however, taking advantage of the confusion in the marches caused by the return to England of Simon de Montfort, Gruffudd annexed the Gorddwr, the Welshry of the lordship of Caus, destroying the Corbet

[167] *Brut*, p. 237; *Littere Wallie*, pp. 54–8; see *AWR*, nos. 110–12, 116, 118 for the submissions of the Welsh princes of Maelienydd and Elfael, dated at Shrewsbury on 14 August 1241; see further the charters by which the native lords of Gwrtheyrnion quitclaimed their rights to that commote to Ralph Mortimer II in 1241 (published in full in J. B. Smith, 'Middle March', pp. 88–90).

[168] *Brut*, p. 245. [169] *Brut*, p. 237.

[170] *Excerpta e Rot. Finium*, ii, pp. 37–8.

[171] Lloyd, *History of Wales*, p. 709; Valle Crucis charters in *Arch. Camb.*, 1st ser., **3** (1848), pp. 228–9, and 3rd ser., **10** (1864), pp. 100–1.

[172] *Cal. Chart. R.*, i, 266. Eyton, x, 263 (Hawise L'Estrange m. to Gruffudd de la Pole); *ibid.* 274–5 cites a fragmentary charter in his possession by which Hawise, with the consent of her husband, Gruffudd, takes custody of the manor of Church Stretton during the absence on the crusade of 1270 of her brother Hamo; cf. *AWR*, nos. 602, 606–7 and especially 609.

[173] *AWR*, nos. 515–20, 526.

border stronghold of Gwyddgrug in the process.[174] By the end of the year, he was allied with Llywelyn,[175] and it is a measure of the traumatic effect which the turmoil around this time had on local society that a deed of Alberbury Priory is dated with reference to the contract between these two Welsh princes and the subsequent depredations on English-held territory.[176] In 1260, the Welsh of Ceri and Cedewain set fire to Knighton, a manor in the Teme valley disputed between Mortimer and Llywelyn; they also appear to have laid waste the bishop of Hereford's manor of Lydbury North, allegedly with the tacit assent of the constable of Montgomery, around this time.[177] Llywelyn captured Maelienydd and the Mortimer castles in the Teme valley in 1262, and had gained control of Tempseter, the Welshry of Clun, by late 1267.[178] The lord of Kinnerley, around this time, faced such pressure from Welsh attacks that he contracted with James Audley to exchange that frontier manor for lands in Staffordshire.[179]

Not only did the Shropshire borders once again fall victim to the depredations of a prince of Gwynedd; they also now increasingly became the stage for the diplomatic efforts of the English king. The traditional meeting point between Welsh and English emissaries had already begun to advance westwards during the 1220s. In October 1223, a council of Marcher lords, including John Fitzalan and Hugh Mortimer, had convened at Montgomery to receive Llywelyn's promise to restore territories captured from the English.[180] After the execution of William Braose, in 1230, it proved difficult to agree on a meeting place, the English delegate having suggested Shrewsbury, and Llywelyn Oswestry; Llywelyn's final offer to meet Ralph, the bishop of Chichester and chancellor, was Myddle, 'a place halfway between Shrewsbury and Ellesmere'.[181] A pact was concluded with Llywelyn at Myddle in 1234.[182] Later, the ford on the Severn at Rhyd Chwima, near Montgomery, replaced Shrewsbury as

[174] On the identification of Gwyddgrug castle, see especially *Cal. Close R., 1261–4*, p. 265; Spurgeon, 'Gwyddgrug Castle and the Gorddwr Dispute', *passim*; for further background, see J. B. Smith, *Llywelyn ap Gruffudd: Prince of Wales* (Cardiff, 1998), pp. 155–7; and below, pp. 158, 169, 176, 178 (n. 20), 231, 257.

[175] See the compact between Gruffudd and Llywelyn in *AWR*, nos. 358 and 601; *Littere Wallie*, pp. 77–80.

[176] Deed of Alberbury Priory of 1263: 'regnante Henrico filio regis Johannis, et Lewelyno filio Griffini tunc existente cum Griffino filio Wenunven cum exercitu non modico ad destruendum Marchiam et maxime Rogerum de Mortuomari', in H. Owen and J. B. Blakeway, *History of Shrewsbury* (1825), i, 125–6, n. 4.

[177] *Cal. Anc. Corr. Wales*, p. 16.

[178] *AWR*, nos. 365, 392; cf. *Cal. Anc. Corr. Wales*, pp. 86–7.

[179] *Cal. Inq. Misc., 1219–1307*, no. 1059. [180] *Cal. Pat R., 1216–25*, p. 411.

[181] *Royal Letters of the Reign of Henry III*, ed. Shirley, i, 366.

[182] *Cal. Pat. R., 1232–47*, p. 59; cf. *Cal. Close R., 1231–4*, pp. 568–9.

the usual site for meetings between the messengers and delegates of the English crown and the princes of Gwynedd, as, for example, in 1258–9.[183] The treaty of 1267 by which the Henry III confirmed to Llywelyn ap Gruffudd the title of prince of Wales, along with most of the wide-ranging territorial gains he had made, was sealed by a homage ceremony for which the king travelled from Shrewsbury to meet Llywelyn at Montgomery.[184] Despite the escheat of Chester to the English crown after 1237, and even though the chief princes of Wales were based in Gwynedd, Shropshire and its borders persisted as the time-honoured setting for the dealings of the king of England with the native rulers of Wales.

The settlement of 1267 at Montgomery, insofar as it was concerned with the Shropshire frontier, can hardly count as a contribution towards a peaceful solution to the conflicts affecting those borderlands. It acknowledged Llywelyn as lord by conquest of Gwrtheyrnion, Ceri and Cedewain and guaranteed him the service his predecessors had received from Whittington. However, it failed to address the burning issue of the uplands of Clun, and the framework envisaging further castle-building by Mortimer and Llywelyn in Maelienydd lit a fuse for further conflict in the area.[185]

It was not long before trouble began again. In 1274, Gruffudd ap Gwenwynwyn plotted against Llywelyn and fled from Welshpool to Shrewsbury, while Llywelyn occupied the Gorddwr.[186] This set off a series of retributive attacks by the Marcher lords over the following two years. Peter Corbet won back the Gorddwr, while Gruffudd ap Gwenwynwyn, now based in Shropshire, harried Llywelyn in Powys, and Ralph Tony seized Elfael.[187] It was probably around this time that the sons of John Fitzalan raided and destroyed the land and the court of Llywelyn ap Gruffudd Maelor of Powys Fadog.[188] The Welsh, needless to say, fought back. By 1276, Llywelyn's men were harrying the country around Montgomery and Oswestry 'by day and night', according to Bogo de Knovill, to whom Edward I had entrusted those castles; the royal serjeants at Oswestry were paid 6s 8d for restocking on arrows after repelling a Welsh attack.[189] Nevertheless, the diplomatic role of this area

[183] *Cal. Pat. R., 1258–66*, p. 27; *Cal. Close R., 1256–9*, pp. 466–7. See J. Davies, 'Rhyd Chwima, pp. 23–36.

[184] J. B. Smith, *Llywelyn*, p. 1; *AWR*, no. 363; *Littere Wallie*, no. 1.

[185] *AWR*, no. 363, p. 539; *Littere Wallie*, pp. 1–2.

[186] *Brut*, p. 261; *Cal. Close R., 1272–9*, pp. 374–5.

[187] *Cal. Close R., 1272–9*, pp. 374–5; Stephenson, 'Politics of Powys Wenwynwyn', p. 45; *AWR*, no. 386; *Cal. Anc. Corr. Wales*, pp. 27–8; *Cal. Pat. R., 1272–81*, p. 169.

[188] *AWR*, no. 535 (dated 1277 × March 1282); cf. *ibid.*, no. 534; *Cal. Anc. Corr. Wales*, p. 98.

[189] *Cal. Anc. Corr. Wales*, p. 82; TNA E 372/121, m. 21r.

remained intact, at least in principle. In 1276, Edward I claimed to have summoned Llywelyn to do homage to him 'either at Montgomery or at John Fitzalan's castle at Oswestry';[190] Bogo de Knovill twice journeyed to Wales to parley with Llywelyn in 1276–7.[191] On the other hand, in 1277 Bogo seized Kinnerley from Llywelyn, and Oswestry Castle, having been refurbished and strongly garrisoned, became the base for raids into Cynllaith as well as for exploiting the commote of Mechain after it was brought under English control.[192]

Moreover, Montgomery played a key tactical role in the royal campaign of 1276–7, in that it formed the base of the operations which forced Llywelyn to retreat from Ceri and Cedewain, and probably Tempseter and Maelienydd as well.[193] It also provided the strategic toehold backing up the siege of Llywelyn's new castle at Dolforwyn commanded by the earl of Lincoln and Roger Mortimer. Yet the Montgomery command was only one of three of Edward's lines of attack, the other two being based at Chester and Carmarthen.[194] The treaty imposing terms on Llywelyn ap Gruffudd after the end of hostilities, moreover, was concluded at Aberconwy, on the northern Welsh coast, and concerned primarily with the restitution of the Perfeddwlad to the crown, although it did also provide for the unconditional release of the hostages of Gruffudd ap Gwenwynwyn in Llywelyn's power.[195] Under the high command of Edward I, the Shropshire frontier began to play a subsidiary role within a larger, integrated military strategy.

The interlude between the two Welsh wars of Edward I was a period of very brittle peace indeed on the Shropshire borders. In 1279, Isabel Mortimer, the widow of John Fitzalan III, committed herself to paying a rent of £200 yearly to the abbey of Vale Royal in return for the custody of Oswestry Castle, a considerable sum which indicates the level of Fitzalan indebtedness to the crown, but also that war was not expected to reduce the value of the estate at that time.[196] Tensions, however, were mounting rapidly. Llywelyn ap Gruffudd Maelor, one of the lords of Powys Fadog, was suing unsuccessfully at the court of the English king in a long-standing dispute with the Fitzalans of Oswestry.[197] Llywelyn ap Gruffudd was meanwhile concentrating his efforts at rebuilding a leading position in Wales on Powys, concluding a secret treaty with Gruffudd

[190] *Rymer*, I, i, 154. [191] TNA E 372/121, m. 21r.
[192] *Ibid.*; cf. *Cal. Pat. R., 1272–81*, p. 223.
[193] *Brut*, p. 265; J. B. Smith, *Llywelyn*, p. 418.
[194] *Brut*, p. 265.
[195] *Littere Wallie*, pp. 118–22; cf. *AWR*, no. 402.
[196] *Cal. Pat. R., 1272–81*, p. 309, 311.
[197] *AWR*, nos. 534–5; *Cal. Anc. Corr. Wales*, pp. 97–8

ap Gwên of Cyfeiliog, the steward of Gruffudd ap Gwenwynwyn, in 1278.[198] The legal dispute between Llywelyn and Gruffudd over Arwystli dragged on for years after 1278, showing that the animosity between the two Welsh lords which had already created so much disturbance in the country west of Shrewsbury was still smouldering. It also gave rise to Edward I's inquisition into the laws of Wales and the March, which did much to incite Welsh resentment by displaying the English king's scepticism about Welsh law, and which involved hearings at Montgomery and Oswestry in 1281.[199] While it is true that, immediately thereafter, Llywelyn concluded a pact with his old enemy Roger Mortimer,[200] in the period leading up to the Welsh rebellion of 1282, unresolved issues involving the lords of the Powys–Shropshire borderland continued to bedevil Anglo-Welsh relations.

This became evident in March 1282, when Llywelyn ap Gruffudd Maelor led a strong force in a lightning raid on Oswestry which was co-ordinated with raids on Hawarden and in south Wales.[201] Edward I's response again made full strategic use of the Shropshire border castles, with Roger Mortimer overseeing operations involving Montgomery, Ellesmere and Oswestry until his death on 26 October 1282.[202] As Roger led the central cohort of Edward I's three-pronged attack on Llywelyn's stronghold in northern Wales, the death of the former significantly weakened that element in the royal strategy, and Edward was not a general to take such a setback lightly. On 29 October 1282, he sent the sheriff of Shropshire and Staffordshire to encourage the garrisons of Roger's castles in the king's name, and appointed Roger Lestrange, one of his most trusted lieutenants and another lord of the Shropshire borders, to Roger's command at Oswestry and Montgomery.[203] It was an astute move. Llywelyn ap Gruffudd had chosen to capitalize on the opportunity afforded by the death of one of Edward's most formidable captains by opening another front in the Wye valley. It was Roger Lestrange, from his post at Montgomery, who gathered the intelligence of Llywelyn's move southwards through Powys Wenwynwyn, and immediately took action to counter it.[204] The final episodes in the war of 1282–3 then took place

[198] *Littere Wallie*, pp. 34–5.

[199] *Cal. Chanc. R. Var.*, pp. 204–8; see the extended discussion of this period in *Welsh Assize Roll*, ed. Davies, pp. 38–86; J. B. Smith, *Llywelyn*, pp. 390–510 and R. R. Davies, *The King of England and the Prince of Wales, 1277–84: Law, Politics and Power* (Kathleen Hughes Memorial Lectures on Mediaeval Welsh History 3, Cambridge, 2002).

[200] *AWR*, no. 425; *Littere Wallie*, pp. 99–100.

[201] *Welsh Assize Roll*, ed. Davies, pp. 352–3.

[202] *Cal. Chanc. R. Var.*, pp. 244, 229.

[203] *Ibid.*, p. 256; *Cal. Anc. Corr. Wales*, p. 65.

[204] *Ibid.*, p. 84; J. B. Smith, *Llywelyn*, pp. 550–67.

in Builth, where Llywelyn ap Gruffudd was killed, and at Castell-y-Bere in western Merioneth, where Dafydd ap Gruffudd made his last stand. But the opening Welsh attacks, as well as Edward I's strategy and choice of lieutenants, had revived, for the last time, the military dimension of the Shropshire frontier.

* * *

The conquest of Wales in 1282–3 concluded an epoch in 'Anglo-Welsh relations'. By imposing direct royal control over *pura Wallia*, it finally succeeded where a series of royal campaigns had failed. On an even longer-term view, the effect of the last Welsh war of Edward I appears yet more momentous. The constellation of power on what became the Powys–Shropshire frontier had remained fundamentally unchanged since the days of the Mercian settlers. The age during which the March of Wales took shape, in that sense, belonged to a chapter in the history of Anglo-Welsh relations which was concluded in 1282–3, but began long before the Normans arrived in the British Isles.

A distinctive political situation therefore persisted throughout the period between the late eleventh century and the close of the thirteenth. Nevertheless, there seems to be no clear-cut answer to the question of how distinctive, in narrowly military terms, the Shropshire borders were during this period. It may be regarded as certain that neither the threat of frontier warfare nor its actual incidence remained equally acute throughout the whole period. It is very probable that the Shropshire borders saw vastly more intense frontier warfare during the age of the Montgomery inroads, between about 1070 and 1102, and during the reign of Stephen, from the mid-1130s to the mid-1150s, than during the reigns of Henry I and Henry II. It is also clear that, even along the Shropshire frontier, which represented only a section of the March of Wales, fighting between English and Welsh was considerably more recurrent in some places than in others. Any generalizations, under such circumstances, must be bold. However, generalizations may still be useful by way of conclusion, and also because the ultimate purpose of this discussion is to compare the Shropshire–Powys frontier both with other parts of the Welsh March and with the county of Shropshire.

To this end, it may be suggested that the threat and actual incidence of frontier warfare on the Shropshire–Powys borders between about 1070 and 1283 was, indeed, so persistent as to contribute considerably towards distinguishing the borders from the county. The March of Wales, did, in the event, become increasingly clearly defined as a land of war, especially after 1102, when the earldom of Shrewsbury lapsed and a military stalemate was created between the frontier lords and the Welsh princes of Powys. Crucially, however, the issues giving rise to border warfare, as well as the scope and intensity of those hostilities, were extremely varied and became transformed over the two hundred years or so under consideration.

The Powys frontier was, on the whole, not the most violent part of the Welsh borders. The reasons for this varied over time. The chief ones have been touched upon repeatedly. Firstly, the Montgomery forfeiture of 1102 meant that no locally based and strong Norman or English force pursued conquests west of Shropshire, with the exception, at the southern limit of the Shropshire frontier, of the Mortimers of Wigmore. Secondly, Powys was one of the most fragmented of the Welsh kingdoms and, even at times when it achieved a measure of unity, its lords were more inclined to ally themselves with the English king against rival Welsh kingdoms than to press for territorial gains to the east. Thirdly, after 1102 and throughout the period under consideration, the forfeited Montgomery lands of Shropshire formed the largest and, crucially, most permanently held concentration of royal lands on any part of the Welsh frontier.

Although this meant that the majority of royal campaigns launched against Wales between 1102 and 1283 involved Shrewsbury and the Shropshire frontier fortresses, it also led to the focus of a singularly sustained royal diplomatic effort on the region. On a long-term view, armed conflict or warfare hardly ever determined Anglo-Welsh relations to the exclusion of other forms of cross-cultural interaction. Admittedly, apart from some crucial periods of *détente*, hostilities were indeed singularly apt to erupt on the frontier. Moreover, it was the destructive border raids which remained etched in people's memories, and became closely associated with the concept of the *marche* in such border epics as *Fouke le Fitz Waryn* and the Mortimer family chronicle. Yet a separate, equally important, strand in Anglo-Welsh relations was intertwined with the military one from the beginning to the end of the period under consideration. From the alliances contracted by the Montgomery earls of Shrewsbury with the descendants of Bleddyn ap Cynfyn, through Richard de Beaumais' manipulative diplomacy conducted from his headquarters at Shrewsbury, to the symbolic ceremony in 1267 at the ford on the Severn near Montgomery, the Shropshire frontier remained an inter-cultural political interface. Frontier parleys and treaties, between *c.* 1070 and the end of Welsh independence at the close of the thirteenth century, were as much a part of this frontierland as border raids, territorial conquest and royal campaigns. Each of these two strands was more dominant at some times than at others. But, throughout the period under consideration, both need to be taken into account. The purpose of this discussion has been to analyse how far the concept of the March of Wales was a product of Anglo-Welsh relations. It has shown that the Shropshire borders frequently played a military role during the two centuries which intervened between the Norman conquest of England and Edward I's conquest of Wales, but also that they became established as political, diplomatic and symbolic frontierlands.

Chapter 4

THE EXTENT AND NATURE OF THE MILITARY FRONTIER

As we have seen, Earl Roger apportioned the westernmost hundreds of his county almost wholesale to his chief followers, Corbet, Warin and Picot de Sai respectively, while he himself built the key castle of Montgomery and retained the surrounding territory, termed a *castellaria* in Domesday Book, in demesne.[1] This particular dispensation of lands formed the mould within which the individual Marcher lordships adjoining Shropshire were to be cast. However, it would be too hasty simply to equate the military frontier zone with the extent of the westernmost hundreds of Shropshire. For one thing, it may be doubted that the men who originally concentrated their military resources here thought they were creating a permanent military frontier. Given the momentum which, it was argued earlier,[2] characterized the Norman advance into Wales, it seems, indeed, probable that the castleries were ad hoc arrangements, to be abandoned once further conquests had been completed. The strategy of grabbing compact tracts of land and organizing them for the defence of a castle was, after all, the tried and tested manner of territorial conquest of Earl Roger's contemporaries. Indeed, Robert of Rhuddlan's conquests in northern Wales have been described as paradigmatic of how the Norman landed settlement advanced in England.[3] The frontier hundreds of Shropshire were not necessarily intended to be a permanent, 'national' military frontier.

The notion that Earl Roger did act primarily to defend the English frontier is a beguiling one for historians. The explanation for this is in part furnished by the state of the evidence. For as it happened, the Shropshire castleries fell within the range of William I's great inquest of 1086. The

[1] See Map 4, p. 25, and above, pp. 59–68. The ways in which the first Norman earls of Chester, Hereford and Shrewsbury distributed the lands among their followers have been authoritatively discussed by C. P. Lewis in his Oxford thesis, 'English and Norman Government and Lordship in the Welsh Borders, 1039–1087' (University of Oxford DPhil thesis, 1985); see also Holden, *Lords*, pp. 32–6.
[2] Above, pp. 108–11. [3] Le Patourel, *The Norman Empire*, pp. 313–15.

tenurial aspect of the castleries therefore became enshrined in the folios of Domesday Book, while the impetus still driving the Norman invasion of Wales from Shropshire appears only in the shape of more or less ambitious claims to tribute from Welsh principalities. When considering the highly detailed, but static, evidence of this monumental source, it is all too easy to forget that the military frontier with Wales had not been fixed by the 1080s. As has been argued, the Anglo-Welsh military border even looked set to be eliminated in the 1070s and 1080s,[4] when the Normans based in Shropshire were leading raids across Wales as far as Anglesey and the Llŷn peninsula. To assume that the frontier hundreds were intended to confirm a territorial *status quo* in western Shropshire may therefore be seriously misleading, because it suggests that the March of Wales was created as a military frontier region purposefully, at one stroke, and successfully.

There may be an element of truth in such a view. After all, the tenurial concentrations on the Shropshire borders did, in part, have a military function. However, in order to assess what role was played by specific military challenges in creating the concept of the March of Wales, we have to take into account the whole period of frontier warfare. That period, as argued in the previous chapter, truly began in the 1090s, as the Norman impetus was met with effective resistance by the Welsh, and continued, not without significant interruptions, until the conquest of Wales in 1282–3. An assessment of the extent and character of the military frontier in western Shropshire during that time is, however, beset with even greater problems of documentation. This is because, for the Shropshire frontier in the twelfth century, contemporary documentation is not so much misleading as lacking almost entirely. Moreover, for the thirteenth century the documentation overwhelmingly presents the point of view of the English crown, and naturally emphasizes the periods when the king took a direct interest in the Welsh frontier, while probably misrepresenting the actual incidence of local border warfare.[5] Even though we may, fortunately, also draw on archaeological evidence and the annalistic entries, we face intimidating problems of documentation in attempting to discuss where exactly, and at what times, the population of Shropshire and the borders had to meet military challenges of a specific frontier nature, and how far it responded to those challenges in such a way as to create a distinctive border society.

* * *

[4] Above, pp. 108–11. [5] Above, pp. 125–35.

THE EXTENT AND NATURE OF THE MILITARY FRONTIER, *c.* 1070–1283: SOME GENERAL REMARKS

A great number of castles were built in Shropshire and the borders between about 1070 and the end of the thirteenth century: the remains of about 170 have survived. Moreover, much valuable work has been done on them. In particular, A. H. A. Hogg and D. J. C. King have examined the castles of Wales and the March collectively, on the basis of the documentary and archaeological evidence, in order to discover whether they were in use as defensive structures before or after 1215.[6] Additionally, the dense distribution of twelfth- and thirteenth-century castles in Glamorgan, Gwynllŵg and Gower has recently been analysed in the light of the advance and consolidation of Norman control by military might in an enduringly hostile country.[7] The spread of castles in Shropshire and the borders clearly provides an essential type of evidence for discussing the making of a distinctive military frontier zone between Shropshire and Wales.

Just as the preceding chronological discussion of the episodes of Anglo-Welsh relations affecting the Shropshire borders needed to strike a balance between the diplomatic and the military dimensions, an analysis of the castle evidence needs to pay due attention to non-military uses of castles. A survey of the distribution of castles in Shropshire and Herefordshire illustrates this point. The spread of the early castles of Shropshire is similar to that of Herefordshire, and may therefore be considered typical of the English counties bordering on Wales.[8] In both cases, castles are far thicker on the ground in the western half of the county, while the area around

[6] Hogg and King, 'Early Castles'; the same, 'Castles in Wales and the Marches: Additions and Corrections', *Arch. Camb.*, **119** (1970), pp. 119–24. The list of Wales and the March may be supplemented by the survey of the whole county of Shropshire in King, *Castellarium Anglicanum*, ii, 419–40; M. Salter, *The Castles and Moated Mansions of Shropshire* (Wolverhampton, 1988); and M. Jackson, *Castles of Shropshire* (Shrewsbury, 1988). I would like to thank Mr M. D. Watson of the Shropshire County Council Archaeology Service for advising me that at present no other updated overview of castle studies in Shropshire has been published (by letter of 18 March 2003). I would like to thank Mr C. J. Spurgeon for pointing out that information on work published on individual castles since the appearance of King's *Castellarium Anglicanum* may be obtained through J. R. Kenyon, *Castles, Town Defences, and Artillery Fortifications in Britain: A Bibliography*, vols. ii and iii (London, 1983 and 1990). I would like to thank Mr J. R. Kenyon for drawing my attention to the *Castle Studies Group Newsletter*.

[7] For the period before 1217 (when the lordship of Glamorgan came into the possession of the Clare family), see Royal Commission on the Ancient and Historical Monuments of Wales (RCAHMW), *An Inventory of the Ancient Monuments in Glamorgan*, vol. iii, part 1a: *Medieval Secular Monuments: The Early Castles – From the Norman Conquest to 1217* (London, 1991), pp. 7–20; for the period 1217–*c.* 1300, see RCAHMW, *An Inventory of the Ancient Monuments in Glamorgan*, vol. iii, part 1b: *Medieval Secular Monuments. The Later Castles – From 1217 to the Present* (Aberystwyth, 2000), pp. 2–6.

[8] See Map 11, on following page; King, *Castellarium Anglicanum*, ii, 419; Hogg and King, 'Early Castles'.

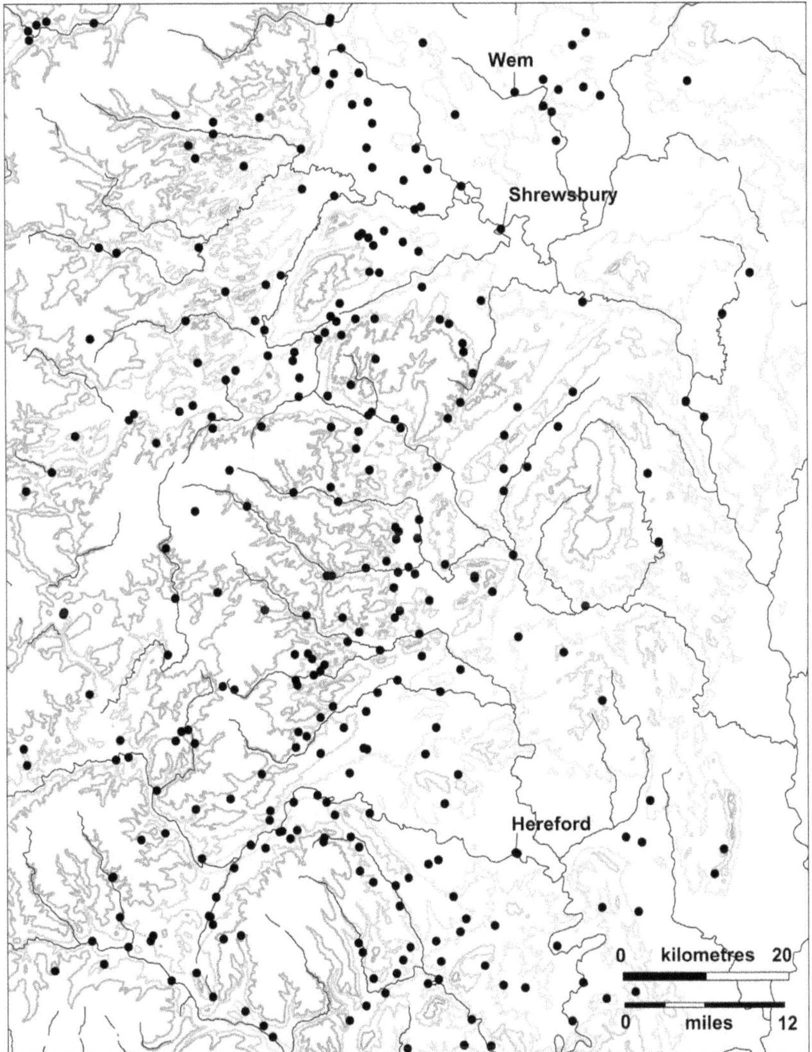

Map 11. The early castles of Shropshire and Herefordshire (to 1215)

the main town is bare of mottes. Thus, it certainly appears at first sight that the construction of castles in great numbers was a typical 'frontier' response to warfare before 1215.

However, on further examination, we may begin to doubt how reliably the spread of castles reflects the extent of the belt of land which suffered most from distinctive forms of border warfare such as plundering raids or territorial disputes. For one thing, there is a concentration of castles north-east of Shrewsbury, around Wem, while no early castles survive in the area to the west of the county town. Given that the latter district must surely have been at greater risk from border raids than Wem, it would appear that such exposure was not the only factor determining where most castles were built. Since Wem was held from the late eleventh century onwards by the Pantulf family,[9] it seems possible to suggest that, around Wem, seigneurial initiative and remoteness from the comital or royal centre offer alternative explanations for castle density to that of the specific challenges of a military frontier. This means that we need to discuss how far similar reasons might explain the density of castles on the western border. Moreover, castles were not constructed exclusively for military purposes during this period. Despite the heavy emphasis on the military purposes of castles in much of modern historiography, it is quite clear that many of the castles in the British Isles were built as a result of other motivations: as administrative or residential centres, as symbols of prestige or of lordship, or for any number of individual concerns which varied widely with date and locality. It is equally clear that the purpose of individual castles could be redefined over time.[10] Recent archaeological work has called into question the strategic purpose of many of the castles constructed by the English in Ireland in the later twelfth century.[11] Moreover, it has come to be recognized that military threats alone do not sufficiently explain the establishment of fortified settlements in Continental Europe. Settlement studies have shown that *incastellamento* in Italy and *encellulement* in France were underpinned by gradual socio-economic developments, especially population growth and the intensified exploitation of economic resources by landlords who were both lay and ecclesiastical.[12] It cannot be assumed that the distribution of castles on the Anglo-Welsh frontier coincides with

[9] Sanders, *English Baronies*, pp. 94–5.

[10] C. L. H. Coulson, *Castles in Medieval Society* (Oxford, 2003) provides a sustained critique of the military emphasis of castle-studies, see esp. pp. 1–2, 29–63; see also N. J. G. Pounds, *The Medieval Castle in England and Wales: A Social and Political History* (Cambridge, 1994), pp. 11–15; J. R. Kenyon, *Medieval Fortifications* (Leicester, 1990), part 2 (chs. 5–9) surveys domestic structures in medieval castles, such as halls, kitchens and chapels; see review by F. Verhaege in *Archéologie Médievale*, **23** (1993), pp. 531–3.

[11] T. E. McNeill, *Castles in Ireland: Feudal Power in a Gaelic World* (London, 1997), pp. 75–8; T. B. Barry, *The Archaeology of Medieval Ireland* (London, 1987), p. 37.

[12] For a succinct survey of the historiography on the *incastellamento* see C. Wickham, 'The *terra* of San Vincenzo al Volturno in the 8th to 12th Centuries: The Historical Framework', in R. Hodges and J. Mitchell (eds.), *San Vincenzo al Volturno: The Archaeology, Art and Territory of an Early Medieval Monastery* (Oxford, 1985), pp. 227–58; for the debates on *encellulement* see R. Fossier, *L'Enfance de l'Europe, Xe–XIIe siècles: Aspects économiques et sociaux* (Paris, 1982); D. Barthélémy and O. Bruand (eds.), *Les Pouvoirs locaux dans la France du centre et de l'ouest (VIIIe–XIe siècles): implantation et moyens d'action* (Rennes, 2004).

a military border region. Only a detailed discussion of the purpose of the castles at different times may indicate how important specific military challenges and responses were in creating a distinctive Marcher region between England and Wales.

The Welsh frontier emerges more clearly as distinct from both central and eastern Shropshire if the distribution of the mottes is considered in terms of their strength. It now becomes apparent that the strongest mottes were built where they could serve primarily as weapons of frontier warfare with the Welsh.[13]

Moreover, we may be highly confident in dating this particular type of castle to the comital period or to the early part of the reign of Henry I at the latest. The distribution of castles which can be dated on documentary evidence to that period is shown on Map 13. The earliest documented castles of Shropshire show that one strategic concern was to guard the approach to Shrewsbury from central England. Nevertheless, the distribution of the datable strong mottes at Oswestry, Wigmore and Richard's Castle does reflect a clear orientation towards Wales. As has been seen, the Gro Tump, a formidable motte, very probably marks an advance beyond Hen Domen Montgomery by Earl Roger and his men.[14] The strong mottes in Herefordshire also convey the impression that this type of castle was associated with a move westwards. The earlier, Richard's Castle, thought to be the first Norman motte in the British Isles, lies to the east of the castle built on a comparable scale at Wigmore, most probably by William fitz Osbern.[15] The pattern is, of course, not universally applicable. Hen Domen, after all, must have represented an advance beyond Caus, but is of a weaker type.[16] We are also well advised to remember that the surviving castle evidence, especially when it comes to assessing size, probably reflects the original situation very imperfectly. What can be said is that the castle evidence, in the state in which it survives, reinforces the argument that the Normans were concentrating their

[13] See Map 12. The map in Salter, *Castles and Moated Mansions*, inside back cover, does not date the castles, and classes them differently, but illustrates a similar concentration of mottes, and in particular strong mottes, in western Shropshire. See King, *Castellarium Anglicanum*, i, lxiv. Shrewsbury is classified as a masonry castle (*ibid.*, ii, 430) and therefore does not appear on Map 12.

[14] See Maps 10 and 12; Spurgeon, 'Castles of Montgomeryshire', pp. 30–1.

[15] Richard's Castle has been identified with the *castellaria* or *castellum* of *Aureton* of DB 185b, 186d respectively; see P. E. Curnow and M. W. Thompson, 'Excavations at Richard's Castle, Herefordshire', *Journal of the British Archaeological Association*, 3rd ser., 32 (1969), p. 106. DB 183c attributes the building of Wigmore castle to William fitz Osbern, earl of Hereford 1067–71; see Renn, 'First Norman Castles in England', p. 129; C. G. Harfield, 'A Hand-List of Castles Recorded in the Domesday Book', *EHR*, **106** (1991), pp. 377–8.

[16] The groundbreaking study of Hen Domen Montgomery has recently been published in its final form: Higham and Barker, *Hen Domen Montgomery. A Final Report.*

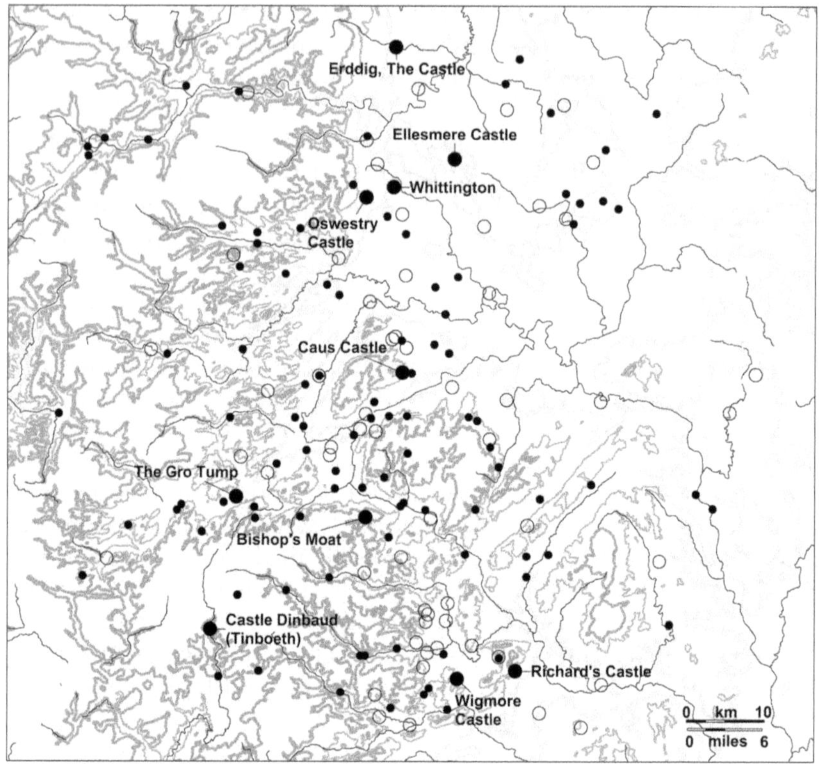

● Classified by Cathcart-King as motte type E1: 'earthworks of exceptionally fine type'

• Classified as E2: 'earthwork of average strength'

○ Classified as E3: 'feeble or damaged earthworks'

Map 12. Mottes in Shropshire and the Welsh borders: relative strengths

military resources in the west of Shropshire in the late eleventh and early twelfth centuries.

This concentration invites comparison with another line of strong castles, that formed by the fortifications which William fitz Osbern built (or in the case of Ewyas Harold, rebuilt) in the late 1060s.[17] The chief mottes on the Shropshire–Powys border came, in effect, to form a continuation of a line of fortifications which extended just over 160 kilometres northwards from Chepstow. William's castles almost certainly pre-date all

[17] See Map 14, below, p. 146. William is recorded in Domesday Book as having built the castles of Chepstow, also called Strigoil (DB 162), of Clifford (DB 183) and of Wigmore (DB 183); and as having refortified Ewyas Harold (DB 186).

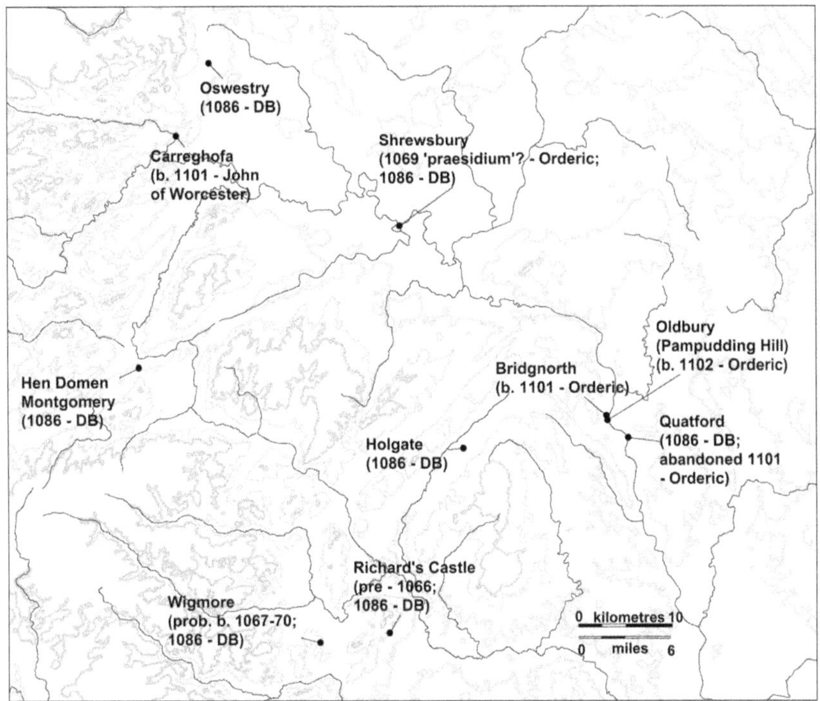

Map 13. Shropshire castles datable to before 1102

of those built by Earl Roger de Montgomery and his men. They would thus have provided a precedent which established the Welsh border as the primary military concern.

This curtain of castles drawn across the Anglo-Welsh borders is comparable to the remarkable distribution of the mottes which are known to have been built by the English in Ireland, in the lordship of Meath, in the thirty years or so after Henry II's grant to Hugh de Lacy of 'the land of Meath with all its appurtenances' in 1172.[18] About 100 mottes have survived in Meath, and some of them must be contemporary with those which are securely datable to 1172–1210. However, the latter are thought to be the most important, and it has been suggested that they represent successive stages in the initial, military occupation of land, successive frontiers formed by the settlement of de Lacy men further and further inland.[19] The documented castles of the middle and lower Boyne,

[18] *Calendar of the Gormanston Register c. 1157–1397*, ed. J. Mills and M. J. McEnery (Dublin, 1916), p. 177.

[19] B. J. Graham, 'The Mottes of the Norman Liberty of Meath', in H. Murtagh (ed.), *Irish Midland Studies. Essays in Commemoration of N. W. English* (Athlone, 1980), p. 47; B. J. Graham, 'Twelfth

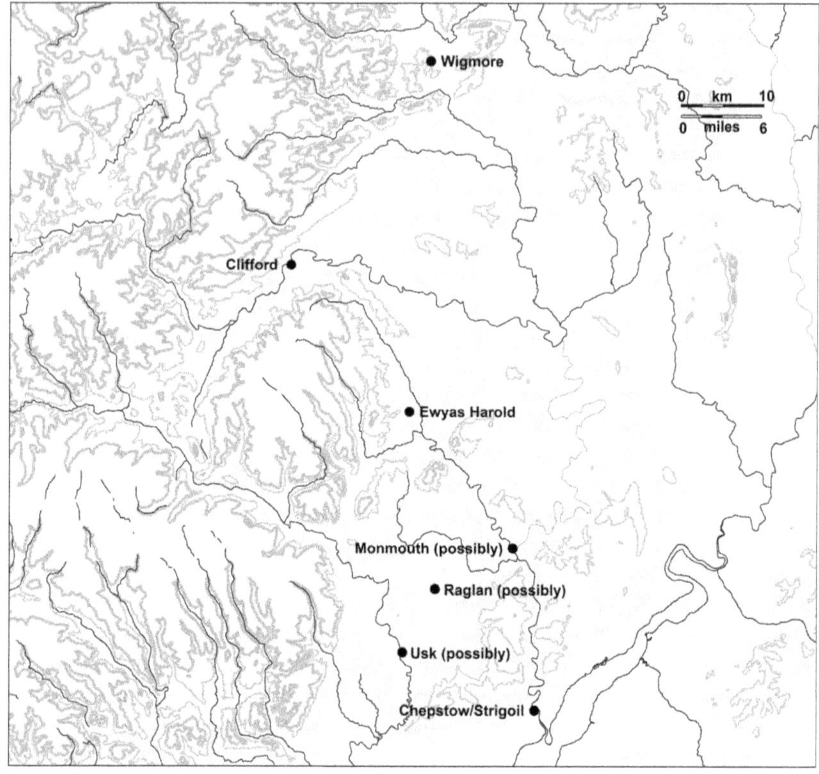

Map 14. Border castles certainly or possibly built or rebuilt by William fitz Osbern (d. 1071 in Flanders)

such as Trim, are mentioned from the 1170s; here, non-fortified seats of men enfeoffed by de Lacy abounded. It also seems possible to discern two later lines of fortifications further west, one on a north-south line at Clonard and one at Durrow (where Hugh was decapitated by an Irishman in 1186).[20] It has been argued that the lordship of Meath was conceived as 'open-ended', and that Hugh de Lacy considered he had been given licence to push the western limits of his new lordship as far as he was able. This view of the Meath castles is not uncontroversial. The distribution of Hugh de Lacy's fortifications was clearly determined by

and Thirteenth-Century Earthwork Castles in Ireland: An Assessment', *Fortress*, **9** (1991), p. 29; R. Bartlett, 'Colonial Aristocracies of the High Middle Ages', in the same and A. Mackay (eds.), *Medieval Frontier Societies* (Oxford, 1989), pp. 31–4.

[20] Bartlett, 'Colonial Aristocracies', pp. 31, 33; *The Annals of Loch Cé: A Chronicle of Irish Affairs, 1014–1690*, ed. W. M. Hennessy, 2 vols. (RS, 1871), i, 173–5.

his propensity for building them within the precincts of major church sites.[21] Moreover, Thomas McNeill has questioned whether these lines of mottes could have provided effective shelter from Irish raiders; and he has argued that mottes tended to be concentrated on the borders of lordships in Ireland after, rather than during, the processes of landed conquest by which those lordships were established.[22] The castles in Meath, then, have been seen both as instruments and as results of conquest.

Comparing the Welsh border castles with those in eastern Ireland in the twelfth century is clearly relevant to this debate on the purpose of Irish castles. However, such a comparison appears in some respects inconclusive. William fitz Osbern's castles shows that strong border fortifications could be erected very quickly, which may support the view that the mottes in Meath were erected while conquest of land was still underway there. However, as will be seen, the accumulation of important castles on the Welsh borders, other than when overseen by William fitz Osbern, took time. It is impossible to gauge accurately how far the Montgomeries faced in Wales in the 1070s and 1080s challenges similar to those of Hugh de Lacy and his men in Meath a century later. But it is not inconceivable that the challenges were comparable. It may be recalled that Earl Hugh of Shrewsbury met his end near Anglesey at the hands of the Vikings in 1098, almost ninety years before Hugh de Lacy's decapitation at Durrow. Moreover, Durrow is about eighty kilometres from the Irish coast, and it is only slightly longer to ride from Shrewsbury to the Welsh coast by way of Hen Domen and the upper Severn valley. It took Hugh de Lacy fourteen years, from Henry II's grant of Meath to him in 1172 until his death in 1186, to establish his furthest line of castles. This supports the view that the castles west of Hen Domen do indeed date to the 1070s and 1080s. It is probably true to say that the distribution of documented castles in Meath does make it safer to assume that the Montgomeries and their men raided up the Severn valley at the same time as they entrenched their position in Shropshire, and perhaps even before. Furthermore, both in Shropshire and in Meath, the strongest castles formed lines and corresponded to the settlement of fief-holders. Thus, it certainly seems possible that, early on, some of the strong castles on the Welsh borders were intended to consolidate a stage in a conquest that was expected to progress further westwards. The situation as it existed there by *c.* 1215 may therefore

[21] See Graham, 'Earthwork Castles in Ireland', p. 29; T. M. Charles-Edwards, 'Ireland and its Invaders, 1166–1186', *Quaestio Insularis*, **4** (2003), pp. 1–34.

[22] McNeill, *Castles in Ireland*, pp. 68, 75–8; the same, *Anglo-Norman Ulster: The History and Archaeology of an Irish Barony, 1177–1400* (Edinburgh, 1980), pp. 69–70.

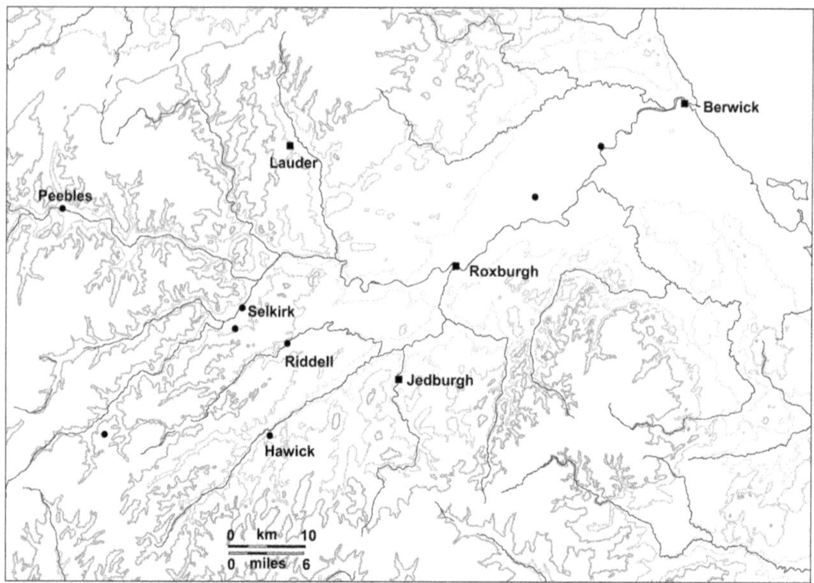

Map 15. Castles and mottes in the Tweed Valley

have been the result of a combination of offensive and defensive castle-building.

The distribution of mottes in Scotland also has interesting implications for our interpretation of the castles of the Welsh borders. Grant Simpson and Bruce Webster have provided maps of mottes, together with castles which can be dated to before 1249, for the Tweed valley and for south-west Scotland (especially Galloway).[23] The stark difference in motte density between the Welsh border counties and the Tweed valley is immediately apparent. It is only slightly further from Berwick to Peebles than from Hereford to Shrewsbury, but in the depicted section of the Scottish Border only eight mottes have so far been located.[24] This was partly due to a dearth of military frontier castles of the kind which, it seems, were built in Shropshire and in Meath. Norman and English settlement in south-eastern Scotland proceeded, during the twelfth

[23] Map 15 is based on G. G. Simpson and B. Webster, 'Charter Evidence and the Distribution of Mottes in Scotland', in K. J. Stringer (ed.), *Essays on the Nobility of Medieval Scotland* (Edinburgh, 1985), p. 8 (fig. 6).

[24] G. Stell, 'Provisional List of Mottes in Scotland', in Stringer (ed.), *Essays on the Nobility of Medieval Scotland*, pp. 16, 20–1.

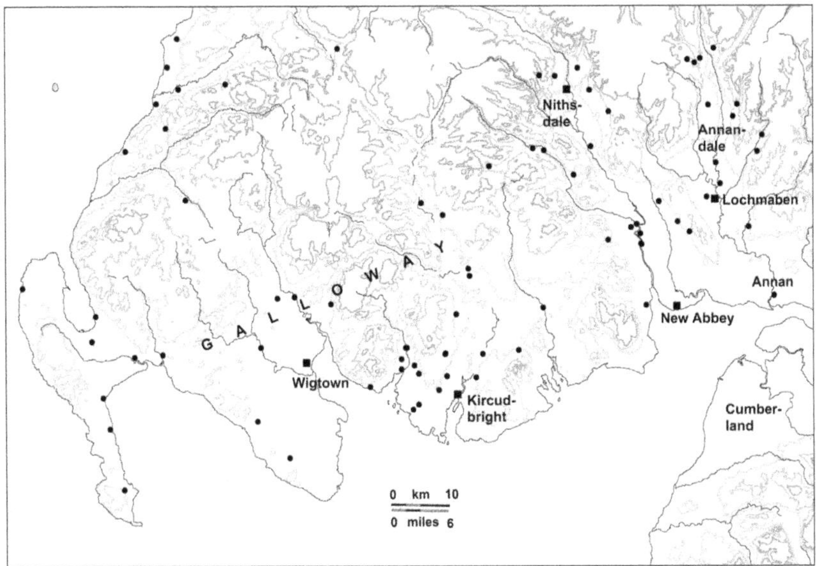

Map 16. Castles and mottes in south-west Scotland

century, by the invitation of the Scots kings, and the Tweed valley was predominantly 'an area of administrative castles'.[25]

By contrast, the map of south-western Scotland shows a dramatically greater density of mottes. Documentary evidence which can be associated with these mottes suggests that they were the result of the settlement of Normans and Englishmen in a hostile environment. This was particularly true of those which can be dated to about 1161–85. At that time, the Scots king was encouraging Anglo-Continental military settlers to infiltrate Galloway, which was then ruled as an almost independent principality by a native dynasty. Although even Galloway cannot rival the motte density of the Shropshire–Powys borders or of Meath, its early castles suggest that mottes were thicker on the ground where they needed to be built quickly, by local fief-holders engaged in territorial conquest. As will be seen, this may well provide a useful tool for the interpretation of a number of the mottes in the Welsh marches.

As for the later castles of Shropshire, the following map shows that the fortifications in Shropshire and the March in use between 1215 and 1307 were equally not restricted to the borders. One specific type, the surviving

[25] Map 16 is based on Simpson and Webster, 'Charter Evidence and Mottes', p. 9 (fig. 7).

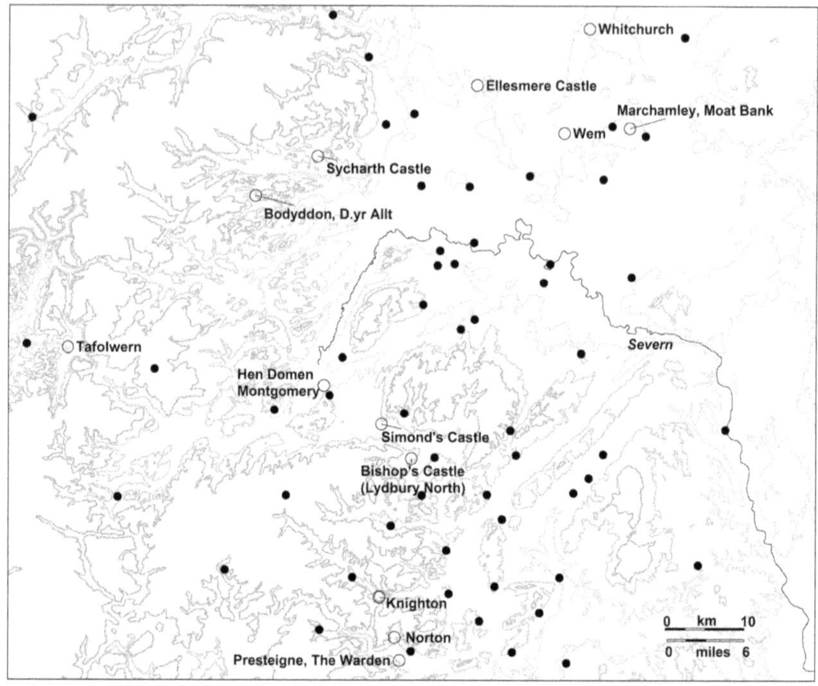

Map 17. Later castles in Shropshire and the Welsh borders

timber castle, reflects the distribution of the earlier castles, in that it is most common along the geographical frontier, where the land was higher, and around Wem. It is true that the distribution of surviving timber castles is particularly likely to come under revision through excavation, if masonry is uncovered, or if the survival of further timber castles after 1215 is proved, as at Hen Domen Montgomery.[26] Hen Domen shows that frontier concerns might help to ensure the survival of timber castles until the end of the thirteenth century. Even after the building of a strong masonry castle on a rocky outcrop above Montgomery in the early 1220s, Hen Domen was maintained as a strategic outpost, probably because it afforded better views of the Vale of Montgomery and because it lay near the ford on

[26] On the excavation of masonry see P.A. Barker, 'Pontesbury Castle Mound, Emergency Excavations, 1961', *TSAS*, **57** (1961–4), pp. 206–23; W. G. Snape, 'Excavation of a Motte and Bailey at Ryton, Shifnal', *TSAS*, **57** (1961–4), pp. 191–3. The archaeological evidence indicating that the timber castle at Hen Domen survived from the late eleventh to the late thirteenth century is summarized in Higham and Barker, *Hen Domen Montgomery. A Final Report*, pp. 13–14 and 159–63.

the Severn which became one of the most important meeting points of English and Welsh embassies during the thirteenth century.[27]

Hen Domen Montgomery, regardless of its fabric, was clearly important as a military and political frontier site throughout the period 1070–1284, a fact that is established on the basis of archaeological and historical evidence. It may be pointed out that its position, near a ford on the river Severn and in the centre of the Montgomeryshire gap, could not have been more symbolic of the Anglo-Welsh border. The case-studies which follow now provide a way of discussing which other Shropshire castles fulfilled a military frontier function, starting with the other key fortresses in the Vale of Montgomery.

THE MILITARY FRONTIER, *c.* 1070–1283, I: THE LORDSHIPS OF CAUS AND OF MONTGOMERY

It is just possible to discern the advance of the Norman military frontier through Rhiwset and Whittery hundreds, between Shrewsbury and Montgomery. The probable original site of Corbet's castle, the ringwork at Hawcock's Mount, already represented a foothold beyond an old English military frontier post.[28] Westbury, a village whose D-shaped street layout and name show it to have been, originally, a frontier settlement with military defences, was quite possibly the Westbury where an English border patrol was killed by a band of Welsh raiders in 1053.[29] Corbet's lands thus originally, albeit probably only for a brief period, represented the vanguard in Earl Roger's conquest operation, possibly holding the position while the new castle at Shrewsbury was being built and the next step was being scouted out. That step was undertaken by building the timber castle at Hen Domen Montgomery and further mottes in the upper Severn valley. Hen Domen's bailey was probably already strongly defended by a clay rampart, ditch and palisade, a pole-supported fighting platform and possibly towers. There also appear to have been a tower on the motte, and a bridge leading up to it.[30] Hawcock's Mount may have continued to play a strategic role, controlling communications

[27] P. A. Barker and R. Higham, *Hen Domen Montgomery: A Timber Castle on the English–Welsh Border* (London, 1982), p. 20. The simultaneous occupation of Hen Domen and New Montgomery castles was shown by the discovery of similar pottery at both sites: *ibid.*, p. 81; Higham and Barker, *Hen Domen Montgomery. A Final Report*, pp. 161–2.

[28] R. Higham and P. A. Barker, *Timber Castles* (London, 1992), pp. 27–8.

[29] *Saxon Chronicles*, i, 184 (Anglo-Saxon Chronicle, C version (Abingdon Chronicle), *sub anno*). The English killed are described as 'guardian men'. The reference could also be to Westbury-on-Severn in Gloucestershire, near the Forest of Dean.

[30] Higham and Barker, *Hen Domen Montgomery. A Final Report*, pp. 13–14, 35–40, 65–70 and 163.

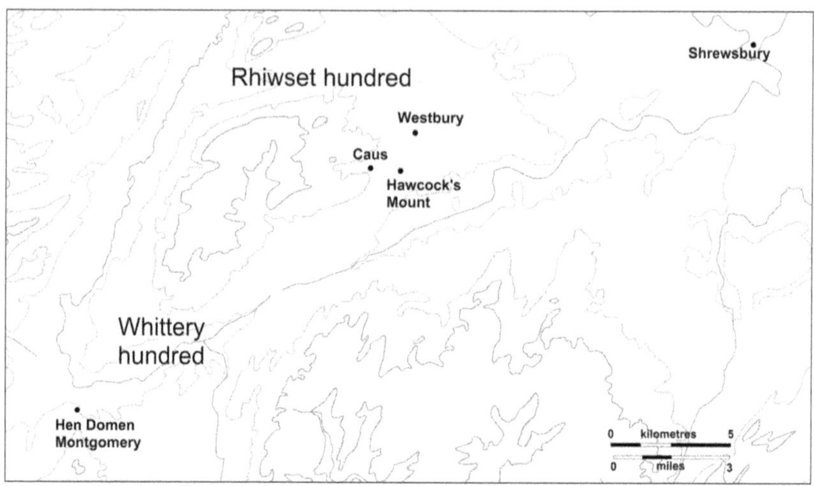

Map 18. The context of the Corbet castles, late eleventh century

and keeping open supply lines for the military operations further west. However, it seems that, when the Montgomery *castellaria* to the west of Rhiwset was established, the need for the military defence of the area was considered to be less imperative. For one thing, the Corbet castlery was no longer kept intact – by 1086 Corbet's lands had been split between his two sons, Roger and Robert.[31] The structure at Hawcock's Mount probably did originally have a strategic purpose, yet it may soon have been converted primarily into the social, judicial and administrative centre of the Corbet estate.

The fortification at Caus very probably replaced Hawcock's Mount, since the name 'Hawcock' derives from 'Old Caus'.[32] It has often been stated that Caus parallels Montgomery in being named after the Norman homeland of its builders,[33] and this might suggest an early date for the transfer of the castle's site. As against this, it was argued above that the Corbets' ancestral home did not lie in the Pays de Caux, but in the Gouffern.[34] Recent place-name studies have also cast doubt on the traditional etymology of 'Caus'.[35] Moreover, the name 'Caus' is first mentioned

[31] DB 255c–256b; above, p. 60.

[32] *VCH*, viii, 300, 303; Gelling, *Place-Names. Part 2*, p. 58, citing the Longleat MSS. The field-name 'Aldecaus' is attested for 1361.

[33] Eyton, vii, 6; *VCH*, viii, 308. [34] Above, pp. 63–5.

[35] Gelling, *Place-Names. Part 2*, pp. 56–7, deems the most probable derivation to be from Old French *caus*, modern *chaux*, 'chalk, lime', possibly referring to materials used in building the castle; Morgan, *Welsh Place-Names*, p. 21, notes that disyllabic contemporary spellings with infixed -r- such as 'Caures' may show a Welsh influence (Welsh *cawres*, 'giantess').

by Orderic, in the passage referring to the burning of the castle in 1134.[36] Conceivably, Orderic was referring to the motte at Hawcock's Mount, and it could therefore be argued that the new castle was built to replace that structure after the reign of Henry I. Despite these objections, it seems reasonable to suggest an earlier date for the construction of the second Caus castle. The move of the Corbet centre was evidently dictated by considerations of defence. The formidable motte on the hilltop above Hawcock's Mount was built on a scale comparable to the most powerful earth-and-timber castles on the Shropshire and Herefordshire frontier; and as has been seen, many of these are documented before 1102.[37] The new site was apparently chosen to take advantage of the protection afforded by the remains of an Iron Age hillfort.[38] The need for a good defensive position clearly outweighed that for accessibility. Thus, the borough which grew up within the bailey of Caus Castle began to shrink soon after Edward I's Welsh wars removed its *raison d'être* as a safe haven for commerce.[39] The castle and borough at Caus were, in origin, products of a defensive military frontier. This would suggest a date for the castle's initial construction during or soon after the 1090s, when it became evident that the Welsh principalities lying a mere fifteen kilometres or so to the west would remain strategic challenges to be reckoned with for the foreseeable future.

The same is clearly true of most of the mottes in the valley of the Rea and Camlad rivers, the Vale of Montgomery. A majority of these mottes are of a striking steep-sided type with flat tops only about eight to fifteen metres in diameter.[40] On account of their distinctive shape and the fact that they were all associated with small settlements, D. J. C. King and C. J. Spurgeon suggested, in an influential article, that these mottes were designed according to a single master plan for 'the settlement or resettlement' of 'small military tenants', most probably in the days of the Montgomery earls of Shrewsbury.[41] It should be noted that Domesday Book is of limited help in identifying their purpose. The meaning of 'waste' in the survey is uncertain,[42] and so therefore is the case for seeing the Vale mottes as part of a strategy of re-establishing

[36] *Orderic*, vi, 442–3. See above, p. 75. [37] Above, pp. 143–5.

[38] *VCH*, viii, 308. [39] *VCH*, viii, 310.

[40] D. J. C. King and C. J. Spurgeon, 'The Mottes in the Vale of Montgomery', *Arch. Camb.* **114** (1965). See also L. F. Chitty, 'Interim Notes on Subsidiary Castle Sites West of Shrewsbury', *TSAS*, **53** (1949/50), pp. 83–90.

[41] King and Spurgeon, 'The Mottes in the Vale of Montgomery', esp. pp. 83–6.

[42] D. M. Palliser, 'Domesday Book and the "Harrying of the North"', *Northern History*, **29** (1993), pp. 1–23; J. J. N. Palmer, 'War and Domesday Waste', in M. Strickland (ed.), *Armies, Chivalry and Warfare in Medieval Britain and France. Proceedings of the 1995 Harlaxton Symposium* (Stamford, 1998), pp. 256–75.

deserted settlements. Nor can Domesday Book be relied upon to reflect accurately the distribution of settlements or castles. A consultation of the most recent maps showing the places mentioned in Domesday Book shows that there was considerable overlap between the distribution of the Vale mottes and the tenurial pattern as it had been established by 1086 (as in the case of Rorrington and Dudston).[43] On the other hand, Brompton Hall and Binweston are examples of mottes associated with settlements which have not been identified as mentioned in Domesday Book. But the mottes, and the settlements, may well have existed nevertheless.

The uniformity of the Vale mottes is remarkable, and strongly suggests a master plan of some kind. It is probable that these mottes were built more or less simultaneously, and separately from nearby but dissimilar castles such as Lady's Mount.[44] However, the fact that the construction of the Vale mottes no doubt required a considerable effort is more ambivalent.[45] While this does also point to co-ordination, it is possible that a great defensive effort would have been considered wasted at the peak of the Montgomery raids into Wales. Perhaps Robert de Bellême, who became earl in 1098, not long after Hen Domen's destruction by the Welsh in 1095, should be credited with the conception and execution of the Vale mottes. His interest in castles is well attested, although the one frontier castle he is known to have built on the Powys–Shropshire borders, Carreghofa, was probably of a very different type.[46] It is also possible, however, that the Vale mottes were built after 1102. The uneasy lull in frontier hostilities during the early part of Henry I's reign, or even the renewed outbreak of cross-border violence in the mid-1130s, may have afforded more ideal conditions for the construction of these mottes than the early phase of Montgomery expansion in the late eleventh century. In any case, the Vale mottes were certainly built with frontier concerns foremost in mind. Brompton Hall motte is particularly indicative of this, since it actually stands on Offa's Dyke. This site was no doubt chosen for the fine view it affords up the Caebitra valley, and must have served as a watchtower guarding against raids launched from Ceri. The motte at Upper Gwarthlow stands on an elevated ridge, presumably for the same strategic reason, and the settlement it protected may have been deserted at a period when it was safe to abandon this militarily stronger, but windy, site in favour of a more sheltered one half a kilometre away

[43] *Alecto Facsimile Edition of Domesday Book*, map 20, 'Shropshire'.

[44] See Spurgeon, 'Castles of Montgomeryshire', pp. 13 (no. 11) and pp. 51–4 (app. 1) on the problems surrounding the identification of Lady's Mount (a possible candidate for the castle near Welshpool attacked by the English in 1196; cf. *Brut*, p. 177).

[45] King and Spurgeon, 'The Mottes in the Vale of Montgomery', p. 83.

[46] Below, pp. 161, 164–5.

to the west.[47] The Vale of Montgomery, as has been seen, was one of the prime channels of communication between England and Wales during the twelfth and thirteenth centuries.[48] The characteristic mottes dotting this region strongly suggest, by their physical type and siting, that the borderlands between Caus and Montgomery were indeed a war zone, or at least a defensive frontier, early in that period.

Other archaeological evidence certainly chimes with this view. In the early twelfth century, the castle at Hen Domen Montgomery became the residence of the de Bollers family.[49] It was probably then that it developed more overtly domestic functions. A hall and a granary are believed to have survived from the first castle; further buildings within the bailey, as well as a cistern, were early additions.[50] However, it should be noted that many of these features were as central to withstanding sieges as they were to domestic life. The new castellans certainly remained mindful of the fact that their abode had been destroyed by the Welsh in 1095.[51] The motte continued to support a tower and bridge, and it was probably during the twelfth century that outer defences were added to the castle, namely a second ditch and another fighting platform on a rampart.[52] The de Bollers lords of Montgomery took no chances in securing the defensibility of their residence.

We need not imagine that the inhabitants of this region remained in arms throughout the twelfth century. In the aftermath of Henry II's 1165 campaign, the Montgomery area even saw some military co-operation between the Welsh and Anglo-Normans. Owain Cyfeiliog availed himself of the support of a host of 'French' knights in 1167 in his successful attempt to capture the castle of Caereinion, in the Welsh hills across the Severn and ten kilometres to the north-west of Montgomery.[53] However, the existence of Caereinion Castle, perhaps built in 1156 by Madog ap Maredudd (d. 1160),[54] Owain's uncle, testifies to a dispute between Madog's heirs in which, by 1167, members of the neighbouring Welsh ruling families of Gwynedd and Deheubarth had begun to meddle.[55] On the other hand, the castle evidence in this area also bears witness to some dramatic frontier campaigns, as in 1196, when Hubert Walter led an army

47 King and Spurgeon, 'The Mottes in the Vale of Montgomery', p. 80.

48 Above, p. 26. 49 Above, pp. 70–72.

50 Higham and Barker, *Hen Domen Montgomery. A Final Report*, pp. 41–53, fig. 3.16 (p. 52).

51 *Saxon Chronicles*, i, 230–1 (Anglo-Saxon Chronicle, E version (Laud MS), *sub annis* 1094–5).

52 Higham and Barker, *Hen Domen Montgomery – A Final Report*, pp. 70–1, 157–60.

53 *Brut*, p. 149; see Map 20, p. 159.

54 *Brut*, p. 133. Note that Stephenson, 'Madog ap Maredudd', pp. 10–11 argues that the Caereinion built in 1156 was in fact at Mathrafal.

55 *Brut*, p. 149.

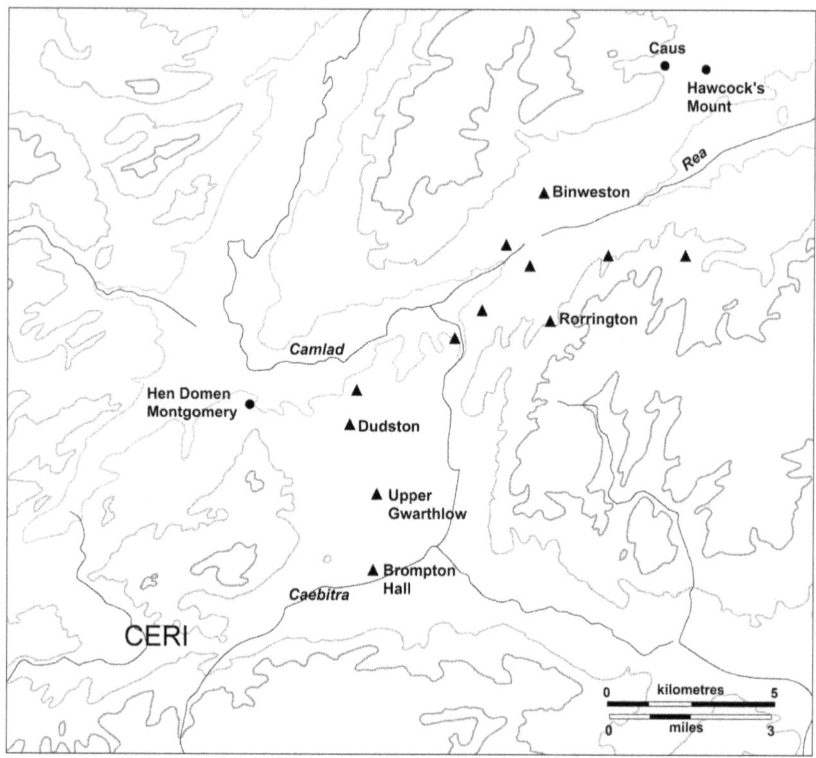

Map 19. The distinctive vale mottes near Montgomery, early to mid-twelfth century (possibly earlier)

against Gwenwynwyn of Powys, and the castle at Welshpool was taken by English sappers tunnelling under its walls.[56]

The evidence of the castles appears to reflect the fact that the border could be a region of both war and peace. On the one hand, it was fully realized that vigilance was still paramount at the turn of the twelfth and thirteenth centuries. Hen Domen is thought to have been, by this time, a highly elaborate earth and timber fortification with inner and outer ramparts and ditches, a partitioned bailey and a motte complete with drawbridge and tower.[57] Caus Castle had been garrisoned by the crown in 1165 and by 1198 Robert Corbet had received a grant of 10 marks for work on the castle, which probably ushered in 550 years of existence as a

[56] *Brut*, p. 177.

[57] Higham and Barker, *Hen Domen Montgomery. A Final Report*, pp. 14–18, 70–1.

stone castle, during most of which time a borough existed in its bailey.[58] On the other hand, Hen Domen had become yet more clearly residential, with the probable addition of a chapel to the hall, granary and other buildings situated within the bailey.[59] Moreover, the mottes in the Vale seem to have been neglected, at least for a while. By 1225, Henry III, concerned about Llywelyn's recent raids into the plains near Oswestry, enjoined 'those who have mottes in the Vale of Montgomery to fortify them without delay with solid palisades for their own security and that of the country around them.'[60]

Henry III's remarkable letter, of course, also shows his concern about the renewed Welsh military activity on the Shropshire frontier during the 1220s. Montgomery had been in royal hands since 1207, when the de Bollers family had failed in the male line. In 1223, the young king Henry III gave orders for the construction of a stone castle on a rock above Montgomery 'because of the exceedingly frequent raids of the Welsh.'[61] Nevertheless, the small characteristic mottes of the Vale apparently still had a defensive role to play, despite the advances in military technology dramatically symbolized by the new castle towering above them. It is notable that the archaeological evidence at Hen Domen for structures with a military purpose is far scantier for the later building phases of this castle.[62] However, this is thought to be so not because the castle lost its military significance, but rather because the timber defences at Hen Domen began to be erected on sill beams rather than posts. Domestic occupation apparently continued throughout the thirteenth century, albeit probably at a reduced level and with an interruption at the height of the frontier troubles late in John's reign.[63] This evidence for domestic uses of castles should perhaps give us pause in dismissing ancient structures with a less clear military function, such as Hawcock's Mount, as abandoned.[64] On the other hand, dramatic evidence for the military

58 *Pipe Roll 11 Henry II, 1165* (P. R. S., 8), p. 98 (Montgomery castle was garrisoned by the crown the same year; the cost, in both cases, was £14 9s 8d); *Pipe Roll 10 Richard I, 1198* (P. R. S., NS 9), p. 108. The castle was demolished soon after it had been garrisoned for the king in 1645: *VCH*, viii, 309.

59 Higham and Barker, *Hen Domen Montgomery. A Final Report*, pp. 14–16.

60 *Rot. Claus.*, ii, 42a: 'precipias omnibus illis qui motas habent in valle de Muntgumery quod sine dilacione motas suas bonis bretaschiis firmari faciant ad securitatem et defensionem suam et parcium illarum'.

61 Matthew Paris, *Chron. Maj.*, iii, 64. On New Montgomery see J. Knight, 'Montgomery. A Castle of the Welsh March, 1223–1649', *Château Gaillard*, **11** (1983), pp. 169–82; Stephenson, 'Llywelyn the Great, the Shropshire March and the Building of Montgomery Castle'.

62 Barker and Higham, *Hen Domen Montgomery* (1982), pp. 41–51.

63 Higham and Barker, *Hen Domen Montgomery. A Final Report*, pp. 18–24, 174.

64 For the view that Hawcock's Mount, or Old Caus, was not abandoned until about 1200, see P. A. Barker, 'Caus Castle and Hawcock's Mount', *Archaeological Journal*, **138** (1981), p. 34.

frontier at this time is the possible site of Hubert's Folly, built in 1228 in the hills of Ceri, which shows that once more the lord of Montgomery had an appetite for territorial conquest in Wales, although Hubert de Burgh's was thwarted even sooner than that of the Montgomeries had been more than a century previously.[65]

As we have seen, the Montgomery area saw the renewal of bitter fighting between English and Welsh during the first half of the thirteenth century, as when Hubert de Burgh waylaid, captured and beheaded a band of Welshmen who had been devastating the countryside near Montgomery Castle in 1231. Tellingly, Llywelyn retaliated by targeting the Marcher lords: he is said to have 'ground down the lands and possessions of the barons who lived on the borders of Wales with a terrifying raid of destruction.'[66] It was in this area, too, that Llywelyn ambushed and defeated an English expeditionary force sent from Montgomery Castle to capture him.[67] Taken together, the evidence of the Vale mottes during the latter part of the twelfth and the early years of the thirteenth century fits in very neatly with the view that the incidence of frontier warfare on the Shropshire–Powys border was dramatically reduced during the reigns of Henry II and Richard I, but that the borders became a specific target for raids, apparently of reprisal, after the rise of Llywelyn ap Iorwerth.

The castles at Montgomery lie at the centre of a frontier zone staked out in the later thirteenth century by the castles of Nantcribba to the west, and Dolforwyn to the east.[68] Nantcribba, or Forden Castle, is identified with Gwyddgrug, a frontier outpost of the lordship of Caus, built for purely military purposes in inhospitable territory to guard the Corbet territory from Welsh inroads. It is thought to be the Gwyddgrug Castle which was destroyed in 1263 by Gruffudd ap Gwenwynwyn of southern Powys, who had long disputed the territory known as the Gorddwr with Thomas Corbet of Caus.[69] Dolforwyn Castle was built

[65] Matthew Paris, *Chron. Maj.*, iii, 159; 'Cronica de Wallia', ed. Jones, p. 37; C. J. Spurgeon, 'Hubert's Folly: The Abortive Castle of the Kerry Campaign, 1228', in J. R. Kenyon and K. O'Conor (eds.), *The Medieval Castle in Ireland and Wales* (Dublin, 2003), pp. 107–20.

[66] Roger of Wendover, *Flores Historiarum*, iv, 221: 'Loelinus … terras baronum, qui in limbo Wallie degebant, et possessiones gravi depopulatione contrivit …'.

[67] Matthew Paris, *Chron. Maj.*, iii, 202–3.

[68] L. Butler, 'Dolforwyn Castle, Montgomery, Powys', *Arch. Camb.*, **144** (1997 for 1995), pp. 133–203; the same, 'Dolforwyn Castle, Powys, Wales: Excavations 1981–4', *Château Gaillard*, **12** (1985), pp. 167–77; 'Dolforwyn Castle', *Archaeology in Wales*, **25** (1985), p. 42; *Archaeology in Wales*, **30** (1990), pp. 19–20; see also **25–8** (1985–8) on Symon's (or Simond's) Castle, Churchstoke and **25** (1985) on Welshpool.

[69] *Brut*, p. 255; *Cal. Close R., 1261–4*, p. 265; *Annales Cambriae*, p. 101; Spurgeon, 'Gwyddgrug Castle', pp. 125–36; Lloyd, 'Border Notes', pp. 48–54. The earliest reference to Gwyddgrug now known dates to 1256: *The Roll of the Shropshire Eyre of 1256*, ed. A. Harding (London, 1981), no. 813.

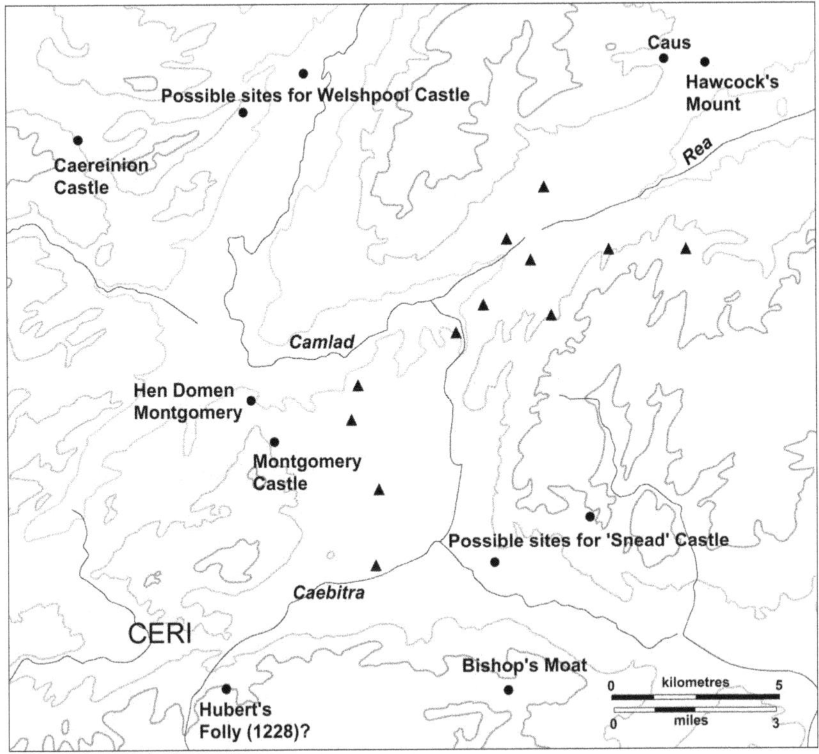

Map 20. Caus and the Vale of Montgomery in the age of Llywelyn ap Iorwerth (d. 1240)

by Llywelyn ap Gruffudd, the prince of Gwynedd, in 1273, partly with the aim of entrenching his domination over Cedewain. Soon after, he occupied the Gorddwr as far as Bausley.[70] In 1277, Dolforwyn became the target of a campaign led by the earl of Lincoln and the Marcher lord Roger Mortimer, and was taken after a fortnight's siege.[71] Again, the evidence of the castles helps to chart the extent of the military frontier zone.

It should be re-emphasized that the Vale of Montgomery formed one of the principal passage routes between Wales and England.[72] Under these circumstances, the evidence for almost continuous domestic occupation

[70] *Rot. Hund.*, ii, 90; *Cal. Anc. Corr. Wales*, p. 82 for Bausley.
[71] *Brut*, p. 265. [72] *VCH*, viii, 300.

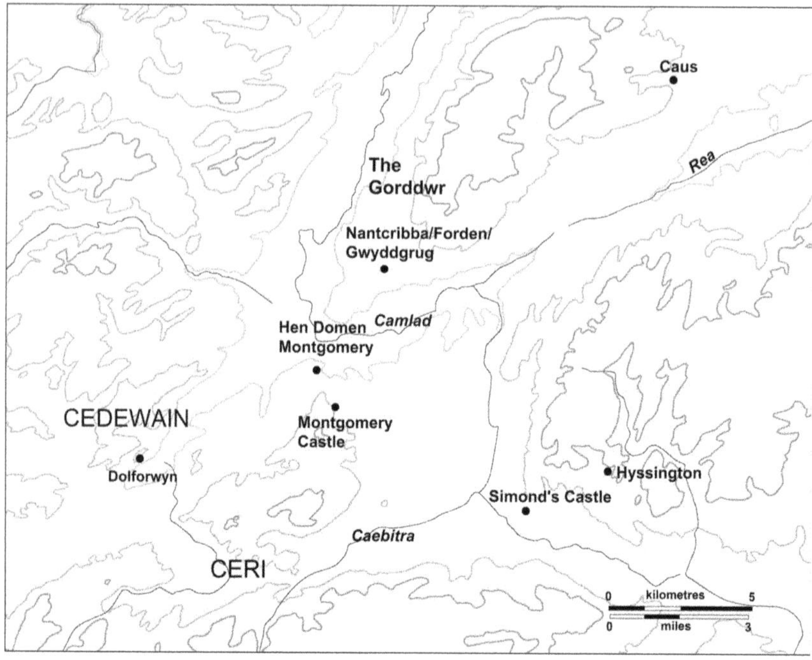

Map 21. Castles in the Vale of Montgomery in the later thirteenth century

at Hen Domen serves as a doubly powerful reminder that the Shropshire frontier was not purely military during the period *c.* 1070 to 1283. The castle evidence for the Vale of Montgomery reinforces the argument advanced in the previous chapter, that phases of frontier warfare alternated with phases of relative peace, and that a diplomatic frontier coexisted with the military frontier at all times.

THE MILITARY FRONTIER, *c.* 1070–1283, II: THE LORDSHIP OF OSWESTRY

The discussion of the mottes in the Vale of Montgomery was able to draw on the evidence of the distinctive Vale mottes and the uniquely thorough excavations at Hen Domen. Inevitably, the less well understood castles to the north and south of the Severn gap will be influenced by the preceding investigation. Yet it seems clear that the situation at Oswestry was potentially very different. The lord of Mersete hundred may have spearheaded territorial conquests of his own into Welsh territory, for he could call on the military manpower supported by his vast Shropshire fief. Warin the Bald, certainly, had a reputation for oppressing the Welsh, and, as has been seen, is found in the late 1070s participating in a campaign against Gruffudd ap Cynan.[73] By 1086, the successor to his territories and position on the Welsh frontier was claiming that the Welsh districts of Cynllaith and Edeirnion owed him tribute, while Earl Roger asserted that the Welsh lord of Nanheudwy held his land by his grant.[74] It may be suggested that Sycharth Castle, which by the late fourteenth century had become the residence of Owain Glyn Dŵr, originated on the initiative of a Norman lord of Oswestry, and indeed that one of the castles in the Dee valley, possibly Rhûg, marks an outpost originally designed to enforce control in Edeirnion.[75] Rhûg is thought to be the 'cruc' in Edeirnion to where Gruffudd ap Cynan was lured by 'two earls of the marches', those of Chester and Shrewsbury, sometime after 1081.[76] The imprisonment of Gruffudd ap Cynan would seem to have offered an opportunity for establishing control over Edeirnion, possibly by building a castle.

There is thus some evidence that the frontier was pushed into Wales in the early days of the Norman conquest, but that this advance was very soon repelled seems clear. Robert de Bellême, earl of Shrewsbury between 1098 and 1102, was an avid and experienced castle-builder, as is shown not only by his English foundations, such as Bridgnorth Castle,[77] but also by the *fossés Robert* in the Saosnois on the western frontier of the *seigneurie* of Bellême,[78] built apparently as part of a strategy to create a highly independent border territory between the respective orbits of power of the French king and the duke of Normandy.[79] That a man of such enterprise chose a site further east from Sycharth for his castle at Carreghofa, completed in 1101–2,[80] may thus represent a calculated retreat from previous acquisitions – since Robert may well already have been planning his rebellion, he needed to reduce the risk of attack on his western flank. It is true that Orderic accused him of harassing the Welsh throughout his period as earl of Shrewsbury,[81] but the Welsh account

73 Above, p. 110; *Orderic*, ii, 262; *Gruffudd ap Cynan*, ed. Jones, p. 123; *Historia Gruffud vab Kenan*, ed. Simon Evans, pp. 12–13; *Life of Gruffudd ap Cynan*, ed. Simon Evans, p. 34; *Vita Griffini*, ed. Russell, pp. 66–7 (§16).

74 DB 255a (cited above, p. 110, n. 46), 253c.

75 R. Richards, 'Sycharth', *Mont. Coll.*, **50** (1949 for 1948), p. 186; Spurgeon, 'Mottes and Castle-Ringworks', p. 28.

76 *Gruffudd ap Cynan*, ed. Jones, pp. 130–2, 172; *Historia Gruffud vab Kenan*, ed. Simon Evans, pp. 16–17; *Life of Gruffudd ap Cynan*, ed. Simon Evans, p. 38; *Vita Griffini*, ed. Russell, pp. 70–3, (§19); Lloyd, *History of Wales*, p. 385.

77 *Orderic*, iv, 32–3; A. Roe, 'Bridgnorth, Shropshire', *West Midlands Archaeology*, **26** (1983), pp. 86–7.

78 J. Le Goff (ed.), *Dictionnaire raisonné de l'Occident médiéval* (Paris, 1999), p. 185.

79 *Orderic*, iv, 228–30 and n. 1; Lemarignier, *Hommage en marche*, pp. 63–4.

80 *John of Worcester*, iii, 100–1.

81 *Orderic*, v, 225.

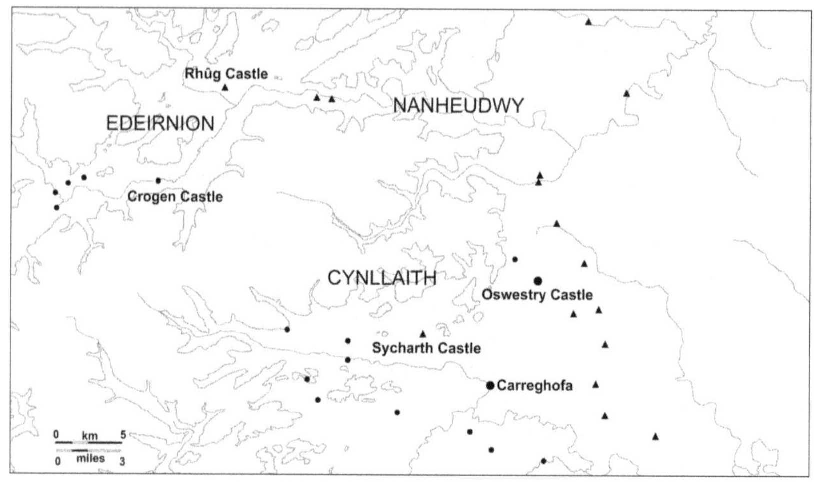

Map 22. Castle distribution in Mersete hundred and adjoining Welsh territories in the late eleventh century

represents him as having taken a more conciliatory approach, ordering 'that trust should be placed in the Britons', and sending 'all his flocks and herds and wealth and all his treasures to be among the Britons …'; though the hope that this would avoid Welsh attacks on what he claimed as his territory was to prove vain.[82]

We may be on surer ground with the castles in the lower country surrounding Oswestry. The large motte at Oswestry itself may already, by 1086, have served as a base for troops of mounted knights equipped to scour the neighbouring country and to counter border raids.[83] The smaller size of most of the other mottes in the area, however, indicates that they can have afforded protection only to petty lords and their households. All are associated with the hamlets dotting the country around Oswestry whose lords were probably subordinated tenurially to the chief castle at Oswestry. In all these respects, these fortifications closely parallel the Vale mottes lying in the Rea and Camlad valley between Caus and Hen Domen Montgomery, which are thought to have originated in the days of Earl Roger.[84] Again, it is very possible that the uneasy lull in frontier

[82] *Brut*, p. 45.

[83] On the *muntatores* see Suppe, *Military Institutions*, pp. 63–87.

[84] King and Spurgeon, 'The Mottes in the Vale of Montgomery', pp. 69–86; above, pp. 153–6.

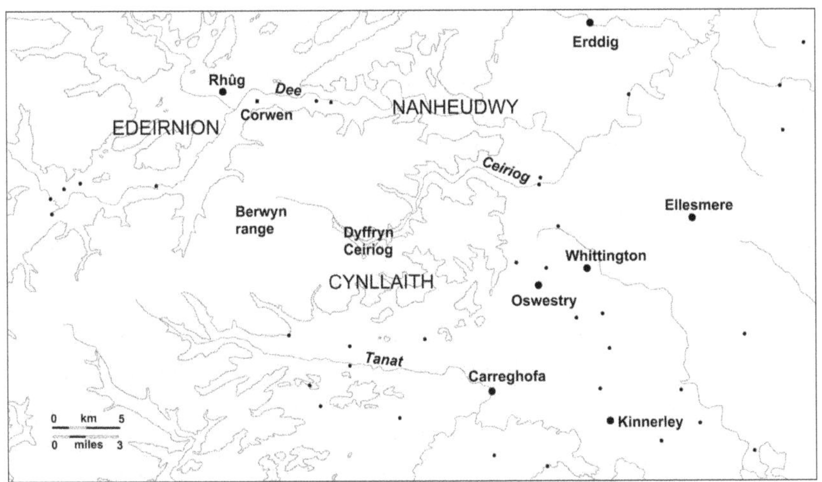

Map 23. Oswestry and adjoining Welsh districts in the twelfth century

hostilities during the early part of Henry I's reign would have afforded even more ideal conditions for the construction of the mottes in the lowlands which are tenurially associated with the large seigneurial castles in Shropshire. However, we may conclude that the mottes in the frontier hundreds of Shropshire very probably date from the time when the units of Norman aristocratic power there were first being consolidated.

By contrast, the strong mottes at Whittington and Ellesmere probably represent an effort at consolidating the Norman position as the impetus of the westwards advance flagged. They are documented as having been fortified against King Stephen in 1138.[85] Admittedly, this hardly suggests their use as typical frontier castles on that occasion, but their geographical position does suggest that the strength of the mottes at Ellesmere and Whittington was principally intended for defence. Oswestry itself, of course, exemplifies a strong motte which was occupied by the Welsh in the mid-twelfth century.[86] Although it and the small mottes surrounding it doubtless reflect, in part, the largely non-military stage of Norman settlement which was due to Henry I's vigilance, Oswestry's status as a frontier castle, and perhaps a military frontier castle, was dramatically clear at the beginning of Henry II's reign.

It is a different story for the mottes, many of them small and not associated with settlements, which are scattered throughout the upper

[85] *Orderic*, vi, 518–19. [86] Above, p. 119.

reaches of the Tanat valley. They do not trace a path along any vital lines of long-distance communication likely to have been of importance to Earl Roger and his men, unlike the mottes in the Rea, Camlad and upper Severn vales or even the mostly feeble constructions in the lower Clun valley. These are far more likely to be Welsh foundations, and as such probably do not much pre-date 1180. The same is true of the mottes in the higher Dee valley, where Crogen is first mentioned as a Welsh castle in 1202, when it was granted to Elise ap Madog, a member of the dynasty of northern Powys, after he had first been deprived of his lands because he had remained neutral during the stand-off between Gwenwynwyn of southern Powys and Llywelyn ap Iorwerth in that year.[87] Since the conflicts revolving around these castles involved only the Welsh, they fall outside the true frontier zone between England and Wales.

It seems clear, therefore, that Henry II's 1165 campaign succeeded only in briefly pushing the frontier westwards from Oswestry. There is some documentary evidence suggesting that royal investment in the castles in the Dee valley preceded this campaign.[88] But it was of little avail, for in 1165 his army, as has been seen, advanced up the Ceiriog valley, only to be ambushed by Welsh raiders in the woods at Dyffryn Ceiriog and bogged down in a summer storm on the Berwyn range.[89] The Welsh force which had come to meet him had encamped at Corwen, opposite the castle which was possibly fortified by the English crown in 1160. It has already been mentioned that the path followed by Henry II's army up to its rain-drenched camp came to be known as 'Ffordd y Saeson', the English road.[90] Yet an even truer symbol of the frontier stood a little further south. Carreghofa Castle, originally one of Earl Robert de Bellême's Shropshire fortifications,[91] was to change hands between the English and Welsh so frequently as to become a quintessential frontier castle. Having been refurbished by the crown in 1159–62,[92] it was captured by the Welsh the following year, although by 1164 it appears to have been retaken by the English.[93] As has been seen, before 1175, and probably after 1173, during the minority of William Fitzalan II,[94] Henry II confirmed Owain Fychan, one of the sons of Madog ap Maredudd, in the possession of

[87] *Brut*, p. 185.

[88] *Pipe Roll 6 Henry II, 1159–60* (P. R. S., 2), p. 26, mentions 'Dernio', which may have been the name for a castle in Edeirnion, possibly Rhûg. Erddig was also fortified at this time.

[89] Above, p. 9.

[90] Lloyd, *History of Wales*, p. 517; above, pp. 121–2.

[91] Above, pp. 161–2.

[92] *Pipe Roll 5 Henry II, 1158–9* (P. R. S., 1), p. 62; *Pipe Roll 6 Henry II, 1159–60* (P. R. S., 2), p. 26; *Pipe Roll 7 Henry II, 1160–61* (P. R. S., 4), p. 38; *Pipe Roll 8 Henry II, 1161–2* (P. R. S., 5), p. 15.

[93] *Pipe Roll 11 Henry II, 1164–5* (P. R. S., 8), p. 90: mill at 'Carrecoen' guarded by the crown.

[94] William Fitzalan II had seisin of his lands in 1175: Eyton, vii, 239–40.

Mechain, in parts of Oswestry lordship 'and [in] all the land and embankment of Carreghofa' (though he explicitly excluded the castle and its vill).[95] In 1187, Carreghofa witnessed Owain Fychan's killing.[96] During Richard I's reign, Hubert Walter, the justiciar, took a close interest in Carreghofa Castle because of its proximity to a silver mine. In 1194–5 a ringwall came to enclose the structure,[97] but in 1197 the castle was surrendered to Gwenwynwyn of Powys in return for a Welsh prisoner.[98] By 1212 the English had regained possession, for they are said to have 'rebuilt' it that year;[99] it was certainly refurbished and garrisoned on King John's orders.[100] The castle is mentioned as remaining in English hands in 1213 and 1215,[101] but it does not appear in our sources again, probably because it was destroyed in Llywelyn ap Iorwerth's raids in the area,[102] possibly in the early 1220s, when Kinnerley and Whittington Castles were captured. Although Oswestry had fallen into Welsh hands in 1149 and fell victim to Welsh raids on many other occasions, it was Carreghofa that came to be seen as a fulcrum of the Shropshire frontier. The years when it changed hands between English and Welsh were used as temporal reference points for dating clauses, just as later, in the 1260s, the raids of Gruffudd ap Gwenwynwyn and Llywelyn ap Gruffudd furnished the bad memories which structured history for the scribes of Alberbury Priory.[103] A charter of 1194, by which Thomas Burnell granted Lilleshall Abbey land in Shropshire, was dated, with a note of triumph and relief, 'on the first eve of Ascension-day after the castle of Carreghofa was returned by the Welsh to the king through the offices of the lord of Canterbury.'[104] In the minds of contemporaries, Carreghofa was a place where the frontier could be located on the ground.

Map 24, showing thirteenth-century castles north of the Severn gap, probably errs on the generous side. It illustrates, however, the mosaic of

95 See above, pp. 123–4; *Welsh Assize Roll*, ed. Davies, p. 237; cf. Morgan, 'Barony of Powys', p. 38, n. 2; Stephenson, 'Supremacy', pp. 48–9 and n. 15.

96 *Brut*, p. 171 (here called Owain ap Madog).

97 *Pipe Roll 6 Richard I, 1194* (P. R. S., NS 5), p. 141; *Pipe Roll 7 Richard I, 1195* (P. R. S., NS 6), p. 244.

98 *Annales Cambriae*, p. 61: Gwenwynwyn receives Carreghofa in exchange for one of the sons of the Lord Rhys, Gruffudd, who had been captured and delivered to Gwenwynwyn by his brother, Maelgwn ap Rhys.

99 'Cronica de Wallia', ed. Jones, p. 34.

100 *Pipe Roll 14 John, 1212* (P. R. S., NS 30, London, 1954), p. 88.

101 *Rot. Claus.*, i, 132a; *Rot. Pat.*, p. 100a and b.

102 See H. M. Colvin and A. J. Taylor, *The History of the King's Works*, 2 vols. (London, 1963), pp. 602–3.

103 See above, p. 131.

104 *Lilleshall Cart.*, no. 199: 'in vigilia Ascensionis proxima postquam Castellum de Karrethove redditum fuit a Walensibus domino Regi per dominum Cantuariensem' (that is, Hubert Walter).

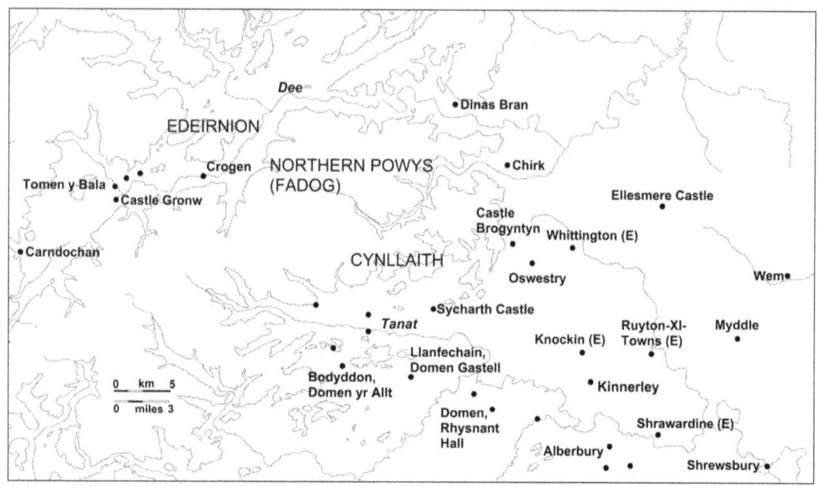

Map 24. Castles near Oswestry and in neighbouring Welsh districts in the thirteenth century

English and Welsh castles on the Shropshire borders which was largely a result of royal patronage, especially during the reigns of Henry II and John. We should note in particular how Ellesmere, which was often granted to Welsh princes at this time, lay well to the east of Oswestry. The map also demonstrates how the diplomatic and military frontiers overlapped during this period. Myddle, where Llywelyn ap Iorwerth concluded truces with English embassies during the 1230s, lay thirteen kilometres to the east of such disputed estates as Kinnerley and Whittington. English and Welsh estates in this region did not so much lie cheek-by-jowl with each other as constitute a jumbled-up muddle of interlocking border manors. Such a situation, as has been argued throughout this work, was just as conducive to coexistence and diplomacy as to military confrontation.

THE MILITARY FRONTIER, *c.* 1070–1283, III: THE LORDSHIPS OF CLUN AND OF WIGMORE

The castle evidence of Clun is strikingly different from that for the area further north. Neither of the early castles at Clun or Bryn Amlwg are typical mottes.[105] Although both provided strong defences and probably originated in the first half of the twelfth century at the latest, the early castle at Clun consisted of a bluff in the bend of a stream, scarped to form

[105] See illustration of Bryn Amlwg, below, p. 179.

a motte, while Bryn Amlwg is a ringwork.[106] It seems clear that neither castle was built under the supervision of Earl Roger, who, as has been seen, favoured large mottes such as the Gro Tump.[107] A further distinctive point about the Clun castle evidence is the high concentration of very weak early castles in the lower Clun valley. On its own, the feeble state of the surviving castle evidence could certainly not be taken as an indication that this area ceased to form part of the border vanguard of Shropshire at an early date. Carreghofa itself, after all, survives as little more than a place-name. As at Oswestry and Caus, many of these mottes are associated with twelfth-century sub-enfeoffments, which suggests that, at the period when subtenants were forced to encastellate, this district was certainly similarly heavily under threat. However, there is the cumulative aspect to be considered: it is the only concentration of weak and early castles in any of the frontier hundreds. Moreover, none of the lower Clun mottes is documented, which further indicates that their importance, in strategic terms as otherwise, was minor. It was on Clun Castle, not the lower Clun mottes, that Henry II spent money in 1160–4. Moreover, it is striking that this area coincides exactly with the extent of Purslow hundred, whose ambiguous status vis-à-vis the English state in the thirteenth century will be discussed in Chapter 7. No castles from this area can be dated with any certainty to the thirteenth century. Some masonry has been excavated at Clungunford, and at Hopton evidence for what may have been a tower about ten metres in diameter has been discerned.[108] The extraordinary castle surviving at Hopton, however, appears to be entirely fourteenth-century stone on a twelfth-century plan,[109] and looks as if it had been fashioned as a mock border castle. Cheney Longville is a fourteenth-century stone mansion.[110] Thus, the lower Clun valley may well have been an exposed area at an early period which then formed a part of Shropshire more securely in both strategic and administrative respects.

It was a very different matter in the uplands of Clun. As was argued earlier, the borough quite clearly fits the pattern of the border town, the castle being juxtaposed to a church whose frontier character is

[106] King, *Castellarium Anglicanum*, p. 423.

[107] Above, pp. 109–10, 143.

[108] P. R. Remfry, *Hopton Castle 1066 to 1305* (Worcester, 1994), p. 7. See P. E. Curnow 'The Tower House at Hopton and its Affinities' in C. Harper-Bill, C. J. Holdsworth and J. L. Nelson (eds.), *Studies in Medieval History Presented to R. Allen Brown* (Woodbridge, 1989), pp. 81–102, for the view that the masonry structure at Hopton castle had a military purpose.

[109] A. H. A. Hogg and D. J. C. King, 'Masonry Castles in Wales and the Marches. A List', *Arch. Camb.*, **116** (1967), p. 107; Remfry, *Hopton Castle*, even suggests that it was built in the 'post-medieval' period, p. 8.

[110] Salter, *Castles and Moated Mansions*, p. 30.

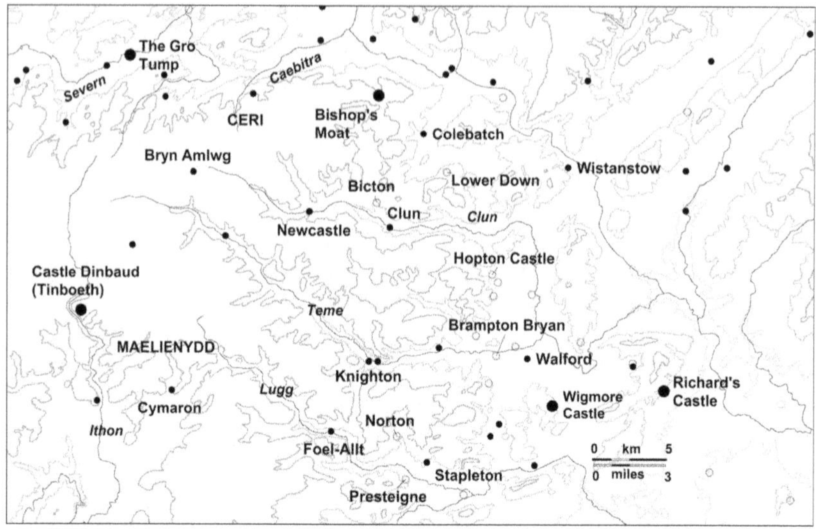

● Classified by Cathcart-King as motte type E1: 'earthworks of exceptionally fine type'

• Classified as E2: 'earthwork of average strength'

○ Classified as E3: 'feeble or damaged earthworks'

Map 25. The castles connected with Clun and Wigmore

highlighted by its starkly massive early English tower and flying buttresses.[111] Early mottes survive at Bicton and Newcastle, on the Clun and Unk rivers respectively, suggesting forward defences against Welsh attacks coming from the ridgeways.[112] The hypothesis that these mottes were primarily defences, rather than, say, instruments of exploitation, is strengthened by the fact that they are mirrored on the northern side of Yr Hen Ffordd ridgeway. Here, we find mottes at Lower Down, Acton and Colebatch, possibly fitting the pattern of mottes built by free tenants of the lord of Clun.[113] If so, they may well have been a response to the threat from the ridgeways, dating to the first half of the twelfth century. Finally, to the west of these castles lies Bryn Amlwg, in its way the epitome of a border stronghold.[114] It is comparable to

[111] Above, p. 42.

[112] For the ridgeways, see Rees, *Map of South Wales and the Border*; L. F. Chitty, 'The Clun–Clee Ridgeway: A Prehistoric Trackway across South Shropshire', in I. Ll. Foster and L. Alcock (eds.), *Culture and Environment* (London, 1963), pp. 171–92. For the suggestion that the ridgeways posed a threat to the Normans throughout the twelfth century, see Suppe, *Military Institutions*, p. 35.

[113] For these places' tenurial dependency on Clun, see Eyton, xi, 242–3.

[114] See illustration below, p. 179 and p. 178.

Bishop's Moat and Gwyddgrug in that it stands on a lordship's frontier in uncultivated territory. Very possibly built as an outpost in the late 1130s or early 1140s, when Elias de Sai joined forces with Mortimer of Wigmore against the neighbouring Welsh dynasties, it may have continued to be refortified at the critical moments early in the reign of Henry II, although by the mid-1190s the lady of Clun may have had to retreat and concentrate her forces on Newcastle.[115] Bryn Amlwg's frontier character is further underscored in that it is thought to have been refortified in stone during Llywelyn ap Gruffudd's occupation of the Clun uplands in the 1260s. Masonry existed at Clun Castle itself possibly as early as the eleventh century,[116] but the great tower recalls the later castles in the lower Clun valley in that its sole purpose was to dominate the landscape with an impressive symbol of lordship. The supposition that it had a real military purpose is undermined by the small side doors built into the massive north and south stone walls below the table of the motte. The great stone tower at Clun was built at a time when the lord wished to display visually his prestige as a scion of an ancient frontier family, but when he no longer considered his power to be under any threat from Welsh attack. It plainly dates to the time when the military frontier in Shropshire had been consigned to being the stuff of border legend.[117]

An interpretation of the castles around Wigmore may start with a topographical observation. The valleys to the south of Clun, those of the Teme and Lugg, with their narrow, flat beds and steeply rising sides, are topographically very similar to the higher Clun valley. The sites of castles such as Knighton and Presteigne therefore closely parallel that of Clun Castle. All are positioned at the entrance to topographical corridors leading towards the higher country of Maelienydd; all lie at around 160 to 180 metres above sea level, at or near the centre of the valley floor; today, small towns have grown up around all of them. Wigmore Castle, on the other hand, lies in country which may be compared to the lower Clun

115 Above, p. 125. *Pipe Roll 7 Richard I, 1195* (P. R. S., NS 6), p. 244: 'Matefelun' a *domus* of William 'de Boterels', husband of Isabel, lady of Clun, was possibly identical with Newcastle: King, *Castellarium Anglicanum*, ii, 434, 563.

116 Dated to the late thirteenth century in King, *Castellarium Anglicanum*. There is a reference in 1272 to a 'well-built castle' the roof of whose 'tower' was in need of repair with lead: TNA C 132/42 (5), m. 6r; cf. Eyton xi, 231–2. See P. R. Remfry, *Clun Castle* (Worcester, 1994), pp. 15–19 for dating and maps of the surviving masonry.

117 It should be noted that a stone-by-stone examination of Clun Castle's masonry carried out by the Herefordshire Archaeology Unit dated the 'Great Tower' to the late thirteenth or early fourteenth century and therefore judged it to be of 'anachronistic design' intended 'to impress and to imply a military strength and antiquity that it simply did not possess': R. K. Morriss, 'Clun Castle Reappraised', in *Castle Studies Group Newsletter*, 7 (1993–4), pp. 23–4.

valley. Although the ground in which it stands is hillier, Wigmore does not represent an advance into a topographically distinctive country in the same way that Clun does.

Correspondingly, the distribution of the smaller castles near Wigmore follows a different principle. As at Clun, Caus and Oswestry, small castles were built on the estates first granted away by the lord of the chief castle. But, whereas at Clun these estates are clustered in the lower ground to the east of the main fortification, at Wigmore they form an almost complete circle around the lord's motte. Given that they all lie to the west, north and south of Wigmore, it is tempting to conclude that they followed a common principle of forming a protective shield. However, as with the other small castles on sub-enfeoffed border manors, it is safer to say that they reflect the distribution of settlements rather than a common strategy. It does, however, seem probable that they provided shelter for the petty lords of individual estates, and they therefore may well have been built at an early stage, and primarily out of military concerns, just as, for example, the Vale mottes. Many of them were no doubt soon abandoned, and it is clear that those that survived throughout the period, such as Brampton Bryan, did so because they became the residential centres of local lords.

The explanation for the pattern of castle-building around Wigmore, then, is in part the distribution of the most valuable manors. In part, also, we need to consider that Wigmore Castle was built by William fitz Osbern. It may therefore be seen as belonging to a string of castles reaching down to Chepstow whose purpose was perhaps not an advance into Wales, but more probably the defence of the English frontier. Cymaron Castle, therefore, may represent a new departure, as well as the scope of the ambition of the Mortimers, who came to be based at Wigmore not long after the death of fitz Osbern. It is said to have been repaired by Hugh Mortimer in 1144, on which occasion Hugh, according to the Welsh chronicle, 'a second time gained possession of Maelienydd'.[118] The river valley castles to the east of Cymaron may well, therefore, date to the first half of the twelfth century, and reflect, primarily, a straightforward bid for territorial conquest, or more probably for the imposition of tribute-based control. As has been observed, Preston and Knighton are comparable, with respect to their topographical position, to Clun, and possibly were built in the hope of achieving a similarly successful foothold on the Welsh frontier. To that extent, these castles were probably intended soon to progress beyond the military stage. Even Cymaron

[118] *Brut*, p. 119.

Castle, after all, which occupies a position considerably further advanced to the west, eventually became the seat of its own judicial court.[119]

★ ★ ★

Military functions are prominent among the purposes for which castles were built on the Shropshire frontier between the late eleventh and the thirteenth centuries. Despite the tendency of the lords of Powys, and especially of southern Powys, to ally themselves with the kings of England, the density of the mottes strongly suggests that there were prolonged periods when those living on the western border of Shropshire were at serious risk from Welsh attacks. Indeed, the explanation for the high number of castles on the Shropshire frontier with Powys would appear to have been, overwhelmingly, the specific military challenge posed by the proximity of the Welsh principalities. It is certainly true that the castle density in the area around Wem strongly suggests that castles were built in greater numbers in places which were both close to seigneurial centres and remote from the county town, and both of these conditions, of course, apply to the western frontier hundreds. Yet the explanation for the high castle density along the frontier does seem to be primarily military. Although castles had been erected on the southern Shropshire frontier as well as the western by 1102, the strongest were built, at that time, to the west. This suggests that, already at an early date, it was the western frontier which was perceived to pose the greatest strategic challenge. Moreover, it would appear that the need to protect small settlements, which more than any other factor led to the high density of castles, was restricted to the borders. The mottes protecting the small settlements from the threat of border raiders in the Vale of Montgomery were typical of a distinctive frontier situation. The Shropshire–Powys border was a region which was exposed to highly specific military challenges.

However, in the light of the chronological analysis supplied in the previous chapter, it seems necessary to ask how evident this military distinctiveness would have been at different times between *c.* 1070 and 1283. On this point, the archaeological evidence can be shown to corroborate the view that there were episodes during which the specific frontier threat was very significantly reduced. Thus, the palisades of the characteristic mottes in the Vale of Montgomery appear to have been neglected during the reigns of Henry II and his sons. This very probably indicates that their military purpose diminished or even disappeared at this time. But they appear to have continued as residential centres – in Henry III's

[119] *Cal. Pat. R., 1292–1301*, p. 290.

reign, a writ was addressed 'to those who have mottes' – and it seems that their military purpose could be resurrected at times when the English king was particularly worried about the strategic situation on the Welsh frontier. Such, too, was the case at Hen Domen Montgomery. Yet the fact that Hen Domen was probably retained, in part, because of its proximity to the ford on the Severn serves to remind us that castles could serve as instruments for diplomacy as well. The evidence of the castles in the Vale of Montgomery fits in very neatly with the arguments advanced in the preceding chapter.

However short-lived the practical military purpose of castles may often have been, there can be no doubt that on the level of perceptions, at least, the evidence of the castles provides a very useful way of determining the existence and extent of a distinctive area on the Shropshire–Powys frontier. Especially at the peak periods of castle building, the sheer visual presence of the mottes must immediately have set the border landscape apart from the rest of the county, on the one hand, and Wales on the other. Castles always had a psychological impact. On the Shropshire frontier, as elsewhere, the military element of that impact was, at times, illusory. Yet, where the making of a separate identity in the minds of contemporaries is concerned, castles which were retained primarily as residences or as administrative centres, and even ruined castles, could be just as evocative of frontier warfare as occupied and garrisoned ones. After all, they stood as monuments to border conflicts which must have remained in living memory, even when they were not directly experienced, throughout the period from *c.* 1070 to 1283. The castles played a substantial role in creating and reaffirming the character of the March as a land of war, both in practice and, more persistently, in perception.

Chapter 5

THE MILITARIZATION OF SOCIETY

Besides the threat and incidence of frontier warfare, treated chronologically in Chapter 3, and the evidence of the castles, analysed in Chapter 4, another approach to discussing the distinctiveness in military terms of the Shropshire–Powys border is to investigate the effects of frontier warfare on society. Again, there is a historiographical context to this approach. It has been argued, particularly by R. R. Davies, that the strategic exigencies of border warfare ensured that military institutions which were characteristic of early Norman England survived in the March long after they had become obsolete in England.[1] The issue impinges, moreover, on debates on the meaningfulness and survival of the honor in England in the twelfth and thirteenth centuries, particularly insofar as that debate is concerned with the question of military retinues.[2] It is also relevant to the question of how far the Welsh borderlands of Shropshire in the thirteenth century may have been similar to the marches in Ireland, to which military service had been exported from England and where it continued, throughout the thirteenth and fourteenth centuries, to be performed as an obligation arising from tenure of land.[3] Given these ramifications, it is clearly important to ask whether frontier warfare created a distinctively militarized society on the Welsh borders.

Military characteristics could certainly, in the eyes of contemporaries, create separate identities. The writing of Gerald of Wales, in particular, calls attention to this. In recording his advice to future would-be

[1] Davies, *Lordship and Society*, ch. 3; the same, 'Kings, Lords and Liberties', p. 50.

[2] For example, D. Crouch, *William Marshal: Court, Career and Chivalry in the Angevin Empire 1147–1219* (London, 1990), pp. 4, 160–2; D. A. Carpenter, 'The Second Century of English Feudalism', *Past & Present*, **168** (2000), pp. 30–71; most recently Holden, *Lords*, esp. pp. 48–62.

[3] A. J. Otway-Ruthven, 'Knight Service in Ireland', *Journal of the Royal Society of Antiquaries of Ireland*, **89** (1959), pp. 4, 13; R. Frame, 'Military Service in the Lordship of Ireland 1290–1360: Institutions and Society on the Anglo-Gaelic Frontier', in Bartlett and MacKay (eds.), *Medieval Frontier Societies*, pp. 101–26.

conquerors of Wales, he pays tribute to the fighting qualities of his kinsmen, who had held on against all the odds to a different part of the Welsh frontier, the country around Pembroke, in the following words:

In my opinion the Welsh marches would have been better controlled under the English occupation if their kings, in governing these regions and in repelling the attacks of a hostile people, had from the beginning taken the advice of the marcher lords ['marchionum et baronum patriae'], and used their tactics, instead of those of the Angevins and the Normans … [T]roops who have lived all their lives in the marches will be by far the most suitable, for they have had long practice in waging war in local conditions. They are bold, speedily deployed and experienced in all that they do. As military circumstances dictate, they ride well and they advance quickly on foot … [Continental troops] are used to fighting on the level, whereas here the terrain is rough; their battles take place in the open fields, but here the country is heavily wooded; with them the army is an honourable profession but with us it is a matter of dire necessity; their victories are won by stubborn resistance, ours by constant movement …'[4]

To a considerable extent, what distinguished the Marchers of south-west Wales from their contemporaries in England and on the continent was therefore, in Gerald's view, their ability to conduct a specific kind of warfare. Gerald, it is true, was concerned with according his relatives the prominent place in history which they, in his view, deserved. Moreover, his eloquent remarks on frontier warfare are reminiscent of those of armchair generals. They are an instance, however, of a widespread tendency at the time Gerald was writing of identifying people, and even peoples, by the arms and tactics they used.[5] It is clearly relevant, then, to investigate whether the people who lived on the Shropshire borders might have been considered to be 'Marchers' because they distinguished themselves by their military way of life.

⋆ ⋆ ⋆

There is good reason to think that the impact on society of the specific challenges of border warfare was, at times, great. The demands made on the military resources of the lords holding castles on that border could clearly be both high and unrelenting. The lord of Oswestry, for example, concentrated the military resources of his vast fief largely on the defence of that castle, granting land as far away as Staffordshire in return for the

[4] Gerald of Wales, *Wales*, transl. Thorpe, pp. 268–9; *Giraldus*, vi, 218–22 (*Descriptio Kambrie*, ii, 8). The passage appears almost *verbatim* in book 2, chapter 38 of Gerald's *Expugnatio Hibernica* (*Giraldus*, v, 395–7), since he believed that the same military conditions prevailed in both countries.

[5] P. Contamine, 'Heer, Heerwesen. Allgemeine Grundzüge', in *Lexikon des Mittelalters*, vol. iv (Munich and Zurich, 1989).

service at Oswestry of mounted soldiers often referred to as *muntatores*, who generally were armed with hauberk, iron cap and lance.[6] That Oswestry was privileged in this way identifies the frontier as the single most important military concern of the lord of the shrieval fief of Shropshire.[7] It would seem clear that the provision of *muntatores* was a measure taken during the reign of Henry I at the latest. All those said in 1166 to owe the service of these frontier knights had received their lands before 1135.[8] Many of the lands owing muntatorial service had already been granted to subtenants by 1086, and it is possible that the service had already been specified by then.[9] After all, the fact that a very strong motte had been erected at that time already shows an awareness that the region had a special military significance. Yet the need to defend Oswestry probably became more urgent after 1086. Moreover, the *muntatores* catered to the very specific needs of a frontier castle, since knights armed only with hauberks and lances were best suited to the task of harrassing raiders trying to remove their booty to the safety of the Welsh hills. It seems quite possible that muntatorial service was introduced as the threat to Oswestry Castle grew more pronounced. This may well not have been until after 1102, when the aggressive Montgomery earls had been removed and it had become clear that the frontier would not advance further. In any case, the *muntatores* show that, during Henry I's reign and possibly earlier, even a lord of a fief which could provide a considerable military manpower found it necessary to focus all the forces he could muster on the defence of one frontier castle and the area it commanded.

The situation at Montgomery, Caus and Clun in the early twelfth century may well have been direr yet, since the territories which could supply garrisons for those castles, though more compact, were far smaller than the vast fief which had come to be focused militarily on the stretch of the frontier near Oswestry. The mottes protecting the hamlets and villages in the vicinity of these castles suggest that the tenants must often have been preoccupied with the defence of their own homesteads. It seems plausible that the lord would have called upon them to contribute towards guarding his chief castle when he could. This, after all, was almost certainly the original purpose of the tenurial concentrations in the frontier hundreds of Shropshire.

6 Suppe, *Military Institutions*, pp. 63–87; see e.g. *Rot Hund.*, ii, 55, 114; on castle-guard and social militarization in Herefordshire, see Holden, *Lords*, pp. 54–7, 116–19.

7 On the fief of the twelfth-century sheriffs of Shropshire, see above, pp. 59–61, 66, 70.

8 *Red Book of the Exchequer*, ed. Hall, i, 271–4.

9 Suppe notes that those owing muntatorial service in 1166 were mostly descended from the 1086 tenants, but observes that this is not conclusive proof that muntatorial service was already being performed at the time of the Domesday inquest: Suppe, *Military Institutions*, p. 86.

Although, in the heady days of Earl Roger's inroads into Wales, these concentrations may well not have been intended to be permanent, the fact that the lord and his tenants lived in close proximity provided several strategic advantages, foremost among them ease of communication in case of an emergency. From Caus Castle, perched as it is on a high point at the eastern end of the Long Mountain, it is possible to survey almost all of the most populous lower land of that long lordship stretching towards Montgomery. A beacon burning on top of the tower of Caus, therefore, would have alerted the entire Corbet military following to danger almost immediately. The newly born frontier castleries had been designed for military co-operation; it seems entirely possible that use was made, occasionally at least, of that advantage. That the military relationship between the lords of Caus and their tenants remained strong in the thirteenth century further supports this argument.[10] Thus, in the 1260s and 1270s, the Corbets' frontier castle of Gwyddgrug was being guarded, albeit somewhat inefficiently, by their tenants Roger Godmund and Roger le Venur.[11]

Military co-operation between the lord and his tenants was in origin based on the common interest of a small colonial occupying force. We know that the chief Norman leaders, such as William fitz Osbern or Odo of Bayeux, took with them men upon whom they could rely. The Norman settlers who followed them to Herefordshire and Kent respectively had probably already been bound to them by ties of kinship or tenure in Normandy, and had fought under their command during the conquest of England.[12] Very possibly, the men whom Corbet, Picot de Sai and Warin the Bald enfeoffed had been their familiars or neighbours in Normandy, just as they themselves had followed their lords, the Montgomeries, from there to the Welsh borders.[13] Whether or not this was so, once a common interest of primary and subordinated landlords had been established, they were destined to co-ordinate their military defence.

Just as the *muntatores* probably began serving for specified periods of time at Oswestry during the reign of Henry I at the latest, so castle-guard at the other Shropshire frontier castles is likely to have been put on a regular footing at a very early date. Admittedly, the chief evidence for this comes from the thirteenth century,[14] but it seems highly probable that it

[10] *VCH*, viii, 325.

[11] *Welsh Assize Roll*, ed. Davies, pp. 31, 334.

[12] Le Patourel, *The Norman Empire*, pp. 32–5.

[13] Above, pp. 59–66.

[14] Although see, for instance, *Haughmond Cart.*, no. 700, for a grant made in the 1150s by the bishop of Hereford on terms of castle-guard service at Bishop's Castle; above, p. 44.

reflects the situation in the twelfth century faithfully.[15] For example, the Hundred Rolls of 1255 for Shropshire contain information on castle-guard obligations at Clun, probably returned by the jurors in response to the sixth article of Henry III's inquiry of that year, which ordered the collection of information on the services due at royal castles.[16] The burdens on the fourteen tenants who owed castle-guard at Clun totalled 185 days' service 'in time of war', although the amounts owed varied widely. Walter of Hopton held Hopton, Bradford and Coston for the service of one knight throughout the year *per reseanciam*, that is, 'by residence', as well as for forty days in time of war; but Adam of Acton only owed the service of a foot-soldier for four days *tempore guerre*.[17] It seems improbable that the tenants of 1255 were expected to perform the service themselves: Peter de Bosco and Roger and Nicholas of Edgton together owed 'forty days in time of war by one knight or two sergeants'. Nor would it appear probable that the garrisoning of Clun Castle could have been entirely the responsibility of these fourteen tenants: Clunbury does not appear in the 1255 roll yet, as late as 1333, Joan 'Symflewas' [*sic*], the lady of Clunbury, did fealty and acknowledged that she held the manors of Clunbury and Brompton for the service of a knight staying at Clun Castle for twenty days in time of war, 'in the same way as the lords of Clunbury had used to perform it'.[18] However, the fact that castle-guard in Clun had not been converted into a money payment, but was specified in days (usually fractions of forty), does strongly suggest that it was a customary duty which had survived since Norman times. The organization of the tenantry of Clun for the defence of the lord's chief castle is likely to have been a very early response to the creation of the Shropshire frontier.

Castle-guard and muntatorial service had the potential to raise considerably the level to which local society was inured to fighting, if those services were regularly demanded and performed. And we have every reason to believe that they were indeed in high demand on the Shropshire frontier during the first half of the twelfth century.

15 See Stenton, *First Century*, p. 205 on the value of thirteenth-century inquisitions for the study of twelfth-century castle-guard.

16 D. Roffe, 'The Hundred Rolls of 1255', *Historical Research*, **69**: 169 (1996), p. 209. Why the details on castle-guard at Clun were submitted is unclear, since the lord of Clun Castle, John Fitzalan II, was alive and had entered into full possession of his estates in 1244. Cf. T. F. Tout's article in *DNB*.

17 *Rot. Hund.*, ii, 76–7; cf. I. W. Rowlands, 'William de Braose and the Lordship of Brecon', *BBCS*, **30** (1982–3), p. 130.

18 SA 552/1/2, m. 11: 'Ead' Johanna fecit fidelitatem et cognouit tenere manerium de Clonebur' et Bromton' cum pertin' de castro de Clone pro seru' unius feod' militis sect' cur' de Clone de tribus septimanibus in tres septimanas et tempore Werre comorand' in dicto castro per viginti dies secundum quantitatem tenure eo modo quod domini de Clonebur' facere consueuerunt'.

For example, the military resources of Clun must have been strained to their very limits in the 1140s. During this period of bitter hostilities with the neighbouring Welsh dynasties of Maelienydd and Elfael, Clun Castle would have needed to be strongly garrisoned. But that was not the only demand made on the troops which Elias de Sai could raise. It was at this time that a singular castle was constructed at the utmost limit of the territory which can have been under Elias' control, at Bryn Amlwg.[19] The extraordinary site of this castle, in inhospitable, uncultivated territory on the higher ground west of Clun, sets this fortification well apart from any castles in England, and indeed from most of the castles on the frontier. Its purpose can only have been military; it was most probably devised as a base for a garrison to contain the threat from raiders, presumably mostly Welsh, into the Clun valley. Such a garrison would therefore have needed to be well trained in exactly the kind of frontier warfare which Gerald of Wales describes. The troops at Bryn Amlwg would have found themselves at some distance, and isolated, from the more populous parts of the lordship. They could easily have been outflanked, but would nevertheless have been in a good position to attack raiders trying to transport booty, or to alert the heartland of the lordship of approaching danger.[20] Bryn Amlwg Castle testifies to the acuteness and persistence of the threat of border raids into Clun in the mid-twelfth century, for its construction and maintenance was considered justified even though the required effort can have been no mean feat for a lordship of relatively limited military resources on which high demands were being made.

Because the lords of Clun found themselves desperately short of military manpower, they worked hard at consolidating and expanding the tenurial basis of the castlery of Clun throughout the first half of the twelfth century. Clun therefore became one of those castleries which were augmented, as military units, during the twelfth century.[21] Thus, by the early 1130s, Henry de Sai had exchanged the manor of Brompton

[19] See illustration. L. Alcock, D. J. C. King, W. G. Putnam and C. J. Spurgeon, 'Excavations at Castell Bryn Amlwg', *Mont. Coll.*, **60** (1967–8), p. 25: the ringwork at Bryn Amlwg 'surely' dates to the first half of the twelfth century at the latest.

[20] See description of this type of castle, termed 'border stronghold', in RCAHMW, *An Inventory of the Ancient Monuments in Glamorgan: The Later Castles*, p. 14. Further parallels noted by Alcock *et al.*, 'Excavations at Castell Bryn Amlwg', pp. 25–6: Bishop's Moat, Gwyddgrug Castle (Forden or Nantcribba), Hen Domen Montgomery, Old Hall Ffrydd (Hubert's Folly), and in Glamorgan Penlle'r Castell (Llangyfelach, SN 665096, 'a strange and remote site on the northern border of the lordship of Gower') and Morlais Castle (Merthyr Tydfil, SO 049096), on the northern border of the lordship of Glamorgan. See also Bartlett, *Making of Europe*, p. 134.

[21] The area described as the *castellaria* of Richmond in 1086, for example, grew to include several fees which came to owe castle-guard service there later: Stenton, *First Century*, pp. 194–5.

The Site of Bryn Amlwg Castle

for Cheney Longville with Shrewsbury Abbey.[22] It seems clear that the purpose of this transaction was to provide the lord of Clun with a conveniently close estate on which to enfeoff a military tenant: according to the 1166 *carta* of Geoffrey de Vere,[23] one Roger son of Eustace of 'Langefeld' owed the service of a knight; in 1242, one Roger Waudin held half a knight's fee at 'Langefeud'; and the 1255 Hundred rolls state that Cecilia de Wolvereslawe, the ward of Roger Waldin's heir, owed a knight for twenty days at Clun in times of war.[24] The efforts of the lords of Clun to avail themselves of more military tenants peaked, as one would expect, during the 1140s. According to a short history of St Alkmund's church preserved in the cartulary of Lilleshall Abbey,[25] Elias de Sai unlawfully seized Wistanstow from the monks at Lilleshall during the reign of King Stephen, bestowing it upon one Baldwin of Stapleton for the service of one knight. The account goes on to state that, after Baldwin was succeeded by his son Philip, Isabel de Sai received the service of one knight at Clun.[26] Given that 'Baldewinus de Stepeltone' appears

[22] *Salop. Cart.*, nos. 47d, 350b.

[23] Geoffrey was at the time lord of Clun by right of his wife, Isabel, daughter of Elias de Sai.

[24] On Cheney Longville see Eyton, xi, 369–75.

[25] Possibly compiled on oral testimony to assist in a court case in around 1190: *Mon. Angl.*,VI, no. xvi, p. 75; cf. *Lilleshall Cart.*, nos. 258 and 212.

[26] *Lilleshall Cart.*, no. 258: 'Helyas de Say dedit eam Baldwino de Stepelton pro servicio unius militis ... Isab. de Say, filia Heliae, recepit servicium unius militis ad Cluna de Philippo filio Baldwini.'

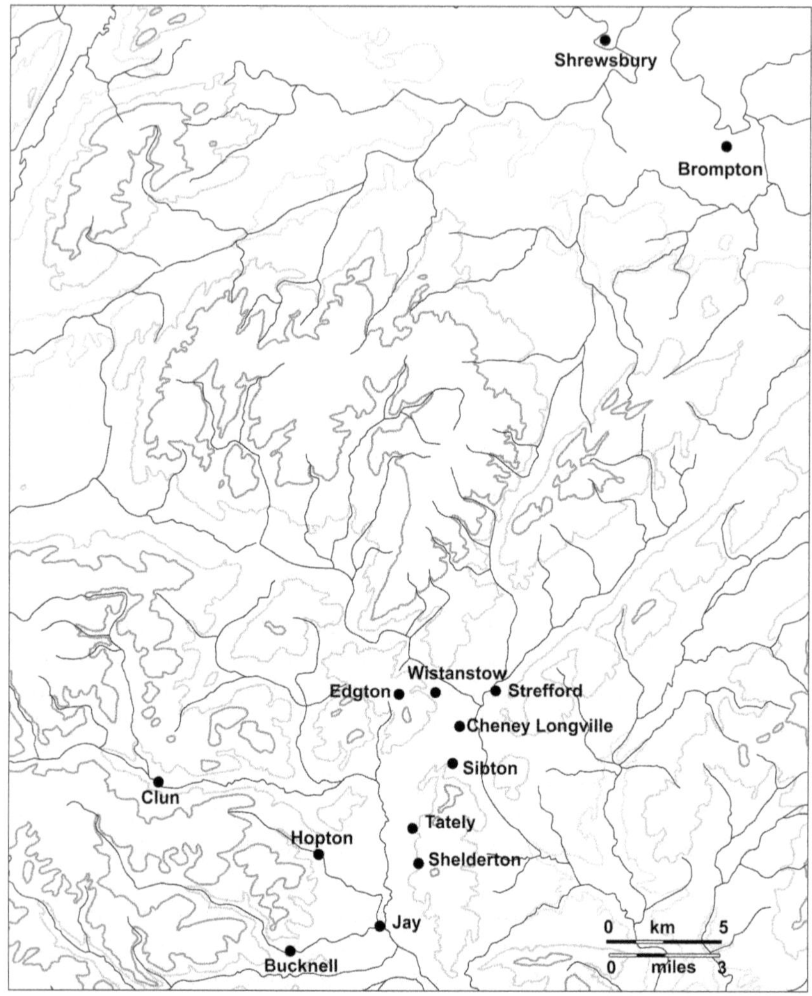

Map 26. The elaboration of the castlery of Clun during the twelfth century

in Geoffrey de Vere's 1166 *carta*, owing the service of one and a half knights,[27] it would appear that Philip succeeded afterwards, and that his father, Baldwin, already owed knight service, probably at Clun, in 1166. Perhaps the service owed was then slightly reduced for Philip because of

[27] *Red Book of the Exchequer*, ed. Hall, i, 274–5. See below, pp. 198–9.

the relative lull in cross-border hostilities which followed Henry II's 1165 campaign. The lords of Clun certainly seem also to have expanded their tenurial network southwards: Jay and Bucknell were added before 1135, if the 1166 *carta*'s toponymics of Hugo 'de Bukwel' and Elias 'de Chay' may be trusted on this point (the tenants of these two estates certainly owed castle-guard and suit of court at Clun in 1255). Eyton thought that Stow and Weston provided a further knight for Clun from 1166 at the latest.[28] Edgton, Hopton and Sibton were subenfeoffed from the de Sai demesne before 1135. Three other estates, Strefford, Tately and Shelderton, originally belonged to the shrieval fief of Shropshire, therefore forming part of the Fitzalan inheritance; it is interesting to note that, immediately after the Fitzalans became lords of Clun, these manors were subordinated to that castle.[29] Tenure-based castle-guard clearly remained a real source of military manpower in the middle decades of the twelfth century and involved a significant part of the Clun tenantry in border warfare.

The lord of Oswestry, too, continued to rely on his lands in Shropshire specifically for support in concerns arising from frontier warfare. In around 1180, Fulk Fitzwarin II granted a village called *Eluretona* (probably Alderton near Myddle) to Shrewsbury Abbey, free from all service except that due to the chief lord, which consisted in providing, once a year, when summoned, an archer with bow and arrows for fifteen days for the custody of the castle of Oswestry, and a man to lead the lord's sumpter horse, at the lord's expense, when the said lord went in the host into Wales.[30] The lords of Oswestry clearly tailored the service owed to them by their tenants to the specific needs of their frontier castle. Moreover, this isolated reference to a relatively minor obligation indicates that the system of tenure-based military service owed at Oswestry had grown strikingly complex, and must have involved a very great proportion of the tenants, even those of relatively minor means, in border warfare. Roger Mortimer's grant of 1199 to Cwmhir Abbey for the souls of his men and of 'those who had died in the conquest of Maelienydd' also demonstrates that, by the turn of the twelfth and thirteenth centuries, border warfare had contributed much to shaping the outlook of the frontier lords and their men, and still acted as a powerful tie between them.[31]

[28] Eyton xi, 313–16.

[29] Eyton xi, 366–9, 300–1.

[30] *Salop. Cart.*, pp. 252–3: 'salvo tantomodo servicio summo domino illius feudi quod tale est monachi semel in anno de predicta terra cum summoniti fuerint invenient unum hominem cum arcu et sagittis per quindecim dies ad custodiam castelli de Osewaldestr' et quando predictus dominus inerit in exceritum [*sic*] in Walliam invenient unum hominem cum volgio ad ducendum sumarium eius et ad logiam suam faciendam in expensis domini'.

[31] See above, p. 125; below, p. 185.

Despite the efforts of the lords, it is doubtful that castle-guard can be envisaged as a system that guaranteed sufficient garrisons for castles. The detailed sources based on thirteenth-century inquests should not let us forget situations such as the plight of the castle of Carmarthen in 1116, which the Normans were forced to hand over to Welsh allies, formally entreating them to 'keep the castle ... which belongs to the king, each one of you in his appointed time in this wise: Owain ap Caradog to keep the castle for a fortnight, and Rhydderch ap Tewdwr for a fortnight, and Maredudd ap Rhydderch ap Caradog for a third fortnight'.[32] There can be no doubt that, on the Shropshire border, too, garrisons had, on some occasions, to be scraped together as best they could.

However, the impact which the principle and practice of castle-guard and military service had on society must have lessened dramatically during the period under consideration. Population growth, for one thing, must have meant that the military resources of the borders became less constrained, and this in turn would have reduced the pressure of military obligations on the individual members of border society. No doubt castle-guard and muntatorial service continued to evolve and adapt, or become obsolete, as convenience, resources and necessity varied. Yet, just as the military border survived almost throughout the thirteenth century, so customary means of levying the necessary troops proved resilient on the frontier. Customary castle-guard may have retained its value over mercenary garrisons because local troops had acquired specific military expertise, and because they could be levied more quickly, something which was essential on the treacherous Shropshire frontier. Henry III certainly appears to have thought so. In 1229, after the disaster of the Ceri campaign, he transferred the castle-guard services at the royal castle of Shrawardine to the new castle at Montgomery, recently granted to Hubert de Burgh, specifying that 'all the guards, due at Screwardin, that is to say that all the knights and free tenants, who were wont to do guard there in the time of the king's ancestors, shall in future do the same for the said Hubert at the castle of Muntgomery'.[33] In an emergency, the king might even commandeer military resources from a frontier castlery. During the Marshal rebellion of 1233, Henry III ordered 'all knights, tenants of the castellany of Clune, to be answering for their guard and service due to the said

[32] *Brut*, p. 89.

[33] *Cal. Chart. R., 1226–57*, p. 83. Castle-guard service at Shrawardine Castle apparently dated back to the first half of the twelfth century at least. As early as 1166, Philip fitz Helgod answered for the service of one knight for forty days at Shrawardine Castle, as performed by his ancestors; Hugh de Lacy, in the same year, admitted to owing £10 for as many knights to do guard service at that castle: *Red Book of the Exchequer*, ed. Hall, i, 277, 66.

castle, to Baldwin de Vere, constable thereof, to do the said guard at his summons whenever necessary'.[34]

It is a paradoxical truth that details about castle-guard service preserved in the thirteenth- and fourteenth-century sources are often better evidence for earlier periods than for the survival of castle-guard. In 1313, the lord of Abergavenny, John Hastings, was said to have owed the king the duty of guarding the country of Upper Gwent 'if there shall be common war between the king and the prince of Wales'.[35] This was clearly a duty agreed after the middle of the thirteenth century, when the title of prince of Wales had come to be commonly used – it may date to 1272, when the Hastings family became lords of Abergavenny. Yet it is also clear that by 1313, when the duty was recorded, it can no longer have applied literally, since the title of prince of Wales had by then been conferred on the son of the English king. That it was fossilized in its literal, though obsolete, form serves as a reminder of the caution with which the statements of inquests need to be approached.

Nevertheless, it is not easy to dismiss the evidence of the 1255 Hundred Rolls for Shropshire. The information on muntatorial services owed at Oswestry which the Shropshire jurors provided in the 1255 inquest is highly detailed, a fact which may indicate that they had not been commuted.[36] John of Chetwynd, said to owe the service of three *muntatores* at Oswestry in 1255, had bound himself in 1250–5 to provide a 'munitor' for the village of Howle, situated about halfway between Stafford and Shrewsbury, to serve in time of war at the castle of Oswestry.[37] It certainly seems that there was some ambiguity about the matter of commuted services. In 1242, Thomas Corbet of Caus asserted that 'when an army is levied in the March of Wales ... the custom in those parts is that whoever holds by military service must do that service by providing a soldier *per corpus hominis*.'[38] Yet he lost his case against Herbert fitz Peter of Pontesbury, who had claimed to owe only a money payment. It seems that between 1240 and 1256,

[34] *Cal. Pat. R., 1232–47*, p. 32. For the suggestion that this source reveals the difficulties in obtaining castle-guard services, see M. Prestwich, 'The Garrisoning of English Medieval Castles', in R. P. Abels and B. S. Bachrach (eds.), *The Normans and Their Adversaries at War: Essays in Memory of C. Warren Hollister* (Woodbridge, 2001), p. 194. This implies that the Clun tenants normally performed their castle-guard at royal behest. In light of the evidence discussed in this chapter, it seems more probable that it was still exceptional in 1233 for the military tenants of a frontier castle not in royal custody to be levied by the king's order.

[35] *CIPM*, v, no. 412, p. 232. 'A prince of Wales' is another possible reading of this document, in which case the service might pre-date the mid-thirteenth century.

[36] *Rot. Hund.*, ii, 55–6, 114.

[37] *Rot. Hund.*, ii, 57; *Haughmond Cart.*, no. 645: 'Ego vero et heredes mei acquietabimus dictam villam de Howle de quodam munitor cum pertinentiis et servicio quod pertinet de villa de Houle tempore guerre apud Album Monasterium Johannis filii Alani ...'

[38] *Curia Regis Rolls*, vol. xvii: *1242–3*, ed. A. Nicol (London, 1991), no. 631.

during the period of English ascendancy on the Shropshire–Powys border, a variety of attitudes towards castle-guard competed with each other. Non-commuted, tenure-based military service persisted as a principle, but it was beginning to be considered old-fashioned.

Nevertheless, as a principle it remained very much alive, at least at Clun, until the end of the thirteenth century. As has been seen, the obligations determined at the outset did not remain immutable throughout two centuries of intermittent frontier warfare: the Clun tenants appear to have owed, by the later thirteenth century, amounts of castle-guard which were appropriate to their status and economic resources. This strongly suggests that their obligations could be renegotiated as their fortunes grew or declined, or as new tenants received grants of land near Clun Castle. As mentioned, the knight service owed at Clun for Wistanstow may have been reduced from one and a half knights to one when a new tenant inherited after 1166.[39] Castle-guard at Clun was certainly never commuted into payments in cash by the tenants to the lord. It is true that in 1272 the money value of the castle-guard services at Clun was assessed at £6 15s,[40] but it seems probable that this was an attempt to express the money value of services which had not yet been commuted.[41] This is suggested by the fact that the money value was said to apply only to services owed in times of war, while in times of peace castle-ward duty at Clun was worth nothing. The tenants at Clun asserted in the same year that their castle-guard should not be assessed as part of Fitzalan revenue due from the estate, since they performed it at their own cost.[42] It would seem that at Clun castle-guard remained, in principle, a useful source of military manpower for as long as the Welsh military frontier existed.

It does not necessarily follow that the lords of Clun could still actually garrison their castle by drawing on the guard services of their tenants in the second half of the thirteenth century. It was argued above that the lords and tenants of Clun, from the late eleventh century to the late thirteenth, periodically faced specific military challenges over and beyond those encountered by local aristocracies elsewhere in the British Isles.[43] Yet castle-guard was not an automatically functioning 'system'; the lord

[39] Above, pp. 176–7, 179–80.

[40] *Cal. Close R., 1268–72*, p. 506.

[41] S. Painter, *Studies in the History of the English Feudal Barony* (Baltimore, 1943), p. 134.

[42] *Cal. Close R., 1268–72*, p. 511.

[43] Above, pp. 176–80. See also F. C. Suppe, 'Castle Guard and the Castlery of Clun', *Haskins Society Journal*, I (1989), pp. 123–34; the same, 'The Persistence of Castle-Guard in the Welsh Marches and Wales: Suggestions for a Research Agenda and Methodology', in Abels and Bachrach (eds.), *The Normans and their Adversaries at War*, pp. 201–21.

needed to earn the loyalty and co-operation of his tenants, be it through dispensing gifts of land or privileges or by providing charismatic and successful military leadership. On a less inspiring note, threats provided another means by which a lord might ensure the performance of castle-guard, as is suggested by the case of Cardiff Castle in the lordship of Glamorgan on the south-eastern Welsh border. The background to this is that, under Earl William of Gloucester (1148–83), castle-guard services owed by tenants were being commuted to wardsilver.[44] However, King John, who had become lord of Glamorgan in 1189, reasserted the importance of personally performed castle-guard in 1208, writing to 'all the barons and knights of the honor of Glamorgan and of the honor of Cardiff', insisting that they repair his houses in the castle bailey at Cardiff, as was customary, and discharge their castle-guard there as they were wont to do or risk forfeiting their fees.[45] If castle-guard at Clun and other border castles was kept alive, then, this was not achieved by the threat of frontier warfare alone. The choices made by the individual lords, and the bargains they were able to strike with their tenants or their own lords, decided in equal measure where and when castle-guard would be performed. Castle-guard, like all other facets of the complex ties between lords and their men, needed to be constantly reinforced by the practice of good lordship;[46] this is a further fact of life on the Shropshire–Powys frontier which is revealed by Roger Mortimer's Cwmhir grant of 1199.[47]

However, customary castle-guard services are but one indication of social militarization. It was argued above that the castellan lords of the Shropshire–Powys frontier routinely acted as military captains in the service of the crown – and this circumstance furnishes a few glimpses of the role still played by these lords, in the later thirteenth century, as the military leaders of their tenants.[48] Thus, in 1263, Thomas Corbet received a letter of protection from legal prosecution 'during the war in Wales' for himself, his son, his brother and the twenty-three other men under his command; sixteen, and probably more, of these held land of him.[49] In the same year, Roger Mortimer received a similar grant of protection 'during the Welsh war' for himself and his thirty-four troops, at least half

44 *Cartae*, i, no. 108; cf. *ibid.*, no. 113.

45 *Rot. Pat.*, p. 79; there is archaeological evidence for the knights' houses in the bailey of Cardiff castle: RCAHMW, *An Inventory of the Ancient Monuments in Glamorgan. The Early Castles*, pp. 165–6 and nn. 20 and 30.

46 For the importance of good lordship in maintaining the loyalty of tenants, see R. R. Davies, 'Lordship or Colony?', in J. F. Lydon, *The English in Medieval Ireland* (Dublin, 1984), pp. 142–60.

47 See above, pp. 126, 181.

48 See Davies, *Lordship and Society*, pp. 77–8; above, pp. 79–84.

49 *Cal. Pat. R. 1258–66*, p. 287; *VCH*, viii, 325.

of whom were border tenants such as Brian of Brampton and John of Lingen.[50] Peter Corbet, Thomas's son, was at the head of six Caus tenants in 1277,[51] and on 6 December 1287, during the revolt of Rhys ap Maredudd, Edward I ordered him to lead his 'horses and arms and reasonable power' to Cardiganshire and not to 'allege now the state of wintry weather or the lack of money for him and his footmen'. Fulk Fitzwarin V and John Lestrange V, together with Owain ap Gruffudd ap Gwenwynwyn, or Owain de la Pole, were to accompany him: even the last generation of thirteenth-century Marcher lords did not escape military duty at the head of their men, no matter how unpleasant the meteorological conditions.[52]

To consider the wider context of the thirteenth-century March of Wales is to add further reasons for thinking that the military retinues of the Corbets and the Mortimers remained a reality until well into Edward I's reign. Great Marcher lords could command veritable personal armies. The earl of Pembroke apparently did so in 1233,[53] and the earl of Gloucester had several Glamorgan tenants in his retinue in 1245.[54] But it is also striking that lesser Marcher barons prided themselves on performing military service in Wales at their own cost. Thus, during Edward I's Welsh campaigns of 1282, Geoffrey de Camvill, the lord of Llansteffan, himself footed the bill for his military service and for that of his men.[55] In May 1282 he paid for the service in Wales of a troop of thirteen lances for one week; the men had been raised from his English fief, but he accepted royal wages only for the period during which they were mobilized in England.[56] It is possible that, when Edward I insisted in the cold winter of 1287–8 that Peter Corbet lead his men to Cardigan, he commented that Peter should not cite as an excuse any 'lack of money' precisely because it was customary for Marcher lords to perform service in Wales at the head of their own retinues and at their own cost. It may be that it was partly due to such traditions that the role of the lords of Caus and Wigmore as the military leaders of their tenants was kept alive.

Provisions for the levying of local troops during royal campaigns provide yet more evidence for the militarization of the border population. There was certainly no shortage of military manpower in the Marcher lordships west of Shropshire in the later thirteenth century. In 1276–7,

[50] *VCH*, viii, pp. 248, 299. [51] Eyton, vii, 33.

[52] *Cal. Chanc. R. Var.*, pp. 317–8; cf. pp. 306–7.

[53] *Cal. Anc. Corr. Wales*, p. 33. Cf. Walker, 'Supporters of Richard Marshal'.

[54] M. Altschul, *A Baronial Family in Medieval England: The Clares, 1217–1314* (Baltimore, 1965), p. 72.

[55] *Cal. Chanc. R. Var.*, p. 229.

[56] J. E. Morris, *The Welsh Wars of Edward I: A Contribution to Mediaeval Military History, Based on Original Documents* (Oxford, 1901), p. 61.

300 moat-builders were dispatched from Oswestry and Montgomery to Chester, and 200 moat-builders and carpenters to Rhuddlan.[57] During Edward I's Welsh wars, the garrisons of the frontier castles may well have been recruited locally; in 1276–7, that at Oswestry consisted of thirty-four soldiers, ten of them mounted.[58] At the height of the campaigns of 1282–3, royal agents were sent to pick armed footmen in Ellesmere, Knockin, Whittington, Clun and Wigmore.[59] In 1287, Edward I levied 400 foot in Clun and 200 in Oswestry to help suppress the revolt of Rhys ap Maredudd, remarkably high numbers considering that the sheriff of Shropshire and Staffordshire was enjoined to provide only 2,000 fighting men from those two counties,[60] while Shropshire owed the service of only 63 knights in 1279 × 1280.[61] The recruitment of troops for royal campaigns was generally most demanding in the areas closest to the fighting; and the population of the Marcher lordships was equal to the task. It would appear entirely possible that those living in the borders were, by the later thirteenth century, considerably more accustomed to warfare than the population of the border counties.

* * *

The military challenges posed by the proximity of the Welsh had a significant impact on the population of the Shropshire borders. Very early on, the lords of the westernmost castles of Shropshire concentrated all their military resources on defending those fortifications. It is probable that occasionally at least a large part of the tenantry of Clun, Caus and Oswestry would have been involved in border warfare, as garrisons or as light cavalry, until the mid-twelfth century. Thereafter, the evidence suggests that in Shropshire, and particularly on the borders, the principle that castle-guard services should not be commuted was distinctively well established, even in the second half of thirteenth century, by when it had begun to be disputed by tenants. However, throughout the period under consideration, it seems probable that castle-guard could not actually be levied equally effectively in all the Shropshire border baronies. Even at the regional level of the Powys–Shropshire frontier, then, the meaningfulness and survival of the honor in the twelfth and thirteenth centuries may well have varied considerably so far as military retinues and obligations were concerned. Nevertheless, during Edward I's reign

[57] TNA E 372/121, m. 21 r.

[58] *Ibid.* [59] *Cal. Chanc. R. Var.*, pp. 279–80.

[60] *Rymer*, I, iii, 17–18; *Cal. Chanc. R. Var.*, pp. 311–13.

[61] Morris, *Welsh Wars of Edward I*, p. 36; the number of knights owed by English barons had of course been reduced dramatically over the century after 1166: see Painter, *Studies*, ch. 2, esp. pp. 38–45.

border castellans such as Corbet and Mortimer still expected to lead their own tenants on royal campaigns in Wales, and there was certainly no shortage of military manpower in the small frontier lordships of the late thirteenth century. It is quite possible that this was, in part, because non-commuted castle-guard services had survived not only as a notion, but also in practice, in the border lordships.

Chapter 6

THE SHAPING OF ADMINISTRATIVE TERRITORIES

The honors on the Shropshire borders, like the Norman and English conquest lordships in Wales, were compact seigneurial territories. Accordingly, the perceived similarities between the two may well not have been limited to the military sphere. Certainly both military and 'civilian' elements inform the modern historical category of the March of Wales, for instance when summarized as 'the area defined by the military enterprise and seigneurial power of the Anglo-Norman lords in the two centuries or so between 1066 and 1284'.[1] The lords of the border honors and conquest lordships rightly saw themselves as military leaders, but their impact extended beyond what could be achieved by the sword. In the longer term, the purpose of military conquest was exploitation of land and of men for the lord's profit. There were various means to achieve that end in the twelfth and thirteenth centuries, but the lords of the Shropshire borderlands faced the distinctive challenge of finding ways to rule both the English and the Welsh population of their honors. How far did the lords' efforts at securing administrative, fiscal and judicial control over their lordships create distinctive administrative territories? And might this have contributed towards setting the borderlands apart from both Shropshire and Powys, while rendering them more similar to the conquest lordships in Wales?

⋆ ⋆ ⋆

The part of Shropshire bordering on Powys already consisted of a chain of administrative territories when Earl Roger began dispensing land there to his chief followers. Like all Anglo-Saxon shires, Shropshire was parcelled out into hundreds for administrative, fiscal and judicial purposes,

[1] Davies, *Lordship and Society*, p. 16.

probably soon after it was first established in the early tenth century.[2] The administrative functions of the hundred, by the mid-eleventh century, were acting powerfully to entrench the cohesion of local territorial units. The laws and ordinances of the tenth- and eleventh-century kings of England demonstrate the importance attached by the royal government to the role of hundredal courts in local governance.[3] According to these normative texts, the hundredal courts were to convene monthly, and there is no reason to doubt that they routinely involved the free men, and probably also many of the unfree, in official business, such as settling disputes, bringing thieves to justice or levying taxes.[4] This must have meant that a strong sense of local identity was the norm in eleventh-century England; the men of relatively compact territories were welded together through regular contact, and also because they routinely acted as the guarantors of one another's rights in the hundredal courts.[5] The administrative institution of the hundred was, then, a solid social cement.[6] Moreover, by its nature it acted not only, or even primarily, on a social level. Since its basis was not fundamentally personal, but territorial, it helped bind together small settled districts, or groups of estates. This effect is likely to have been especially pronounced in the border counties of England, Cheshire, Shropshire and Herefordshire, since in these territorial fragmentation of hundreds was unusually rare.[7]

Local cohesion must, then, have been fostered in the westernmost hundreds of Shropshire – but this can have done little to set them apart from the county, particularly as the most substantial of the inhabitants of these hundreds, in any case, probably also attended shire meetings. It is in fact difficult to pinpoint any characteristics which would have distinguished the westernmost hundreds of Shropshire, in the mid-eleventh century, from the other hundreds of that county. The hundreds of Mersete and Rhiwset contrasted with their four neighbours to the east – Baschurch, Condover, Hodnet and Wrockwardine – in that the latter were abnormally large and named after royal manors. This provides indirect evidence

[2] F. R. Thorn, 'Hundreds and Wapentakes', in A. Williams and R. W. H. Erskine (eds.), *The Shropshire Domesday* (Alecto County Edition of Domesday Book, 19, 1990), p. 29.

[3] *Die Gesetze der Angelsachsen*, ed. F. Liebermann, 3 vols. (Halle, 1896–1916), i, 192–5; iii, 130–3; H. R. Loyn, 'The Hundred in England in the Tenth and Early Eleventh Centuries', in H. Hearder and H. R. Loyn (eds.), *British Government and Administration: Studies Presented to S. B. Chrimes* (Cardiff, 1974), pp. 1–15; *The Laws of the Kings of England from Edmund to Henry I*, ed. A. J. Robertson (Cambridge, 1925), pp. 16–19 and notes.

[4] H. R. Loyn, *The Governance of Anglo-Saxon England, 500–1087* (London, 1984), p. 140; on the unfree attending hundredal meetings: S. Reynolds, *Kingdoms and Communities in Western Europe, 900–1300* (Oxford, 1984), pp. 114–15.

[5] *Gesetze*, ed. Liebermann, i, 192.

[6] Lewis, 'English and Norman Government', p. 37.

[7] *Ibid.*, p. 53.

that they may have been created by earlier, smaller hundreds being joined together by royal edict.[8] Yet this was not particular to the hundreds in the body of the county. Leintwardine, the southernmost of the western Shropshire frontier hundreds, was sizeable. It consisted of two detached parts, and was named, or possibly renamed, after a royal manor.[9] Moreover, almost all hundreds on the westernmost frontier depended upon royal manors, and may therefore be numbered among those hundreds which originated, and functioned, as districts dependent upon a royal estate.[10] In this, too, they were similar to several of the hundreds in the body of the county. The hundreds which were not dependent on manors lay on the border with Herefordshire.[11] Before the arrival of the Normans, the westernmost hundreds of Shropshire had few features setting them apart from the rest of the county.

The first Norman lords of the Shropshire border, Picot de Sai, Corbet and Warin the Bald had no tenurial *antecessores*; they did not step into the shoes of mid-eleventh-century landholders. Rather, the compact blocks of estates which Earl Roger had, by 1086, bestowed on these three men were each focused on one of the hundreds on the western borders of Shropshire.[12] It seems very possible that Picot de Sai was originally granted the territory of Rinlow hundred as a whole, perhaps prospectively; the same may well be true of Warin the Bald and Mersete hundred, and of Corbet and Wittery hundred. This may well parallel the way in which the Normans and the English acquired land in Wales, in Ireland and on the Anglo-Scottish border.[13] In Cumbria, it seems possible that the compact Norman honors created there reveal the contours of earlier, arguably Celtic, territorial units. In Ireland, from the 1160s, the leading English magnates such as Strongbow or Hugh de Lacy were granted whole kingdoms, albeit prospectively; the basis for land-grants to knightly settlers from England and Wales appears sometimes to have been sub-kingdoms or *tuatha*.[14] Moreover, it is directly relevant that Earl Roger and his men provide a fair share of the evidence that, when the Normans seized, or at least claimed, land in Wales, they targeted whole commotes, rather than individual vills. Rainald the sheriff was said in 1086 to have two 'fines' in

[8] *Ibid.*, p. 52. [9] *Ibid.*, p. 52.

[10] Thorn, 'Hundreds and Wapentakes', *Shropshire Domesday*, p. 30.

[11] *Ibid.*, p. 36.

[12] Lewis, 'English and Norman Government', pp. 228–31, 233, 244.

[13] J. G. Edwards, 'The Normans and the Welsh March', *Proceedings of the British Academy*, **42** (1956), pp. 155–77; G. W. S. Barrow, 'The Pattern of Lordship and Feudal Settlement in Cumbria', *Journal of Medieval History*, **1** (1975), pp. 117–38; the same, *The Anglo-Norman Era in Scottish History* (Oxford, 1980), esp. ch. 2; P. G. B. McNeill, H. L. MacQueen and A. M. Lyons (eds.), *Atlas of Scottish History to 1707* (Edinburgh, 1996), pp. 412–13.

[14] R. Frame, *Colonial Ireland, 1169–1369* (Dublin 1981), pp. 70–1.

Wales, Cynllaith and Edeirnion; Earl Hugh of Chester to hold the 'terra' of Iâl of Earl Roger; and one 'Tudur the Welshman' to hold a *finis terrae* of Earl Roger which may be identified with the commote of Nanheudwy.[15] In the eyes of late eleventh-century English administrators, Welsh territorial divisions could certainly be the equivalents of hundreds: the cantred of Arwystli is referred to in Domesday Book as a 'hundretum'.[16] Thus, if Earl Roger did indeed bestow the three frontier hundreds of Shropshire wholesale on three of his chief men, this would indicate that the border hundreds were appropriated by the Normans in the same way as they seized Welsh territories.

One possible reason for seizing on commotes was that these territories were administrative units inextricably tied to Welsh rights of lordship. Their purpose was probably to make possible the collection of tributes and renders, and they therefore provided the ready-made and transferable means of controlling the population and resources of Welsh districts.[17] Similarly, it is conceivable that, by allocating hundreds, Earl Roger intended to put to use existing administrative structures to establish as firm a hold on the border territories as possible. Earl Roger himself, apart from having been put in charge of Shropshire, was one of the five Normans among whom William the Conqueror had divided the 'rapes' of Sussex;[18] it seems certain that he was familiar with the practice of granting land by conferring existing administrative units. Bestowing on his chief men whole hundreds – including hundredal courts – may well have been intended to enhance the control his lieutenants exercised over the freemen in their districts.[19] Tenure of the hundredal manor in 1086 seems to have conferred control over the hundredal court, particularly in Shropshire and other western border counties, where many of the hundreds were associated with royal manors before the Norman conquest.[20] Earl Roger certainly appears to have paid special attention to the hundredal manors while dispensing lands in Shropshire. He retained in demesne seven of the nine Shropshire manors to which hundreds were attached. However, in Mersete and Rhiwset hundreds, he included

[15] DB 255a (Cynllaith and Edeirnion); 254b (Iâl); 253c (Tudur the Welshman); Edwards, 'Normans', pp. 138–9; Lloyd, *History of Wales*, ii, 389.

[16] DB 269a; cf. DB 269b: 'Robert (of Rhuddlan) also claims a Hundred, Arwystli, which Earl Roger (de Montgomery) holds. The Welshmen testify that this Hundred is one of the (Hundreds) of North Wales.'

[17] Edwards, 'Normans', pp. 169–71.

[18] *VCH*, i, 288; note that the number and nature of the Sussex rapes before 1086 is uncertain: J. F. A. Mason, 'William I and the Sussex Rapes' (Historical Association, 1066 Commemoration Lectures, 3, 1966, repr. 1972).

[19] On individual Normans controlling hundredal courts see Green, *Aristocracy*, p. 197.

[20] H. M. Cam, 'Manerium Cum Hundredo: The Hundred and the Hundredal Manor', in her *Liberties and Communities in Medieval England* (Cambridge, 1933; repr. London, 1963), pp. 75–7.

the hundredal manors, Maesbury and Alberbury respectively, among those estates he granted to his chief men.[21] Given that he kept a valuable manor to himself in both cases – Whittington in Mersete hundred and Ford in Rhiwset – it appears all the more probable that Warin and Corbet received the hundredal manors because it enhanced their control over the tenurial blocks they had received. Picot's case is less clear-cut, but probably only because Rinlow hundred appears not to have been attached to a manor. It parallels Mersete and Rhiwset in that Earl Roger retained Lydham, a valuable but peripheral manor of Rinlow hundred.[22] Earl Roger and his men, like all of the Norman adventurers bent on making conquests in Wales and the borders, were not primarily concerned with administrative and judicial matters, but with exercising military domination.[23] Nevertheless, they may well have appreciated that the hundreds provided, like the commotes, a well-established means of territorial control. A distinctive link between the three men holding compact territories in western Shropshire and the hundreds in which they held those lands does seem to have been created by 1086.

The territorial correlation between the new tenurial units and the old hundreds should not be exaggerated. Even if Picot had originally been assigned only Rinlow hundred, the situation soon changed. By 1086, the territory held by Picot in Rinlow hundred was almost doubled by the estates he had received from the two parts of Leintwardine hundred to the north and south. Strategic concerns may have played a role in this expansion, but, possibly, it was meant to compensate him for those Rinlow estates held by Earl Roger and the bishop of Hereford.[24] Be that as it may, the new tenurial unit extended beyond the boundaries of the hundred.[25] There were several Rhiwset estates, besides Ford, which were not included in Corbet's fief. On the other hand, Roger fitz Corbet had a considerable interest in Wittery hundred, which included Earl Roger's new castle of Montgomery. This may have been because Roger, and his father before him, were meant to act as guardians of that fortification. The case of the lord of Mersete hundred is most distinctive in this respect, as the compact territory he held on the Welsh borders constituted only a small part of the vast fief he had been granted in Shropshire.[26] The three border lords were by no means all in the same position in 1086, and none

[21] DB 253b–c. Leintwardine manor, possibly the hundredal manor of the eponymous hundred during the reign of King Edward the Confessor, was held in chief by Ralph of Mortimer: DB 260b; on Roger's grants to his chief men see above, pp. 59–68.

[22] DB 253c. [23] Davies, 'Kings, Lords and Liberties', p. 44.

[24] DB 252b. The bishop of Hereford held Lydbury North in chief; this formed the nucleus of the lordship of Bishop's Castle.

[25] Lewis, 'English and Norman Government', p. 244; Maps 34 and 35.

[26] *Ibid.*, pp. 228–31 and Map 3.

of their holdings exactly fitted the mould formed by the original hundreds of Shropshire.

Moreover, that mould was not immediately broken. Rinlow hundred, parts of Leintwardine, Rhiwset, Wittery and Mersete may have been overlaid by novel and unusually compact tenurial interests, but it seems that these interests did not displace the old hundredal structure. Hundredal meetings may well have been disrupted when Earl Roger and his men first arrived, but, at the time of the Domesday survey, all the westernmost hundreds certainly fulfilled the same administrative functions as the other hundreds of Shropshire.[27] Thus, in 1086, the old hundreds still mattered; they continued to determine where administrative and territorial boundaries ran. Although radical changes in the tenurial structure had been effected, the administrative units that had shaped the Shropshire–Powys frontier during the eleventh century remained in place. The distinction between the territorial basis of seigneurial power and that of the hundreds remained valid.

Thus, the origins of the link between the lords of the tenurial blocks in western Shropshire and the westernmost hundreds seem somewhat ambiguous. That link may have originally been meant to involve little more than a prospective claim to the financial profits of the hundredal court. But it seems, on balance, more probable that Earl Roger and his men expected to engage more fully and directly with the existing administrative and judicial structures – after all, this could only be to their advantage. In any case, the way in which Earl Roger chose to distribute land meant, first, that the compartmentalized nature of the borderlands was to be preserved, second, that the potential, at least, for the development of territories defined by non-military – judicial and administrative – seigneurial power was maintained, and third, that the relationship between such territories and the hundredal structure needs to be considered. In what follows, the fate of the administrative territories in westernmost Shropshire between the late eleventh and late thirteenth centuries will be examined by focusing on three geographical regions in turn: the valley and uplands around Clun, the area surrounding the castle of Oswestry, and finally the Rea–Camlad valley and Severn gap.

ADMINISTRATIVE TERRITORIES, *c.* 1100–1300, I: THE CLUN VALLEY AND UPLANDS

There are several indications that, by the end of the reign of Henry I, the compact tenurial block once held by Picot de Sai was developing into a seigneurial honor along lines familiar from the history of other

[27] Thorn, 'Hundreds and Wapentakes', *Shropshire Domesday, passim.*

nascent Anglo-Norman baronies. As has been seen in a previous chapter, Picot's lands descended to male and female heirs during the twelfth century without being divided, and this established the identity of those lands as an integral family inheritance.[28] By 1166, when Geoffrey de Vere, the husband of Picot's granddaughter, returned a *carta* in response to the national inquiry into tenure by knight service, that block of family land had as much claim as any in England to being a barony.[29] The castle at Clun had certainly been built by this time, and almost certainly much earlier, providing a focus, or *caput*, for this new unit of aristocratic power. The lord's demesne was being steadily reduced by grants to lay followers[30] and, since it was focused on the upper Clun valley, it provides further evidence that the castle at Clun was indeed a seigneurial centre by 1135. The territory granted to Picot de Sai by 1086 came to correspond to a textbook example of a seigneurial honor early in the twelfth century.

What precisely did this mean for the administrative structure in this region? According to the textbook view, the lords of Clun during the twelfth century would have presided over an honorial court[31] and, given that most of their tenants held land in the Clun valley, the relationship between such a court and the court of Rinlow hundred needs to be considered. Newly fledged honors which were territorially coterminous with eleventh-century hundreds have attracted some scholarly attention, so a few cases can be adduced for comparison. During the twelfth century, the counts of Aumale controlled the entire territory of Holderness in eastern Yorkshire, and appear to have converted into a single wapentake the three hundreds into which that district had been divided in the tenth century.[32] As all the suitors to the wapentake court were men holding land of the counts, and the higher-ranking among them were more likely to attend, the court of the wapentake, in practice, also served as the court of the honor.[33] Similarly, the court of the honor of Clitheroe in Lancashire was, originally, also the wapentake court of Blackburn[34] and it is thought that a comparable situation existed in the Isle of Axholme

[28] Above, pp. 68–9, 73–84. [29] *Red Book of the Exchequer*, ed. Hall, i, 274–5.

[30] The details of subenfeoffment in the twelfth-century lordship of Clun are set forth by Eyton, xi, 225–75; 297–316; 355–75.

[31] Stenton, *First Century*, esp. pp. 42–6.

[32] B. English, *The Lords of Holderness, 1086–1260: A Study in Feudal Society* (Hull, 1991), pp. 109–12.

[33] *Ibid.*, pp. 113–21.

[34] *Ibid.*, p. 114; *The Court Rolls of the Honor of Clitheroe, in the County of Lancaster*, ed. W. Farrer, 3 vols. (Manchester, 1897–1913), i, v.

in Lincolnshire, where the lords of the Mowbray honor held the entire wapentake in demesne.[35]

The honor centred on Clun was of a size roughly comparable to these examples. Moreover, the Clun valley was sparsely populated even by twelfth-century standards,[36] which must have meant that proportionally fewer courts were necessary. Certainly, regularized social and judicial meetings were both customary and in the best interest of the lords and their men. Given these circumstances and the parallels mentioned above, it seems possible that in the case of the nascent honor of Clun, too, the old hundredal structure facilitated the creation of the honorial court, and in so doing was subsumed by it. This need not mean that there was an orchestrated, intentional transition; the lords of Clun would have retained an interest in the potential for territorial control and financial profit offered by hundredal organization. Nevertheless, demographic changes, as well as military and political disruption, make it seem probable that confusion existed at times over the nature or identity of local courts.

In any case, it is evident that the hundredal structure was not obliterated, at least not permanently, in this part of westernmost Shropshire. It is true that 'Rinlow' and 'Leintwardine' did not survive as hundredal names, a fact which suggests that the situation did not remain unchanged. However, a new hundredal name, 'Purslow', which first appears in 1183, testifies both to a hundredal organization and to a close tie to the lordship of Clun, for Purslow was a demesne manor of Picot de Sai in 1086.[37] The relationship between the lords of Clun and Purslow hundred comes into clearer view during the reign of Henry III. In 1255, the tenants of a number of estates in the lower Clun valley were said to hold of John Fitzalan II, then lord of Clun, and owe 'suit at his court at Clun and at the hundred of Purslow'.[38] Soon afterwards, John's claim to Purslow hundred was being interpreted in terms of thirteenth-century royal administration: in 1256, he was said to have leased custody of Purslow hundred from the king for one pound annually.[39] During 1291–2, when Richard Fitzalan I, the earl of Arundel, was pressed to state by what warrant he claimed custody of the hundred of Purslow, he declared that he

[35] *Charters of the Honour of Mowbray, 1107–1191*, ed. D. Greenway (London, 1972), pp. lviii–lix, lxxii (Map ii A), no. 369; for a survey of honorial courts in Herefordshire and the adjoining conquest lordships, see Holden, *Lords*, pp. 62–72.

[36] Above, pp. 28–30.

[37] *Pipe Roll 29 Henry III, 1182–3* (P. R. S., 32, London, 1911), p. 3; the second appearance of this hundredal name dates to 1203: *Pleas before the King or his Justices, 1198–1212*, ed. Stenton, p. 69; DB 258b.

[38] *Rotuli Hundredorum*, ed. W. Illingworth, ii (London, 1812–18), 76–7: eg. 'Rogerus Bardolf [...] facit sectam curie de Clonna et hundredi de Posselawe'.

[39] *Roll of the Shropshire Eyre of 1256*, ed. Harding, no. 509.

held it 'from time immemorial'.[40] Again, the link between the lord of Clun and Purslow hundred appears couched in contemporary governmental terms. In this case, in response to the terms of the *quo warranto* inquiry,[41] specific reference is made to its antiquity. In practice, Richard's plea to the *quo warranto* inquiries failed, for it was apparently judged that he could not base a claim to custody of a hundred on 'time immemorial', and Edward I confiscated Purslow hundred in 1294.[42] However, Edward II restored the hundred to Edmund, the son of Richard Fitzalan, in 1308.[43] Moreover, twenty years later, a man who had been indicted in the hundred of Purslow was imprisoned and convicted at Clun[44] and, by the later fourteenth century, the records of the Purslow hundredal meetings were being kept on the dorse of the 'Hallimot Anglicorum' court rolls, the records of the manorial court for the lord's unfree English tenants. By then, the hundred of Purslow formed part of the administrative structure of the lordship of Clun.[45] Nevertheless, it seems probable that both the honorial court and the hundred of Purslow functioned as separate administrative entities in the mid-thirteenth century. Hundred and honor certainly had separate identities in the later thirteenth and fourteenth centuries.[46]

Determining the precise relationship of Purslow hundred to the honor of Clun before 1255 is rendered difficult by the fragmentary nature of the sources. It is certain that, even at the time when it first appears in the sources, Purslow hundred was not territorially coterminous with the lordship of Clun. By 1203, Clun itself no longer formed part of the hundred whose focus lay in the Clun valley. The fact that Purslow, rather than Clun, was chosen as the hundredal name already indicates this. Moreover, Clun is referred to, in 1203, as a township, a 'villata'.[47] This indicates that Clun had a separate administrative identity by then. A burghal court was certainly in existence by 1218 × 1224, when one Meyler son of Richard granted a small rent from his bakehouse 'in the town of Clun' to Haughmond Abbey.[48] Although the court in question was referred to as 'the whole hundred of Clun', and was still being described as the

40 *Placita de Quo Warranto*, ed. W. Illingworth (London, 1918), p. 681a.

41 *Ibid.*, pp. xv–xvii.

42 TNA E/159/67, m. 11r.

43 *Cal. Pat. R., 1307–13*, p. 52; cf. Davies, *Lordship and Society*, p. 21 and n. 21.

44 Raspin, *Transcript*, p. 22.

45 SA 552/1/719, m. 6 verso (1389); 552/1/720 m. 2 verso (1391).

46 In 1397, Richard II granted his cousin Edward, the earl of Rutland, 'the castle and town of Clone with the land and lordship of Cloneslond in the Welsh March, and the hundred of Posselowe annexed to the lordship ...', indicating that by then lordship and hundred were conceived of as distinct units: *Cal. Pat. R., 1396–9*, p. 205.

47 *Pleas before the King or his Justices, 1198–1212*, ed. Stenton, p. 69.

48 *Haughmond Cart.*, no. 242.

'hundred of the town of Clun' in the 1330s and 1340s,[49] it seems certain that it was a burghal court.[50] The territorial structure in the early thirteenth century was, then, in part determined by the fact that the manor of Clun had grown into a new centre of population during the twelfth century.

It seems plausible that the hundredal structure in the lower Clun valley, too, was profoundly affected by the increase in population. Demographic growth can only have acted to increase the importance, for purposes of governance, of hundredal organization. It would therefore have given the lord of Clun an added incentive to strive to preserve and instrumentalize the traditional administrative structure. This was, after all, what he was doing by the mid-thirteenth century. There seems to be no obvious reason to doubt, then, that the relationship between the lords of Clun and Purslow hundred – or its predecessor – prefigured ever more clearly, during the twelfth century, the way in which the Marcher lords of Clun governed the populace of the lower Clun valley during the later Middle Ages.

The correspondence between the hundredal and honorial boundaries, insofar as they can be determined, supports such a view. The estates constituting Purslow hundred in 1183 cannot be identified from contemporary evidence. However, we may gain an approximate picture of the thirteenth-century situation from the list of suitors provided by the 1255 Hundred Rolls, from the place-names appearing in the Purslow hundred presentments to the Shropshire eyre of 1256 and from the fourteenth-century court rolls of the Fitzalan lordship of Clun.[51] As Map 27 shows, Purslow hundred, rather than mirroring Rinlow hundred, related more closely to the distribution of the estates granted to Picot de Sai, with the significant exception of Clun itself. Purslow hundred embraced almost all of the estates held by Picot de Sai in the two parts of the former Leintwardine hundred. Moreover, the close correlation between Purslow hundred and the lordship of Clun is not limited to the estates which we know to have been granted to the lord of Clun by 1086. Wistanstow, originally a Leintwardine manor, was held, in 1086, not by Picot, but by Nigel the physician.[52] As has been seen, it was said, sometime between

[49] SA 552/1/6, m. 2 recto; 552/1/9, m. 6 recto.

[50] Among the various meanings of the term 'hundred' that of 'burghal court' is well established: H. M. Cam, 'North Gate of Oxford', in her *Liberties and Communities in Medieval England* (London, 1963), p. 109.

[51] *Rot. Hund.*, ii, 76; *Roll of the Shropshire Eyre of 1256*, ed. Harding, pp. 196–203; for examples of the Clun court rolls listing places paying suit to Purslow hundred in 1389 and 1391 see SA 552/1/719, mm. 1v, 6v; 552/1/720 mm. 2v, 5v. It should be noted that Map 27 shows all the estates that can be shown to have paid suit to Purslow hundred, and therefore takes no account of the way in which the boundaries of that hundred fluctuated between 1256 and *c.* 1390.

[52] DB 260d.

1166 and 1190, to have been unlawfully appropriated by Elias de Sai during Stephen's reign, and granted, in return for knight service, to one Baldwin of Stapleton. In 1166 Baldwin of Stapleton appears among the knights of Geoffrey de Vere, then lord of Clun.[53] This, along with the geographical position of Wistanstow, seems to have helped to determine that manor's incorporation into Purslow hundred. In the records of the Shropshire eyre of 1256 Wistanstow appears among the Purslow presentments[54] and, in the late 1380s and early 1390s, it paid suit to Purslow hundred.[55] A territorial extension of the lordship of Clun in the mid-twelfth century, thus, appears to have contributed towards delimiting the boundaries of Purslow hundred in the late Middle Ages.

Besides demographic changes and seigneurial interests, the fate of hundredal organization in the Clun valley was shaped by geography. Around 1200, two Welsh tenants of Medlicott, a member of the Corbet manor of Wentnor, paid one Ralph son of Picot to take responsibility for the suit they owed to Purslow hundred court.[56] At the time, they were plainly tenants of the lord of Caus: their transaction was witnessed and sealed in the court of Robert Corbet (d. 1222). However, Wentnor had been a member of Rinlow hundred,[57] and it is separated from Caus by the mountainous range of the Stiperstones. The Medlicott tenants also owed suit at the court of Lydham, north of Purslow hundred, around 1200,[58] and Lydham, too, can be found among the Purslow suitors by the late fourteenth century, even though it was a manor belonging first to the lords of Montgomery and later to the bishop of Hereford.[59] Purslow hundred, it would appear, doubled as a means for the lords of Clun to increase their influence over parts of the population of the Clun valley which held land from different lords, and this probably accounts for the northwards extension of Purslow hundred which had occurred by the end of the fourteenth century.

It would follow that, if hundredal organization was reformed primarily in response to demographic growth in the Clun valley, there is good reason to believe that the lords of Clun had a hand in any administrative innovations which were undertaken in this area. Besides Shropshire, hundredal boundaries changed most dramatically, after the arrival of the Normans, in Herefordshire, Derbyshire and Dorset.[60] It would seem that everywhere seigneurial initiative had a strong part to play in these hundredal rearrangements. In Herefordshire hundreds were amalgamated

[53] *Lilleshall Cart.*, no. 258; *Red Book of the Exchequer*, ed. Hall, i, 274–5. See above, pp. 179–80.

[54] *Roll of the Shropshire Eyre of 1256*, ed. Harding, no. 496.

[55] SA 552/1/719 m. 6v; 552/1/720 m. 2v. [56] *Haughmond Cart.*, no. 743; below, p. 215.

[57] DB 255c. [58] *Haughmond Cart.*, no. 743. [59] SA 552/1/720v; Eyton xi, 275–82.

[60] H. M. Cam, *The Hundred and the Hundred Rolls: An Outline of Local Government in Medieval England* (London, 1930), p. 9.

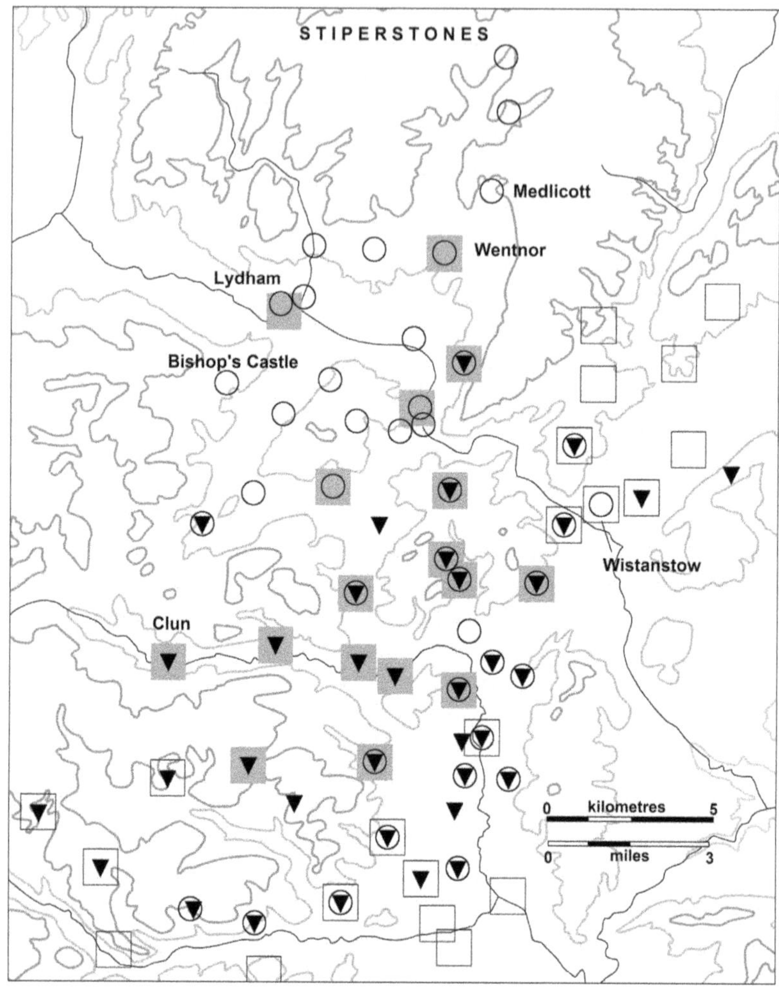

Map 27. Picot de Sai's estates and the development of the Clun Valley hundreds, 1086–*c.* 1350

after losing territory to Marcher lordships; in Dorset, all hundreds had lords, and this is thought to have had a determining influence on the way in which boundaries were redrawn after 1086.[61] In the case of the

[61] F. R. Thorn, 'Hundreds and Wapentakes', in A. Williams and R. W. H. Erskine (eds.), *The Herefordshire Domesday* (Alecto County Edition of Domesday Book, 1988), p. 29; F. R. Thorn,

hundredal rearrangements in the lower Clun valley, it is possible that some were the work of William Fitzalan II, who inherited the barony of Clun after the death of his mother, Isabel de Sai, in about 1199.[62] William was sheriff of Shropshire from 1189 until Easter 1201.[63] This would have placed him in an ideal position to create a burghal court and to establish, or re-establish, a hundred and name it after one of his own demesne manors. He certainly demonstrated a particular interest in the town of Clun in 1204, when he gave King John a courser to obtain the right to hold a fair.[64] By the time of Meyler's grant of a bakehouse rent to Haughmond Abbey, Clun's burghal court was firmly integrated into the seigneurial administration of that lordship: the grant was witnessed both by John Fitzalan's seneschal and by the constable of Clun.[65] Like the building of the castle which had encouraged the growth of a borough, the establishment of that borough's court was most probably a seigneurial initiative, and it seems very probable that the same is true of the naming of Purslow hundred. It is true, however, that there is a further complicating factor. Although Purslow hundred was probably a seigneurial creation, that hundredal name may have referred to a slightly different territory when it was used by the agents of the royal administration such as justices in eyre. For one thing, it should not necessarily be assumed that agents of seigneurial governance always co-operated fully with agents of royal governance, and a lack of co-operation alone would have provided plenty of scope for confusion. The administrative boundaries of the eastern part of the frontier honor of Clun were probably singularly difficult to define throughout the period under consideration.

The territory over which the lords of Clun came to claim control was not limited to the borough of Clun and the hundred of Purslow, but also comprised Welsh-populated land to the west. The fully fledged lordship comes to life in the court rolls surviving from the first half of the fourteenth century.[66] By that time, the Fitzalan earls of Arundel exercised precise control over their lordship through a small army of seigneurial officials and a plethora of courts convening as often as every three

'Hundreds and Wapentakes', in A. Williams and G. H. Martin (eds.), *The Dorset Domesday* (Alecto County Edition of Domesday Book, 1991), pp. 39–40. In Derbyshire, where none of the wapentakes was dominated by a single landholder, the evidence for boundary changes is less clear: F. R. Thorn, 'Hundreds and Wapentakes', in *The Derbyshire Domesday*, ed. A. Williams and R. W. H. Erskine (Alecto County Edition of Domesday Book, 1990), pp. 32–4.

62 On Isabel see Eyton, vii, 237, xi, 228–9, 235–6; *Lilleshall Cart.*, no. 258.

63 *Pipe Roll 4 John, 1202* (P. R. S., NS 15), p. 41.

64 *Rot. Oblat.*, p. 215.

65 *Haughmond Cart.*, no. 242: 'Wilelmo de Draytona tunc senescallo domini Johannis filii Alano, toto hundredo de Cluna, Helia de Costentin tunc constabulario de Cluna …'

66 Preserved in the Shropshire Archives in Shrewsbury (see Bibliography for references).

weeks. Moreover, this efficient administrative machine extended over a large Welsh-populated territory in the uplands surrounding Clun. Here, seigneurial administration operated, during the fourteenth century, in a thoroughly Welsh environment.[67] It therefore compares interestingly to the administrative organization of Purslow hundred. In some respects, the tenants of the Welsh part of Clun lordship were governed by their lord by the same means as they would have been on a Welsh royal or princely demesne township, or *maerdref*. Thus, the lord's officers derived at least part of their recompense by collecting *cylch*, a traditional Welsh circuit-render, from the unfree tenants.[68] The bailiffs received small contributions from the belongings of fugitives; they were also entitled to a due 'called maintenance of the lord's followers and dogs', all customs familiar from the native Welsh context.[69] The free tenants of Tempseter collectively owed, every other year, a commuted cattle-tribute known as the eight-pound tax (*treth wythbunt*);[70] as late as 1375, a Welsh officer of Clun lordship could be accused of unjustly collecting *commorth*, a traditional cow-render, from the serfs at Whitcott Keysett.[71] It was doubtless the prevalence of the Welsh language which determined that several of the numerous offices within the seigneurial organization of Clun were known by the names of their Welsh equivalents or at least rough counterparts. The reeve of Tempseter was frequently referred to as that district's *rhingyll*, a term which in Wales would have denoted an officer assigned specific duties within a commote.[72] The bailiff of Cerifaldwyn was known as a *wasmair*, and so was the bailiff of Upper and Lower Purlogue.[73] The 'Keysett' element in the place-name 'Whitcott Keysett' probably derives from Welsh *ceisiad*, 'sergeant of the peace, catchpole, inquisitor'.[74] It is first documented in 1284 and thereby provides the earliest trace of customary Welsh local administration in Clun lordship.[75] Both with regard to nomenclature and, to some extent, in practice, seigneurial administration in Clun incorporated elements of a traditional Welsh estate.

[67] See above, pp. 42–51.

[68] SA 552/1/8a, m. 8r: Welsh officer charged with unjustly levying *cylch* from the lord's unfree Welsh tenants of Hobendred (1339).

[69] Belongings of fugitives: SA 552/1/7, m. 8r (1337); followers and dogs (*seruicium dictum potura satellitum et canum domini*): SA 552/1/7, m. 7r (1337); Rees, *South Wales and the March*, pp. 9, 103–4.

[70] SA 552/1/7, m. 11r: 'tretheroythpunt' (1337); cf. Davies, *Lordship and Society*, p. 134.

[71] SA 552/1/18, m. 5r: 'kymortha'.

[72] SA 552/1/8a, m. 2r: William ap Howel Vaghan gives pledges to receive the office of *rhyngill* of Tempseter (1338).

[73] SA 552/1/7, m. 11r: 'Wasmair' in Keribaldwyn ... Wasmair' in Isporlog' et Vgwporlog" (1337).

[74] Morgan, *Welsh Place-Names*, p. 57; cf. Rees, *South Wales and the March*, pp. 103–4.

[75] *Cal. Cl. R., 1279–88*, p. 261.

However, by the time of these fourteenth-century rolls, the administrative organization of the western part of the lordship of Clun also bore clear marks of English influence. As on aristocratic estates in England, a steward, a receiver and a constable oversaw, respectively, the overall business of the lordship, financial and military matters. Moreover, the seigneurial courts were clearly modelled on English parallels: the unfree tenants on the lord's demesne were justiciable in a court that was known as the 'hallmoot of the Welsh', which presumably met either at Clun Castle or at one of the demesne vills nearby, such as Bicton.[76] The free Welshmen owed suit at a court of 'Tempseter', which resembled English manorial courts in a variety of ways. Like the Welsh and English manorial courts, the free Welsh judicial assembly convened regularly, about once a month; records were painstakingly kept for it throughout the fourteenth century, as they were for the hundredal court of Purslow and the manorial courts; and tenants from the English parts of the lordship owed suit at it, being allowed to find essoins for a maximum of three consecutive sessions.[77] The court was, on different occasions, presided over by officials with English and Welsh names.[78] The fourteenth-century Welsh courts of Clun formed a hybrid system of seigneurial governance, where Welsh and English elements of seigneurial administration coexisted. Clun possessed a truly 'frontier' seigneurial administrative organization, closely akin to that existing in such Marcher lordships as Dyffryn Clwyd.[79]

At Dyffryn Clwyd, a Welsh administrative structure probably developed over the thirteenth century and was brought under English control in the aftermath of 1282–3. At Clun, the organization of seigneurial governance may well also have been long in the making. By the early fourteenth century, it certainly does not appear to be the creation of a single moment. Its complex, and in some respects inefficient, attributes give it the feel of an organically grown whole. Indeed, it was still being adjusted, by trial and error: in 1317, the freemen of the Welshry complained about the number of bailiffs in the lordship, and Edmund Fitzalan, earl of Arundel and lord of Clun, reduced it to one provost with his servant, one steward with two under-bailiffs, and one servant for 'Keryvaldewyne'.[80] As has been seen,

[76] e.g. SA 552/1/5a, m. 2v: 'Halimot Wallicorum' (1335).

[77] e.g. SA 552/1/7, m. 2r; John 'of Edgton', a manor held of the lordship of Clun in the lower Clun valley, had essoins for the three consecutive sessions of Tempseter court of 1 April, 29 April and 20 May 1337: SA 552/1/7, mm. 7r, 9r, 10r.

[78] e.g. SA 552/1/5b, m. 2r (1336).

[79] A. D. M. Barrell, R. R. Davies, O. J. Padel and Ll. B. Smith, 'The Dyffryn Clwyd Court Roll Project', in Z. Razi and R. Smith (eds.), *Medieval Society and the Manor Court* (Oxford, 1996), pp. 260–97.

[80] 'Ancient Documents Relating to the Honor, Forest and Borough of Clun', ed. T. Salt, *TSAS*, 11 (1888), p. 249.

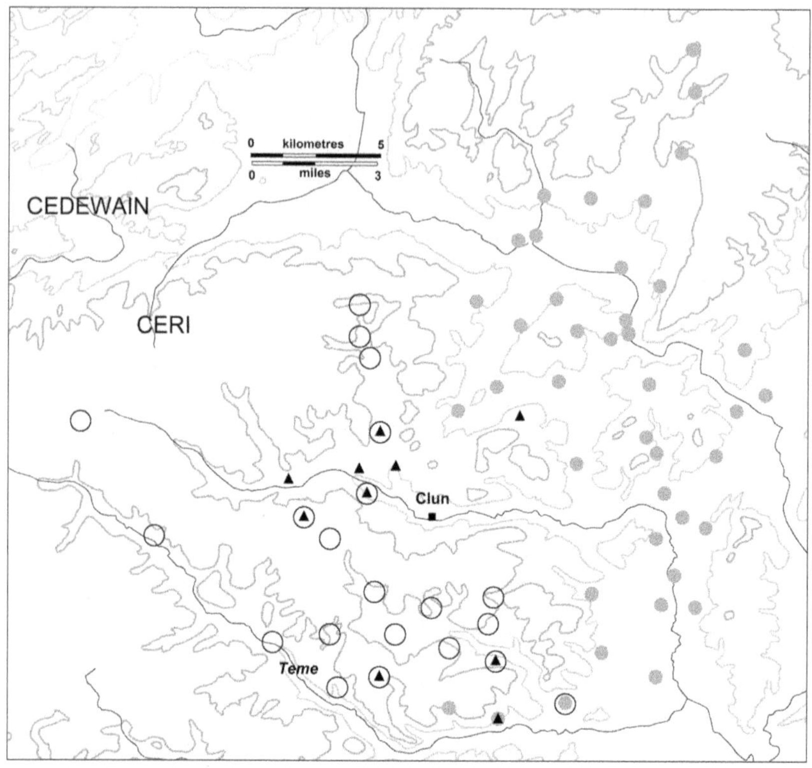

Map 28. Administrative districts in fourteenth-century Clun

by 1284 the Welsh office of *ceisiad* was already so well established in the lordship of Clun as to become incorporated into a formerly exclusively English place-name.[81] Another sign that there was a long tradition of seigneurial governance of the Welsh districts around Clun is the fact that in the fourteenth century, ancient Welsh laws were being enforced in the Welsh courts of Clun lordship. Most strikingly, cases were being adjudged by invoking the law of *galanas*, which regulated compensation payable in cases of murder by the murderer's kin to that of the victim.[82] By the time the splendid court rolls which have come down to us were being kept, *galanas* existed purely as a means to augment seigneurial income,

[81] Whitcott Keysett, see above, p. 202.

[82] For an instance which occurred in 1345, see SA 552/1/11, m. 13r: 'Galanas viij. li' – De parentela Meur' Vaghn' pro morte Dauid ap Ll' ap Meur' quem interfec' viij. li'.'

rather than as a living institution central to Welsh society in the lordship of Clun. However, it may well have been, in the fourteenth century, a fossilized survival from an earlier period;[83] and the traditional nature of the Welsh renders further suggests that seigneurial administration of the Welsh uplands had roots which went back before 1282 in time. Indeed, it is not fanciful to envisage the lords of Clun and their officials presiding over the resolution of bloodfeuds between their Welsh tenants during the thirteenth century. The alternative, after all, is that the Fitzalans themselves introduced Welsh customs in the fourteenth.

When did 'hybrid' forms of seigneurial administration begin to underline the distinctiveness of the lordship of Clun? The manorial courts for the English and the unfree Welsh probably pre-dated the court of Tempseter. The name of the latter territory is first recorded in 1292, when the occupants of 'Tempsiter Manor' paid Richard, the earl of Arundel, £200 for right of chase and for protection against oppression.[84] The precise reach of seigneurial control over it appears to have been established only by degrees, and with some setbacks. The *post mortem* inquisition of John Fitzalan III, in 1272, lists a number of the vills which were later to constitute the Welshry of Clun, but remarks that some of them could not be extended because they were unwilling to come before the escheator, while others were 'in the hands of the prince'.[85] Although Llywelyn ap Gruffudd therefore still controlled the upland portion of the future Clun lordship at the beginning of Edward I's reign, this still represented an improvement from the point of view of the Fitzalans. For in 1267, all that the *post mortem* inquest into the possessions of John Fitzalan II had been able to say was that 'in the forest of Clun there was a large Welshry which used to be worth much to the lord both in demesne renders and in other perquisites and dues which we cannot now extend because of the disturbances wrought by the Welsh'.[86] As the phrasing of the 1267 inquisition suggests, it does appear that, during the tenure of John Fitzalan II, some advances were made in bringing seigneurial demands to bear more effectively on the uplands surrounding Clun. In 1242, two years after the death of John Fitzalan I, and while John Fitzalan II was still a minor, the sheriff of Shropshire accounted for the revenues of the lordship of Clun. The revenues for the biannual period totalled £349 3s 7d and included renders from the borough of Clun, the demesne lands, the free tenants

[83] As is suggested by the title of R. R. Davies' article, 'The Survival of the Bloodfeud in Medieval Wales', *History: The Journal of the Historical Association*, **54**:182 (1969), pp. 338–57, which discusses the evidence of the Clun court rolls.

[84] *A Concise Account of Ancient Documents Relating to Clun*, ed. Salt, p. 6.

[85] *CIPM, Henry III*, no. 812; TNA C 132/42 (5), m. 6v.

[86] *CIPM, Henry III*, no. 684; TNA C 132/35 (18), m. 3r.

of Clun, six mills, tolls and revenue from the fairs, the forests, aids, pleas, perquisites, autumn services, pannage and profits from the sale of hay.[87] No explicit mention was made of any Welsh renders. Though it is possible that these were included under one of the headings, at the very least, the way in which revenues were accounted for in 1242 shows that the Welsh territory had not yet acquired its well-established identity as a separate administrative part of Clun lordship.

However, it may be that, immediately afterwards, seigneurial control over Clun and the hills around it intensified noticeably. The royal custody of the lordship during the minority of John Fitzalan II (1240–4) came at the beginning of the period of Henry III's predominance over Wales which intervened between the death of Llywelyn ap Iorwerth (1240) and the rebellion of Llywelyn ap Gruffudd of 1256.[88] It would appear that this was a time when the administrative methods of the English crown were being brought to bear on the Shropshire–Powys borders with unprecedented effectiveness. The Welsh lords of Ceri and Cedewain each fined £50 to receive seisin of their lands in 1248, agreeing to terms of payment in instalments; the royal bailiff of Montgomery was mandated to take pledges.[89] A Welsh royal seneschal was active in Elfael and Maelienydd in 1252.[90] This was a time, then, when novel English methods of administration were being exported into the Welsh principalities bordering on Shropshire, and it may well be that this quickened the pace of administrative innovation in the lordship of Clun. It was also a time when other Marcher barons, particularly the Clare lords of Glamorgan transformed their overlordship over the Welsh territories within their Marcher dominions into an intensive and well-circumscribed territorial authority.[91] It seems quite plausible that the 1240s and 1250s may be singled out as a period during which the administration of the lordship of Clun, and in particular of the Welsh territories, made a great leap forward.

The Fitzalan lords of Clun of the early thirteenth century would already have had every incentive to exploit their lordship as efficiently as possible. In 1214, when King John was making the heaviest financial demands on his magnates, William Fitzalan II had incurred a debt of 10,000 marks for succession to the Fitzalan barony.[92] This debt had still

[87] *Great Roll of the Pipe, 1241–2*, ed. Cannon, p. 8.

[88] In 1244, John fined £1,000 to have seisin of his inheritance: *Excerpta e Rot. Finium*, i, 417; he received the castle of Arundel in the same year: *Cal. Pat. R., 1232–47*, p. 426.

[89] *Excerpta e Rot. Finium*, ii, 37–8. [90] *Brut*, p. 245.

[91] Altschul, *The Clares*, p. 261; Davies, *Lordship and Society*, pp. 88–90, dates this 'second conquest of Glamorgan' to the period 1245–90.

[92] *Pipe Roll 16 John, 1214* (P. R. S., NS 35, London 1962), p. 120; Holt, *Magna Carta*, p. 190.

not been paid in 1242; indeed, Richard Fitzalan, earl of Arundel, still owed a large part of it to Edward I in the 1290s.[93] It is worth noting also that the Fitzalans certainly did not escape the effects of the spiralling inflation between 1180 and 1220 which appears to have been one of the developments that encouraged lords of English estates to take a direct interest in the management of their demesnes.[94]

But even before the burden of debt and the added incentive of inflation, it seems that the lords of Clun were keenly aware of the potential for profit offered by the Welsh territories. The main clue to this is provided by the situation of the main honorial castle. Its location on the western periphery of Picot's Domesday estates shows that, by the early twelfth century at the latest, a high priority of the lords of Clun was to facilitate and intensify the collection of tributes, such as that of the two *animalia* which is attested in Domesday Book and was in all probability a customary Welsh cattle due owed to the Norman lord.[95] It is very possible that Welsh administrators were already involved at this time. As early as *c.* 1070, the lands William fitz Osbern claimed in Gwent were overseen by 'prepositi' or 'meiri', very possibly Welshmen holding an office dating to before the arrival of the Normans.[96] In 1116, in the nascent Marcher lordship of Cantref Bychan in south Wales, one Maredudd ap Rhydderch ap Caradog 'held stewardship under' the Norman on whom Henry I had bestowed the chief castle of the district, Llandovery.[97] This Maredudd was none other than the son of one of the two co-rulers of Deheubarth of the 1070s.[98] He was seen as distinct from 'the keepers of the castle', although he participated in its defence against Welsh attackers. His role was presumably that of a seigneurial representative, or possibly a client lord, overseeing collection of the renders owed by the Welsh population of the cantred.[99] It is conceivable that the lords of Clun of the

93 *Great Roll of the Pipe, 1241–2*, ed. Cannon, p. 4; M. Prestwich, *War, Politics and Finance under Edward I* (London, 1972, repr. Aldershot, 1991), pp. 236–7.

94 E. Miller, 'England in the Twelfth and Thirteenth Centuries: An Economic Contrast?', *EHR*, 2nd ser., **24** (1971), pp. 1–14; K. J. Stringer, *Earl David of Huntingdon, 1152–1219: A Study in Anglo-Scottish History* (Edinburgh, 1985), p. 112; for 'economic lordship' in Herefordshire and the south-eastern March, see Holden, *Lords*, pp. 72–81.

95 DB 258b. Note that this characteristically Welsh tribute is owed by two *radmans*. On castles as 'collection-points' for native Gaelic tribute-payments see Stringer, *Earl David*, pp. 71–6.

96 DB 162a; cf. *Domesday Book*, gen. ed. J. Morris, vol. xv: *Gloucestershire*, ed. and transl. J. S. Moore (Phillimore, London and Chichester, 1982), W 2 and note; and D. Longley, 'Status and Lordship in the Early Middle Ages', in M. Aldhouse-Green and R. Howell (eds.), *The Gwent County History*, vol. i: *Gwent in Prehistory and Early History*, pp. 312–14.

97 *Brut*, pp. 86–7. I would like to thank Professor Thomas Charles-Edwards for drawing my attention to this passage.

98 *Brut*, pp. 28–9.

99 *Brut, Peniarth 20*, p. 40, has Maredudd holding a 'chieftainship' rather than a 'stewardship'.

early twelfth century similarly arranged for the co-operation of a Welsh steward, who perhaps was based at the honorial *caput*.

Competition with native Welsh lords for the tributes due from the free Welsh population of the Clun uplands may well have underlain the conflicts with the dynasties of Elfael and Maelienydd which the de Sais pursued in the 1140s.[100] If so, this would create a link to the later thirteenth and fourteenth centuries. For, as elsewhere in the fully fledged March of Wales, the Welsh population of Clun did not at that time owe their dues as tenants of their lord's land, as would have been normal on a manor in England. Rather, those dues were owed to the lord personally, just like the Welsh rulers' customary services from which they evidently derived.[101] By the 1260s, the lord of Clun drew profit from a converted kitchen rent;[102] by 1302, we first hear that he was owed *cylch* and *trethcanteidion* (a render of 100 oxen).[103] The story of the exploitation of the free Welsh populace by the lords of Clun, though it certainly did not continue in an unbroken line from the late eleventh to the early fourteenth century, thus appears always to have been one of the collection of personal rents by increasingly sophisticated means. The highly distinctive 'frontier' seigneurial administration which appears in its fully fledged form in fourteenth century Clun may well have had antecedents dating back to the mid-thirteenth century, and roots reaching back even further.

ADMINISTRATIVE TERRITORIES, *c.* 1100–1300, II: OSWESTRY

Like the territories which came to constitute the lordship of Clun, the estates originally bestowed on Warin the Bald must soon have begun to be organized for exploitation by the lord and his household. However, the size of the shrieval fief means that its development during the twelfth and thirteenth centuries has to be envisaged along slightly different lines.[104] The compact border territory centred on Mersete hundred was only a comparatively minor part of the estates which were granted to Warin more or less contemporaneously, as part of the distribution of land undertaken by Roger de Montgomery after he had been given control of Shropshire. However, the Mersete estates came to occupy a special position among Warin's lands. By 1086, Rainald, Warin's successor, had built

[100] See above, pp. 119, 168–9, 177–80.
[101] Davies, *Lordship and Society*, pp. 134–6; 356–7.
[102] TNA C 132/35 (18), m. 3r: 'dominus recepit annuatim ad sustent[ationem] lardar' sui .x. s. de Walecheria quod est in manu sua'.
[103] *CIPM*, iv, no. 90: inquisition *post mortem* of Richard Earl of Arundel (d. 1302).
[104] On the 'shrieval fief', above, pp. 59–61, 66, 70, 175.

his own castle at Oswestry.[105] Originally, this choice of a location close to the borders was doubtless determined, in part, by expected returns from domination of neighbouring Welsh territories. In any case, it provided a seigneurial focus, and therefore had a profound effect on how the shrieval fief came to be organized as an honor. Although the lords of Oswestry retained demesne estates in most of the Shropshire hundreds, and although they enfeoffed men on some Mersete hundred estates, their main demesne landed interest was to remain the compact territory around Oswestry Castle.[106] As has been seen, it was on the castle of Oswestry that the military resources of the shrieval fief came to be concentrated.[107] Moreover, mid-thirteenth century sources reveal that many of the estates in central and eastern Shropshire owed suit at the lord's court at Oswestry;[108] if it is uncertain how regularly that suit was paid by that time, those obligations do testify to the process by which the shrieval fief of Shropshire acquired the lineaments of an honor during the twelfth century. They therefore show that it was the castle at Oswestry that had come to be singled out as that honor's chief estate, its *caput*. Nevertheless, the fact that the frontier territory of the lords of Oswestry formed only part, if a privileged part, of a larger honor will have meant that, compared to Clun, the distinction between honorial and hundredal administration will always have tended to be clearer.

With respect to how they were transmitted to successive tenants, the Mersete estates had, of course, a more chequered history than Picot's lands. Neither Rainald de Bailleul nor Alan fitz Flaald were the heirs of their predecessors, though Rainald was at least married to Warin's niece. Moreover, the castle of Oswestry, and presumably the territory around it, was captured by the Welsh in the 1140s, and only restored to William, the heir of Alan fitz Flaald, in 1155. Despite these disruptions, the notion of a barony of Oswestry which was the successor of the shrieval fief developed, no doubt mainly because the estates were not split up during the twelfth century. Indeed, that notion was well established by 1201 at the latest for, although subsequently both the barony of Clun and that of Oswestry were held by the Fitzalans, both honors continued to be viewed as separate parts of the family inheritance.

Moreover, the idea that the part of the shrieval estates which was focused on Mersete hundred formed a coherent territory seems to have survived – that notion was not obliterated by the formation of the 'barony of Oswestry'. Thus, a hundred named after Oswestry is first mentioned in

[105] DB 253c. [106] Eyton, x, 316–20; 360–80; xi, 1–3; 7–9.
[107] Above, pp. 174–5. [108] *Rot. Hund.*, ii, 55–8.

1241–2.[109] It seems highly probable that the 'hundred of Oswestry' did not always refer to a clearly defined territory. And the term 'hundred' seems also, on occasion, to have meant simply a district centred on a castle, as when it was applied to Ellesmere in the early thirteenth century or, as in 1282, when Edmund Mortimer was put in custody of 'the castle and hundred of Oswestry'.[110] In what sense might the hundred of Oswestry be seen as the direct successor, or a direct development, of Mersete hundred? 'Mersete' last appears as a hundredal name in Domesday Book. In 1203, William Fitzalan II prevented a case concerning land near Oswestry being heard before justices in eyre at Shrewsbury on the grounds that they lay 'within his hundred', indicating that he thought of his border demesne as a hundred at that time.[111] It is reasonable to suppose that, during the twelfth century, Oswestry Castle provided the focal point for such local administrative life as survived in the area; after all, 'Oswestry' became the new hundredal name. Arguments for the – at least intermittent – survival of hundredal organization in westernmost Shropshire were advanced in the discussion of Purslow hundred. It does seem possible to say that, between the late eleventh century and the mid-thirteenth century, local administrative structures around Oswestry were never disrupted for long enough to efface permanently the memory of hundredal organization.

As in Clun, the administrative structures centred on Oswestry were shaped, to some extent, by the local tenurial structure. In particular, the Mersete estate of Whittington had never been part of the shrieval fief, but had passed from Montgomery demesne to the crown, later being held in chief by both Welsh lords and the Fitzwarins. By the late fourteenth century, and probably earlier, seigneurial administration in the lordship of Oswestry had adapted to the fact that Whittington effectively split Oswestry hundred in two. At both Clun and Oswestry, two major administrative territories existed. At Clun, these corresponded to the English and Welsh parts of the honor. At Oswestry, on the other hand, the division did not run along ethnic lines, but was dictated by the geography of lordship. By 1383, the Fitzalan lands around Oswestry lying to the south of Whittington owed suit at the court of Duparts, a name deriving from the size of that district, which corresponded roughly to two thirds of Oswestry hundred.[112] The remainder of the Fitzalan demesne vills,

[109] *Great Roll of the Pipe, 1241–2*, ed. Cannon, p. 8.

[110] *Haughmond Cart.*, no. 657; *Cal. Pat. R., 1281–92*, p. 32.

[111] *Pleas before the King or his Justices, 1198–1212*, ed. Stenton, p. 96.

[112] BL Harleian 1970, f. 83r; and *ibid.*, f. 88r for the suit paid by the vill of Cynynion. The following owed suit at the court of Duparts: Aston, Bryn, Crickheath, Hisland, Llanforda, Llanyblodwel, Llwyntidmon, Llynclys, Maesbury, Sandford, Sweeney, Sychtyn, Treflach, Trefonnen, Twyford, Weston (Coton), Woolston and Wootton.

most of which were situated to the north of Whittington, owed suit at the court of Traean, a name deriving from the Welsh for 'one third'.[113] In the 1380s, the correspondence was not always exact, but in 1393 a survey of the lordship of Oswestry confirmed that the two administrative units of Oswestry hundred were indeed a result of the geographical position of Whittington.[114] It seems plain that the existence of a rival seigneurial claim to Mersete territory always complicated the structure of local administration. Yet the honorial organization at Oswestry paralleled that at Clun and Purslow hundred, in that courts referred to as 'small' were convened for the Duparts and the Traean on a regular basis, about once a month. Two 'general' courts were in session quarterly, one for each part of Oswestry hundred, just as 'great hundreds' assembled for Purslow hundred in the 1380s and for the borough of Clun earlier in the fourteenth century.[115] Additionally, a burghal court had been created by 1241–2.[116] Another parallel to Clun is provided by the fact that forinsec courts convened in both lordships.[117] In the case of Oswestry, courts normally were held in or at the seigneurial castle; this makes it more probable that this was customary in Clun as well. In 1383–4, all the suitors at the courts of the Duparts and the Traean had Welsh names.[118] It may therefore be that these assemblies were considered the 'Welsh courts' of Oswestry hundred; the existence of such courts is implied by the fact that in 1401, the earl of Arundel granted the burgesses of Oswestry the right to be tried only in his 'English courts'.[119] True, an ethnic division between courts does appear to have existed at Oswestry; by the same token, possibly the court of Clun borough was originally considered to be reserved for the English tenants of the Fitzalans.

Seigneurial instruments of governance must have had to adapt to the extensive Welsh settlement of the area around Oswestry. The Fitzalan surveys of the 1390s reveal that the area covered by Mersete hundred had been almost entirely overlaid by the Welsh tenurial units of *gwely* and *gafael*. It seems reasonable to link this Welsh settlement directly with the occupation of Oswestry Castle by Madog ap Maredudd in the 1140s, especially given that, by the late fourteenth century, the *gwelyau* around Oswestry

[113] *Ibid.*, f. 78r: Bron-y-garth, Dudleston, Ifton Rhyn, Middleton, Treprennal, Weston and Wigginton.

[114] *Ibid.*, f. 89v; Slack, *The Lordship of Oswestry*, pp. 153–71: Weston and Treprennal were considered part of the Duparts in 1393.

[115] BL Harleian 1970, ff. 78r–91v (Traean and Duparts); SA 552/1/719, m. 6v (Purslow); SA 552/1/6, m. 2r (Clun borough).

[116] *Great Roll of the Pipe, 1241–2*, ed. Cannon, p. 8.

[117] BL Harleian 1981, f. 35r (Oswestry); SA 552/1/6, m. 2v (Clun).

[118] BL Harleian 1970, ff. 78r–89v.

[119] BL Harleian 1981, f. 37r.

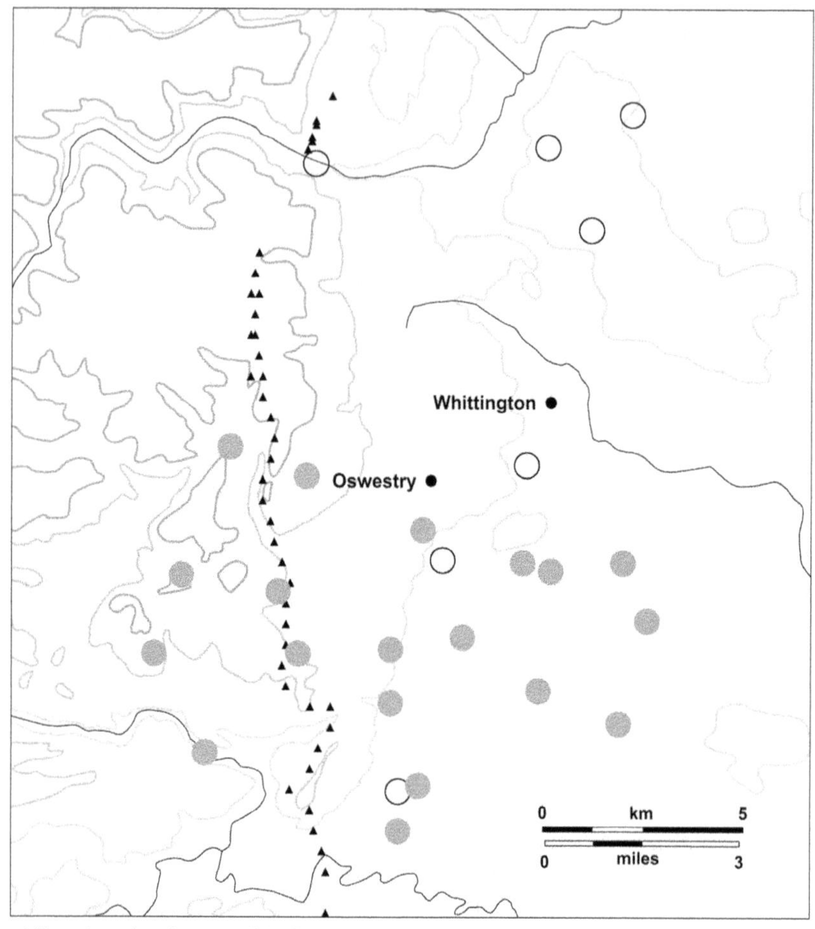

Map 29. Administrative districts in fourteenth-century Oswestry (1383–4)

had been subject to some repartitioning – an effect brought about by the workings of Welsh inheritance law over several generations.[120] It comes as no surprise to find the references to the 'hundred' of Oswestry occasionally displaced by those to the 'cantred' of Oswestry – an indication that, for all the lords' pretence to be preserving English administrative structures, in the eyes of Edward I's commissioners there seemed to be little difference between the district of Oswestry and Welsh territories

[120] See above, pp. 42–51, esp. Map 8, p. 43.

further west such as the commotes of Mechain or Cyfeiliog.[121] 'Oswestry hundred' was still being reorganized as a result of Welsh settlement in the fifteenth century. In 1401, the 'Welshmen of the hundred of Oswestry', who owed guard-service at the four gates of the town for three days and three nights during fairs, were relieved of their duty, having been accused of participating with the followers of Owain Glyn Dŵr in a raid on the town in the previous year.[122]

No doubt the extent to which administrative structures functioned effectively varied, depending on the interest taken in administrative affairs by the lords of Oswestry. In 1203, the administrative organization of Oswestry hundred was efficient enough for William Fitzalan II to be able to identify the estate of Eardiston as lying within 'his hundred'. Details are extremely sketchy for the twelfth century, although we do know that William Fitzalan I had a steward in the 1120s and 1130s, and the fact that Fulk Fitzwarin II, the lord of Alberbury and Whittington, was said to employ bailiffs on his estates during the 1180s is some indication that his contemporary, William Fitzalan II, may have done the same.[123] References to the typical seigneurial officials such as steward and constable only become common during the thirteenth century. In 1265, John Fitzalan III addressed a charter to the constable of Oswestry, the bailiff of Wroxeter 'and his other bailiffs and loyal men in the March'; in 1277, we hear of the 'three beadles of the hundred of Oswestry'.[124] What we know of the value of the lordship of Oswestry suggests that the development of seigneurial administration there paralleled Clun in several ways. Oswestry was worth £44 12s 5½d annually to its lord in 1267, and yielded £88 17s 3d in 1272;[125] its royal custodians accounted for values of 'the castle and manor of Oswestry' of £187 17s 6d (over two years) in 1242, for £112 19s 4d in 1275 and for £101 16s 3½d in 1277. These figures all included 'renders of the Welsh'; but in 1277 it was noted that no fair had been held in that year because of the war with Llywelyn ap Gruffudd.[126] As at Clun, therefore, royal influence appears to have increased the efficiency of seigneurial administration after 1241 and again in the 1270s, but setbacks occurred as a result of exposure to Welsh attacks.

Although it seems clear that Oswestry was exploited more efficiently in the second half of the thirteenth century, the capacity of seigneurial administration in the twelfth century should not be dismissed too lightly.

[121] *Cal. Chanc. R. Var.*, p. 202. [122] BL Harleian 1981, ff. 36r–v.

[123] *Haughmond Cart.*, no. 900; *Salop. Cart.*, no. 351.

[124] *Haughmond Cart.*, no. 10: 'ceteris ballivis ac fidelibus suis de Marchia'; TNA E 372/121, m. 21r.

[125] Eyton, x, 329–30; cf. TNA C 132/42 (5), m. 5r (defaced), *post mortem* inquisition of John Fitzalan III; *CIPM, Henry III*, no. 812.

[126] *Great Roll of the Pipe, 1241–2*, ed. Cannon, p. 8; TNA E/372/119, m. 40r; TNA E/372/121, m. 21r.

Thus, remarkably, the lord continued to levy the Danegeld from the burgesses of Oswestry until 1383–4.[127] This English tax had roots in the Viking age,[128] and it had been abolished by Henry II in 1162. It may be that the lords of Oswestry first started levying Danegeld themselves as part of assuming control of Mersete hundred, for the hundred was the administrative unit charged with assessing the Danegeld.[129] Alternatively, it is conceivable that the right to levy it was granted to them by one of the kings of the twelfth century. Although there appears to be no record of the right to collect and keep Danegeld being granted to lords, it does seem probable that it could occasionally be retained by earls.[130] In any case, the survival of the Danegeld in the lordship of Oswestry looks like a truly striking instance of continuity in the seigneurial exploitation of that lordship between the second half of the twelfth century and the later Middle Ages.

It would appear, then, that in Oswestry lordship customary dues could be preserved for centuries. This means it is possible that the Welsh renders recorded in the surveys of the Fitzalan lordships of the late fourteenth century were also ancient. These surveys aimed at providing a maximum view of the profits which the lord could, customarily, reap from his estates. The conservatism of this kind of source can indeed rarely be demonstrated as clearly as by comparing the Fitzalan surveys of the fourteenth to sixteenth centuries.[131] In Oswestry, it was still understood even in the sixteenth century that Welsh renders were owed to the lord as personal dues, rather than being rents issuing from the land. The intrinsic propensity of these sources to reflect the past, perhaps even more faithfully than the present, together with the evidence for the survival of Danegeld, mean that Welsh renders may first have been levied by the lords of Oswestry at a very early period. However the collection of seigneurial dues may have been organized at different periods, it is quite possible that it began shortly after William Fitzalan I was reinstated as lord of Oswestry, after the area surrounding that castle had been settled by Welshmen. The Welshmen who owed the service of guarding the gates of Oswestry town

[127] BL Harleian 1981, f. 36v.

[128] 'Danegeld' was originally the name sometimes given to an annual *heregeld* ('army-tax'). It was levied on land and instituted in 1012 by King Æthelred (not to pay tribute to Vikings but to fund a 'Danish' mercenary fleet): S. Keynes, 'The Historical Context of the Battle of Maldon', in D. Scragg (ed.), *The Battle of Maldon AD 991* (Oxford, 1991), p. 101. Cf. most recently R. Abels, 'Paying the Danegeld: Anglo-Saxon Peacemaking with Vikings', in P. De Souza and J. France (eds.), *War and Peace in Ancient and Medieval History* (Cambridge, 2008), pp. 173–92.

[129] J. A. Green, *The Government of England under Henry I* (Cambridge, 1986), p. 112.

[130] Green, *Aristocracy*, p. 236; J. A. Green, 'Financing Stephen's War', *Anglo-Norman Studies*, **14** (1992), p. 104; see also her 'The Last Century of Danegeld', *EHR*, **96** (1981), pp. 241–58.

[131] Davies, *Lordship and Society*, p. 140, n. 38; Slack, *The Lordship of Oswestry*, *passim*.

during fairs were said in 1401 to do so 'ex antiquo', and 'together with all the Welshmen called *cais*'.[132] This suggests that traditional Welsh serjeanty service survived at Oswestry because it was adapted to the needs of a market town on the Anglo-Welsh border. It seems perfectly possible that the castle at Oswestry became a centre for the routine collection of traditional Welsh renders by an Anglo-Continental *seigneur* and his officials in the latter half of the twelfth century.

ADMINISTRATIVE TERRITORIES, *C.* 1100–1300, III: CAUS

The territory originally granted to Corbet differs considerably from the extent of the lordship of Caus in the thirteenth and fourteenth centuries; considerably more so than was the case with the territories around Oswestry and Clun granted respectively to Warin the Bald and Picot de Sai. For one thing, the compact Corbet territory had evidently been split into two adjacent parts by 1086 in order to provide two of Corbet's sons with a share. The subsequent fate of the two shares provides an illuminating contrast. The lesser share of the Corbet lands was further subdivided among the two daughters of the younger of Corbet's sons, Robert, and descended as the estates of the Shropshire families of Fitzherbert and de Botreaux.[133] By contrast, the greater share remained intact, and had, by the end of the thirteenth century, been bequeathed to male heirs five times, if the claims of Thomas Corbet to have had five ancestors since the conquest are to be believed.[134] Moreover, a strong castle came to be erected at Caus, while the eastern share of the Corbet inheritance never acquired a comparable fortified focus. By 1200, Robert Corbet, the lord of Caus, could confirm, with his own seal, a transaction between his English and Welsh tenants completed in his court.[135] In 1222, his son, Thomas, was charged the £100 relief levied by the crown on estates considered to be baronies.[136] The contrast between the two shares into which Corbet's estates had been divided in the late eleventh century serves to illustrate that there was nothing deterministic about the development of frontier honors; only if certain conditions were fulfilled could a barony be created.

The relationship of the developing lordship centred on Caus and the hundredal structure in the Rea–Camlad valley took a different course. Caus, like Oswestry, gave its name to a hundred, although the 'Hundred of

[132] BL Harleian 1981, ff. 36r–v: 'cum cuncto numero hominum Wallice vocatorum "Kayes"'.

[133] Eyton, vii, 144–70. [134] TNA E 368/24/12v.

[135] *Haughmond Cart.*, no. 743; above, p. 199.

[136] *Excerpta e Rot. Finium*, i, 94–5.

Caus' is not mentioned until 1353.[137] However, the Domesday hundredal names of Wittery and Rhiwset did not survive, but were replaced by those of Chirbury and Ford respectively. The hundred of Caus is likely to have been the burghal court. However, the lords of Caus failed to establish control over the hundredal structure in the Rea–Camlad valley, despite holding a considerable share of the estates. Neither Chirbury nor Ford were Corbet manors, which suggests that the rearrangement of the hundreds named after those two estates was not controlled by the lords of Caus: they do not seem to have succeeded in emulating the lords of Clun in establishing a hundred based on one of their demesne manors. Indeed, when Thomas Corbet of Caus sought to extend the territorial basis of his lordship in the 1240s by withdrawing to his court the suits of some vills of Chirbury hundred, the jurors of that hundred themselves were free to protest. As will be discussed in the following chapter, for a variety of reasons the hundreds of the Rea–Camlad valley failed to be incorporated into the lordship of Caus.[138]

As was the case at Clun and Oswestry, the lordship based at Caus had to adapt to the settlement of Welshmen in the period between *c.* 1086 and 1300. The Corbets held several estates in westernmost Shropshire in 1086, but Welshmen are recorded only at Trewern and at Bausley.[139] By 1300, however, the western parts of the Corbet estates had come to be defined in terms of three Welsh districts, going by the names of Lower Gorddwr, Upper Gorddwr and Bachelldre.[140] That the district name was Welsh, meaning 'land beyond the water', suggests that its currency was the result of Welsh settlement. That the region came to be subdivided, at least in the eyes of English administrators, suggests a reorganization by seigneurial governance. The need for subdivision is perhaps an indication that the influx of Welsh settlers was quite considerable. Certainly, by 1300, there were forty-four Welsh free tenants in the Lower Gorddwr, twenty-eight in the Upper Gorddwr and ten in Bachelldre.[141] As at Oswestry, Welsh settlement of the area may have begun in the twelfth century. In about 1200, the abbey of Cwmhir was granted the estate of Forden by one Hywel ap Cadwallon, son of Cadwallon ap Madog, lord of Maelienydd.[142]

137 *VCH*, viii, 325, citing Longleat MSS., unbound 3670.

138 Below, pp. 228–32, 238–45.

139 DB 253c ('certain Welshmen' and two further Welshmen at Trewern); DB 255c (two Welshmen with one plough at Bausley).

140 TNA C 133/94 (6) m. 2r; cf. *CIPM*, iii, no. 600.

141 TNA C 133/94 (6), m. 2r.

142 *Rotuli Chartarum*, ed. Hardy, p. 206; Lloyd, 'Border Notes', p. 49. Note that Lloyd's identification of *Fortun'* with Forden in the Gorddwr has been called into question. Cf. *AWR*, no. 109; R. Morgan, 'The Territorial Divisions of Medieval Montgomeryshire (I)', in *Mont. Coll.*, **69** (1981), p. 23 and n. 53; D. H. Williams, *Atlas of Cistercian Lands in Wales* (Cardiff, 1990), p. 40, which identify *Fortun'*

At around the same time, Trewern was bestowed in 'frank marriage' on Gwenwynwyn (d. 1216), the lord of Powys, when he married Margaret, daughter of Robert Corbet (d. 1222).[143] The Gorddwr continued to be disputed between the Corbets and the Welsh lords of southern Powys until the 1270s.[144] It is probable here, as in the uplands of Clun, that efforts at setting seigneurial administration on a routine footing met with frequent setbacks during the thirteenth century.

* * *

It has been suggested that the Normans worked with what they found to hand in seeking to establish themselves as the lords of diverse cultures and populations throughout Europe.[145] It would appear that the lords of the Shropshire–Powys borderlands displayed such versatility to a remarkable degree. The lords here made use of some existing administrative structures, but over time they also created an interesting amalgam of different methods of seigneurial governance. In the English-populated parts of their lordships, hundredal and honorial organization interacted in a way which is difficult to disentangle, no doubt because some fudge and confusion existed. Rival traditions and perceptions survived. It may be, for instance, that the name 'Purslow hundred' was used in different ways by seigneurial and royal officers. The way in which administrative territories were created in the Welsh-populated areas appears more clear-cut. Here, exploitation was initially quite restricted, limiting itself to the collection of tribute. Possibly, this task was performed by Welsh stewards in the twelfth century. Only after the middle decades of the thirteenth century were court-centred districts created in Welsh territory and, even though they could be short-lived, they did pave the way for the distinction between Englishries and Welshries which was to be so characteristic of all 'Marcher' lordships of the fourteenth century.[146] The way in which both the English and the Welsh parts of the border honors of Shropshire were organized into administrative territories certainly assimilated those honors to other lordships of the Welsh frontier and in Wales, while tending to differentiate them from seigneurial lands in Shropshire and the rest of England.

as Hopton in Ceri. I should like to thank Dr David Stephenson for his help in identifying Hywel ap Cadwallon.

143 *Registrum Ricardi de Swinfield, Episcopi Herefordensis*, ed. W. W. Capes (Canterbury and York Society 6, 1909), p. 209; Morgan, 'Trewern in Gorddwr', p. 131.

144 Spurgeon, 'Gwyddgrug Castle'.

145 Davies, 'Kings, Lords and Liberties', pp. 50–1.

146 Davies, *Lordship and Society*, pp. 200–2, 308–10; Rees, *South Wales and the March*, p. 28.

Chapter 7

THE BORDER LORDSHIPS AND THE ENGLISH STATE

Towards the end of the period under consideration, the distinctiveness of the lordships of the 'March' had already become a matter for debate. It was argued above that the *barones Marchie* formed an identifiable group in various respects, and that their honors overlapped with a cultural and strategic borderland. However, when their lordships came to be perceived more clearly as a special category of seigneurial estate, it was not primarily because they lay on an ethnic and military frontier. In the thirteenth century, and particularly from the 1240s and 1250s onwards, the truly contentious issue concerning those lordships, and the single most important reason why their distinctiveness came to be more clearly perceived, was the question of whether they lay beyond the full reach of English royal governance.[1] It was with regard to claims to exemption from royal governance, and in response to challenges by the agents of an increasingly effective royal governmental machine, that the distinctiveness of the lordships of the Welsh 'March' first became an issue for sustained and systematic investigation.

The issue of Marcher liberties was not entirely contentious. In 1268, Henry III himself declared that the *marchiones* in the March of Wales had regality in their lands, and that their writ, not his, ran there.[2] Contentious or not, 'Marcher' liberties certainly had the potential to establish links between the lordships of south Wales and those of the borders. For instance, Richard de Clare, the earl of Gloucester and lord of Glamorgan, had to defend his claim to 'Marcher' regality in 1247, when Richard Siward, whom he had found guilty of felony in the court of Glamorgan lordship, appealed against that sentence to the king.[3] More famously, in

[1] Davies, 'Kings, Lords and Liberties', p. 59; the same, *Lordship and Society*, pp. 217–22; for Herefordshire and the adjoining 'March', see Holden, *Lords*, 151–65.

[2] *Cal. Pat. R., 1266–72*, p. 299.

[3] *Cartae*, ii, no. 535; Altschul, *The Clares*, pp. 70–5; D. Crouch, 'The Last Adventure of Richard Siward', *Morgannwg*, 35 (1991), pp. 7–30.

1292, Edward I condemned to prison the lord of Glamorgan (the earl of Gloucester and Hertford) and the lord of Brecon (the earl of Hereford), declaring their lands forfeit, explicitly accusing them of carrying on a local conflict and expecting to escape unpunished by claiming Marcher liberty.[4] In the charged political atmosphere of thirteenth-century England, liberties clearly became relevant to the medieval concept of the March. The purpose of this chapter is to discuss how far the lordships on the Shropshire–Powys border shared with the lordships of south Wales a claim to lie beyond the reach of the medieval English state.

It was argued in the previous chapter that, in terms of administrative structure, the lordships of Oswestry, Caus, Clun and Wigmore had much in common in the twelfth and thirteenth centuries. Moreover, they were all of roughly similar size and all positioned on the Welsh borders. All of them incorporated territory which had once been shire-ground; all descended within the same families for generations. It might reasonably be expected that these lordships would also prove broadly similar with regard to exemption from the instruments of royal governance. However, a survey of the lordships of the Shropshire–Powys frontier in the first half of the fourteenth century does not support such a view. By the beginning of the reign of Edward III, the medieval English state had evolved highly sophisticated methods of governance. In particular, the year 1334 saw a milestone in the development of royal taxation, as the fifteenth and tenth granted to finance Edward III's Scottish campaigns came to be levied not by assessing individuals' movable wealth, but by negotiating fixed quotas for vills and townships. As the assessments for Shropshire survive, it is a straightforward task to ascertain how far westwards the arm of the English state extended in 1334. While neither the borough of Clun, nor Wigmore, nor any of the manors in the hundred of Oswestry even appear in the rolls for that subsidy, the assessors assigned quotas to the borough of Caus, the manor of Worthen and several other vills in the lordship of Caus, considering them to lie in the hundreds of Ford and Chirbury.[5] The Fitzwarin manor of Alberbury and the Fitzalan hundred of Purslow were also assessed. Nor was this pattern a unique occurrence; it had already been revealed in 1327, when a twentieth on movables was collected.[6] Thus, royal taxation at the beginning of Edward III's reign revealed stark contrasts between the different lordships on the Shropshire–Powys borders. As the assessment of those

[4] *The Parliament Rolls of Medieval England, 1275–1504*, gen. ed. C. Given-Wilson, 16 vols. (London, 2005), vol. i: *Edward I (1275–94)*, ed. P. Brand (London, 2005), pp. 499–516, esp. pp. 509, 512.

[5] *The Lay Subsidy of 1334*, ed. R. E. Glasscock (London, 1975), pp. 122, 249, 252–3, 256–7.

[6] *The Shropshire Lay Subsidy Roll of 1 Edward III (1327)*, ed. Fletcher, *passim*.

taxes involved assigning manors to hundreds, it forced the issue of which territories lay in the county, and therefore in the English kingdom, and which did not.

A natural first step in explaining the contrasts which Edward III's taxes threw into relief is to point to the different fates undergone by the Fitzalans, the Corbets and the Mortimers during the reign of Edward II and the first years of his successor. Neither Edmund Fitzalan nor Roger Mortimer III of Wigmore survived until 1334; the former, the earl of Arundel, after a stint as justiciar of the Principality of Wales, was executed in 1326 on the order of the latter;[7] Roger, in turn, having seized the Fitzalan border castles and been proclaimed earl of March in 1328, was put to death two years later, after Edward III had come into full power.[8] A swiftly revolving political wheel of fortune had ensured that both briefly advanced to the foremost rank among Marcher lords before meeting a violent end, but by 1334 both had been succeeded by their heirs. The contrast with the Corbets could scarcely be starker. Peter Corbet II, anticipating that he would die without an heir, and probably induced by penury, would have sold the reversion to the lordship of Caus to Edmund Fitzalan in 1315 had Edward II not vetoed such a deal.[9] Peter did indeed die childless in 1322, leaving the castle and lordship of Caus in the hands of his widow, Beatrice, who did not remarry. In trying to explain the differences with respect to fiscal exemption between Caus on the one hand and Oswestry, Clun and Wigmore on the other, it is natural to suggest that they were due to the fact that the earls of Arundel and March had recently established themselves as Marcher lords who were forces to be reckoned with on a national political stage, while the Corbet barons of Caus had just died out in the male line.

However, there are equally strong arguments for not accepting these considerations as the whole explanation for the apparent differences in the relation of the Shropshire–Powys lordships to the English state in the first third of the fourteenth century. To maintain that the inclusion of the lordship of Caus within the county rested purely on contemporary factors would be to raise fundamental questions about the nature and conditions of the exemption of Oswestry, Clun and Wigmore. Did maintenance of Marcher liberties depend on the survival of the male line, and could all Marcher lordships simply slot back into the county once their

[7] *Chronicles of the Reigns of Edward I and Edward II*, ed. W. Stubbs, 2 vols. (RS, 1882–3), i, 321; ii, 87, 289, 312.

[8] *Ibid.*, i, 342, 352; ii, 102, 291; C. Given-Wilson, 'Edmund Fitzalan, Second Earl of Arundel', in *ODNB* (2004); *ibid.*, R. R. Davies, 'Roger Mortimer (V), First Earl of March (1287–1330)'.

[9] *Cal. Pat. R., 1313–17*, p. 266; *Cal. Close R., 1313–18*, pp. 226–7; BL Additional Charters 20438; BL Harleian 1240, f. 49v; cf. Davies, *Lordship and Society*, pp. 56–7.

lords died out? This should not be assumed without fuller consideration of how far these lordships may have been exempt from the English state between the late eleventh and the early fourteenth century. After all, Purslow hundred, an integral part of the Fitzalan lordship of Clun, was also taxed in 1327 and 1334,[10] which suggests that the extent of the territory liable to English taxes was not determined purely by the recent fate of the local aristocratic families. Moreover, Caus continued to be taxed after it had been bestowed on the Staffords in 1347, which indicates further that fiscal exemption was not, or at least not entirely, tied to the position of the lords of that castle.[11] The differences between the lordships clearly had deeper-lying reasons than the different status of their lords at the beginning of Edward III's reign, and it is these deeper-lying reasons that will be explored in this chapter.

I: THE GEOGRAPHICAL EXTENT OF THE COUNTY OF SHROPSHIRE, *c.* 1070–1300

The question of how far westwards the administrative boundary of the county of Shropshire extended during the twelfth century is not straightforward. It should not be taken for granted that the territory which effectively fell within the purview of the county officials such as Richard de Beaumais and his aides was always coextensive with the territory of the county as it appears in Domesday Book, and again in the thirteenth and fourteenth centuries. After all, Welsh-populated areas, both on the Shropshire borders and, especially, in the case of Archenfield on the Herefordshire frontier, were included in the Domesday inquest. 'Pembroke', possibly already organized as a shire, submitted an account to Henry I's exchequer in 1129–30, as did the knights of the 'honor of Carmarthen'.[12] The fact that Herefordshire was consistently referred to as lying 'in Waliis' or 'in Wallia' further suggests that the English state, during the twelfth century, saw no obstacle in principle to including within the ambit of its governance territories it apparently regarded as part of Wales.[13] On the Shropshire borders, as in south-west Wales, military

[10] *The Shropshire Lay Subsidy Roll of 1 Edward III (1327)*, ed. Fletcher, pp. 125–44; *Lay Subsidy of 1334*, ed. Glasscock, p. 253.

[11] To give some examples, Caus – and Purslow hundred – were taxed, while Oswestry, Clun and Wigmore were exempt, in 1352 (TNA E 179/166/14, rot. 1, m. 2r); in 1373 (TNA E 179/166/19, rot. 1, mm. 2r–3r); and in 1377 (TNA E 179/166/22, rot. 1, m. 1r); cf. the National Archives' E 179 catalogue online: www.nationalarchives.gov.uk/e179/. The same pattern of taxation still persisted in the 1520s, shortly before the March of Wales was shired: *The Lay Subsidy for Shropshire 1524–7*, ed. M. A. Faraday (Keele, 1999).

[12] *Pipe Roll 31 Henry I*, ed. Hunter, pp. 136–7, 89–90.

[13] e.g. *Pipe Roll 12 Henry II, 1166* (P. R. S., 9), p. 82.

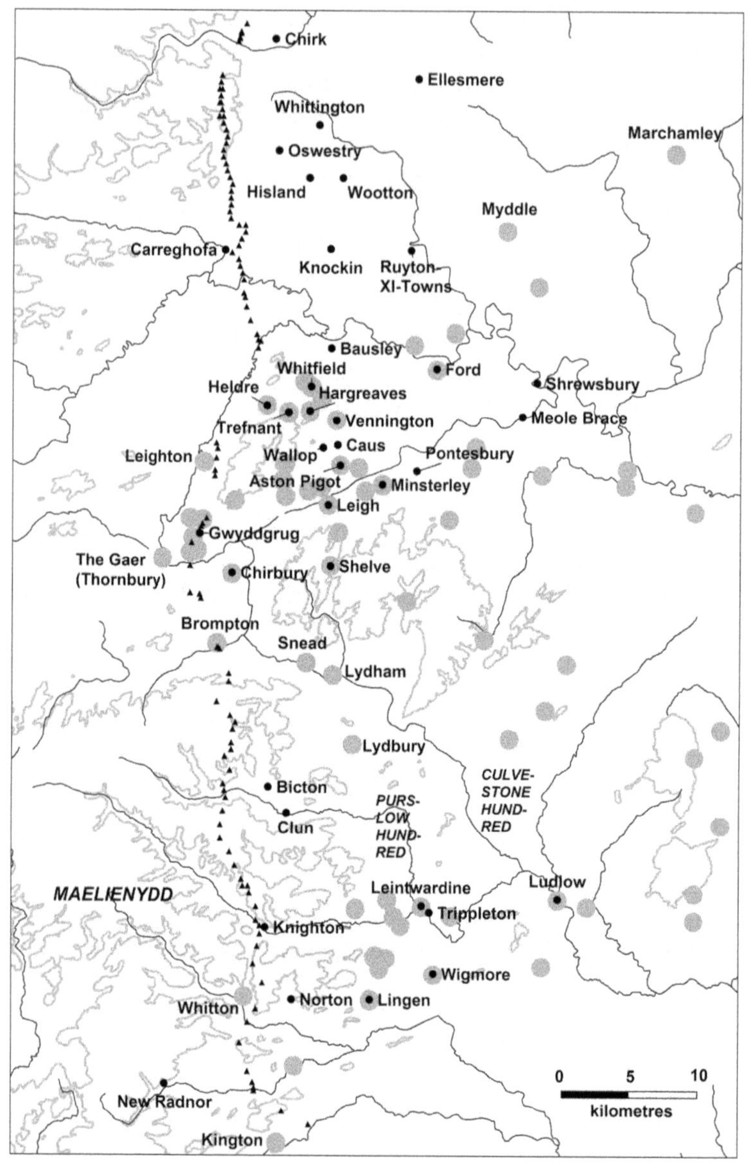

Map 30. The Shropshire borders and the English state in the thirteenth century

advances into Welsh territory had been made during the late eleventh century, and Earl Roger and his men had laid claim to domination over Welsh districts adjacent to shire ground.[14] It should not be assumed that domination could not have been converted into incorporation within county governance.

On the other hand, the borders of the county of Shropshire, during the twelfth and thirteenth centuries, were not moving westwards. On the contrary, they were retreating to the east, because the establishment of border lordships resulted in the loss of county ground.[15] What follows is a re-examination of the evidence with two aims. The first aim is to discuss how far, and when, the individual frontier honors either withdrew from the range of county or royal government, or came to exclude novel instruments of that government as they developed. The first part of this chapter examines the different lordships in turn, leaving a general discussion of the Welsh fifteenth granted to Edward I in 1291 until the end. The second aim is to consider the possible reasons for withdrawal or exclusion; this is the topic of the second part of this chapter.

Oswestry and Clun

The former territory of Mersete hundred appears to have taken the lead in being removed from the county. In 1203, a case over land at Eardiston, within the lordship of Oswestry, was brought before the justices at Shrewsbury.[16] However, William Fitzalan II was backed by the county assembly when he protested that Eardiston lay 'in his hundred, which owes no suit to the county court of Shropshire, neither for cases of death nor arson, nor in answer to any summons do the men of that hundred come before the justiciars or before the sheriff'. It is true that not all former estates of Mersete hundred which had been granted to the ancestors of William Fitzalan II escaped the jurisdiction of the itinerant justices at Shrewsbury in 1203. An assize of *mort d'ancestor* of the lands held by Reginald de Hesding concerned, among other estates, Wootton and Hisland, both of which lay west of the river Perry, well within the orbit of the compact Fitzalan honor centred on Oswestry.[17] However, use of possessory assizes was quite commonly being made even in conquest lordships which were established on land which remained part

[14] Above, pp. 110–11, 161, 191–2.

[15] G. C. Baugh, 'The Franchises', in *VCH*, iii, esp. pp. 34–42 ('The Marcher Lordships and the Border with Wales').

[16] *Pleas before the King or his Justices, 1198–1212*, ed. Stenton, p. 96.

[17] *Ibid.*, pp. 108–9.

of Wales when the Normans arrived, for example Glamorgan.[18] While it is true that Glamorgan was held by King John at the time, the heirs to the lordship of Knockin had concluded their negotiations by final concord before the royal court at Westminster in the late 1190s, despite the fact that Oswestry was not in royal custody then.[19] It is more significant, therefore, that the 'township' of Clun, which had passed to William Fitzalan II the previous year, was summoned to appear before the justices in eyre at Shrewsbury.[20] Although the township apparently made no presentments, this does pinpoint the crucial difference between the old Fitzalan inheritance and the recent acquisition by that family.[21] Whereas it could be established, by 1203, that Oswestry 'hundred' lay outside the county, such a claim was not yet advanced at that time for the 'township' of Clun.

However, it is not possible to be certain whether the lordship of Oswestry was already exempt from taxation during John's reign. No account of the names of those who paid the thirteenth on movables of 1207 is known to have survived;[22] it can only be said that William did not owe any debts from that tax, for these would have been entered in the Pipe Rolls. As for scutage, William was charged for twenty-seven and a half knights' fees during the reign of Richard I, which certainly represents a reduction of the total of fees which had been returned in 1166 – but it is not clear that this reduction reflects the fiscal exemption of a part of the Fitzalan fief.[23] The case of Clun shows that scutage exemption was not automatic for border estates, even if they were held by a Fitzalan: the husbands of Isabel de Sai were charged for their *honor* or *feodum* of Clun in the 1190s and until 1201; and even after the 'fee of Clun' had passed to William Fitzalan II, Isabel's son, it remained liable for scutage throughout John's reign.[24] Moreover, it should be recalled that King John installed his own custodians at the castles of Oswestry, Chirk, Carreghofa and Shrawardine during the Fitzalan minority between

[18] *Cartae*, i, nos. 40 (1197), 69 (1205); cf. R. R. Davies, 'The Peoples of Britain and Ireland, 1100–1400, 3: Laws and Customs', *TRHS*, 6th ser., **6** (1996), p. 4.

[19] *Feet of Fines, 7–8 Richard I, 1196–7* (P. R. S., 20), pp. 57–8, 65–6; *Feet of Fines, 9 Richard I, 1197–8* (P. R. S., 23), pp. 78–9; *Feet of Fines, 10 Richard I, 1198–9* (P. R. S., 24), p. 184.

[20] *Pleas before the King or his Justices, 1198–1212*, ed. Stenton, p. 69; Baugh, 'Franchises', p. 36; Eyton, xi, 229.

[21] See genealogical diagram above, p. 88, for the marriage of William Fitzalan I to Isabel de Sai in *c.* 1155.

[22] *Pipe Roll 9 John, 1207* (P. R. S., NS 22), pp. xviii–xxi.

[23] *Red Book of the Exchequer*, ed. Hall, pp. 86, 105, 271–4.

[24] *Pipe Roll 7 Richard I, 1195* (P. R. S., NS 6), p. 245; *Red Book of the Exchequer*, ed. Hall, p. 105; *Pipe Roll 1 John, 1199* (P. R. S., NS 10), p. 78; *Pipe Roll 3 John, 1201* (P. R. S., NS 14), p. 282; *Pipe Roll 4 John, 1202* (P. R. S., NS 15), p. 46; *Pipe Roll 16 John, 1214* (P. R. S., NS 35), p. 122 (owed by Thomas de Erdinton, custodian of William Fitzalan III).

c. 1210 and 1214; when he wrote to the sheriff of Shropshire to ensure delivery of scutage collected from Fitzalan's lands in 1214, it may well be that Oswestry contributed to the total.[25] It is remarkable that John should have paid such close personal attention to the Welsh borderlands, particularly as the Poitevin scutage was only incompletely collected because of the short notice at which it was imposed.[26] Whatever his reasons may have been, as far as the Fitzalan border estates were concerned, their exemption from the English state was not unambiguously established during John's reign.

To all appearances, the lordships of Clun and of Oswestry continued to differ with respect to their status vis-à-vis the English state after John Fitzalan I succeeded to his father's Shropshire estates in 1218. Justices in eyre had suspended their activities after 1208, and did not visit Shropshire again until 1221.[27] In that year, no cases concerning vills lying in the 'hundred' of Oswestry appear to have been brought before the justices. However, John Fitzalan I had to intervene when an English tenant claimed that a Welshman had wrongfully disseised him of his free tenancy at 'Bygyton', probably Bicton near Clun. Once again, the county upheld Fitzalan's claim that 'that land is of his fief and of his liberty, where the lord king does not lay his hand and his writs do not run.'[28] But it would seem that, while the judicial immunity of the lordship of Oswestry had been well established by the time of the minority of Henry III, that of the lordship of Clun still needed defending. That situation changed only gradually, and apparently with some setbacks. In 1225, John Fitzalan I was involved in bringing to Gloucester the fifteenth levied on movables in Shropshire and Staffordshire, but no mention was made of any exemption.[29] In 1229, 1230, 1231 and 1232, John Fitzalan I was assessed both on nine fees 'of Geoffrey de Vere' and on twenty-two and a half fees of his own, but never paid anything on the first item, and received acquittances for the latter only.[30] However, Henry III levied his second tax on movables in 1232, and the royal account roll for the fortieth of that year records that a fiscal exemption was granted to 'the lands of John Fitzalan beyond "Coluestan"'.[31] This reference is most probably Culvestone hundred in southern Shropshire, which bordered on the eastern limits of Purslow

[25] *Rot. Pat.*, p. 100; *Rot. Claus.*, i, 132, 170a, 212.

[26] *Pipe Roll 16 John, 1214* (P. R. S., NS 35), p. xv.

[27] Baugh, 'Franchises', p. 24.

[28] *Rolls of the Justices in Eyre, 1221, 1222*, ed. Stenton, no. 1020.

[29] *Rot. Claus.*, ii, 74b. [30] Eyton, xi, 230–1, n. 4.

[31] *Roll of Divers Accounts for the Early Years of the Reign of Henry III*, ed. F. A. Cazel (P. R. S., NS 44, 1982), p. 65. The lands 'infra hundredum de Chirebir" were also granted exemption; as Purslow hundred lay to the south of Chirbury hundred, there appears to have been some redundancy.

hundred. It therefore appears to exempt that hundred, and possibly Clun itself as well. Thus, it seems as if fiscal exemption for the southernmost of the two Fitzalan border lordships still depended on explicit royal favour at the time of Llywelyn ap Iorwerth's attacks on the castles of the Anglo-Welsh borders. In this respect, Clun continued to differ from Oswestry. Eyton believed that John Fitzalan I was assessed on Clun for Henry III's thirtieth on movables in 1235; moreover, John Fitzalan II was charged on that lordship for taxes or scutage in 1245, 1246, 1254 and 1260, although he was mostly acquitted from actually paying.[32]

By contrast, as was just argued, there is reason to believe that, after 1203, the lordship of Oswestry retained an unchallenged immunity. That argument is certainly not weakened by the fact that in 1254, when John Fitzalan II obtained a royal charter of free warren, it extended only to those of his demesne estates lying east of Oswestry lordship, possibly implying that no such grant was perceived necessary or appropriate for Oswestry itself.[33] It was, after all, in the first half of the thirteenth century that the Fitzalans explicitly retained regal prerogatives when they granted Shrewsbury Abbey free use of the market of Oswestry.[34] Moreover, the – albeit negative – evidence of the 1255 Hundred Rolls also supports this line of argument. Oswestry 'hundred' made no presentments. Also, while the jurors of Pimhill hundred, which adjoined the lordship of Oswestry on the east, accused both the lord of Ellesmere and the abbot of Shrewsbury of withdrawing suits from the hundredal court, John Fitzalan II's withdrawal of Ruyton-XI-Towns, which had been effected by 1203, elicited no comment.[35] More positive evidence of Oswestry's exemption at this time is provided by the records of the Shropshire eyre of 1256, for the county court found that it could not prosecute Fulk Fitzwarin IV for having killed a man, since the deed had been committed 'beyond Oswestry within the land of Wales.'[36] By contrast, Purslow hundred made its own presentments both in 1255, when it revealed that most of the suitors of the lord's court at Clun also performed suit at the hundredal court of Purslow, and at the eyre of 1256.[37] The fiscal exemption for Purslow hundred which was granted in 1232 clearly was not the preliminary to that territory's removal from the county.

It is, on balance, more probable that Oswestry was considered automatically exempt between *c.* 1203 and 1256 than that the lack of evidence

[32] Eyton, x, 231.

[33] *Cal. Pat. R., 1247–58*, p. 263.

[34] *Salop. Cart.*, nos. 304 (1215–33), 306 (1247).

[35] On Ruyton-XI-Towns, see Baugh, 'Franchises', p. 35; *Rot. Hund.*, ii, 75–6.

[36] *Roll of the Shropshire Eyre of 1256*, ed. Harding, no. 858; 'ultra Oswaldestr' infra terram Walliensis [*sic*]'.

[37] *Rot. Hund.*, ii, 76–8; *Roll of the Shropshire Eyre of 1256*, ed. Harding, pp. 196–203.

showing it to lie within the county is due to the accidents of documentary survival. By the same rationale, as Clun itself did not make any separate presentments in the 1250s, it seems probable that its immunity remained unchallenged after 1221. Thus, by 1269, when John Fitzalan III responded to a royal letter by asserting that 'in the parts of the March of Wales where he now resided, he was not bound to do anything at the king's mandate, and nothing would he do',[38] his sweeping claim was bolstered by the extent to which the workings of county government had indeed come routinely to bypass his border estates at that time. The immunity of his border territories from local governance no longer needed to be defended; it had become so well established that it could be invoked against directives from the centre of royal administration.

How well does the evidence of the reign of Edward I fit in with this argument? In 1281, Oswestry, besides Montgomery, Chester, Rhuddlan and Llanbadarn Fawr, numbered among the places visited by Edward I's jury-based inquiry into Welsh law conducted in that year.[39] This was not purely determined by its geographical position close to the borders. At Montgomery and Chester the subject of inquiry was laws in the Welsh-settled districts of Ceri, Cedewain and Iâl respectively, but at Oswestry the inquiry aimed to ascertain what laws were used in Oswestry lordship itself. Finally, the argument that Oswestry was considered to lie outside the county of Shropshire is supported by the evidence of the Shropshire *quo warranto* inquiry in 1292. When Richard Fitzalan I was called upon to explain by what warrant he claimed the right to hold pleas of the crown, the inquiry was concerned only with those of his demesne estates which lay in central and eastern Shropshire.[40] Moreover, the difference between Oswestry lordship and Purslow hundred was again highlighted, for while the former escaped notice, Richard was challenged to outline the legal basis for his claim to what was referred to as 'custody' of Purslow hundred.[41]

After Richard Fitzalan's death in 1302, during the minority of his son Edmund and the royal custody of Oswestry, the agents and methods of the English king's judiciary repeatedly intruded into the lordship. In 1302, Roger Mortimer of Chirk was charged with providing for a commission of *oyer* and *terminer* at Oswestry to settle a complaint of the tenants of Oswestry against the count of Savoy, to whom Edward I had granted the custody of the lordship.[42] Edward ordered another commission of

[38] *Excerpta e Rot. Finium*, ii, 486.

[39] *Cal. Chanc. R. Var.*, pp. 190–210; for Oswestry see *ibid.*, pp. 202–4.

[40] *Plac. de Quo Warranto*, p. 687b.

[41] *Ibid.*, p. 681a. [42] *Cal. Pat. R., 1301–7*, p. 287.

oyer and *terminer* to assemble at Oswestry in 1307.[43] However, on both occasions, it was from the lordships of Whittington, Caus and Ellesmere that the juries for the *oyer* and *terminer* proceedings were to be summoned, and this may have been a nod towards the traditional principle that the lords of the frontier settled their disputes among themselves.[44] But we should also note that, on these occasions, the Fitzalan lordship was referred to as 'the liberty of Oswestry of the county of Salop'. Even Oswestry hundred might, in exceptional circumstances, be considered to be simply an English franchise.

Caus

The Corbet estates surrounding the castle of Caus were, during the thirteenth century, more clearly subject to county governance than the lordships of Clun and Oswestry.[45] However, that contrast was not yet very stark at the outset of John's reign. It is true that at the Shropshire eyre of 1203, Robert Corbet (d. 1222), the lord of Caus, was forced, in an assize of *mort d'ancestor*, to surrender sixty acres of land in Minsterley, which lay close to the castle of Caus and had been a Corbet manor in 1086. It is also true that he was amerced half a mark for wrongful testimony.[46] However, it was observed above that possessory assizes were also available in both Oswestry and Glamorgan at around that date. Nor did Caus differ starkly from its neighbours with regard to fiscal exemption. Robert Corbet's ancestor in 1166 seems to have returned no *carta*. Even so, Robert himself was charged for the scutages of the 1190s, his lordship being assessed at five knights' fees. Nor did he escape the first three scutages of John's reign (1199–1202), nor the sixth (1205); and, while he was acquitted by writ from paying the seventh (1206), this did not mean he could avoid paying the Poitevin scutage in 1214.[47] In considering the evidence for scutage, it should be borne in mind that the estates of the Corbets of Caus were almost entirely restricted to the compact territory in the Rea–Camlad vale; unlike the Fitzalans, they held little land in central and eastern Shropshire. We may be confident, therefore, that

[43] *Ibid.*, p. 544–5.

[44] Richard Fitzalan had insisted in 1293 that barons of the 'Welshry' customarily convened to settle their disputes: 'Ricardus dicit quod ipse est baro de Walescheria ubi est consuetudo approbata quod barones parcium illarum quando hujusmodi discordia est inter eos orta accedere debent ad aliquem certum locum et ibi per amicos utriusque partis debet discordia illa pacificari' (*Abbreviatio Placitorum*, p. 231a).

[45] Baugh, 'Franchises', p. 37; Lieberman, 'Striving for Marcher Liberties: The Corbets'.

[46] *Pleas before the King or his Justices, 1198–1212*, ed. Stenton, pp. 100, 120; DB 253c.

[47] *Red Book of the Exchequer*, ed. Hall, pp. 87, 105; *Pipe Roll 7 Richard I, 1195* (P. R. S., NS 6), p. 245; *Pipe Roll 1 John, 1199* (P. R. S., NS 10), p. 79; *Pipe Roll 3 John, 1201* (P. R. S., NS 14), p. 282; *Pipe Roll 4*

John's scutages were indeed levied on a frontier honor, just as they were on the 'fee of Clun'. The evidence for the lordship of Caus, then, further supports the view that, during John's reign, the border lordships were not exempt from scutage.

It was argued above that the judicial immunity of Oswestry and Clun became established after 1203 and 1221 respectively. If the Corbets sought to transform their border lordships into similar sanctuaries from the interference of the royal judiciary, they were far less successful. It is true that neither Caus, nor Worthen, nor the hundred of Chirbury made presentments at, or were involved in, cases brought before the general eyre at Shrewsbury in 1221. However, the justices did outlaw one William Jeago for a murder committed at the manor of Pontesbury, which estate had been part of the Corbet block of lands since the late eleventh century.[48] Moreover, Thomas Corbet, lord of Caus from 1222 to 1274, was himself recurrently indicted in disputes over manors in Shropshire and the borders. In the Shropshire eyre of 1221, he vouched John Fitzalan II to warranty in a case concerning Tasley, just north of Bridgnorth. In 1236 and in 1242, Thomas Corbet and Herbert fitz Peter, the tenant of Pontesbury, appeared before the King's Bench to settle disputes over seisin of that manor and the military service due from it.[49] Thomas Corbet was also arraigned before the royal court in 1247, when Fulk Fitzwarin III was suing him over the manor of Bausley, the suit being enrolled under the heading of 'Wales', rather than of 'Salop'.[50] The lordship of Caus had received a grant of free warren in the year previous to this intrusion into the westernmost Corbet territories,[51] and this provides an example of how such a grant could represent less a retrenchment of crown control than an early symptom of increasing royal interference. For a lord of the Welsh borders to be tried by the English judiciary was not unusual.[52] It is worth noting, however, that, as far as the Corbet estates were concerned, the territorial reach of that judiciary extended further and further west during the first half of the thirteenth century.

John, 1202 (P. R. S., NS 15), p. 46; *Pipe Roll 7 John, 1205* (P. R. S., NS 19), p. 90; *Pipe Roll 8 John, 1206* (P. R. S., NS 20), p. 111; *Pipe Roll 16 John, 1214* (P. R. S., NS 35), p. 122.

48 *Rolls of the Justices in Eyre, 1221, 1222*, ed. Stenton, no. 1309.

49 *Curia Regis Rolls*, vol. xv: *1233–37* (London, 1972), p. 162, 420; *Curia Regis Rolls*, vol. xvii: *1242–3*, ed. A. Nicol (London, 1991), no. 631, p. 127. See also his dispute in 1233 with Robert fitz John, the tenant of Stratton: *Curia Regis Rolls*, vol. xv: *1233–37* (London, 1972), p. 162.

50 Meisel, *Barons of the Welsh Frontier*, p. 91; TNA KB 26/159, m. 6r; KB 26/159, m. 9r.

51 TNA C/143/1/4: the grant extended to the manors of Worthen, Forton, 'Caus in Westbury', Minsterley, Yockleton, and Wentnor.

52 Davies, *Lordship and Society*, pp. 251–4; in about 1255, a royal commission was appointed to investigate the dispute between Thomas and Gruffudd ap Gwenwynwyn, the lord of southern Powys: *Cal. Pat. R., 1247–58*, p. 438.

It is in keeping with this that the lordship of Caus was considered to lie fully within the purview of the inquest which Henry III conducted into royal rights in the localities in 1255. This was in stark contrast to Oswestry, which was entirely bypassed, and to Clun, which was only marginally touched. Thus, the jurors of Chirbury hundred stated that Thomas Corbet had withdrawn pleas originating in his fief 'of felony, bloodshed, of theft and of the hue and cry' which had pertained to the hundred.[53] They further specified that he had been doing so for five years, and that the king had therefore sustained financial losses of 40 shillings. They also stated that Thomas's manor of Worthen, with all its members, was part of Chirbury hundred and had performed suit until the eyre of justice Sir William 'de Ewerwyke',[54] but that since then it had made presentments separately. They further testified that the manor of Caus was not within Chirbury hundred and did not owe suit at it. However, they also accused Thomas of withdrawing from Chirbury hundred the suit of the vill of Leigh while it was in his custody as a result of the minority of its tenant, Hugh Hagar. Hugh, they further specified, did suit to the hundred, except when Thomas withdrew pleas belonging to the hundred to 'his court and liberty of Caus', which he had done for sixteen years. Similarly, according to jurors of Ford hundred, Thomas had withdrawn the suit of land in Minsterley from that hundred four years before the 1255 inquest.[55] Thus, whereas the immunity of Clun and Oswestry no longer even needed defending by 1255, Thomas Corbet's attempts at establishing a similarly exempt status for his territories became the subject of precise accusations founded on detailed evidence.

The findings of the 1255 inquest are exactly mirrored by the proceedings of the Shropshire eyre of the following year. The townships of Caus and Wallop claimed never to have been accustomed to appear before justices, although they admitted that they lay within the county.[56] The manor of Worthen, on the other hand, made separate presentments of crown pleas by means of five jurors, proving correct the statement to that effect made by Chirbury hundred in the previous year.[57] Furthermore, the cases involving the Corbet lords of Caus continued to demonstrate the limits of the English crown's jurisdiction. Thus, on the one hand, it was not questioned that the quarrel between Thomas Corbet and Fulk Fitzwarin IV over the manor of Alberbury, which lay close to the Welsh

[53] *Rot. Hund.*, ii, 60.

[54] Justices in eyre visited Shropshire from 27 October to 25 November 1248: D. Crook, *Records of the General Eyre* (London, 1982), pp. 110–11.

[55] *Rot. Hund.*, ii, 66.

[56] *Roll of the Shropshire Eyre of 1256*, ed. Harding, no. 864.

[57] *Ibid.*, p. 209.

borders, should be adjudicated before the justices at Shrewsbury.[58] On the other, it also emerged that three of Thomas' serjeants had seized two mares near Chirbury and driven them to 'Wythigruk' in Welshry', no doubt the Corbet castle of Gwyddgrug, in distraint for a debt.[59] In this case the justices were content with Thomas Corbet's explanation that it was 'the custom between the land of Wales and Englishry that if anyone from the land of England is indebted to anyone from the land of Wales or vice versa they may take distress from either region until the party has been satisfied.'

The position of the westernmost Corbet manors on the very fringe of the county continued to give rise to ambiguities and contradictions in Edward I's reign. The Ford hundred jurors stated in 1274 that the men of Robert Pigot had, for about thirty years, been compelled by Thomas Corbet to hold their lands by Welsh tenure ('per legem Walensem'), even though they had been used to hold by English tenure and 'follow the king's peace as Englishmen', and despite the fact that Robert held his land as a knight's fee.[60] As they were probably referring to the men of the Robert Pigot who held Aston Pigot of the lords of Caus, this represented an intrusion into that lordship by the hundredal inquiry of 1274. In 1277, an inquisition before the sheriff of Shropshire into the history of Bausley manor and the adjacent Welsh-settled territory east of the Severn known as the Gorddwr was held 'in the full county of Salop'. This was with the express intention of adjudicating a violent frontier dispute in which the Corbets, the Fitzwarins and the Welsh lords of Gwynedd and southern Powys had, within living memory, been involved.[61] On the other hand, four years later, Edward I's inquiry into Welsh laws concluded that 'le Gordur' lay 'in the Welshry and outside the county', and that Thomas Corbet and Gruffudd ap Gwenwynwyn had, on one occasion, sought to settle their dispute by the decision of a jury of twenty-four knights.[62]

At the time of the *quo warranto* inquiries, then, the Corbet estates offered a wealth of unresolved issues. In 1291–2, Peter Corbet was charged with defending his right to hold pleas reserved to the crown in his manors of Worthen, Minsterley and Shelve; he was also called upon to justify withdrawing the suits of twenty-two vills in the Rea–Camlad valley and in the hills surrounding it from the hundreds of Ford and Chirbury as well as from the county court of Shropshire. Essentially the entire lordship of Caus was coming under scrutiny.[63] Peter managed to deflect the legal challenge at first by questioning the form of the writ which had initiated

[58] *Ibid.*, pp. 138–9.
[59] *Ibid.*, no. 813. [60] *Rot. Hund.*, ii, 96.
[61] *Cal. Inq. Misc., 1219–1307*, p. 329.
[62] *Cal. Chanc. R. Var.*, p. 204. [63] *Plac. de Quo Warranto*, pp. 677, 681.

the *quo warranto* inquiry into his claims. However, he was later forced to acknowledge that he had no claim to try pleas of the crown in Worthen or Shelve.[64] He claimed that the vills of Vennington, Trefnant, Whitfield, Heldre and Hargreaves were 'in Welshry and entirely outside the county', although the jurors stated that they lay in Ford hundred. Peter acknowledged that the townships of Caus and Wallop lay in the county, but held that 'no sheriff, coroner or other royal servant should enter those vills to do his office, and that those vills did not owe suit at hundred or county or have to come before the justices of the king or his coroners or escheators or other servants to make presentments or do anything that might pertain to the crown'. The king's attorney objected that 'those aforesaid liberties constituted the royal crown (*faciunt Coronam Regis*)', and that none might lay claim to them without explicit royal licence. The outcome of this plea is not recorded; but this vill-by-vill bargaining could hardly have contrasted in a more pronounced way with the case of Fitzalan, whose border territories – apart from Purslow hundred – entirely escaped the notice of Edward I's *quo warranto* inquiry.

Wigmore

The most striking respect in which the Mortimer lordship of Wigmore differed from its northern neighbours during John's reign is the extent to which it appears to have escaped scutage. The Mortimers, like the Corbets, appear not to have returned a *carta* in 1166; moreover, they were never charged for scutage during the twelfth century for Wigmore, even though their neighbours on the Welsh borders of Shropshire and Herefordshire generally were.[65] Roger Mortimer (d. 1214) is not entered in the Shropshire or Herefordshire Pipe Rolls as owing debts for any of the seven scutages John levied between 1199 and 1206. Although in theory this may have meant that he had performed military service personally, even though none of his neighbours to the north did so, it appears more probable that he was not charged. Thus, in the case of John's second scutage, Roger Mortimer was acquitted by writ from scutage and fines for not accompanying the king to Normandy for his holdings in

[64] *Ibid.*, p. 686a.

[65] *Red Book of the Exchequer*, ed. Hall, pp. 24 (1160–1); cf. *ibid.*, pp. 41–2 (1167–8), for 'Hereford in Wallia': Robert of Ewias and Hugo de Lacy, but not Mortimer; p. 49 (1171–2): bishop of Hereford only; p. 66 (1186–7): bishop of Hereford, Robert of Ewias, Hugh Lacy, Walter of Cormeilles only; p. 74 (1190–1): Robert of Ewias, Walter of Cormeilles, Baderun of Monmouth, Robert Chandos, Walter Lacy only; pp. 85–6 (1194–5): Roger Mortimer acquitted by writ for his Lincolnshire estates; not mentioned under Herefordshire; pp. 106, 113–14 (1196–7): Roger Mortimer acquitted by writ for Nottingham and Derby, not mentioned under Herefordshire.

six English counties;[66] the fact that no such comment appears on the Pipe Rolls for Herefordshire or Shropshire suggests that Wigmore was automatically exempt from scutage. This argument is strengthened by the evidence for John's remaining five scutages. In 1202, Mortimer is again absent from the Herefordshire and Shropshire rolls, but acquitted by writ from scutage for his fiefs in Oxfordshire and Devon;[67] he is not entered as owing scutage for any of his English lands for John's fourth and fifth scutages; but for John's sixth and seventh scutages, Wigmore appears to have been automatically exempt from scutage, unlike Roger Mortimer's estates in different parts of England.[68]

Even during John's reign, at a time when the government of England, faced with inflation and the heaviest territorial losses on the Continent it had ever encountered, was desperately seeking to raise its level of income from the regalian rights pertaining to the English crown, Roger Mortimer's lands on the Welsh borders seem, for fiscal purposes, to have been treated much as if they had lain outside England. To be sure, the Mortimers did not quite escape the novel methods of squeezing money from the barons with which King John and his agents experimented. In 1214, Roger Mortimer, falling ill towards the end of his life, was made to fine 500 marks for permission to bestow his lands in Shropshire on his son Hugh.[69] Although this payment is reminiscent of a baronial relief rather than indicative of a fiscal innovation, the succession of a young Mortimer lord seems also, temporarily at least, to have weakened the resolve with which that family was able to resist taxation in Herefordshire. In May 1214, Roger Mortimer had been acquitted of the scutage of Poitou, because his son was personally serving in that province.[70] Despite this, Hugh was noted on the Pipe Roll for Herefordshire as owing 46 marks for the Poitevin scutage levied in 1214, just as the lords of the Shropshire–Powys frontier owed varying amounts for the same scutage that year.[71]

During John's reign, Roger Mortimer (d. 1214) was involved in lengthy litigation over a Shropshire manor with the de Bracy family, before the justices both in eyre in Shrewsbury and at the royal court at Westminster, but the manor in question, Meole Brace, lay just to the

[66] Lincolnshire, Wiltshire, Northamptonshire, Berkshire, Oxfordshire, Leicestershire: *Pipe Roll 3 John, 1201* (P. R. S., NS 14), pp. 22, 83, 186, 200, 214, 241.

[67] *Pipe Roll 4 John, 1202* (P. R. S., NS 15), p. 209, 253.

[68] Roger Mortimer (Berkshire): *Pipe Roll 9 John, 1207* (P. R. S., NS 22), p. 187 (also said to owe 5th scutage John, though later acquitted); Roger Mortimer (Rutland): *Pipe Roll 10 John, 1208* (P. R. S., NS 23), p. 75; *Pipe Roll 11 John, 1209* (P. R. S., NS 24), p. 107; Shropshire lords: *Pipe Roll 7 John, 1205* (P. R. S., NS 19), pp. 90–1; *Pipe Roll 8 John, 1206* (P. R. S., NS 20), p. 111.

[69] *Pipe Roll 16 John, 1214* (P. R. S., NS 35), p. 120; *Rot. Oblat.*, pp. 530, 535–6.

[70] *Rot. Claus.*, i, 201.

[71] *Pipe Roll 16 John, 1214* (P. R. S., NS 35), p. 137; *ibid.*, pp. 121–2.

south of Shrewsbury, in central Shropshire.[72] As was the case elsewhere on the borders, the Mortimer frontier estates did not prove immune to the possessory assizes. Much as Oswestry had been invaded by an assize of *mort d'ancestor* in 1203, in 1221 a case concerning the estates of Trippleton and Leintwardine was heard at Shrewsbury.[73] It is more striking that the fiscal exemption of Wigmore was no longer taken for granted. Rather, in 1232, 'the lands of Ralph Mortimer in the valley of Wigmore' were included in the specific royal exemption from the fortieth of that year which also extended to the lands of John Fitzalan.[74]

Overall, Wigmore and its vicinity are paralleled most closely by Clun and Oswestry in the extent to which the Wigmore area apparently escaped the notice of the royal judiciary and crown inquiries before 1292. Possessory assizes continued to provide the only exception: at the Shropshire eyre of 1227, Ralph Mortimer conveyed forty acres of land in Lingen, a hamlet six kilometres to the west of Wigmore, on one John of Lingen, building the transaction around an assize of *mort d'ancestor*, concluding it by final concord and receiving 25 marks from John in return.[75] But one searches the records of the Shropshire eyres in vain for litigation over the Mortimer estates that lay nearest to Wales, although, in 1256, Hugh Mortimer was charged with disseisin in a case concerning Chelmarsh in central Shropshire.[76]

Wigmore is also best comparable to Clun and Oswestry as far as the hundredal inquest of 1255 is concerned. Wigmore did not make its own presentments before the inquest, although the castle at Wigmore, like those at Clun and Oswestry, is mentioned because estates in central Shropshire owed ward-service at it.[77] In 1274, Wigmore again escaped making its own presentments, as did Clun and Oswestry. However, the burgesses of Ludlow and the jurors of Munslow hundred lodged complaints against the constable of Wigmore.[78] Moreover, the jurors of Overs hundred in southern Shropshire noted that, since the battle of Evesham, Hugh Mortimer had withdrawn the suits of several of his manors from that hundred.[79]

The Mortimers, like the Fitzalans and the Corbets, did not escape the *quo warranto* inquiry of 1292. During the inquiry for Shropshire, Edmund Mortimer was called upon to explain by what warrant he had

[72] *Pleas before the King or his Justices, 1198–1212*, ed. Stenton, p. 63; *Curia Regis Rolls*, vol. iii: *1203–1205* (London, 1926), pp. 111, 142, 149; iv, 163; v, 177. Cf. Eyton, vi, 350–7.

[73] *Rolls of the Justices in Eyre, 1221, 1222*, ed. Stenton, pp. xlv, 460, 488–9.

[74] *Roll of Divers Accounts*, ed. Cazel, p. 65.

[75] *TSAS*, 4th ser., **4** (1914), p. 166.

[76] *Roll of the Shropshire Eyre of 1256*, ed. Harding, no. 47.

[77] *Rot. Hund.*, ii, 81–2. [78] *Rot. Hund.*, ii, 99, 101.

[79] *Rot. Hund.*, ii, 103.

withdrawn the suits of over forty estates. Although Wigmore itself was not among these, a number of the vills listed in the *quo warranto* proceedings were close to the Welsh borders.[80] One of these, Whitton, even lay beyond Offa's Dyke, in the Lugg valley – precisely the area which two centuries previously had been referred to as lying 'in Marcha de Walis' in Domesday Book.[81] The Mortimer lordship of Wigmore was coming under very close scrutiny in the early 1290s; a dramatic reversal from the previous picture. A possible explanation may be suggested by looking at the Welsh fifteenth which was being collected at exactly this time.

The Welsh fifteenth granted in 1291 and the lordships of the Shropshire–Powys frontier

In 1290, the barons of England granted King Edward I a fifteenth on movables in aid of his campaign in Gascony. Just over a year later, that levy was also requested from the magnates of Wales.[82] This represented a new departure in the fiscal experimentation of the English crown: Wales had never been taxed before. The collectors in charge of levying the Welsh fifteenth therefore had to engage, to an unprecedented degree, with the question of exactly which territories lay in Wales, the March and England. It is therefore of central importance to the question of how far the lordships of the Shropshire borders were considered to lie outside the county.

As perhaps was to be expected, the collection of the Welsh fifteenth did not proceed smoothly on the Shropshire–Powys border. In 1293–4, Edmund Mortimer (d. 1304), then lord of Wigmore Castle on the Welsh borders and of several estates in southern Shropshire, was accused of having resisted the collection of the original, English fifteenth 'in the county of Shropshire', intending to 'remove his lands from the county and add them to his liberty outside the county.'[83] In his defence, Edmund stated that he had not hindered the collection of the fifteenth in Shropshire, 'except at Wigmore', claiming that there 'his tenants, since time immemorial, do not answer the summons of the itinerant justices and the king's writ does not run there and the jurisdiction belongs solely to the lord of the liberty', and moreover that the 'tenants there are free from the royal taxes'. He also stated that one year later, when the king had requested the Welsh fifteenth from Mortimer, 'as from other lords of Wales', Mortimer had given 'a special concession of a fifteenth of the

[80] *Plac. de Quo Warranto*, 677, 681b.
[81] Above, pp. 5–6 and Map 2, p. 7.
[82] *Cal. Pat. R.*, *1281–92*, p. 419.
[83] *List of Welsh Entries in the Memoranda Rolls, 1282–1343*, ed. N. Fryde (Cardiff, 1974), no. 68.

goods of tenants inside the aforesaid liberty [of Wigmore]'. This dispute reflects the ambiguities within which the agents of royal government might become embroiled when they ventured towards the western limits of the English state. Nor was the confusion about the status of Wigmore resolved. Edmund Mortimer was careful to obtain a royal document guaranteeing that the grant of the Welsh fifteenth would not constitute a precedent,[84] but his son had to defend Wigmore's exemption from royal taxation at some point between 1302 and 1322.[85] Nevertheless, despite the confusion, some notions were well developed. Edmund Mortimer bolstered his claim to fiscal exemption by propounding a classic catalogue of Marcher liberties. The tax collectors had acknowledged the existence of a Mortimer 'liberty outside the county'. The idea that the border lordships of Wales should be exempt from routine English taxation was clearly becoming as well articulated as, and associated with, other Marcher liberties by the end of the thirteenth century.

It was not a simple matter then to convict Edmund Mortimer of tax evasion in the 1290s; it is even more difficult today. Tax jurors and assessors were certainly appointed not only from the Welsh districts he held at the time – the 'cantreds' of Cedewain and Maelienydd and the 'commotes' of Gwrtheyrnion and Ceri – but also from the 'valley of Wigmore'.[86] The thirteen subsidy rolls that survive to testify to the Welsh fifteenth indicate that the tax was also actually assessed on territories from which assessors and jurors had been appointed. Further, they constitute the best evidence we have that it was indeed collected.[87] Certainly neither Edmund's lordship of Radnor nor his border manors of Knighton and Norton escaped assessment, and therefore almost certainly collection, of the Welsh fifteenth.[88] No subsidy rolls survive for the 'valley of Wigmore', which precludes final certainty. But it does seem as if, in the specific circumstances of the collection of the Welsh fifteenth from Mortimer lordships, the tax was indeed levied from the territories whose population was assessed for it. Wigmore lordship may well have paid the Welsh fifteenth of the early 1290s.

In any case, it is highly significant that jurors and assessors for the Welsh fifteenth were also appointed, mainly in March and April 1293, at Oswestry, Clun, Whittington, Knockin and Caus.[89] As in southern Wales, so on the

[84] *Cal. Pat. R., 1292–1301*, p. 56 (1293).

[85] *Cal. Anc. Corr. Wales*, pp. 101–2; it is possible that the Roger Mortimer of this document was Edmund's father (d. 1282), and that the reference is therefore to the fifteenth of 1275.

[86] As is evident from the schedules of jurors and assessors of the fifteenth on movables granted by the Marcher lords for South Wales and the March: TNA E 179/242/48, m. 6v.

[87] *The Merioneth Lay Subsidy Roll 1292–3*, ed. K. Williams-Jones (Cardiff, 1976), pp. ix–x.

[88] M.A. Faraday, 'The Assessment for the Fifteenth of 1293 on Radnor and Other Marcher Lordships', *Transactions of the Radnorshire Society*, **43** (1973), pp. 79–85.

[89] TNA E 179/242/48, mm. 5v (Knockin, Whittington, Caus); 6v (Oswestry, Clun).

Shropshire borders, it was the lordships which constituted the territorial units within which the tax was to be assessed. Thus, at Oswestry the jurors and assessors were appointed 'on the land of Richard Fitzalan, the earl of Arundel'. This was the simplest, perhaps the only, way of proceeding; yet in the circumstances it unavoidably produced clashes with established practice. At Clun, jurors and assessors of the Welsh fifteenth were assembled 'from the whole land of the aforesaid earl both in the hundred of Purslow and elsewhere in his lands in Wales', despite the fact that Purslow hundred, as has been seen, was generally regarded as lying within the county. Similarly, the fact that the Welsh fifteenth was to be assessed at Caus is not, at first sight, compatible with that lordship's being liable for English taxes during the fourteenth century. However, at Caus in 1293 both tax assessors and all twelve jurors had Welsh names, and it seems apparent that the Welsh tax was only to be assessed on those of the Corbet territories which were Welsh-populated. The ethnic distinction was certainly upheld at Knockin, where the Welsh and English communities both contributed six jurors towards the standard total of twelve; here it would appear that both were considered liable. At Oswestry, the two taxable sub-units of the lordship were the borough, which presented two jurors with Welsh names and six Englishmen, and the Welsh-populated hinterland, whose twelve jurors were referred to as coming 'de forinsec'. As for Whittington, it appears to have been too small and too Welsh-dominated for distinctions to be made among the jurors: three of these bore English names, but they were not considered a separate body within the jury of twelve, as they were at Knockin. Thus, great attention to local circumstances was paid in providing for the assessment of the Welsh fifteenth on the Shropshire borders. Moreover, apart from Purslow hundred, there appears to be no exception to the rule that the Shropshire border territories which came to evade the scope of county and royal government during the thirteenth century were, for the purposes of the assessment of the Welsh fifteenth, considered to lie within the March of Wales.

As was pointed out in the case of 'the valley of Wigmore', whether or not the tax was actually collected is often difficult to say. None of the Shropshire lords, as far as we know, emulated Edmund Mortimer in acquiring written royal guarantees that the Welsh fifteenth would not be considered a precedent. The other Marcher lords who are known to have done so, besides Edmund Mortimer, were:[90]

- John de Warenne, earl of Surrey, for Bromfield
- Humphrey de Bohun, earl of Hereford and Essex, for Brecon

[90] *Cal. Pat. R., 1281–92*, pp. 500, 502, 503, 510, 511; *Cal. Pat. R., 1292–1301*, p. 52.

- Theobald de Verdon, for Ewyas Lacy
- John Giffard, for Clifford and Middlewood, Glasbury and Bronllys, Hirfrin, Cwmwd Perfedd and Iscennen
- Edmund, the king's brother, for Monmouth, Grosmont, Skenfrith and White Castle
- Gilbert de Clare, earl of Gloucester and Hertford, 'within his liberties in Wales'
- Roger le Bigod, earl of Norfolk and marshal of England, for Strigoil
- John de Hastings, for Abergavenny and Cilgerran
- Roger de Montalt, for Mold and Hawarden.

Roger de Montalt parallels the lords of Oswestry, Clun, Whittington, Caus or Knockin in that he was a relatively minor frontier baron whose lordship had been established during the twelfth century. The fact that he appears in the list means that there is no obvious reason why the Shropshire lords should not have acquired royal guarantees against precedent; if his name had been absent, that would have provided a reason for thinking that only high-ranking aristocrats who received their lands in Wales in 1282–3 applied for the guarantees. In the circumstances, however, the fact that none of the Shropshire lords applied might be considered an argument for thinking that there was no need for them to do so, since the tax was not collected on their estates. However, the royal guarantees seem to date to the period during which the tax was negotiated with the Marcher lords, and therefore to have been granted before jurors and assessors were appointed. Moreover, lay subsidy rolls survive for the lands in Powys of Roger Mortimer (including Chirk and Carreghofa) and the sons of Gruffudd ap Gwenwynwyn, but none of these appears to have acquired a royal guarantee against precedent.[91] On balance, it is reasonably safe to assume that collection of the Welsh fifteenth did proceed in the Shropshire border lordships. In any case, it seems clear that, in the early 1290s, they were not considered to lie in England.

II: FACTORS DETERMINING THE EXTENT OF THE COUNTY OF SHROPSHIRE, *c.* 1070–1300

What factors may have helped to determine the extent to which the lordships came to be withdrawn from the county, or to be exempt

[91] TNA E 179/242/55; 'A Powys Lay Subsidy Roll, 1293', ed. R. Morgan, *Mont. Coll.*, **71** (1983), pp. 91–112.

from novel instruments of royal governance? It has been argued that the Fitzalans 'withdrew their lordship from the county', that is, established the estates around Oswestry as a territory with judicial immunity, before Easter 1201, while they were still sheriffs of Shropshire.[92] It would seem highly plausible that the Fitzalans were in a particularly favourable position to take the lead, as they seem to have been able to lay a quasi-hereditary claim to the office of sheriff of Shropshire during the twelfth century. After all, Thomas Corbet very clearly seized the opportunity of his tenure of the office from 1248 to 1250 to withdraw the suits of several manors of Ford and Chirbury hundreds to his court at Caus; in 1255, he was accused of having done so 'five years previously'.[93] However, it should not be assumed without argument that tenure of the shrieval office guaranteed that frontier estates could be withdrawn successfully. Geoffrey de Vere, sheriff of Shropshire from 1165–70, had no permanent success in establishing Clun, which he held by right of marriage to Isabel de Sai, as lying outside the county, if indeed he attempted to do so. As was argued above, the judicial immunity of Caus, unlike that of Oswestry, was not tacitly accepted, but rather became the subject of intricate legal argument in 1292. Nor does it appear that a lord had necessarily to be sheriff in order to establish or maintain that his border estates lay outside the county; after all, the Fitzalans lost their grip on the office in 1201 – two years previous to the Shropshire eyre which first drew attention to Oswestry's claim to immunity – and did not regain it for the rest of the thirteenth century. The Mortimers, moreover, never held the office at all.[94] Although it is clear that the office of sheriff can only have assisted attempts at redrawing the borders of the county, it does seem as if it was neither a guarantee nor a necessary precondition.

A similar point could be argued about the importance of royal favour to the establishment and maintenance of frontier exemptions. It stands to reason that the goodwill or acquiescence of the king could, and no doubt on occasion did, assist the lords of the Shropshire–Powys frontier in achieving greater freedom from interference and from the obligations of county administration.[95] Yet it does not seem to have been a condition *sine qua non*. In 1203, William Fitzalan II had recently been removed from the office of sheriff, possibly because he had incurred King John's disfavour during the rebellion of Fulk Fitzwarin III of Whittington. Besides, it is worth recalling that in 1203 and in 1221 it was, after all, the county assembly that decided how far the jurisdiction

[92] Baugh, 'Franchises', p. 35.
[93] *Rot. Hund.*, ii, 60. [94] Baugh, 'Franchises', p. 37.
[95] *Ibid.*, pp. 35, 37; compare Holden, *Lords*, 158–63.

of the shire extended – exemption from that jurisdiction might be, and was, established without explicit royal consent in thirteenth-century Shropshire. Conversely, when a royal exemption was granted, as it was to Ralph Mortimer and John Fitzalan in respect of their border estates on the occasion of the fortieth of 1232, the implication was that, usually, those estates would not have been exempt, but would normally be considered to lie within the county. The same point was established by grants of free warren and other immunities, such as those to Caus in 1247 and to various central Shropshire estates of the Fitzalans in 1254. It is conceivable that such grants were intended to dispel doubts about the issue of whether or not the favoured estates lay within the county, by driving home the point that liberties could only be assumed with royal permission. Royal favour might insidiously undermine implicit claims to exemption; invoking it certainly does not explain satisfactorily how territories like Clun and Oswestry came to escape entirely the painstaking scrutiny of baronial claims to liberties conducted by Edward I's agents in 1292.

It might also be suggested that exemption from burdens imposed by the English state was granted because the lords of the frontier castles were perceived to fulfil the role of protecting that state's borders. If it seems daring to propose that such a well-defined equation was widely accepted during the twelfth and thirteenth centuries, it does seem clear that, on occasion, the existence of a specific military threat could affect how the crown treated the lords of the Shropshire–Powys frontier. Thus, it seems highly plausible that Henry III's fiscal exemption of 1232 was granted in consideration of the devastation which had been wrought the previous year on Montgomery, Clun and the Mortimer border castles by the raids of Llywelyn ap Iorwerth, in much the same way as the northern counties were sometimes granted fiscal exemption because of Scottish raids. Similarly, it makes sense to assume that lords who sometimes received royal funds to refurbish and fortify their frontier castles – as the Corbets, Mortimers and Fitzalans all, on occasion, did – would recurrently have been granted exemption from royal taxes because of the imminence of a military threat from the Welsh. Moreover, in 1274, when the amount of knight's service and scutage owed by Peter Corbet was assessed, it was taken into account that Llywelyn ap Gruffudd had recently occupied a third of his barony.[96] It does seem that the frequent involvement of the lords of the Welsh frontier castles in border diplomacy and conflict contributed, in practice, towards the way in which their status vis-à-vis the English state was perceived and defined. As has been seen, by 1236, shortly

[96] *Rot. Hund.*, ii, 90.

after their border castles had been devastated yet again, the Mortimers and the Fitzalans were claiming that they fulfilled a role parallel to the lords of the Cinque Ports;[97] although that was not considered justified at the time, it is easy to see how the perception that special privileges were tied to their frontier existence might have become widespread.

One respect in which the lordship of Caus differed from Oswestry, Clun and Wigmore was its geographical position relative to Wales and the county of Shropshire. After the de Bollers lordship escheated to the crown in 1207, Caus was alone in straddling an important connecting road between two royal castles, Montgomery and Shrewsbury. This inevitably drew attention to the question of how far Caus was included in the county. In 1226, while the new castle at Montgomery was being built, Henry III ordered an inquiry into whether Thomas Corbet owed suit at 'the hundred of Montgomery'.[98] Relative geographical remoteness was an advantage in creating a distance from county administration, one which the Corbets of Caus did not enjoy to the extent that the lords of Wigmore, Clun and Oswestry did. Moreover, Caus did not unequivocally share a frontier with Powys, being sandwiched between the two Shropshire hundreds of Ford and Chirbury. This was a result of the fact that the twelfth-century lords of Caus did not succeed in replacing with their own seigneurial administration the hundredal organization which survived in the Rea–Camlad valley, despite holding a fair share of the vills which came to constitute Chirbury hundred. As the case of Wigmore shows, contiguity with Wales did not guarantee that a lordship's claims to exemption from county administration would go unchallenged. However, the geographical position of Caus meant that the efforts of the Corbet lords at withdrawing it from county administration were more clearly akin to attempts at creating liberties in central Shropshire.[99] Geographical contiguity with Wales, then, provided an additional reason why border territories should be exempt from the English state: the issue of whether or not they might lie in Wales or the March. Especially after 1207, Oswestry, Clun and Wigmore were far more likely than Caus to be considered not as English franchises, but as lying entirely outside the county.

Besides what might be called geopolitical considerations, the difference in timing should also be taken into account. The Corbet lords of Caus may have compounded their geographical disadvantage in attempting to withdraw their lordship from the county simply because they set about doing so half a century after the Fitzalans. The Fitzalans, in turn,

[97] Above, p. 83. [98] *Rot. Claus.*, ii. 114a, 154–5.
[99] Baugh, 'Franchises', pp. 45–53.

may have been less successful in asserting the exemption from taxes and scutage of Clun than of Oswestry because they came to inherit the former lordship only in *c.* 1199.[100] Such an interpretation would certainly be in keeping with modern scholarship on the making of English franchises and Marcher liberties.[101] The franchises of England, Cam argued, developed in response to the evolution of the English kingdom between the eleventh century and the reign of Edward I, acquiring a precise meaning only within the context of, and in relation to, a developed bureaucratic state. Similarly, Davies argued that the degree to which Marcher liberties came to be perceived and defined as such corresponded to the precision and frequency with which Marcher lords were challenged to defend them by the agents of the crown; and that the thirteenth century was the key period during which those challenges were made and definitions occurred. These considerations certainly help to explain the extent of exemption on the Shropshire–Powys borders. There is good reason to believe that, had Fitzalan advanced his claims only thirty years later, they would have attracted more comment from the inquests of the latter half of the thirteenth century. Moreover, being a sheriff in 1248 brought with it an altogether less exalted status than it had in the twelfth century, when the Fitzalans were so successful in monopolizing the shrieval office.[102] Nevertheless, although the Fitzalans had established a claim to Purslow hundred well before they asserted the immunity of Clun in 1221, that did not mean that that claim went uninvestigated. The same is true of Wigmore, as is shown by the specific fiscal exemption of 1232. Not even early timing could guarantee unchallenged withdrawal of a frontier territory from the county of Shropshire.

This focuses attention on the final ingredient in the successful establishment of such withdrawal: the ethnicity of the population of the frontier districts in question. Again, modern scholarship provides a possible key to an understanding of this factor, because it has illustrated the ways in which the English state became not only more elaborate and bureaucratic over the thirteenth century, but also grew ethnically exclusive in its outlook and operation.[103] It is primarily the foremost exponents of Edward I's government that displayed this outlook: it is evident from the

[100] For the date, see Eyton, xi, 229.

[101] H. M. Cam, 'The Evolution of the Mediaeval English Franchise', *Speculum*, xxxii (July 1957), pp. 427–42; repr. in her *Law-Makers and Law-Finders* (London, 1962), pp. 22–43; Davies, 'Kings, Lords and Liberties', pp. 41–61.

[102] D. A. Carpenter, 'The Decline of the Curial Sheriff in England', *EHR*, **91** (1976), p. 1.

[103] R. R. Davies, 'The English State and the "Celtic" Peoples, 1100–1400', *Journal of Historical Sociology*, **6** (1993), pp. 1–14; see also his *Domination and Conquest*, chs. 3 and 6; and his *The First English Empire: Power and Identities in the British Isles, 1093–1343* (Oxford, 2000), pp. 140–1.

expostulations and exhortations of Archbishop Pecham in 1284 and from the tone of Edward I's ordinances of 1295.[104] By the end of the thirteenth century, the effects of this outlook were being felt in the localities. In the Irish context, it underlay the enactment against degeneracy passed by the Dublin parliament of 1297.[105] It manifested itself in the applicability of the common law, which came to be both restricted to and mandatory for Englishmen throughout the British Isles during the thirteenth century.[106] It may explain why the Welsh of Archenfield paid their share of Henry III's fifteenth on movables in 1225, but were able later on to claim exemption from English taxes by asserting that Archenfield was part of the Welsh March.[107]

It was argued above that the districts of Oswestry lordship and the uplands of Clun saw a considerable influx of Welsh settlers during the second half of the twelfth century, while Purslow hundred and Wigmore remained largely English-populated.[108] The correlation between Welsh- and English-settled territories and districts which escaped the scrutiny of the thirteenth-century royal inquiries is a very close one for these Fitzalan and Mortimer lordships. The same is true for Caus and its 'Welshry', the Gorddwr. It was argued earlier that the Welsh fifteenth was levied, in 1293, from the Welsh-populated areas of the Corbet frontier honor alone. Moreover, those territories also seem to have eluded the *quo warranto* proceedings which had been conducted in 1291–2. A comparison between the Fitzalan claims to exemption in 1203 and 1293 also supports the view that the increased ethnic exclusiveness of the English state had an effect on the Shropshire borders. At the beginning of the thirteenth century, William Fitzalan II had simply laid a claim to a private hundred. But his great-great-grandson, ninety years later, found that his best defence against having to answer before the royal court for raiding the Fitzwarin lordship of Whittington was to proclaim that he was 'a baron of the Welshry.'[109] By the 1290s, the exemption of the Welsh-settled districts of Caus did not need defending. At the same time, Welshness had become a trump-card in the hands of those lords who did need to cement the

[104] *Registrum Epistolarum Johannis Peckham*, ed. Martin, ii, 741–2; iii, 776–7; *Record of Caernarvon*, ed. Ellis, pp. 131–2; Davies, *Age of Conquest*, pp. 385–6.

[105] S. Duffy, 'The Problem of Degeneracy', in J. F. Lydon (ed.), *Law and Disorder in Thirteenth-Century Ireland: The Dublin Parliament of 1297* (Dublin, 1997), pp. 87–106; R. Frame, ' "Les Engleys nées en Irlande": The English Political Identity in Medieval Ireland', *TRHS*, 6th ser., **3** (1993), pp. 83–103.

[106] Davies, 'The Peoples of Britain and Ireland, 1100–1400. 3. Laws and Customs', pp. 5–6.

[107] *Foreign Accounts of Henry III 1219–34*, ed. F. Cazel (P. R. S., 44, 1974–5), p. 56; Davies, *Lordship and Society*, p. 17.

[108] Above, pp. 42–51.

[109] *Abbreviatio Placitorum*, p. 231a.

claim of their border territories to lie outside the county. True, nothing was set in stone. In 1292 × 1293, as has been seen, sixteen Welshmen evicted by Roger Lestrange from the manor of Ellesmere were granted the right to a commission of *oyer* and *terminer* to determine whether they had been unjustly ejected.[110] They had had to wait for eight years, though. The evidence of the Shropshire–Powys lordships suggests that, during the thirteenth century, the English state became less ethnically inclusive not only in its rhetoric and in central government, but in the practice of how it brought its governmental machine to bear on the localities.

⋆ ⋆ ⋆

The deeper-lying reasons for the different ways in which the English state treated Caus, Clun, Oswestry and Wigmore during the first third of the fourteenth century thus directly reflect the way in which that state developed during the thirteenth century. During the twelfth, and arguably still at the beginning of the thirteenth, there was no objection in principle to including territories which were regarded as lying 'in Wales' within the routine operation of the English government. However, during the thirteenth century, that operation both became more elaborate and precise and began to work on the assumption that it applied only to Englishmen. The different extent to which the lordships of the Shropshire–Powys frontier, and indeed the English and Welsh districts within them, escaped the reach of the English state can be explained to a considerable extent by those twin developments. By Edward II's reign, when Fitzalan and Mortimer came to direct high politics, while the ancient line of the Corbets of Caus was about to be extinguished, the border honors of these lords had been shaping their relationship with the English state in diverging ways for over a century.

Nevertheless, the attempts of the thirteenth-century Corbet lords at withdrawing their estates from the county are highly telling. They reflect precisely the way in which exemption from the English state had come

[110] *Cal. Chanc. R. Var.*, p. 285; *Cal. Pat. R., 1281–92*, p. 521; above, pp. 44–5 and n. 103. For some recent work on the attitudes of the English and their state towards their 'Celtic' neighbours during the thirteenth and fourteenth centuries, see M. Lieberman, 'The English and the Welsh in *Fouke le Fitz Waryn*', in J. Burton, P. Schofield and B. Weiler (eds.), *Thirteenth-Century England*, 12 (Woodbridge, 2009), pp. 1–11; A. Ruddick, 'Ethnic Identity and Political Language in the King of England's Dominions: A Fourteenth-Century Perspective', in L. Clark (ed.), *Identity and Insurgency in the Late Middle Ages (The Fifteenth Century, 6)* (Woodbridge, 2006), pp. 15–32; the same, 'National and Political Identity in Anglo-Scottish Relations, *c.* 1286–1377: A Governmental Perspective', in A. King and M. Penman (eds.), *England and Scotland in the Fourteenth Century: New Perspectives* (Woodbridge, 2007), pp. 196–215.

to be perceived as an attribute, a distinctive badge of a certain group of lords and lordships: those able to claim that they were part of the March of Wales, *Marchia Wallie*. It seems clear that, in Shropshire, exemption from the English state was perceived to be, from *c.* 1200 at the latest, an attribute typical of the lordships of the 'March'. The extent to which the lordships of the Powys–Shropshire frontier achieved that exemption therefore constitutes a further measure of how far they were included, in practice as well as perception, within a distinctive region embracing both the lordships in south Wales and those on the Anglo-Welsh borders.

CONCLUSION

The introduction to this book proposed that the border between Shropshire and Powys provides a showcase for studying the creation and perception of the medieval March of Wales. That border shifted strikingly little during the two centuries or so which elapsed between the Norman conquest of England in 1066 and the English conquest of Wales in 1282–3. It therefore contrasted sharply with certain parts of Wales, particularly the north, south and west coasts, where the Normans and the English made spectacular territorial gains and often suffered equally spectacular losses. But, while the medieval Shropshire–Powys border remained remarkably fixed in terms of its geographical position, the way in which it was conceptualized changed dramatically. As far as we can tell, it was the Welsh borders of Shropshire which from 1166 inspired a new fashion for the term *Marchia Wallie*, even though the compact border honors clustered around the Severn gap were established mostly on English rather than Welsh territory.[1] However, by the fourteenth century, the category *Marchia Wallie* routinely included the Shropshire 'March' as well as the conquest lordships in south Wales. Thus, at first there was a discrepancy between the medieval and the modern concepts of the March of Wales. More than a century elapsed before the medieval concept of the March came to routinely embrace the compact honors on the Anglo-Welsh borders as well as the conquered parts of Wales. The preceding chapters have sought to explain this conceptual change. They have taken a thematic approach, discussing how far the 'actual' conditions on the Welsh borders of Shropshire shaped the medieval concept of the March of Wales; that is, how far that concept was determined by such features as the distribution of settlements and of castles and castellan

[1] In the late 1080s, it was recorded in Domesday Book that certain vills on the Welsh borders of northernmost Herefordshire lay in a 'March of Wales': DB 183d ('in marcha de Wales'), 186d ('in Marcha de Walis').

families, the degree of social militarization, the hybrid institutions of seigneurial administration, or claims to 'Marcher' regality. It remains to knit together the different strands of this thematic argument. One way of doing so is to proceed chronologically.

On the eve of the Norman conquest of England, the political frontier between Shropshire and Powys had been in existence for centuries.[2] But although the Normans based at Richard's Castle may already have begun speaking of a 'marcha de Walis' during the 1050s and early 1060s, the Anglo-Welsh frontier was still generally thought of as a line; that was the outlook that had inspired the construction of Offa's Dyke.[3] In the early 1060s, certain border districts were still being digested into the English governmental framework.[4] Eadric the Wild and men of his ilk may have thought of themselves as a special group of 'border' aristocrats, and considered that their estates in westernmost Shropshire had a distinctive status.[5] Wales was a strategic concern of the authorities of the English state.[6] The population of 'Mersete' hundred may still have thought of themselves as 'the settlers on the boundary'. But, in 1065, there were no signs that the status quo which had been established on the Anglo-Welsh border would be radically altered.

The story of how a 'Marcher' region between Shropshire and Powys was created really begins with the arrival of Roger, *vicomte* of the Hiémois, and earl of Shrewsbury. Earl Roger first brought Shropshire under his control, establishing a distinctive chain of tenurial blocks on its borders, among them the *castellaria* centred on a castle named after Montgommery, his Norman home town. In this way, he created the mould within which the lordships of the Shropshire borders were to be cast. Earl Roger also placed those honors in the hands of his most able and loyal men, who appear, moreover, to have gained experience in dealing with political frontiers on the southern borders of Normandy. It may be that these men were given control of the hundredal administrations of westernmost Shropshire, in the hope that this would strengthen their hold on the local population. The castles definitely built by the Montgomeries and their men between *c.* 1070 and 1102 aimed to guard approaches to the county of Shropshire from central England as well as from Wales. At the same time, however, the independence of Powys from foreign rule hung in the balance. In the late eleventh century, the Normans based in Shropshire conducted harrying raids to the farthest reaches of Wales, probably building strings of castles up the Welsh river valleys of the Severn, the Tanat

[2] Above, pp. 103–7. [3] Above, pp. 5–8.

[4] Lewis, 'English and Norman Government', pp. 347–8.

[5] Above, pp. 56–8. [6] Above, p. 107.

and the Dee, and certainly gaining footholds as far away as Ceredigion and Dyfed.[7] It is possible that the Montgomeries hoped to assert a level of domination over the Welsh territories adjoining Shropshire commensurate with the control they had over the county itself. But any hope they had of achieving that was diminished when Welsh resurgence began in earnest in the mid-1090s, and lost in 1102, when Henry I removed the Montgomery family and with it the force driving further large-scale conquests of Welsh territory.

Indeed, the reign of Henry I (1100–35) has emerged as the period of pivotal importance in the creation of a region between Shropshire and Powys which could be referred to as 'Marcher'. Henry's decision to allow the earldom of Shrewsbury to lapse ushered in a new 'frontier' period in the military history of the western limits of Shropshire. It is symptomatic of this that the strongest castles built during the twelfth century came to form a line along the border with Powys.[8] The castles erected by Robert de Bellême, between 1098 and 1102, Carreghofa in the west and Bridgnorth in the east, were already defensive in nature.[9] The Welsh had destroyed Hen Domen Montgomery in 1095, and that castle subsequently became a true frontier fortress, built, rebuilt and maintained for a military purpose long after similar castles further east in the county and in other parts of England had been abandoned or become purely residential and administrative in function. While Hen Domen was being rebuilt for the first time, the honors of western Shropshire came to wear a common, distinctive border aspect in that they all – Caus, Clun, Oswestry and Montgomery – became focused on strong castles with a clear defensive purpose. In particular, Caus Castle was erected on a hilltop site near a motte whose name derives from 'Old Caus'. Moreover, a multitude of small mottes was built near the many isolated settlements in the lowlands around Oswestry, in the lower Clun valley and in an arc around Wigmore; of these, a highly distinctive group, steep-sided and with a narrow platform, may have been constructed in the Rea–Camlad valley even before 1102.[10] The evidence of the castles, together with stray references in the Welsh chronicles, indicates that Henry I's campaigns against Powys in 1114 and 1121 were provoked by sporadic Welsh raids.[11] The existence of a military border zone had a profound impact on society. Place-name evidence suggests that, in the borderlands, the growth and multiplication of settlements lagged behind, compared to the uplands in south-eastern Shropshire.[12] This was a time when the tenants

[7] Above, pp. 107–11.
[8] Above, pp. 143–4.
[9] Above, pp. 161–2.
[10] Above, pp. 153–6.
[11] Above, pp. 118–19.
[12] Above, pp. 34–7.

of the frontier lords were often, indeed regularly, called upon to help defend the border strongholds and counter Welsh raids. Evidence from the thirteenth and fourteenth centuries suggests that as a rule they did so in person, serving as lightly armed cavalry or in the garrisons at Clun, Oswestry, Montgomery and Caus.[13]

As the lords of the westernmost honors of Shropshire struggled to come to terms with living on a military frontier, they also confronted the reality of having to redefine their relationship with each other and with their Welsh neighbours, the dynasty of Powys. The original personnel of the Shropshire borders had all been Montgomery men: Picot de Sai, Corbet and Rainald de Bailleul all came from the Gouffern, the heartland of the Montgomery lordship on the borders of Normandy. They had followed their lord to westernmost England, and considered themselves junior partners in the Montgomery land-grabbing enterprise whose theatre of operations extended from Holderness in north-eastern England to Pembroke in south-western Wales. That perspective disappeared at a stroke in 1102. The potential for further co-operative ventures into Wales was reduced dramatically. It disappeared entirely when Henry I introduced Alan fitz Flaald, a Breton, and Baldwin de Bollers, probably a Fleming, as tenants of key castles and offices in Shropshire. Although Richard de Beaumais, a former Montgomery man, became a local justiciar, based at the county town, the Montgomery border aristocracy was permanently transformed. Henry I had incorporated the Shropshire border within a grand policy of creating his own group of frontier castellans on the Welsh marches and in south Wales. The lords of the castles between Oswestry and Clun came to hold their compact border territories directly of the king; their main territorial interests lay on the frontier; but they had little else in common. In this respect, they were assimilated to their southern neighbours, such as the Mortimers. Thereby, the likelihood that they were to share a similar fate and outlook and come to be perceived as one of a kind increased.[14]

The monastic endowments made at Haughmond by the lords of Oswestry and at Wigmore by the Mortimers belong to this period, and show that these lords had come to see the border counties as the focus of their family estates.[15] The different locations of these two new religious houses, however, may indicate that Alan fitz Flaald and his descendants were now focusing more on the county, while the Mortimers still harboured ambitions for extending their dominion further into Wales. Both the Fitzalans' hereditary hold on the shrievalty and their marriage choices

[13] Above, pp. 174–7. [14] Above, pp. 68–74.
[15] Above, pp. 74–5.

point in the same direction, while the Mortimers certainly continued to pursue further territorial conquests westwards.[16] Meanwhile, all the frontier honors began to descend hereditarily and in the male line. This was more straightforward in the cases of Clun and of Caus (at least the larger of the two parts into which the Corbet fief had been split) than at Montgomery, Whittington or Oswestry. Nevertheless, all of these honors acquired an ever more justifiable claim to be considered baronies. Each had a closely knit social and administrative identity which was focused on a seigneurial castle, and which strengthened and grew as lords continued to grant parts of their demesne lands in fee to their followers.[17] It fits this picture that at Hen Domen there is archaeological evidence for domestic occupation as well as military use during the first half of the twelfth century.[18] The lords of the frontier thus thought of themselves, at an early stage, as holding responsibility for local governance, and of their castles as centres of the social, administrative and judicial organization of their honors. All the frontier lords may have bolstered their non-military authority from a very early stage by making use of the existing hundredal organization.[19] They had also, very early on, begun to claim, and with varying success to collect, regular tribute-payments from the Welsh population living within the districts they sought to control.[20]

Finally, Henry I's reign was a period when principles of cross-border diplomacy were created which were to endure until 1282–3. One channel of Anglo-Welsh relations, that of marriage diplomacy, had already been pioneered by Picot de Sai, the first Norman lord of Clun. Moreover, the Montgomery earls of Shrewsbury had sought to establish alliances with, and ultimately domination over, the Welsh princes of Powys – for instance, they laid claim to overlordship over Arwystli, and may have had a castle in that cantred to reinforce that claim. But, after 1102, Shropshire and its borders first became established as the diplomatic interface between the Welsh and the English royal government. One effect of the Montgomery forfeiture had been to give the English crown a vast landed interest in the county of Shropshire, by far the largest such interest in any border shire until Cheshire was brought into royal ownership in 1237–41. As it happened, Richard de Beaumais was appointed as the first permanent royal deputy to the borders, just in time to exploit the bitter rivalry between the members of the dynasty of Powys, the descendants of Bleddyn ap Cynfyn (d. 1075).[21]

[16] Above, pp. 84–6. [17] Above, pp. 194–5, 208–9, 215.
[18] Above, pp. 151–9. [19] Above, pp. 192–4.
[20] Above, pp. 207–9, 213–15, 216–17.
[21] Above, pp. 113–19.

On the eve of the Anarchy of Stephen's reign (1135–54), then, the contours of a 'Marcher' region between Shropshire and Powys had taken shape. The compact border honors had survived as a chain of tenurial blocks held directly of the king of England, and the situation of their lords was assimilated to that of their neighbours to the south, such as the Mortimers, while being differentiated from the situation both in Cheshire to the north and Shropshire to the east. The Shropshire frontier honors had, as a group, been set on the same historical track as other nascent baronies on the Anglo-Welsh borders to the south.

It was not certain, however, that they would remain on that same track. After the death of Henry I, all the large castles on the Shropshire–Powys frontier came under severe Welsh attack. Caus Castle was burned, Cymaron in Maelienydd destroyed and Oswestry occupied.[22] Hen Domen Montgomery, as far as we know, escaped – no archaeological evidence of destruction dating to the middle of the twelfth century has been discovered. The castle appears to have continued to be used for both military and domestic purposes.[23] However, Stephen de Bollers, son and heir of the lord of the castle, was killed by the son of Madog ap Maredudd of Powys in 1152.[24] Moreover, William Fitzalan I spent much of Stephen's reign in exile. During the Anarchy, it seemed distinctly possible that the frontier aristocracy which had begun to take shape in Henry I's reign, not least under the leadership of Payn fitz John and Miles of Gloucester, might lose its northernmost members. On the other hand, the lords of Clun and of Wigmore both went on the offensive against the Welsh dynasties of Elfael and Maelienydd; Cymaron was rebuilt, and the border stronghold of Bryn Amlwg has also been dated to this period.[25] Meanwhile, the military enfeoffments in the eastern, lowland part of the honor of Clun continued, even though the de Sai lords were running short of estates lying close to their castle. In order to establish the Stapletons at Wistanstow, they seem to have seized that border estate from the monks at Lilleshall. Given the military situation at this period, it seems very probable that the Stapletons and other free tenants of Clun often helped with the defence of their lord's castles.[26]

In another sense, too, the future shape of the Shropshire–Powys 'March' seemed uncertain at this time. It was quite probably in the middle of the twelfth century that a significant wave of Welsh settlement swept into the lowlands around Oswestry. If so, then it is plausible to date a similar increase in Welsh population in the valleys and uplands west of Clun to

[22] Above, pp. 119–20. [23] Above, p. 155.
[24] Above, pp. 76, 119. [25] Above, pp. 177–9.
[26] Above, pp. 179–81.

about the same time. The *gwelyau*, the customary Welsh tenurial units, which appear in fourteenth-century surveys and other records relating to these lordships, were in any case probably established before the end of the twelfth century. And it also seems probable that thereafter no further large-scale migrations of either Welsh or English settlers westwards or eastwards occurred. Certainly the *gwelyau* near Oswestry survived even though the Fitzalans were reinstalled there by Henry II in 1155.[27]

Part of the reason was no doubt the long period of relative peace which characterized the last third of the twelfth century and the beginning of the thirteenth, at least north of the Mortimer lordship of Wigmore. No English king led a campaign to Wales for a period of almost half a century, between Henry II's disastrous military venture of 1165 and King John's of 1211 and 1212; Powysian princes such as Madog ap Maredudd and Owain Cyfeiliog maintained quite amicable relations with the Angevin kings of England.[28] As was argued in the introduction, this was the period during which the phrase *Marchia Wallie* began to be commonly used, originally to refer to the borderlands between Shropshire and Powys, later to the rest of the Anglo-Welsh borderlands as well. By the early 1200s, King John was speaking of 'his' March of Wales and writing to William Fitzalan II about the *barones Marchie*. It was at this time that a 'Marcher' region was more widely perceived to exist between the county of Shropshire and the Welsh kingdom of Powys.[29]

By the turn of the twelfth century, the Shropshire–Powys 'March' was solidifying in several respects. The contours it had begun to acquire at the end of Henry I's reign were triumphantly re-established. Indeed, they seemed better defined than in some other parts of the Anglo-Welsh borders. While many of the lords of the Welsh frontier died childless during the later twelfth century, the border estates of Shropshire continued to descend hereditarily in the male line. At least, this was true of Fitzalan, Corbet and Mortimer.[30] The de Bollers did disappear from the scene in 1207, and their honor escheated permanently to the crown. But the Fitzalans, by that time, had acquired a further important Shropshire border interest through the marriage of William Fitzalan I to Isabel de Sai, the lady of Clun. Their son, William Fitzalan II, entertained Gerald of Wales at Oswestry in 1188; shortly afterwards, he became sheriff of Shropshire, as his father and grandfather had been. It must have been he who led the way in strengthening the fabric of civilian administration in the frontier lordships, at least in English-populated places such as Purslow hundred or the borough of Clun.[31] Despite the

[27] Above, pp. 45–6.
[28] Above, pp. 122–5.
[29] Above, pp. 6–10.
[30] Above, pp. 98–9.
[31] Above, pp. 196–7.

upheavals that Oswestry had experienced during the middle of the twelfth century, seigneurial administration survived there as well: William Fitzalan II continued to levy the Danegeld from the burgesses, and in 1203 he was able to identify precisely which vills belonged to his 'hundred' of Oswestry.[32] He did try to curtail further Welsh immigration.[33] However, in view of the fact that he must have felt the financial pinch caused by inflation there can be no doubt that he made every effort to collect such traditional Welsh renders and dues as he could from the tenants of the Oswestry *gwelyau*.[34]

Signs of growth went hand in hand with such symptoms of consolidation. Apparently, settlement at last began to expand, on the borders, at a rate comparable to that in the county proper.[35] The burgeoning of the castle-boroughs on the frontier also began during the second half of the twelfth century and, as these nascent towns very probably remained English-dominated at first, they contributed towards creating a zone of mixed settlement, while also introducing burghal courts into Welsh-populated districts.[36] Religious houses, too, began now to be founded much closer to the Shropshire border: Chirbury by the de Bollers and Alberbury by the Fitzwarins.[37] During the later twelfth century, the border between Shropshire and Powys looked like an area which was settling down, where a *modus vivendi* was being worked out, where certain features which had proved viable were acquiring an air of permanence. Around 1203, at the time of Fulk Fitzwarin III's rebellion against King John, then, the Shropshire frontier baronies had retained and developed common, typical characteristics to such an extent that they had – arguably – come to form a region. Several of these characteristics, moreover, derived from their frontier position.

As a result, the creation of a 'Marcher' society also progressed further. The military obligations which the tenants of the frontier lordships owed may often have lain dormant, and some of the royal serjeants now settled on the borders owed services relating to diplomacy, not war.[38] But the presence of a military frontier never quite ceased to make itself felt. Carreghofa Castle was captured and recaptured by the Welsh and English until the end of John's reign, when it seems to have been permanently destroyed.[39] The upkeep of the distinctive Vale of Montgomery mottes was apparently neglected at this period.[40] But the Mortimer efforts at acquiring Maelienydd by force of arms peaked in the later twelfth century; and a stone tower was built at Caus Castle, partly financed by the

[32] Above, pp. 214–15. [33] Above, p. 44.
[34] Above, pp. 207–8. [35] Above, pp. 36–7.
[36] Above, pp. 37–42. [37] Above, pp. 74–5.
[38] Above, pp. 182–3, 122–3. [39] Above, pp. 164–5.
[40] Above, p. 157.

crown.[41] Military obligations were certainly not forgotten or universally converted into money payments.[42] However, more and more marriages occurred between the lords of the frontier castles and members of the Powysian dynasty, which enjoyed a brief hegemony within Wales at the end of the twelfth century.[43] Moreover, the Fitzalans and the other lords of frontier castles were increasingly coming to play a role in keeping oiled the wheels of Anglo-Welsh diplomacy, which itself was becoming transformed through the increased use of written documents. It was no coincidence that the phrase *barones Marchie* became fashionable at this time.[44]

The process by which the 'Marcher' lords of the Shropshire–Powys frontier came to see themselves as guardians of the English realm was closely contemporaneous with another development: that by which they began to assert that their border territories lay beyond the reach of the English state. Both of these new trends intensified over the thirteenth century, and transformed the way in which the frontier baronies were viewed as distinct from the county. For a variety of reasons, however, they also served to heighten the differences between the lordship of Caus on the one hand and those of Oswestry, Clun and Wigmore on the other. In 1203, even before the lordship of Montgomery became a small but significant royal dominion, William Fitzalan II asserted that a dispute over an estate near Oswestry ought to be judged not by the royal justices at Shrewsbury, but by himself.[45] In 1199, William de Braose, the lord of Brecon, Builth, Elfael and Radnor, had already made a similar claim, which indicates that exemption from royal governance was already regarded as a defining characteristic of the lordships on the Welsh borders of the English state.[46] This became a very widely shared view over the following decades, as the English government evolved new, more intrusive and precise fiscal and jurisdictional instruments. However, whereas the exemption of the lordship of Oswestry and of the upland part of the lordship of Clun soon remained undisputed, and that of Wigmore seems never even to have been at issue, that of Caus and of Purslow hundred was never securely established.[47] This was due to such factors as royal favour, the geographical position of the districts in question, the timing with which their lords claimed exemptions and, increasingly, the ethnicity of their population.[48] As a result, the issue of whether or not the frontier lordships lay outside the county came to differentiate them from each other. But, because it was often a contentious issue, and sometimes

[41] Above, pp. 81, 124. [42] Above, pp. 183–4.
[43] Above, p. 125. [44] Above, pp. 79–82.
[45] Above, p. 210. [46] *Rot. Curiae Regis*, i, 426.
[47] Above, pp. 221–35. [48] Above, pp. 238–44.

one for litigation, it came to rival other features of the border honors as the main reason both why they were distinctive and why they were perceived to be so.

Nevertheless, those honors retained, during much of the thirteenth century, the characteristics which had come to distinguish them from the county over the twelfth. For one thing, they remained a military frontier. Llywelyn ap Iorwerth's capture of Shrewsbury in 1215 was a warning shot across the English bows. During the 1220s, Henry III worried about the safety of the Shropshire–Powys border to such an extent that he revived ancient obligations of castle-guard in the area and exhorted the local lords and smallholders to refortify their castles. He also rebuilt and re-garrisoned Hen Domen, which had been abandoned, and invested in a masonry castle nearby at New Montgomery. His fears were justified: in 1228 he experienced one of his earliest military disasters, on the occasion of his campaign to Ceri. In the early 1230s, the border castles of Shropshire shared the fate of other 'Marcher' fortresses to their south, when they were specifically targeted for destruction by the prince of Gwynedd. This may have been the reason for the exemption of the border lordships from the fortieth levied in 1232. If so, the practice of such border privileges surely explains why, in 1236, Ralph Mortimer II and John Fitzalan I were claiming, at the coronation of Eleanor of Provence, a right to the same ceremonial rights as the lords of the Cinque Ports. Although, in 1220, John Fitzalan I had made a marriage which was, arguably, to divert the primary focus of his family from the Powys border to the d'Aubigni castle of Arundel in Sussex, this great-grandson of Alan fitz Flaald clearly still thought of himself as a member of a select group of frontiersmen. The Mortimers, meanwhile, became more focused on Wales and the borders than they had ever been before, in terms both of marriage policy and of political ambition.

It could be argued that Llywelyn ap Iorwerth prevented the Shropshire–Powys 'March' from becoming fully fledged. His death in 1240 ushered in a crucial period of royal dominance in Wales during which yet another ingredient in the creation of a 'Marcher' region on the Powys borders was added. For it may have been then that English-style methods of seigneurial governance began to be exported to the Welsh districts under the control of the *barones Marchie* of the Shropshire frontier. It seems very possible that, at Oswestry and Clun, this was done on royal initiative: the Fitzalan estates were in the custody of the crown between 1240 and 1243. The intra-dynastic rivalry in the house of Gwynedd, which lasted until 1255, provided the opportunity, at least, for demesne and free courts and seigneurial officers to become fairly well established in Welsh-populated districts like Tempseter or the hinterland of Oswestry. As government became more precise, English and Welsh districts became better defined, which further contributed towards preventing large-scale population movements from Wales into England or vice versa. To be sure, after 1256, when Llywelyn ap Gruffudd had made himself sole ruler of Gwynedd and border hostilities flared up again, initial progress in the establishment of 'Welshries' was reversed. As the *post mortem* inquisition of John Fitzalan II stated in 1267: 'in the forest of Clun there was a large Welshry which used to be worth much to the lord both in demesne renders and in other perquisites and dues which we cannot now extend because of the disturbances wrought by the Welsh'.[49] The Shropshire–Powys 'March' was still being transformed in new ways by the mid-thirteenth century; but at least one of these, the establishment of seigneurial governance in Welsh districts, was an intermittent process.

On the other hand, various long-established distinctive traits continued to play a role. After the middle of the thirteenth century, the borders appear to have overtaken the county as an area still offering possibilities for settlement expansion, and the growth of the castle-boroughs on the frontier gathered momentum (with Y Trallwng/Welshpool, a Welsh foundation, receiving burghal privileges at around this time). Welshmen may have begun moving into border boroughs such as Clun or Oswestry.[50] Meanwhile, the old frontier families, Mortimer, Fitzalan, Fitzwarin and Corbet, survived the second wave of mortality which swept away such Marcher dynasties as Braose, Lacy, Marshal and Clifford.[51] By reason of their survival in the male line, the families of the Shropshire–Powys March were, by this time, truly exceptional among the subjects of the English king, and well aware of it. The Fitzwarins and the Mortimers, at least, developed a keen interest in family legends and chronicles in the second half of the thirteenth century; the Corbets could cite their unbroken ancestral line when defying demands for the payment of baronial relief.[52] On the other hand, new families such as the Audleys or the Lestranges joined the first rank of border lords through service to the crown which was often specifically related to Anglo-Welsh diplomacy or frontier military commands.[53] Lords still demanded castle-guard or muntatorial service from their tenants, although there are signs that these obligations were beginning to be considered old-fashioned.[54] Part of the evidence for military obligations was gathered in 1255 by the fullest inquiry into government in the localities that had been launched since

[49] *CIPM, Henry III*, no. 684; TNA C 132/35 (18), m. 3r.
[50] Above, p. 41.
[51] Davies, *Lordship and Society*, p. 37.
[52] Above, p. 99. [53] Above, pp. 82–4.
[54] Above, pp. 183–4.

1086. This inquiry also once again highlighted the difference, with regard to exemption from the English state, between Caus and Purslow hundred on the one hand and Clun and Oswestry on the other.

Anglo-Welsh relations in the age of Llywelyn ap Gruffudd were highly complex. The Shropshire borders continued to play a central role as the time-honoured stage for royal diplomacy; even though Chester had been brought into crown tenure after 1237, thirty years later Henry III concluded his last treaty with the prince of Wales at Montgomery. But that was after war had once again erupted on the border between Shropshire and Powys: around 1263, Gruffudd ap Gwenwynwyn destroyed the Corbet border stronghold at Gwyddgrug, while Llywelyn ap Gruffudd seized and rebuilt in stone that at Bryn Amlwg, west of Clun.[55] In that lordship, the principle of castle-guard certainly survived, and it seems quite plausible that it also continued in practice.[56] Moreover, under Edward I's generalship, Montgomery and the other castles of the Shropshire borders became integrated into the larger campaign strategies which aimed at subduing independent Wales in 1276–7 and 1282–3.[57] Considerable proportions of the frontier lordships' tenantry were mustered for military service in the royal armies on these occasions. Lords such as Roger Mortimer and Peter Corbet still, at this time, expected to lead their tenants on military campaigns into Wales.[58]

Edward I's conquest and occupation of Wales after 1283 did transform the Shropshire–Powys borders in that it marked the end of their long existence as a military and diplomatic frontier.[59] However, the other distinctive traits of the Shropshire–Powys March survived, and indeed developed further. Edward I's inquiries in 1274 and in 1292 continued to reveal differences between the border lordships. The way in which the Welsh fifteenth was levied demonstrates that the lordships of Oswestry, Whittington, Knockin, Caus, Clun and Wigmore were considered to lie in the March in the early 1290s.[60] It also illustrates that the March between Shropshire and Powys was still being moulded by developments external to it. The English state had begun to operate on assumptions of ethnic exclusivity, and it was probably for this reason that only the Welshry of Caus lordship, the Gorddwr, was taxed as part of the March. It may also have been the reason why the Fitzalans struggled to have English-populated Purslow hundred recognized by the crown as part of their Marcher lordship of Clun during the 1290s.[61]

[55] Above, pp. 130–2. [56] Above, pp. 184–5.
[57] Above, pp. 132–5. [58] Above, pp. 185–7.
[59] Above, p. 135. [60] Above, pp. 235–8.
[61] Above, pp. 242–4.

Another external influence which helped to determine the final shape of the 'March' between Shropshire and Powys was of course Edward I's grants of Cedewain and Ceri to Roger Mortimer of Wigmore and his grant of Chirkland to Roger Mortimer's son, another Roger.[62] These lordships were compact honors territorially adjacent to the patchwork of lordships which formed a frontier district between the county of Shropshire and what was soon to be widely known as the Welsh barony of Powys. They immediately acquired those characteristic traits which had more recently begun to set the lordships of Oswestry, Clun and Caus apart from the county. Thus, English methods of seigneurial governance were introduced into them, and they were considered to lie beyond the county within the March of Wales.[63] These were among the chief characteristic traits which contributed towards demarcating a 'Marcher' region between England and Wales in the fourteenth and fifteenth centuries.

On the other hand, there were profound differences between these new lordships and the original Shropshire–Powys 'March'. That 'March' had already been in existence before exemption from the reach of the English state and the institution of English-style instruments of seigneurial governance had even come to play a role in creating a distinctive region on the Welsh borders of Shropshire. Its history was more than the sum of the histories of the honors which had first been created by Earl Roger in the western part of that county. Those honors were gradually moulded into a distinctive region because together they formed a frontier, or rather a variety of frontiers. Border raids, Anglo-Welsh diplomacy and marriages, migratory movements, inter-cultural borrowings and settlement expansion all, at different times, served both to highlight the similarities between the frontier lordships and to set those lordships apart from the county and from Wales. Many differences persisted between the individual frontier lordships and several more were thrown into relief during the thirteenth century. Not all of them straddled military or ethnic boundaries to the same extent, or escaped the reach of the English state equally successfully. But the differences were outweighed, in practice and in the minds of contemporaries, by the many ways in which they shared a common fate for over two centuries. There was indeed an overarching theme to their histories: the story by which the individual jigsaw pieces on the Shropshire–Powys frontier came to form a recognizable picture, a

[62] *Cal. Chart. R., 1257–1300*, p. 211; *Cal. Chanc. R. Var.*, p. 223.

[63] In the early 1290s, they were taxed as part of Wales and the March: TNA E 179/242/48, m. 6v (Ceri and Cedewain); TNA E 179/242/55 (Chirk, Carreghofa and other lands of Roger Mortimer the younger in Powys).

whole which could be referred to as *Marchia Wallie*, and whose lords could be dubbed *barones Marchie*.

Thus, a discussion of the Welsh borders of Shropshire does provide a framework for understanding the creation and perception of the medieval March of Wales. The factors which contributed most towards shaping a 'Marcher' district have been highlighted and ordered chronologically. It has also been established that such a district could be created despite significant differences in topography, and despite similarities with Wales proper and with England, in such respects as population density and economic organization. Moreover, this framework elucidates both why the medieval concept of the March came to include the lordships in south Wales and why that inclusion was delayed by perhaps more than a century. The early emphasis of the concept was on lordships on the frontier between England and Wales rather than on conquest territories in Wales itself. However, as further traits came to be considered typical of the 'March', the similarities between the lordships on the Anglo-Welsh borders and those in south Wales made it possible for both these categories, eventually, to be considered part of the same whole.

This can be illustrated by two brief comparisons. First, the Welsh borders may be set beside another 'march' faced by the Norman and Plantagenet kings of England, the 'march' of Normandy.[64] This further exemplifies the characteristics which those kings and their clerks may well have considered typical of 'marches' by the later twelfth century. Second, a brief glance at the lordship of Glamorgan illustrates how both the Anglo-Welsh border honors and the conquest lordships of south Wales could have come to be included in the *Marchia Wallie* by the early fourteenth century.

The high medieval border of Normandy, unlike the Anglo-Welsh border, was not a frontier of peoples.[65] Nevertheless, like the border once marked by Offa's Dyke, it was a political boundary – and it was being identified as a 'march' at precisely the same time as the 'march' of Wales. In 1172, the inquest into knights' service owed to the duke of Normandy, the Norman equivalent of the English inquiry of 1166, found that Richard Silvain – a ducal official and head of a minor castellan family based in the county of Mortain – was in charge of mustering the service of 29 'and a half and one eighth' knights for forty

[64] As mentioned above, p. 12, n. 35, I shall deal more fully with the links and parallels between the medieval frontiers of Wales and of Normandy in a forthcoming article in the *English Historical Review*.

[65] See Power, *Norman Frontier*, pp. 8–10 and ch. 4, on the linguistic and legal dimensions of the Norman border. For a recent discussion of Norman identity, see H. M. Thomas, *The English and the Normans: Ethnic Hostility, Assimilation, and Identity, 1066–c. 1220* (Oxford, 2003).

days 'ad marchiam'; Hugh de Gournay, lord of the eponymous castle on the river Epte, was found to owe the service of all but twelve of his knights 'ad marchiam'.[66] In 1203, King John wrote to the constable of Radepont in the Norman Vexin laying down rules concerning the ransoming of prisoners 'in Marchia'.[67] It is possible to point to some very specific similarities between the Welsh and Norman 'marches' which might well explain why both were thought to be not only borders, but similar kinds of borders. For one thing, the medieval frontier of Normandy is one of the very few areas of continental Europe which can compete with the March of Wales in terms of castle density.[68] That, in turn, meant that the distribution of aristocratic power was structured in similar ways. On both borders, compact lordships of varying sizes abounded.[69] Moreover, as in the Welsh March, many local aristocracies on the Norman frontier survived in the male line from the eleventh and early twelfth centuries until well into the thirteenth, or even later.[70] Further, the border of Normandy was heavily encastellated for good military reasons.[71] At the same time, the role of the Norman 'march', especially of the Vexin, in diplomacy has long been noted.[72] To these structural similarities might be added the personal links which began being forged very soon after 1066. William fitz Osbern was lord of the old Norman frontier fortress of Ivry when he built the castles of Chepstow, Clifford and Wigmore. Roger de Montgomery, as a young man, fought in the Domfront campaign of 1051/2 and married Mabel de Bellême; his ancestors may have been settled in the Montgommery hills as a defensive measure in the mid-tenth century.[73] Other links were provided by Hugh, the first Norman earl of Chester; by Bernard de Neufmarché and the Mortimers. The Braoses, who were at different

[66] *Red Book of the Exchequer*, ed. Hall, ii, 628, 643; cf. Power, *Norman Frontier*, pp. 26–30. For the Silvain family, castellans of Saint-Pois, see *Orderic*, vi, 490–2; Power, *Norman Frontier*, pp. 33, 275, 389; for de Gournay: D. Gurney, *The Record of the House of Gournay*, 4 vols. (London, 1848–58); Power, *Norman Frontier*, pp. 504–5.

[67] *Rotuli Litterarum Patentium in Turri Londinensi Asservati, 1201–16*, ed. by Thomas Duffus Hardy (London, 1835), p. 24b.

[68] For illustrations see the maps in Power, *Norman Frontier*, or in Le Patourel, *The Norman Empire*.

[69] Power, *Norman Frontier*, pp. 208, 246–8, 267, 273, 469.

[70] See the genealogies in Power, *Norman Frontier*, notably, in the Eure and Avre valleys, nos. 9 (Châteaneuf-en-Thymerais with Brézolles); 32 (the Reviers lords of Vernon castle); 31 (the Tosny lords of Conches); 23 (the Donjon lords of Muzy); or in the Vexin, nos. 11 (the Crispin lords of Neaufles); 18 (the lords of Gournay); and 7 (the lords of Beaussault).

[71] Louise, *Bellême*; Bauduin, *La Première Normandie (Xe–XIe siècles)*. Power, *Norman Frontier*, passim, esp. pt iii.

[72] Lemarignier, *Recherches sur l'hommage en marche et les frontières féodales* (Lille, 1945); Power, *Norman Frontier*, pp. 16–17.

[73] *The Gesta Guillelmi of William of Poitiers*, ed. and transl. by R. H. C. Davis and M. Chibnall (Oxford, 1998), p. 26; Thompson, 'Norman Aristocracy', p. 252.

times between the late eleventh and early thirteenth centuries lords of Radnor, Builth, Elfael, Brecon, Abergavenny and Gower, took their name from their Norman border estate of Briouze near Argentan, which they held from the eleventh century until 1204.[74] The parallels between the Norman and Welsh borders may well have contributed to the concept of a 'march' during the twelfth and early thirteenth centuries.

The lordship of Glamorgan, of course, highlights the parallels between the Anglo-Welsh border honors and the south of Wales. The former Welsh kingdom of Morgannwg was even more topographically diverse than the Shropshire–Powys borders, encompassing a coastal vale of fertile soils and starkly contrasting uplands. It was not included within the range of Domesday Book; Robert fitz Hamo, the lord of Creully in Normandy, certainly led his invasion into Morgannwg after 1086, and probably after 1093. However, a chain of castleries was established here as well, the earliest of them focused on mottes which were built near the coast or on estuaries and could be supplied from the sea. The castellan families based here held of the lord at Cardiff, but must soon have shared an outlook similar to that of the barons on the Anglo-Welsh frontier. The castle evidence suggests that the Normans had brought the lowlands of Morgannwg under quite secure control by the early twelfth century. However, all of the new castles, including Cardiff, remained vulnerable to Welsh attack from the upland commotes until the second half of the thirteenth century. Although the lordship of Glamorgan was established entirely on Welsh territory, English methods of governance were being exported there by the early twelfth century. By 1102, a sheriff (*vicecomes*) held office in Glamorgan; the lordship appears in the documents as a *comitatus* in 1107; by the second half of the century, we hear of the 'Welsh hundred of the county of Margam'.[75] This last instance, in recalling the 'Welsh hallmoot' at Clun, provides a particularly striking parallel to the Powys borders. Moreover, the early need to identify the 'Welsh' units of seigneurial administration is one sign that foreign, particularly English, settlement was well underway by the middle of the twelfth century.[76] In the shire-fee of Glamorgan, a frontier society was shaped during the high medieval period: as Gerald

[74] On the Braoses, see Lloyd, *History of Wales*, pp. 402–3; Sanders, *English Baronies*, pp. 21–2; Rowlands, 'William de Braose'; Holden, *Lords*, *passim*.

[75] *Cartae*, i, no. 35; vi, no. 1546, p. 2268; i, no. 126, p. 122: 'Walensi hundredo comitatus de Margan'.

[76] M. Lieberman, 'Anglicization in High Medieval Wales: The Case of Glamorgan', *WHR*, **23** (2006), pp. 1–26.

of Wales recalled, when the Third Crusade was preached at Llandaf in 1188, the 'English stood on one side and the Welsh on the other; and from each nation many took the Cross'.[77] A mixed population, too, enhanced Glamorgan's similarity to the border lordships. As for Marcher regality, there is perhaps no more striking illustration than one which has already been mentioned: the case of Richard Siward, lord of Llanbleddian, Tal-y-fan and Rhuthun.[78] In 1245, Siward was outlawed by Earl Richard de Clare in the county court at Cardiff 'according to the laws and customs of the *patria*' of Glamorgan. He stood accused of breaking a truce concluded between the earl and Hywel ap Maredudd, lord of Meisgyn and Glynrhondda, and of later rebelling against the earl, in league with Hywel.[79] By appealing to the king, Siward forced the earl to defend Siward's outlawing before the royal court, where the earl was accused of behaving in Glamorgan 'quasi rex et iusticiarius'.[80] This foreshadowed the momentous events of 1292, when Edward I and his parliament condemned to prison the lords both of Glamorgan (the earl of Gloucester and Hertford) and of Brecon (the earl of Hereford) for carrying on an armed border dispute in the marches.[81] This was an explicit assertion of royal authority over Marcher immunity. In 1281, Gilbert de Clare, one of the two earls later to be condemned to gaol, had claimed Marcher regality in Glamorgan, since he held that lordship by right of conquest.[82] A fuller discussion would reveal more parallels and differences between the Welsh borders and the conquest lordships in south Wales. Yet even a brief comparison with the Shropshire–Powys frontier shows why Glamorgan was not, in the end, considered to be unique or a part of Wales, but seen to belong to the 'March'. By the later thirteenth century, there could be no doubt in the minds of contemporaries that Glamorgan was part of the March, when it displayed so many of the attributes that then mattered in identifying that region. The history of the lordship of Glamorgan reveals variations on the same overarching theme that unites the history of the lordships on the Shropshire–Powys frontier.

Those lordships were almost entirely carved out of former English shire territory and lay on the northernmost limits of the March of Wales of today's historians – Oswestry, being situated north of the Severn, falls outside the coverage of Professor Rees' magnificent maps of south Wales

[77] Gerald of Wales, *Journey through Wales*, transl. Thorpe, p. 126; cf. *Giraldus*, vi, 67 (*Itinerarium Kambrie*, i, 7).
[78] See above, p. 218.
[79] *Cartae*, ii, no. 535; Altschul, *The Clares*, pp. 70–5; Crouch, 'The Last Adventure of Richard Siward'.
[80] *Cartae*, ii, no. 535, p. 554. Cf. Davies, 'Kings, Lords and Liberties', pp. 41–2.
[81] Above, pp. 218–19. [82] *Cartae*, iii, no. 741.

and the border in the fourteenth century.[83] These honors, then, have been peripheral to the March of Wales of modern political historiography. Yet identifying the characteristics which rendered them distinctive between *c.* 1070 and 1283 has made it clearer how they could come to be seen as the epitome of the region known as *Marchia Wallie*. It has also gone some way towards explaining why that phrase came to refer to a part of the British Isles as diverse and fragmented as the historian's March of Wales.

[83] Rees, *Map of South Wales and the Border*.

SELECT BIBLIOGRAPHY

MAPS AND ATLASES

Alecto County Edition of Domesday Book, Map 14, 'Herefordshire and Worcestershire' (London, 1988).

Alecto County Edition of Domesday Book, Map 20, 'Shropshire' (London, 1990).

McNeill, P.G.B., H.L. MacQueen and A.M. Lyons (eds.), *Atlas of Scottish History to 1707* (Edinburgh, 1996)

Rees, W., *A Map of South Wales and the Border in the Fourteenth Century* (Ordnance Survey, 1932).

An Historical Atlas of Wales: From Early to Modern Times, 3rd edn (London, 1967).

MANUSCRIPT AND ARCHIVAL SOURCES

British Library (London):
BL Additional Charters 20438.
BL Cotton Claudius D VI, f. 12v (Matthew Paris's map of Britain).
BL Harleian 1240.
BL Harleian 1970.
BL Harleian 1981.

Corpus Christi College, Cambridge:
MS 16 (Matthew Paris's map on f. v, verso).

Public Record Office/The National Archives (Kew):
– Chancery: Inquisitions *Ad Quod Damnum*
TNA C/143/1/4.
– Chancery: Inquisitions *Post Mortem*
TNA C 132/35 (18).
TNA C 132/42 (5).
TNA C 133/7 (8).
TNA C 133/20 (14).
TNA C 133/77 (3).
TNA C 133/79 (14).
TNA C 133/91 (2).
TNA C 133/94 (6).

TNA C 133/101 (6).
TNA C 133/113 (2).
TNA C 133/114 (8).
TNA C 133/121 (12).
TNA C 134/4 (1).
TNA C 134/56 (3).
TNA C 134/84.
TNA C 134/50.
TNA C 134/31 (1).
TNA C 134/91 (1).
TNA C 134/92 (1).
TNA C 135/7 (1).
TNA C 135/31 (16).
TNA C 135/26 (11).
TNA C 135/30 (1).
TNA C 135/253 (1).
TNA C 135/14 (3).
TNA C 141/2 (20).
TNA C 141/6 (20).
TNA C 142/59 (78).
– King's Remembrancer: Memoranda Rolls and Enrolment Books
TNA E/159/67.
– Exchequer: Tax Records
TNA E 179/166/14.
TNA E 179/166/19.
TNA E 179/166/22.
TNA E 179/242/48.
TNA E 179/242/55.
– Exchequer: Lord Treasurer's Remembrancer: Memoranda Rolls
TNA E 368/24.
– Exchequer: Pipe Rolls
TNA E/372/119.
TNA E 372/121.
– Records of the Court of King's Bench
TNA KB 26/159.

Shropshire Archives (Shrewsbury):
– Clun Court Rolls, Tempseter Court/ Hallmoot of the Welsh;
SA 552/1/2.
SA 552/1/5a.
SA 552/1/5b.
SA 552/1/7.
SA 552/1/8a.
SA 552/1/10.
SA 552/1/11.
SA 552/1/18.
– Clun Court Rolls, Hallmoot of the English/Purslow Hundred
SA 552/1/719.

SA 552/1/720.
– Clun Court Rolls, Burghal Court of Clun/Forinsec Court
SA 552/1/6.
SA 552/1/9.

PRINTED PRIMARY SOURCES

The Acts of Welsh Rulers, 1120–1283, ed. H. Pryce, with the assistance of C. Insley (Cardiff, 2005).

'Ancient Documents Relating to the Honor, Forest and Borough of Clun', ed. T. Salt, *TSAS*, **11** (1888), pp.244–71.

'The Anglo-Norman Chronicle of Wigmore Abbey', ed. J.C. Dickinson and P.T. Ricketts, *Transactions of the Woolhope Naturalists' Field Club*, **39** (1969), pp.413–45.

'Anglo-Saxon Charters relating to Shropshire', ed. W.H. Stevenson and W.H. Duignan, *TSAS*, 4th ser., **1** (1911), pp.1–22.

Annales Cambriae, ed. J. Williams ab Ithel (RS, 1860).

Annales Monastici, ed. H.R. Luard, 5 vols. (RS, 1864–9).

The Annals of Loch Cé: A Chronicle of Irish Affairs, 1014–1690, ed. W.M. Hennessy, 2 vols. (RS, 1871).

Bede's Ecclesiastical History of the English People, ed. B. Colgrave and R.A.B. Mynors (Oxford, 1969).

Brenhinedd y Saesson: or, The Kings of the Saxons, ed. T. Jones (Cardiff, 1971).

Brut y Tywysogyon, or the Chronicle of the Princes, Peniarth MS. 20 Version, ed. T. Jones (Cardiff, 1952).

Brut y Tywysogyon, or the Chronicle of the Princes. Red Book of Hergest Version, ed. T. Jones (Cardiff, 1955).

Calendar of Ancient Correspondence Concerning Wales, ed. J.G. Edwards (Cardiff, 1935).

Calendar of Charter Rolls, 1226–1300, 2 vols. (London, 1903–6).

Calendar of Close Rolls, 1231–4 (London, 1905).

Calendar of Close Rolls, 1256–9 (London, 1910).

Calendar of Close Rolls, 1261–4 (London, 1936).

Calendar of Close Rolls, 1272–88, 2 vols. (London, 1900–2).

Calendar of Close Rolls, 1313–18 (London, 1893).

Calendar of Documents Preserved in France, ed. J.H. Round (London 1899).

Calendar of Documents Relating to Ireland, ed. H.S. Sweetman *et al.*, 5 vols. (London, 1875–86).

Calendar of the Gormanston Register ca. 1157–1397, ed. J. Mills and M.J. McEnery (Dublin, 1916).

Calendar of Inquisitions Miscellaneous, 1219–1307 (London, 1916).

Calendar of Inquisitions Post Mortem, Henry III (London, 1904).

Calendar of Inquisitions Post Mortem, 6 vols., vols. iii–vii, xiv (London, 1908–13, 1952).

Calendar of Patent Rolls, 1216–25 (London, 1901).

Calendar of Patent Rolls, 1232–66, 3 vols. (London, 1906–10).

Calendar of Patent Rolls, 1266–72 (London, 1913)

Calendar of Patent Rolls, 1272–1301, 3 vols. (London, 1895–1901).

Calendar of Patent Rolls, 1307–17, 2 vols. (London, 1894–8).

Calendar of Patent Rolls, 1348–50 (London, 1905).

Calendar of Patent Rolls, 1396–9 (London, 1909).

Calendar of Various Chancery Rolls: Supplementary Close Rolls, Welsh Rolls, Scutage Rolls. A.D. 1277–1326 (London, 1912).

Cartæ et Alia Munimenta Quæ ad Dominium de Glamorgan Pertinent, ed. G.T. Clark, 4 vols. (Dowlais, 1885–93).

Cartæ et Alia Munimenta Quæ ad Dominium de Glamorgancia Pertinent, ed. G.T. Clark, 6 vols. (Cardiff, 1910).

Cartulaire normand de Philippe-Auguste, Louis VIII, Saint Louis et Philippe-le-Hardi, ed. L. Delisle (Caen, 1882, repr. Geneva, 1978).

The Cartulary of Haughmond Abbey, ed. U. Rees (Cardiff, 1985).

The Cartulary of Lilleshall Abbey, ed. U. Rees (Shrewsbury, 1997).

The Cartulary of Shrewsbury Abbey, ed. U. Rees, 2 vols. (Aberystwyth, 1975).

Chancellor's Roll 8 Richard I, 1196 (P. R. S., NS 7, London, 1930).

The Charters of the Abbey of Ystrad Marchell, ed. G.C.G. Thomas (Aberystwyth, 1997).

Charters of the Honour of Mowbray, 1107–1191, ed. D. Greenway (London, 1972).

The Charters of Norwich Cathedral Priory, Part 2, ed. B. Dodwell (P. R. S., NS 46, London, 1985).

Chronica Magistri Rogeri de Houedene, ed. W. Stubbs, 4 vols. (RS, 1868–71).

The Chronicle of Battle Abbey, ed. E. Searle (Oxford, 1980).

The Chronicle of John of Worcester, vol. ii: The Annals from 450 to 1066, ed. R.R. Darlington and P. McGurk, transl. J. Bray and P. McGurk (Oxford, 1995).

The Chronicle of John of Worcester, vol iii. The Annals from 1067 to 1140 with the Gloucester Interpolations and the Continuation to 1141, ed. and transl. P. McGurk (Oxford, 1998).

The Chronicle of Richard of Devizes of the time of King Richard the First, ed. J.T. Appleby (London, 1963).

Chronicles of the Reigns of Edward I and Edward II, ed. W. Stubbs, 2 vols. (RS, 1882–3).

Chronicon Abbatiae de Evesham, ed. W.D. Macray (RS, 1863).

The Complete Peerage of England, Scotland, Ireland, Great Britain, and the United Kingdom, Extant, Extinct, or Dormant, ed. G.E. Cokayne, 14 vols. (London, 1910–98).

A Concise Account of Ancient Documents Relating to the Honor, Forest and Borough of Clun, ed. T. Salt (Shrewsbury, 1858).

The Court Rolls of the Honor of Clitheroe, in the County of Lancaster, ed. W. Farrer, 3 vols. (Manchester, 1897–1913).

'"Cronica de Wallia" and Other Documents from Exeter Cathedral Library MS. 3514', ed. T. Jones, *BBCS*, **12** (1946), pp. 27–44.

Curia Regis Rolls, vol. iii, 1203–1205 (London, 1926).

Curia Regis Rolls, vol. x, 1221–2 (London, 1949).

Curia Regis Rolls, vol. xii, 1225–6 (London, 1957).

Curia Regis Rolls, vol. xv, 1233–37 (London, 1972).

Curia Regis Rolls, vol. xvii, 1242–3, ed. A. Nicol (London, 1991).

Curia Regis Rolls, vol. xviii, 1243–1245, ed. P. Brand (London, 1999).

Diplomatic Documents Preserved in the Public Record Office, ed. P. Chaplais (London, 1964).

Domesday Book, gen. ed. J. Morris, vol. xv: *Gloucestershire*, ed. and transl. J.S. Moore (Phillimore, London and Chichester, 1982).

Domesday Book, gen. ed. J. Morris, vol. xxv: *Shropshire*, ed. F. Thorn and C. Thorn, from a draft translation prepared by C. Parker (Phillimore, London and Chichester, 1986).

'An Early Charter of the Abbey of Cwmhir', ed. B.G. Charles, *The Transactions of the Radnorshire Society*, **40** (1970), pp.68–73.

The Early Charters of the West Midlands, ed. H.P.R. Finberg, 2nd edn (Leicester, 1972).

Early Yorkshire Charters, vol. vii: Honour of Skipton, ed. C.T. Clay (Wakefield, 1947).

The Ecclesiastical History of Orderic Vitalis, ed. and transl. M. Chibnall, 6 vols. (Oxford, 1969–80).

Excerpta e Rotulis Finium, 1216–1272, ed. C. Roberts, 2 vols. (London, 1835–6).

The First Four Books of the Historia Rerum Anglicarum of William of Newburgh, in *Chronicles of the Reigns of Stephen, Henry II and Richard I*, ed. R. Howlett, 2 vols. (RS, 1884–5), i, 1–408; ii, 409–583.

Foedera, Conventiones, Litterae, ed. T. Rymer, 3rd edn, 10 vols (1745, repr. Farnborough, 1967).

Foreign Accounts of Henry III, 1219–34, ed. F. Cazel (P. R. S. 44, 1974–5).

Fouke le Fitz Waryn, ed. E. Hathaway, P.T. Ricketts, C.A. Robson and A.D. Wilshere (Oxford, 1975).

Four Maps of Great Britain Designed by Matthew Paris about A.D. 1250. Reproduced from Three Manuscripts in the British Museum and one at Corpus Christi College, Cambridge, ed. J.P. Gilson (London, 1928).

Gallia Christiana, various eds., 8 vols. in 22 (Bruges, 1890–1993).

George Owen of Henllys, *The Description of Pembrokeshire*, ed. D. Miles (Llandysul, 1994).

Gerald of Wales, *Expugnatio Hibernica*, ed. A.B. Scott and F.X. Martin (Royal Irish Academy, 1978).

Gerald of Wales, *The Journey through Wales/The Description of Wales*, transl. L. Thorpe (London, 1978).

Die Gesetze der Angelsachsen, ed. F. Liebermann, 3 vols. (Halle, 1896–1916).

The Gesta Guillelmi of William of Poitiers, ed. and transl. by R.H.C. Davis and M. Chibnall (Oxford, 1998).

The Gesta Normannorum Ducum of William of Jumièges, Orderic Vitalis, and Robert of Torigni, ed. and transl. E.M.C. van Houts, 2 vols. (Oxford, 1992–5).

Gesta Regis Henrici Secundi, ed. W. Stubbs, 2 vols. (RS, 1867).

Gesta Stephani, ed. and transl. K.R. Potter, with introduction and notes by R.H.C. Davis (Oxford, 1976).

Giraldi Cambrensis Opera, ed. J.S. Brewer, J.F. Dimock and G.F. Warner, 8 vols. (RS, 1861–91).

The Great Roll of the Pipe, 26 Henry III, 1241–2, ed. H.L. Cannon (New Haven and London, 1918).

The Great Roll of the Pipe for the First Year of the Reign of King Richard I, ed. J. Hunter (London, 1844).

Historia Gruffud vab Kenan, ed. D. Simon Evans (Cardiff, 1977).

The Historical Works of Gervase of Canterbury, ed. W. Stubbs, 2 vols. (RS, 1879–80).

The History of Gruffydd ap Cynan, ed. A. Jones (Manchester, 1910).

Innocentii III, Romani Pontificis, Opera Omnia, ed. J.-P. Migne, 4 vols. (*Bibliotheca Patrum Latina*, 214–18, Paris, 1855).

The Itinerary of John Leland in or about the Years 1536–1539, ed. L.T. Smith, 5 vols. (London, 1906, repr. 1964).

The Law of Hywel Dda, ed. and transl. D. Jenkins (Llandysul, 1986).

The Laws of the Kings of England from Edmund to Henry I, ed. A.J. Robertson (Cambridge, 1925).
The Lay Subsidy of 1334, ed. R.E. Glasscock (London, 1975).
The Lay Subsidy for Shropshire 1524–7, ed. M.A. Faraday (Keele, 1999).
Liber Feodorum. The Book of Fees Commonly Called Testa de Nevill, 3 vols. (London, 1920–31).
Littere Wallie, ed. J.G. Edwards (Cardiff, 1940).
The Lordship of Oswestry: A Series of Extents and Rentals Transcribed and Edited with an Introduction, 1393–1607, ed. W.J. Slack, (Shrewsbury, 1951).
Matthew Paris, *Chronica Majora*, ed. H.R. Luard, 7 vols. (RS, 1872–83).
Matthew Paris, *Historia Anglorum*, ed. F. Madden, 3 vols. (RS, 1866–9).
A Mediaeval Prince of Wales: The Life of Gruffudd ap Cynan, ed. D. Simon Evans (Llanerch, 1990).
The Merioneth Lay Subsidy Roll 1292–3, ed. K. Williams-Jones (Cardiff, 1976).
Monasticon Anglicanum: A History of the Abbies and Other Monasteries, Hospitals, Friaries, and Cathedral and Collegiate Churches, with their Dependencies, in England and Wales, ed. W. Dugdale, new edn by J. Caley, H. Ellis and B. Bandinel, 6 vols. in 8 (London, 1817–30; repr. Farnborough, 1970).
'Mortimer Chronicle (Latin)', *Mon. Angl.*, vi, part 1, pp. 348–55.
The Parliament Rolls of Medieval England, 1275–1504, gen. ed. C. Given-Wilson, 16 vols. (London, 2005), vol. i: *Edward I (1275–94)*, ed. P. Brand (London, 2005).
The Parliament Rolls of Medieval England, 1275–1504, gen. ed. C. Given-Wilson, 16 vols. (London, 2005), vol. ii: *Edward I (1294–1307)*, ed. P. Brand (London, 2005).
The Parliament Rolls of Medieval England, 1275–1504, gen. ed. C. Given-Wilson, 16 vols. (London, 2005), vol. viii: *Henry IV (1399–1413)*, ed. C. Given-Wilson (London, 2005).
Parliamentary Writs and Writs of Military Summons (Edward I-Edward II), ed. F. Palgrave, 2 vols. in 4 (London, 1827–34).
Pipe Roll 31 Henry I, ed. J. Hunter (1833, repr. in facs. London, 1929).
Pipe Rolls 2, 3, 4 Henry II, 1155–8, ed. J. Hunter (London, 1844, repr. in facs. London, 1930).
Pipe Rolls 5–8 Henry II, 1158–62, 4 vols. (P. R. S., 1–2, 4–5, London, 1884–5).
Pipe Rolls 10–14 Henry II, 1163–8, 5 vols. (P. R. S., 7–8, 9–12, London, 1886–90).
Pipe Rolls 16–20 Henry II, 1169–74, 5 vols. (P. R. S., 15–16, 18–19, 21, London, 1892–6).
Pipe Rolls 25 Henry II, 1178–9 (P. R. S., 28, London, 1907).
Pipe Rolls 3–7 Richard I, 1191–5, 4 vols. (P. R. S., NS 2–3, 5–6, London, 1926–9).
Pipe Rolls 9 Richard I–1 John, 1197, 3 vols. (P. R. S., NS 8–10, London, 1931–3).
Pipe Rolls 3–4 John, 1201–1202, 2 vols. (P. R. S., NS 14–15, London, 1936–7).
Pipe Rolls 7–11 John, 1205–1209, 5 vols. (P. R. S., NS 19–20, 22–4, London, 1941–6).
Pipe Roll 14 John, 1212 (P. R. S., NS 30, London, 1954).
Pipe Roll 16 John, 1214 (P. R. S., NS 35, London, 1962).
Pipe Roll 29 Henry III, 1182–3 (P. R. S., 32, London, 1911).
Placita de Quo Warranto, ed. W. Illingworth (London, 1818).
Placitorum in Domo Capitulari Westmonasteriensi Asservatorum Abbreviatio (London, 1811).
Pleas before the King or his Justices, 1198–1212, vol. iii: *Rolls or Fragments of Rolls from the Years 1199, 1201, and 1203–1206*, ed. D. M. Stenton (Selden Society 83, 1967).

'A Powys Lay Subsidy Roll, 1293', ed. R. Morgan, *Mont. Coll.*, **71** (1983), pp.91–112.
Ralph of Diss, *Opera Historica*, ed. W. Stubbs, 2 vols. (RS, 1876).
The Record of Caernarvon, ed. H. Ellis (London, 1838).
Recueil des Actes des Ducs de Normandie, 911–1066, ed. M. Fauroux (Caen, 1961).
Red Book of the Exchequer, ed. H. Hall, 3 vols. (London: RS, 1896).
Regesta Regum Anglo-Normannorum. The Acta of William I (1066–1087), ed. D. Bates (Oxford, 1998).
Regesta Regum Anglo-Normannorum, 1066–1154, vol. ii: Regesta Henrici Primi, 1100–1135, eds. C. Johnson and H.A. Cronne (Oxford, 1956).
Regesta Regum Anglo-Normannorum, 1066–1154, vol. iii: 1135–54 (King Stephen, Empress Mathilda and Geoffrey and Henry, Dukes of Normandy), ed. H.A. Cronne and R.H.C. Davis (Oxford, 1968).
Registrum Epistolarum Fratris Johannis Peckham, Archiepiscopi Cantuariensis, ed. C.T. Martin, 3 vols. (RS, 1882–5).
Registrum Ricardi de Swinfield, Episcopi Herefordensis, ed. W.W. Capes (Canterbury and York Society 6, 1909).
Roger of Wendover, *Chronica, sive Flores Historiarum*, ed. H.O. Coxe, 4 vols. (London, 1841–4).
Roll of Divers Accounts for the Early Years of the Reign of Henry III, ed. F.A. Cazel (P. R. S., NS 44, 1982).
The Roll of the Shropshire Eyre of 1256, ed. A. Harding (London, 1981).
Rolls of the Justices in Eyre, 1221, 1222, ed. D.M. Stenton (Selden Society, 59, 1940).
Rotuli Chartarum, ed. T.D. Hardy (London, 1837).
Rotuli Curiae Regis, ed. F. Palgrave, 2 vols. (London, 1835).
Rotuli Hundredorum, ed. W. Illlingworth, 2 vols. (London, 1812–18).
Rotuli Litterarum Clausarum, 1204–27, ed. T.D. Hardy, 2 vols. (London, 1833–44).
Rotuli Litterarum Patentium, 1201–16, ed. T.D. Hardy (London, 1835).
Rotuli de Oblatis et Finibus, Tempore Regis Johannis, ed. T.D. Hardy (London, 1835).
Rotuli Parliamentorum, ed. J. Strachey, 6 vols. (London, 1767–77).
Royal and Other Letters Illustrative of the Reign of Henry III, ed. W.W. Shirley, 2 vols. (RS, 1862–6).
Sawyer, P.H., *Anglo-Saxon Charters: An Annotated List and Bibliography* (Royal Historical Society, 1968).
The Shropshire Lay Subsidy Roll of 1 Edward III (1327), ed. W.G.D. Fletcher (Oswestry, 1907 – repr. from *TSAS*, various).
Statutes of the Realm, 9 vols. in 10 (London, 1810–28).
Two of the Saxon Chronicles Parallel, ed. J. Earle and C. Plummer, 2 vols. (Oxford, 1892, repr. 2000).
Urkunden und erzählende Quellen zur deutschen Ostsiedlung im Mittelalter, ed. R. Buchner (Freiherr vom Stein-Gedächtnisausgabe, Band xxvi a–b), 2 vols. (Darmstadt, 1968–70).
'Valle Crucis Abbey. Its Origin and Foundation Charter', ed. M.C. Jones, *Arch. Camb.*, 3rd ser., 12 (1866), pp.400–17.
Valor Ecclesiasticus, ed. J. Caley and J. Hunter, 6 vols. (London, 1810–34).
The Valuation of Norwich, ed. W.E. Lunt (Oxford, 1926).
Vita Griffini Filii Conani: The Medieval Latin Life of Gruffudd ap Cynan, ed. and transl. P. Russell (Cardiff, 2005).
The Welsh Assize Roll 1277–84, ed. J.C. Davies (Cardiff, 1940).

William of Newburgh, *The First Four Books of the Historia Rerum Anglicarum*, in *Chronicles of the Reigns of Stephen, Henry II and Richard I*, ed. R. Howlett, 2 vols. (RS, 1884–5), i, 1–408; ii, 409–583.
William Worcestre: *Itineraries*, ed. J.H. Harvey (Oxford Medieval Texts, 1969).

PRINTED SECONDARY WORKS

Abels, R., 'Paying the Danegeld: Anglo-Saxon Peacemaking with Vikings', in P. De Souza and J. France (eds.), *War and Peace in Ancient and Medieval History* (Cambridge, 2008), pp. 173–92.
Abulafia, D., and N. Berend (eds.), *Medieval Frontiers: Concepts and Practices* (Aldershot, 2002).
Alcock, L., D.J.C. King, W.G. Putnam and C.J. Spurgeon, 'Excavations at Castell Bryn Amlwg', *Mont. Coll.*, **60** (1967–8), pp. 8–27.
Altschul, M., *A Baronial Family in Medieval England: The Clares, 1217–1314* (Baltimore, 1965).
Barker, P.A., 'Caus Castle and Hawcock's Mount', *Archaeological Journal*, **138** (1981), p. 34.
'Pontesbury Castle Mound, Emergency Excavations, 1961', *TSAS*, **57** (1961–4), pp. 206–23.
'Timber Castles on the Welsh Border with Special Reference to Hen Domen, Montgomery', in *Les Mondes Normands (VIIIe–XIIe siècles)* (Caen, 1989), pp. 135–47.
and R. Higham, *Hen Domen Montgomery: A Timber Castle on the English–Welsh Border* (London, 1982).
Hen Domen Montgomery: A Timber Castle on the English-Welsh Border. Excavations 1960–1988. A Summary Report (1988).
Barker, P.A., and J. Lawson, 'A Pre-Norman Field System at Hen Domen, Montgomery', *Medieval Archaeology*, **15** (1972 for 1971), pp. 58–72.
Barlow, F., *William Rufus* (London, 1983).
Barnes, P.M., Introduction to *Pipe Roll 14 John, 1212* (P. R. S., NS 30, 1955), pp. xi–xxxi.
Barrell, A.D.M., R.R. Davies, O.J. Padel and Ll. B. Smith, 'The Dyffryn Clwyd Court Roll Project', in Z. Razi and R. Smith (eds.), *Medieval Society and the Manor Court* (Oxford, 1996), pp. 260–97.
Barrow, G.W.S., *The Anglo-Norman Era in Scottish History* (Oxford, 1980).
'Frontier and Settlement: Which Influenced Which? England and Scotland, 1100–1300', in R. Bartlett and A. MacKay (eds.), *Medieval Frontier Societies* (Oxford, 1989), pp. 3–21.
'The Pattern of Lordship and Feudal Settlement in Cumbria', *Journal of Medieval History*, **1** (1975), pp. 117–38.
Barry, T.B., *The Archaeology of Medieval Ireland* (London, 1987).
Barthélémy, D., and O. Bruand (eds.), *Les Pouvoirs locaux dans la France du centre et de l'ouest (VIIIe–XIe siècles): implantation et moyens d'action* (Rennes, 2004).
Bartlett, R., *Gerald of Wales (1146–1223)* (Oxford, 1982).
'Colonial Aristocracies of the High Middle Ages', in R. Bartlett and A. Mackay (eds.), *Medieval Frontier Societies* (Oxford, 1989), pp. 23–47.
The Making of Europe: Conquest, Colonization and Cultural Change 950–1350 (London, 1993).

and A. MacKay (eds.), *Medieval Frontier Societies* (Oxford, 1989)

Barton, P.G., 'Gruffudd ap Gwenwynwyn's Trefnant Market Charter 1279–1282', *Mont. Coll.*, **90** (2002), pp. 69–86.

Bateson, M., 'The Laws of Breteuil (Continued)', *EHR*, 15, no. **58** (1900), pp. 302–18.

'The Laws of Breteuil, Part II: The English Evidence (Continued)', *EHR*, **15**, no. 59 (1900), pp. 496–523.

Bauduin, P., 'Une famille châtelaine sur les confins normanno-manceaux: les Géré (Xe–XIIIe s.), *Archéologie Médievale*, **22** (1992), pp. 309–56.

La Première Normandie (Xe–XIe siècles). Sur les frontières de la haute Normandie: identité et construction d'une principauté (Caen, 2004).

Baugh, G. C., 'The Franchises', in *VCH*, **3**, 33–53.

(ed.), *The Victoria History of the Counties of England*, vol. iii: *A History of Shropshire* (Oxford, 1979).

Beresford, M.W., *New Towns of the Middle Ages*, 2nd edn (London, 1988).

and H.P.R. Finberg, *English Medieval Boroughs: A Handlist* (Newton Abbot, 1973).

Boutruche, R., 'The Devastation of Rural Areas During the Hundred Years War and the Agricultural Recovery of France', in P.S. Lewis (ed.), *The Recovery of France in the Fifteenth Century* (New York and London, 1971), pp.23–59.

Bouvris, J.–M., 'Aux premiers temps d'une grande abbaye normande au XIe siècle: les chartes de fondation de St-Martin de Sées', *Annales de Normandie*, **39** (1989), pp. 452–4.

Brand, P., ' "Multis Vigiliis Excogitatam et Inventam": Henry II and the Creation of the English Common Law', in P. Brand, *The Making of the Common Law* (London, 1992), pp.77–102.

Braund, D.C., *Rome and the Friendly King: The Character of Client Kingship* (London, 1984).

Brooke, C.N.L., *The Church and the Welsh Border in the Central Middle Ages*, ed. D.N. Dumville and C.N.L. Brooke (Woodbridge, 1986).

Brunner, K., 'Die fränkischen Fürstentitel im neunten und zehnten Jahrhundert', in H. Wolfram (ed.), *Intitulatio II: Lateinische Herrscher- und Fürstentitel im 9. und 10. Jahrhundert (Mitteilungen des Instituts für Österreichische Geschichtsforschung, Ergänzungsband 24*, 1973), pp.179–340.

Brunner, O., *Land und Herrschaft: Grundfragen der territorialen Verfassungsgeschiche Österreichs im Mittelalter*, 5th edn (Vienna, 1965, repr. Darmstadt, 1990).

Butler, L., 'Dolforwyn Castle', *Archaeology in Wales*, **25** (1985), p. 42.

'Dolforwyn Castle, Montgomery, Powys', *Arch. Camb.*, **144** (1997 for 1995), pp. 133–203.

'Dolforwyn Castle, Powys, Wales: Excavations 1981–4', *Château Gaillard*, **12** (1985), pp. 167–77.

Cam, H.M., 'The Evolution of the Mediaeval English Franchise', *Speculum*, **32** (July 1957), pp.427–42; repr. in H. M. Cam, *Law-Makers and Law-Finders* (London, 1962), pp.22–43.

The Hundred and the Hundred Rolls: An Outline of Local Government in Medieval England (London, 1930).

'Manerium cum Hundredo: The Hundred and the Hundredal Manor', in H. M. Cam, *Liberties and Communities in Medieval England: Collected Studies in Local Administration and Topography* (Cambridge, 1933; repr. London, 1963), pp.69–40.

'The North Gate of Oxford', in H. M. Cam, *Liberties and Communities in Medieval England. Collected Studies in Local Administration and Topography* (Cambridge, 1933; repr. 1963), pp. 107–23.

Cane, J., 'Excavations on Wat's Dyke at Pentre Wern, Shropshire in 1984/5', *TSAS*, **71** (1996), pp. 10–21.

Cantrill, T.C., 'Geology', in W. Page (ed.), *The Victoria History of Shropshire, vol. i* (London, 1908), pp. 1–46.

Carpenter, D.A., 'The Decline of the Curial Sheriff in England', *EHR*, **91** (1976), pp. 1–32.

The Minority of Henry III (London, 1990).

'The Second Century of English Feudalism', *Past & Present*, **168** (2000), pp. 30–71.

Charles, B.G., *Non-Celtic Place-Names in Wales* (London, 1938).

'The Welsh, their Language and Place-Names in Archenfield and Oswestry', in *Angles and Britons: O'Donnell lectures* (University of Wales Press, 1963), pp. 85–110.

Charles-Edwards, T.M., *Early Irish and Welsh Kinship* (Oxford, 1993).

'Ireland and its Invaders, 1166–1186', *Quaestio Insularis*, **4** (2003), pp. 1–34.

'Wales and Mercia, 613–918', in M.P. Brown and C.A. Farr (eds.), *Mercia: An Anglo-Saxon Kingdom in Europe* (London and New York, 2001), pp. 89–105.

Chibnall, M., *Anglo-Norman England, 1066–1166* (Oxford, 1986).

'Robert of Bellême and the Castle of Tickhill', in *Droit privé et institutions régionales. Études historiques offerts à Jean Yver* (Paris, 1976), pp. 151–6.

Chitty, L.F., 'The Clun–Clee Ridgeway: A Prehistoric Trackway across South Shropshire', in I. Ll. Foster and L. Alcock (eds.), *Culture and Environment* (London, 1963), pp. 171–92.

Colvin, H.M., and A.J. Taylor, *The History of the King's Works*, 2 vols. (London, 1963).

Contamine, P., 'Heer, Heerwesen. Allgemeine Grundzüge', in *Lexikon des Mittelalters, vol. iv* (Munich and Zurich, 1989), pp. 1987–90.

Coplestone-Crow, B., 'From Foundation to Anarchy', in R. Shoesmith and A. Johnson (eds.), *Ludlow Castle: Its History and Buildings* (Logaston Press, 2000).

Coulson, C.L.H., *Castles in Medieval Society* (Oxford, 2003).

Cox, D.C., 'County Government in the Early Middle Ages', in *VCH*, **3**, 1–32.

Craib, T., and others, *Itinerary of Henry III, 1215–1272* (Public Record Office, 1923).

Crook, D., *Records of the General Eyre* (London, 1982).

Crouch, D., 'The Last Adventure of Richard Siward', *Morgannwg*, **35** (1991), pp. 7–30.

'The March and the Welsh Kings', in E. King (ed.), *The Anarchy of King Stephen's Reign* (Oxford, 1994), pp. 256–89.

William Marshal: Court, Career and Chivalry in the Angevin Empire 1147–1219 (London, 1990).

Crump, J.J., 'The Mortimer Family and the Making of the March', in M. Prestwich, R.H. Britnell, and R. Frame (eds.), *Thirteenth-Century England*, 6 (1997 for 1995), pp. 117–26.

Curnow, P.E., 'The Tower House at Hopton and its Affinities' in C. Harper-Bill, C.J. Holdsworth and J.L. Nelson (eds.), *Studies in Medieval History Presented to R. Allen Brown* (Woodbridge, 1989), pp. 81–102.

and M.W. Thompson, 'Excavations at Richard's Castle, Herefordshire', *Journal of the British Archaeological Association*, 3rd ser., **32** (1969), pp. 105–27.

Curta, F., (ed.), *Borders, Barriers and Ethnogenesis: Frontiers in Late Antiquity and the Middle Ages* (Turnhout, 2005).

Darby, H.C., *Domesday England* (Cambridge, 1977).

Davies, J., 'Rhyd Chwima – The Ford at Montgomery – Aque Vadum de Mungumeri', *Mont. Coll.*, **94** (2006), pp. 23–36.

Davies, J.R., 'Aspects of Church Reform in Wales, c. 1093–c. 1223', in *Anglo-Norman Studies*, **30** (2008), pp. 85–99.

Davies, R.R., *The Age of Conquest. Wales 1063–1415* (Oxford, 2000; first published under this title Oxford, 1991; first published as *Conquest, Coexistence and Change: Wales 1063–1415*, Oxford, 1987).

Domination and Conquest: The Experience of Ireland, Scotland and Wales 1100–1300 (Cambridge, 1990).

'The English State and the "Celtic" peoples, 1100–1400', *Journal of Historical Sociology*, **6** (1993), pp. 1–14.

The First English Empire: Power and Identities in the British Isles, 1093–1343 (Oxford, 2000).

'Frontier Arrangements in Fragmented Societies: Ireland and Wales', in R. Bartlett and A. MacKay (eds.), *Medieval Frontier Societies* (Oxford, 1989), pp. 77–100.

'Henry I and Wales', in H. Mayr-Harting and R.I. Moore (eds.), *Studies in Medieval History Presented to R. H. C. Davis* (London, 1985), pp. 132–47.

'The Identity of "Wales" in the Thirteenth Century', in R. R. Davies and G.H. Jenkins (eds.), *From Medieval to Modern Wales: Historical Essays in Honour of Kenneth O. Morgan and Ralph A. Griffiths* (Cardiff, 2004), pp. 45–63.

The King of England and the Prince of Wales, 1277–84: Law, Politics and Power (Kathleen Hughes Memorial Lectures on Mediaeval Welsh History 3, Cambridge, 2002).

'Kings, Lords and Liberties in the March of Wales, 1066–1272', *TRHS*, 5th ser., **29** (1979), pp. 41–61.

'Lordship or Colony?', in J.F. Lydon (ed.), *The English in Medieval Ireland* (Dublin, 1984), pp. 142–60.

Lordship and Society in the March of Wales, 1282–1400 (Oxford, 1978).

'The Medieval State: The Tyranny of a Concept?', *Journal of Historical Sociology*, **16** (2003), pp. 280–99.

'The Peoples of Britain and Ireland, 1100–1400, 3: Laws and Customs', *TRHS*, 6th ser., **6** (1996), pp. 1–23.

The Revolt of Owain Glyn Dŵr (Oxford, 1995).

'Roger Mortimer (V), First Earl of March (1287–1330)', in *ODNB* (2004).

'The Survival of the Bloodfeud in Medieval Wales', *History: The Journal of the Historical Association*, **54**:182 (1969), pp. 338–57.

Davies, W., *Wales in the Early Middle Ages* (London, 1982).

Dhondt, J., 'Le Titre du marquis à l'époque carolingienne', *Archivum Latinitatis Medii Aevi (Bulletin Du Cange)*, **19** (1948), pp. 407–17.

Dictionary of Medieval Latin from British Sources, various eds., 8 fascicules (London, 1975–2003); *Fascicule vi (M)*, ed. D. R. Howlett (Oxford, 2001).

Douglas, D.C., *William the Conqueror* (London, 1964).

Duby, G., 'Youth in Aristocratic Society', in G. Duby, *The Chivalrous Society*, transl. C. Postan (London, 1977), pp. 112–22.

Duffy, S., 'The Problem of Degeneracy', in J.F. Lydon (ed.), *Law and Disorder in Thirteenth-Century Ireland: The Dublin Parliament of 1297* (Dublin, 1997), pp. 87–106.

Edwards, J.F., and B.P. Hindle, 'The Transportation System of Medieval England and Wales', *Journal of Historical Geography*, **17** (1991), pp. 123–34.

Edwards, J.G., 'Henry II and the Fight at Coleshill: Some Further Reflections', *WHR*, **3** (1966–7), pp. 251–63.

'The Normans and the Welsh March', *Proceedings of the British Academy*, **42** (1956), pp. 155–77.

Edwards, N. (ed.), *Landscape and Settlement in Medieval Wales* (Oxford, 1997).

and A. Lane, 'The Archaeology of the Early Church in Wales: An Introduction', in N. Edwards and A. Lane (eds.), *The Early Church in Wales and the West* (Oxford, 1992), pp. 1–11.

Ehlers, J., *Heinrich der Löwe: Eine Biographie* (Munich, 2008).

Ekwall, E., *English River-Names* (Oxford, 1928).

Elrington, C.R. (ed.), *The Victoria History of the Counties of England. A History of Shropshire, vol. iv* (Oxford, 1989).

English, B., *The Lords of Holderness, 1086–1260: A Study in Feudal Society* (Hull, 1991).

Everson, P.L., 'Three Case Studies of Ridge and Furrow, 1: Offa's Dyke at Dudston in Chirbury, Shropshire. A Pre-Offan Field System?', *Landscape History*, **13** (1991), pp. 53–63.

Eyton, R.W., *Antiquities of Shropshire*, 12 vols. (London, 1854–60).

Court, Household, and Itinerary of King Henry II: Instancing Also the Chief Agents and Adversaries of the King in his Government, Diplomacy, and Strategy (London, 1878).

Faraday, M.A., 'The Assessment for the Fifteenth of 1293 on Radnor and Other Marcher Lordships', *Transactions of the Radnorshire Society*, **43** (1973), pp. 79–85.

Favre, L. (ed.), *Glossarium Mediae et Infimae Latinitatis, Conditum a Carolo du Fresne, Domino du Cange*, new edn, 10 vols. (Niort, 1883–7).

Febvre, L., *La Terre et l'évolution humaine* (Paris, 1922).

Fossier, R., *L'Enfance de l'Europe, Xe–XIIe siècles: Aspects économiques et sociaux* (Paris, 1982).

Fox, C., and D.W. Phillips, 'Offa's Dyke: A Field Survey (Fifth Report)', *Arch. Camb.*, **85** (1930), pp. 1–73.

Foxall, H.D.G., *Shropshire Field-Names* (Shrewsbury, 1980).

Frame, R., 'Aristocracies and the Political Configuration of the British Isles', in R.R. Davies (ed.), *The British Isles, 1100–1500: Comparisons, Contrasts and Connections* (Edinburgh, 1988), pp. 142–59.

Colonial Ireland, 1169–1369 (Dublin 1981).

'"Les Engleys nées en Irlande": The English Political Identity in Medieval Ireland', *TRHS*, 6th ser., **3** (1993), pp. 83–103.

'Military Service in the Lordship of Ireland 1290–1360: Institutions and Society on the Anglo-Gaelic Frontier', in R. Bartlett and A. MacKay (eds.), *Medieval Frontier Societies* (Oxford, 1989), pp. 101–26.

The Political Development of the British Isles 1100–1400, 2nd edn (Oxford, 1995).

'Power and Society in the Lordship of Ireland, 1272–1377', *Past & Present*, **76** (1977), pp. 3–33.
Fryde, N. (ed.), *List of Welsh Entries in the Memoranda Rolls, 1282–1343* (Cardiff, 1974).
Galbraith, V.H., 'An Episcopal Land-Grant of 1085', *EHR*, **44** (1929).
Gaydon, A.T., (ed.), *The Victoria History of the Counties of England: A History of Shropshire, vol. ii* (London, 1973).
(ed.), *The Victoria History of the Counties of England: A History of Shropshire, vol. viii* (Oxford, 1968).
Gelling, M., *The Place-Names of Shropshire, Part 1: The Major Names of Shropshire* (Nottingham, 1990).
The Place-names of Shropshire, Part 2: The Hundreds of Ford and Condover (Nottingham, 1995).
The Place-Names of Shropshire, Part 4: Shrewsbury Town and Suburbs and the Liberties of Shrewsbury (Nottingham, 2004).
The West Midlands in the Early Middle Ages (Leicester, 1992).
Gillingham, J., 'Henry II, Richard I and the Lord Rhys', *Peritia*, **10** (1996), pp. 225–36.
Richard the Lionheart (London, 1978).
Given-Wilson, C., 'Edmund Fitzalan, Second Earl of Arundel', in *ODNB* (2004).
Graham, B.J., 'The Mottes of the Norman Liberty of Meath', in H. Murtagh (ed.), *Irish Midland Studies: Essays in Commemoration of N. W. English* (Athlone, 1980), pp. 39–56.
'Twelfth and Thirteenth-Century Earthwork Castles in Ireland: An Assessment', *Fortress*, **9** (1991), pp. 24–34.
Green, J.A., *The Aristocracy of Norman England* (Cambridge, 1997).
'Financing Stephen's War', *Anglo-Norman Studies*, **14** (1992), pp. 91–114.
The Government of England under Henry I (Cambridge, 1986).
'The Last Century of Danegeld', *EHR*, **96** (1981), pp. 241–58.
Griffiths, R.A. (ed.), *Boroughs of Medieval Wales* (Cardiff, 1978).
Le Goff, J. (ed.), *Dictionnaire raisonné de l'Occident médiéval* (Paris, 1999).
Harfield, C.G., 'A Hand-List of Castles Recorded in the Domesday Book', *EHR*, **106** (1991), pp. 371–92.
Harris, B.E., 'The Earldom of Chester 1070–1301', in B. E. Harris (ed.), *A History of the County of Chester, vol. ii* (Oxford, 1979), pp. 1–8.
Harvey, P.D.A., 'Matthew Paris's Maps of Britain', in P.R. Coss and S.D. Lloyd (eds.), *Thirteenth-Century England*, 4 (Woodbridge, 1992), pp. 109–21.
Higham, R., and P.A. Barker, *Hen Domen Montgomery: A Timber Castle on the English-Welsh Border – A Final Report* (Exeter, 2000).
Timber Castles (London, 1992)
Hill, D., 'Offa's Dyke: Pattern and Purpose', *Antiquaries' Journal*, **80** (2000), pp. 195–206.
and M. Worthington, *Offa's Dyke: History and Guide* (Stroud, 2003).
Hilton, R.H., *A Medieval Society: The West Midlands at the End of the Thirteenth Century* (London, 1966).
Hindle, B.P., '*The Towns and Roads of the Gough Map*' (1979, offprint from *The Manchester Geographer*, **1**:1, 1980), pp. 35–49.
Hoffman, R.C., 'Warfare, Weather and a Rural Economy: The Duchy of Wroclaw in the Mid-Fifteenth Century', *Viator*, **4** (1973), pp. 273–405.

Hogg, A.H.A., and D.J.C. King, 'Castles in Wales and the Marches: Additions and Corrections', *Arch. Camb.*, **119** (1970), pp. 119–24.

'Early Castles in Wales and the Marches', *Arch. Camb.*, **112** (1963), pp. 77–124.

'Masonry Castles in Wales and the Marches: A List', *Arch. Camb.*, **116** (1967), pp. 71–132.

Holden, B.W., *Lords of the Central Marches: English Aristocracy and Frontier Society, 1087–1265* (Oxford, 2008).

'The Making of the Middle March of Wales, 1066–1250', *WHR*, **20** (2000), pp. 207–26.

Hollister, C.W., 'The Campaign of 1102 against Robert of Bellême', in C. Harper-Bill, C.J. Holdsworth, J. Nelson and J. Laughland (eds.), *Studies in Medieval History Presented to R. Allen Brown* (Woodbridge, 1989), pp. 193–202.

Henry I (New Haven and London, 2001).

Holt, J.C., '1153: The Treaty of Winchester', in J. C. Holt, *Colonial England*, pp. 271–90. Repr. from E.B. King (ed.), *The Anarchy of King Stephen's Reign* (Oxford, 1994), pp. 291–316.

'Feudal Society and the Family in Early Medieval England, I: The Revolution of 1066', in J. C. Holt, *Colonial England*, pp. 161–78. Repr. from *TRHS*, 5th ser., **32** (1982), pp. 193–212.

'Feudal Society and the Family in Early Medieval England, III: Patronage and Politics', in J. C. Holt, *Colonial England*, pp. 161–78. Repr. from *TRHS*, 5th ser., **34** (1984), pp. 1–25.

Magna Carta, 2nd edn (Cambridge, 1992).

The Northerners. A Study in the Reign of King John (Oxford, 1992).

'Politics and Property in Early Medieval England', in J. C. Holt, *Colonial England* (London, 1997), pp. 113–59. Repr. from *Past and Present*, **57** (1972), pp. 3–52; **65** (1974), pp. 130–2. Also repr. in T. H. Aston (ed.), *Landlords, Peasants and Politics in Medieval England* (Cambridge, 1987), pp. 65–114.

'What's in a Name? Family Nomenclature and the Norman Conquest', in J. C. Holt, *Colonial England*, pp. 179–96. Stenton Lecture, University of Reading (1981).

Isaac, B., *The Limits of Empire*, rev. edn (Oxford, 1992).

Jackson, M., *Castles of Shropshire* (Shrewsbury, 1988).

Jacobs, N., 'Animadversions on Bastardy in the Red Book of Hergest: *Early Welsh Gnomic Poems*, IV.6', *Cambrian Medieval Celtic Studies*, **55** (2008), pp. 51–9.

Jones, E.T., 'River Navigation in Medieval England', *Journal of Historical Geography*, **26** (2000), pp. 60–74.

Kapelle, W.E., *The Norman Conquest of the North: The Region and its Transformation, 1000–1135* (London, 1979).

Keefe, T.K., 'The 1165 Levy for the Army of Wales', *Notes and Queries*, NS, **29**:3 (1982), pp. 194–6.

Kenyon, J.R., *Castles, Town Defences, and Artillery Fortifications in Britain: A Bibliography*, vols. ii and iii (London, 1983 and 1990).

Medieval Fortifications (Leicester, 1990); review by F. Verhaege in *Archéologie Médievale*, **23** (1993), pp. 531–3.

Keynes, S., 'The Historical Context of the Battle of Maldon', in D. Scragg (ed.), *The Battle of Maldon AD 991* (Oxford, 1991), pp. 81–113.

Kimball, E.G., *Serjeanty Tenure in Medieval England* (New Haven, 1936).

King, D.J.C., 'Henry II and the Fight at Coleshill', *WHR*, **2** (1965), pp. 367–73.

Castellarium Anglicanum: An Index and Bibliography of the Castles in England, Wales and the Islands, 2 vols. (New York, 1983).

and C.J. Spurgeon, 'The Mottes in the Vale of Montgomery', *Arch. Camb.*, **114** (1965), pp. 69–86.

Knight, J., 'Montgomery. A Castle of the Welsh March, 1223–1649', *Château Gaillard*, **11** (1983), pp. 169–82.

Latimer, P., 'Henry II's Campaign against the Welsh in 1165', *WHR*, **14:4** (1988), pp. 523–52.

Lemarignier, J.F., *Recherches sur l'hommage en marche et les frontières féodales* (Lille, 1945).

Lewis, C.P., 'The Early Earls of Norman England', *Anglo-Norman Studies*, **13** (1990), pp. 207–23.

'The Formation of the Honor of Chester, 1066–1100', in A.T. Thacker (ed.), *The Earldom of Chester and its Charters: A Tribute to Geoffrey Barraclough* (Chester, 1991), pp. 37–68.

'The Norman Settlement of Herefordshire under William I', *Anglo-Norman Studies*, **7** (1984), pp. 195–213.

'Ralph (I) de Mortimer (fl. c. 1080–1104)', in *ODNB* (2004).

'Walter de Lacy (d. 1085)', in *ODNB* (2004).

Lewis, C., P. Mitchell-Fox and C. Dyer (eds.), *Village, Hamlet and Field: Changing Medieval Settlements in Central England* (Manchester, 1997).

Lewis, S., *The Art of Matthew Paris in the* Chronica Majora (Berkeley and Aldershot, 1987).

Lieberman, M., 'Anglicization in High Medieval Wales: The Case of Glamorgan', *WHR*, **23** (2006), pp. 1–26.

'The English and the Welsh in *Fouke le Fitz Waryn*', in J. Burton, P. Schofield and B. Weiler (eds.), *Thirteenth-Century England*, 12 (Woodbridge, 2009), pp. 1–11.

The March of Wales, 1067–1300: A Borderland of Medieval Britain (Cardiff, 2008).

'The Medieval "Marches" of Normandy and of Wales', *EHR*, forthcoming.

'Striving for Marcher Liberties: The Corbets of Caus in the Thirteenth Century', in M. Prestwich (ed.), *Liberties and Identities in the Medieval British Isles* (Woodbridge, 2008), pp. 141–54.

Lloyd, J.E., 'Border Notes', *BBCS*, **11** (1941–4), pp. 48–54.

A History of Wales from the Earliest Times to the Edwardian Conquest, 3rd edn (London, 1939; repr. in 2 vols. 1948).

'The Welsh Chronicles', *Proceedings of the British Academy*, **14** (1928), pp. 369–91.

Longley, D., 'Status and Lordship in the Early Middle Ages', in M. Aldhouse-Green and R. Howell (eds.), *The Gwent County History, vol. i: Gwent in Prehistory and Early History*, pp. 287–316.

Louise, G., *La Seigneurie de Bellême, Xe–XIIe siècles: évolution des pouvoirs territoriaux et construction d'une seigneurie de frontière aux confins de la Normandie et du Maine à la charnière de l'an mil*, 2 vols. (Flers, 1990).

Loyd, L.C., *The Origins of Some Anglo-Norman Families* (Harleian Soc., **103**, 1951).

Loyn, H.R., *The Governance of Anglo-Saxon England, 500–1087* (London, 1984).

'The Hundred in England in the Tenth and Early Eleventh Centuries', in H. Hearder and H.R. Loyn (eds.), *British Government and Administration: Studies Presented to S. B. Chrimes* (Cardiff, 1974), pp. 1–15.

'Wales and England in the Tenth Century: The Context of the Æthelstan Charters', *WHR*, **10** (1980–1), pp. 283–301.
Lydon, J., 'A Land of War', in A. Cosgrove (ed.), *A New History of Ireland, vol. ii: Medieval Ireland 1169–1534* (Oxford, 1987), pp. 240–74.
Mann, K., 'The March of Wales: A Question of Terminology', *WHR*, **18** (1996), pp. 1–13.
'A Microcosm of Civil War: The Border Shires', *TSAS*, **73** (1998), pp. 8–12.
Mason, J.F.A., *The Borough of Bridgnorth, 1157–1957* (Bridgnorth, 1957).
'The Norman Castle at Quatford', *TSAS*, **57** (1961–4), pp. 37–62.
'The Officers and Clerks of the Norman Earls of Shropshire', *TSAS*, **56** (1957–60), pp. 244–57.
'Roger de Montgomery and his Sons (1067–1102)', *TRHS*, 5th ser., **13** (1963), pp. 1–28.
'William I and the Sussex Rapes' (Historical Association, 1066 Commemoration Lectures, 3, 1966, repr. 1972).
McNeill, T.E., *Anglo-Norman Ulster: The History and Archaeology of an Irish Barony, 1177–1400* (Edinburgh, 1980).
Castles in Ireland: Feudal Power in a Gaelic World (London, 1997).
Maund, K.L., *Handlist of the Acts of Native Welsh Rulers* (Cardiff, 1996).
Ireland, Wales, and England in the Eleventh Century (Woodbridge, 1991).
'The Welsh Alliances of Earl Ælfgar of Mercia and his Family in the Mid-Eleventh Century', *Anglo-Norman Studies*, **11** (1989), pp. 181–90.
Meisel, J., *Barons of the Welsh Frontier: The Corbet, Pantulf, and Fitz Warin Families, 1066–1272* (London, 1980).
Miller, E., 'England in the Twelfth and Thirteenth Centuries: An Economic Contrast?', *Economic History Review*, 2nd ser., **24** (1971), pp. 1–14.
Mitchell, J.B., 'Early Maps of Great Britain', *Geographical Journal*, **81** (1933), pp. 27–43.
Morgan, P., *War and Society in Medieval Cheshire, 1277–1403* (Manchester, 1987)
Morgan, R., 'The Barony of Powys, 1275–1360', *WHR*, **10** (1980), pp. 1–42.
'The Foundation of the Borough of Welshpool', *Mont. Coll.*, **65** (1977), pp. 7–24.
A Study of Radnorshire Place-Names (Llanrwst, 1998).
'The Territorial Divisions of Medieval Montgomeryshire (I)', in *Mont. Coll.*, **69** (1981), pp. 9–44.
'Trewern in Gorddwr: Domesday Manor and Knight's Fief 1086–1311', *Mont. Coll.*, **64** (1976), pp. 121–33.
Welsh Place-Names in Shropshire (Cardiff, 1997).
Morris, J.E., *The Welsh Wars of Edward I: A Contribution to Mediaeval Military History, Based on Original Documents* (Oxford, 1901).
Morriss, R.K., 'Clun Castle Reappraised', in *Castle Studies Group Newsletter*, **7** (1993–4), pp. 23–4.
Murphy, K., 'Small Boroughs in South-West Wales: Their Planning, Early Development and Defences', in N. Edwards (ed.), *Landscape and Settlement in Medieval Wales* (Oxford, 1997), pp. 139–56.
Nelson, L.H., *The Normans in South Wales, 1070–1171* (Austin, Texas, 1966).
Northcote Toller, T. (ed.), *An Anglo-Saxon Dictionary, Based on the Manuscript Collections of the Late Joseph Bosworth*, parts 1–4. A-Y (Oxford, 1898).

An Anglo-Saxon Dictionary: Supplement, with rev. and enlarged Addenda by A. Campbell (Oxford, 1921).
O'Byrne, E., and J. Ní Ghradaigh (eds.), *The March in the Medieval West, 1000–1400* (forthcoming).
Ormerod, G., *The History of the County Palatine and City of Chester*, 3 vols. (London, 1882).
Otway-Ruthven, A.J., 'Knight Service in Ireland', *Journal of the Royal Society of Antiquaries of Ireland*, **89** (1959), pp. 1–15.
Owen, H., and J.B. Blakeway, *History of Shrewsbury*, 2 vols. (1824–5).
Page, W. (ed.), *The Victoria History of the Counties of England. A History of Shropshire, vol. i* (London, 1908).
Painter, S., *Studies in the History of the English Feudal Barony* (Baltimore, 1943).
Palliser, D.M., 'Domesday Book and the "Harrying of the North"', *Northern History*, **29** (1993), pp. 1–23.
Palmer, J.J.N., 'War and Domesday Waste', in M. Strickland (ed.), *Armies, Chivalry and Warfare in Medieval Britain and France. Proceedings of the 1995 Harlaxton Symposium* (Stamford, 1998), pp.256–75.
Parsons, E.J.S., *The Map of Great Britain circa A.D. 1360 Known as the Gough Map: An Introduction to the Facsimile*, 2nd edn (Oxford, 1996).
Le Patourel, J., *The Norman Empire* (Oxford, 1976).
Pearson, M.J., 'The Creation and Development of the St Asaph Cathedral Chapter, 1141–1293', *Cambrian Medieval Celtic Studies*, **40** (2000), pp. 35–56.
Pevsner, N., *The Buildings of England: Herefordshire* (London, 1963).
Peyvel, P., 'Structures féodales et frontière médiévale: l'exemple de la zone de contact entre Forez et Bourbonnais aux XIIIe et XIVe siècles', *Moyen Âge*, **93** (1987), pp. 51–83.
Phillips, A.D.M., and C.B. Phillips (eds.), *A New Historical Atlas of Cheshire* (Chester, 2001).
Pierce, G.O., 'Place-Names', in D. Huw Owen (ed.), *Settlement and Society in Wales* (Cardiff, 1989), pp.73–94.
Pohl, W., I. Wood and H. Reimitz (eds.), *The Transformation of Frontiers from Late Antiquity to the Carolingians* (Leiden, 2001).
Poole, A.L., *Medieval England*, 2 vols. (Oxford, 1958).
Pounds, N.J.G., *The Medieval Castle in England and Wales: A Social and Political History* (Cambridge, 1994).
Power, D., *The Norman Frontier in the Twelfth and Early Thirteenth Centuries* (Cambridge, 2004).
and N. Standen (eds.), *Frontiers in Question: Eurasian Borderlands, 700–1700* (London et al., 1999).
Powicke, F.M., *The Loss of Normandy*, 2nd edn (Manchester, 1961).
Powicke, M.R., *Military Obligation in Medieval England: A Study in Liberty and Duty* (Oxford, 1962).
Prestwich, M., 'The Garrisoning of English Medieval Castles', in R.P. Abels and B.S. Bachrach (eds.), *The Normans and Their Adversaries at War: Essays in Memory of C. Warren Hollister* (Woodbridge, 2001), pp.185–200.
War, Politics and Finance under Edward I (London, 1972, repr. Aldershot, 1991).
Le Prévost, A., *Dictionnaire des anciens noms de lieu du département de l'Eure* (Évreux, 1839).

Pugh (ed.), T.B., *Glamorgan County History, vol. iii: The Middle Ages* (Cardiff, 1971).
Rees, W., *The Act of Union of England and Wales* (Cardiff, 1948).
South Wales and the March 1284–1415: A Social and Agrarian Study (Oxford, 1924, repr. Bath, 1967, re-issued 1974).
Reeves, A.C., *The Marcher Lords* (Llandybïe, 1983).
Remfry, P.R., *Clun Castle* (Worcester, 1994).
Hopton Castle 1066 to 1305 (Worcester, 1994).
Renn, D.F., 'The First Norman Castles in England (1051–1071)', *Château Gaillard*, **1** (1964), pp. 125–32.
Reynolds, S., *Kingdoms and Communities in Western Europe, 900–1300* (Oxford, 1984).
Richards, R., 'Sycharth', *Mont. Coll.*, **50** (1949 for 1948), pp. 183–8.
Roe, A., 'Bridgnorth, Shropshire', *West Midlands Archaeology*, **26** (1983), pp. 86–7.
Roffe, D., 'The Hundred Rolls of 1255', *Historical Research*, **69**:169 (1996), pp. 201–10.
Rothwell, W., L.W. Stone and T.B.W. Reid (eds.), *Anglo-Norman Dictionary* (London, 1992).
Round, J.H., 'The Origin of the Stewarts', in J. H. Round, *Studies in Peerage and Family History* (London, 1901).
Rowlands, I.W., 'The 1201 Peace between King John and Llywelyn ap Iorwerth', *Studia Celtica*, **34** (2000), pp. 149–66.
'King John and Wales', in S.D. Church (ed.), *King John: New Interpretations* (Woodbridge, 1999), pp. 273–87.
'The Making of the March: Aspects of the Norman Settlement in Dyfed', *Anglo-Norman Studies*, **3** (1981), pp. 142–57.
'William de Braose and the Lordship of Brecon', *BBCS*, **30** (1982–3), pp. 123–33.
Royal Commission on the Ancient and Historical Monuments of Wales, *An Inventory of the Ancient Monuments in Glamorgan, vol. iii, part 1a: Medieval Secular Monuments: The Early Castles – From the Norman Conquest to 1217* (London, 1991).
An Inventory of the Ancient Monuments in Glamorgan, vol. iii, part 1b: Medieval Secular Monuments: The Later Castles – From 1217 to the Present (Aberystwyth, 2000).
Ruddick, A., 'Ethnic Identity and Political Language in the King of England's Dominions: A Fourteenth-Century Perspective', in L. Clark (ed.), *Identity and Insurgency in the Late Middle Ages (The Fifteenth Century, 6)* (Woodbridge, 2006), pp. 15–32.
'National and Political Identity in Anglo-Scottish Relations, *c.* 1286–1377: A Governmental Perspective', in A. King and M. Penman (eds.), *England and Scotland in the Fourteenth Century: New Perspectives* (Woodbridge, 2007), pp. 196–215.
Sahlins, P., 'Natural Frontiers Revisited: France's Boundaries since the Seventeenth Century', *American Historical Review*, **95** (1990), pp. 1423–51.
Salter, M., *The Castles and Moated Mansions of Shropshire* (Wolverhampton, 1988).
Sanders, I.J., *English Baronies: A Study of their Origin and Descent, 1086–1327* (Oxford, 1960).
Saunders, V.A., 'Shropshire', in H.C. Darby and I.B. Terrett (eds.), *The Domesday Geography of Midland England*, 2nd edn (Cambridge, 1971), pp. 115–62.
Scammell, J., 'Robert I and the North of England', *EHR*, **73** (1958), pp. 385–403.

Shoesmith, R., and A. Johnson (eds.), *Ludlow Castle: Its History and Buildings* (Logaston Press, 2000).

Silvester, R., 'New Radnor: The Topography of a Medieval Planned Town in Mid-Wales', in N. Edwards (ed.), *Landscape and Settlement in Medieval Wales* (Oxford, 1997), pp. 157–64.

Simpson, G.G., and B. Webster, 'Charter Evidence and the Distribution of Mottes in Scotland', in K.J. Stringer (ed.), *Essays on the Nobility of Medieval Scotland* (Edinburgh, 1985), pp. 1–12.

Smith, J.B., 'Dynastic Succession in Medieval Wales', *BBCS*, **33** (1986), pp. 199–232.

'The Kingdom of Morgannwg and the Norman Conquest of Glamorgan', in T.B. Pugh (ed.), *Glamorgan County History, vol. iii* (Cardiff, 1971), pp. 1–43.

Llywelyn ap Gruffudd: Prince of Wales (Cardiff, 1998).

'Magna Carta and the Charters of the Welsh Princes', *EHR*, **99** (1984), pp. 344–62.

'The Middle March in the Thirteenth Century', *BBCS*, **24** (1970–2), pp. 77–93.

Smith, Ll.B., 'Oswestry', in R.A. Griffiths (ed.), *Boroughs of Medieval Wales* (Cardiff, 1978), pp. 219–42.

'The Welsh Language before 1536', in G.H. Jenkins (ed.), *The Welsh Language before the Industrial Revolution* (Cardiff, 1997), pp. 15–44.

Snape, W.G., 'Excavation of a Motte and Bailey at Ryton, Shifnal', *TSAS*, **57** (1961–4), pp. 191–3.

Spurgeon, C.J., 'The Castles of Montgomeryshire', *Mont. Coll.*, **59** (1965/6), pp. 1–59.

'Gwyddgrug Castle and the Gorddwr Dispute in the Thirteenth Century', *Mont. Coll.*, **57** (1962), part ii, 125–36.

'Hubert's Folly: The Abortive Castle of the Kerry Campaign, 1228', in J.R. Kenyon and K. O'Conor (eds.), *The Medieval Castle in Ireland and Wales* (Dublin, 2003), pp. 107–20.

'Mottes and Castle-Ringworks in Wales', in J.R. Kenyon and R. Avent (eds.), *Castles in Wales and the Marches: Essays in Honour of D. J. Cathcart King* (Cardiff, 1987), pp. 23–49.

Stancliffe, C., 'Where was Oswald Killed?', in C. Stancliffe and E. Cambridge (eds.), *Oswald: Northumbrian King to European Saint* (Stamford, 1995), pp. 84–96.

Stell, G., 'Provisional List of Mottes in Scotland', in K.J. Stringer (ed.), *Essays on the Nobility of Medieval Scotland* (Edinburgh, 1985), pp. 13–21.

Stenton, F.M., *Anglo-Saxon England*, 3rd edn (Oxford, 1971).

The First Century of English Feudalism, 1066–1166, 2nd edn (Oxford, 1961).

'The Road System of Medieval England', *Economic History Review*, **7** (1936/7), pp. 1–21.

Stephenson, D., '*Fouke le Fitz Waryn* and Llywelyn ap Gruffydd's Claim to Whittington', *TSAS*, **78** (2002), pp. 26–31.

'Llywelyn the Great, the Shropshire March and the Building of Montgomery Castle', *TSAS*, **80** (2005), pp. 52–8.

'Madog ap Maredudd, *Rex Powissensium*', *WHR*, **24** (2008), pp. 1–28.

'The Politics of Powys Wenwynwyn in the Thirteenth Century', *Cambridge Medieval Celtic Studies*, **7** (1984), pp. 39–61.

'The "Resurgence" of Powys in the Late Eleventh and Early Twelfth Centuries', *Anglo-Norman Studies*, **30** (2008), pp. 182–95.

'The Supremacy in (Southern) Powys of Owain Fychan ap Madog: A Reconsideration', *Cambrian Medieval Celtic Studies*, **49** (2005), pp. 45–55.

'Welsh Lords in Shropshire: Gruffydd ap Iorwerth Goch and His Descendants in the Thirteenth Century', *TSAS*, **78** (2002), pp. 32–7.

Strickland, M., 'Securing the North: Invasion and the Strategy of Defence in Twelfth-Century Anglo-Scottish Warfare', in M. Strickland (ed.), *Anglo-Norman Warfare* (The Boydell Press, 1992), pp.208–29.

War and Chivalry: The Conduct and Perception of War in England and Normandy, 1066–1217 (Cambridge, 1996).

Stringer, K.J., *Earl David of Huntingdon, 1152–1219. A Study in Anglo-Scottish History* (Edinburgh, 1985).

Stubbs, W., *The Constitutional History of England*, 3 vols. (Oxford, 1874–1903).

Suppe, F.C., 'Castle Guard and the Castlery of Clun', *Haskins Society Journal*, **1** (1989), pp. 123–34.

Military Institutions on the Welsh Marches: Shropshire AD 1066–1300 (Woodbridge, 1994).

'The Persistence of Castle-Guard in the Welsh Marches and Wales: Suggestions for a Research Agenda and Methodology', in R.P. Abels and B.S. Bachrach (eds.), *The Normans and their Adversaries at War: Essays in Memory of C. Warren Hollister* (Woodbridge, 2001), pp.201–21.

'Roger of Powys, Henry II's Anglo-Welsh Middleman, and his Lineage', *WHR*, **21**:1 (2002), pp. 1–23.

'Who Was Rhys Sais? Some Comments on Anglo-Welsh Relations before 1066', *Haskins Society Journal*, **7** (1995), pp. 63–73.

Sylvester, D., *The Rural Landscape of the Welsh Borderland* (London, 1969).

Tait, J., 'Introduction to the Shropshire Domesday', in *VCH*, **i**, 279–307.

Thomas, H.M., *The English and the Normans: Ethnic Hostility, Assimilation, and Identity, 1066–c. 1220* (Oxford, 2003).

Thomas, R.J., *Enwau Afonydd a Nentydd Cymru* (Cardiff, 1938).

Thompson, K., 'The Norman Aristocracy before 1066: The Example of the Montgomerys', *Historical Research*, **60** (1987), pp. 251–63.

Thorn, F.R., 'Hundreds and Wapentakes', in A. Williams and R.W.H. Erskine (eds.), *The Derbyshire Domesday* (Alecto County Edition of Domesday Book, 1990), pp.28–38.

'Hundreds and Wapentakes', in A. Williams and R.W.H. Erskine (eds.), *The Herefordshire Domesday* (Alecto County Edition of Domesday Book, 1988), pp.23–30.

'Hundreds and Wapentakes', in A. Williams and R.W.H. Erskine (eds.), *The Shropshire Domesday* (Alecto County Edition of Domesday Book, 19, 1990), pp.28–37.

'Hundreds and Wapentakes', in A. Williams and G.H. Martin (eds.), *The Dorset Domesday* (Alecto County Edition of Domesday Book, 1991), pp.27–44.

Turner, F.J., *The Frontier in American History* (New York, 1921).

Vallez, A., 'La Construction du comté d'Alençon (1269–1380): Essai de géographie historique', *Annales de Normandie*, **22** (1972), pp. 11–45.

R. Vaughan, *Matthew Paris* (Cambridge, 1958).

Walker, D.G., 'The Norman Settlement in Wales', *Proceedings of the Battle Conference*, **1**, (1978), pp. 131–43.

Walker, R.F., 'Hubert de Burgh and Wales, 1218–1232,' *EHR*, **87** (1972), pp. 465–94.
'The Supporters of Richard Marshal, Earl of Pembroke, in the Rebellion of 1233–1234', *WHR*, **17** (1994–5), pp. 41–65.
Warlop, E., *The Flemish Nobility*, 4 vols. (Kortrijk 1975–6). Originally publ. as *De Vlaamse Adel voor 1300* (Handzame, 1968).
Warren, W.L., *Henry II* (London, 1973).
Watkin, C.W., 'Herefordshire', in H.C. Darby and I.B. Terrett (eds.), *The Domesday Geography of Midland England*, 2nd edn (Cambridge, 1971).
Wickham, C., 'The *terra* of San Vincenzo al Volturno in the 8th to 12th Centuries: The Historical Framework', in R. Hodges and J. Mitchell (eds.), *San Vincenzo al Volturno: The Archaeology, Art and Territory of an Early Medieval Monastery* (Oxford, 1985), pp. 227–58.
Wightman, W.E., *The Lacy Family in England and Normandy, 1066–1194* (Oxford, 1966).
Williams, D.H., *Atlas of Cistercian Lands in Wales* (Cardiff, 1990).
The Welsh Cistercians, 2 vols. (Tenby, 1984).
The Welsh Cistercians: Aspects of Their Economic History (Pontypool, 1969).
Williams, G.A., 'Welsh Raiding in the Twelfth-Century Shropshire/Cheshire March: The Case of Owain Cyfeiliog', *Studia Celtica*, **40** (2006), pp. 89–115.
Wormald, P., 'Offa's Dyke', in J. Campbell (ed.), *The Anglo-Saxons*, pbk. edn (London, 1991; originally Oxford, 1982), pp. 120–1.
Worthington, M., 'Wat's Dyke: An Archaeological and Historical Enigma', *Bulletin of the John Rylands University Library of Manchester*, **79**:3 (1997), pp. 177–96.

UNPUBLISHED THESES

Holden, B.W., 'The Aristocracy of Western Herefordshire and the Middle March, 1166–1246' (University of Oxford DPhil. thesis, 2000).
Lewis, C.P., 'English and Norman Government and Lordship in the Welsh Borders, 1039–1087' (University of Oxford DPhil thesis, 1985).
Lieberman, M., 'Shropshire and the March of Wales, ca. 1070–1283: The Creation of Separate Identities' (University of Oxford DPhil. thesis, 2004).
Raspin, G.E.A., 'Transcript and Descriptive List of the Medieval Court Rolls of the Marcher Lordship of Clun Deposited in the Salop Record Office by the Earl of Powis' (University of London thesis for Diploma in Archive Administration, 1963).
Smith, Ll.B., 'The Lordships of Chirk and Oswestry, 1282–1415' (University of London PhD thesis, 1971).
Thompson, K.M., 'The Cross-Channel Estates of the Montgomery-Bellême Family, *c.* 1050–1112' (University College Cardiff MA thesis, 1983).
Walker, R.F., 'The Anglo-Welsh Wars, 1216–67' (University of Oxford DPhil thesis, 1954).

INDEX

Index

Index

Index

Index

Lightning Source UK Ltd.
Milton Keynes UK
UKHW022154151218
334096UK00018B/351/P

9 781107 650046